THE JAGGED EDGE OF DUTY

THE JAGGED EDGE OF DUTY

A Fighter Pilot's World War II

ROBERT L. RICHARDSON

STACKPOLE
BOOKS

Guilford, Connecticut

Dedicated to peacemakers and to those who, despite their love of peace and their own natural inclinations, fought bravely in the interest of freedom and against oppressors and those who would destroy peace. And to those whose lives were ended, or altered, as a result of that fight.

Published by Stackpole Books
An imprint of Globe Pequot
www.rowman.com

Distributed by
NATIONAL BOOK NETWORK
800-462-6420

British Library Cataloguing in Publication Information available

Library of Congress Cataloging-in-Publication Data

Names: Richardson, Robert L., 1949- author.
Title: The jagged edge of duty : a fighter pilot's World War II / Robert L. Richardson.
Description: Guilford, Connecticut : Stackpole Books, [2017] | Includes bibliographical references and index.
Identifiers: LCCN 2016055525 (print) | LCCN 2016056106 (ebook) | ISBN 9780811718424 (hardcover : alk. paper) | ISBN 9780811765725 (e-book) | ISBN 9780811718424 (hardcover. : alk. paper)
Subjects: LCSH: Knepper, Alan, 1916-1943. | United States. Army Air Forces. Fighter Squadron, 49th—Biography. | Fighter pilots—United States—Biography. | Lightning (Fighter plane)—Anecdotes. | World War, 1939-1945—Aerial operations, American. | World War, 1939-1945—Campaigns—Italy. | World War, 1939-1945—Africa, North. | World War, 1939-1945—Regimental histories—United States.
Classification: LCC D790.262 49th .R53 2017 (print) | LCC D790.262 49th (ebook) | DDC 940.54/4973092 [B] —dc23
LC record available at https://lccn.loc.gov/2016055525

♾™ The paper used in this publication meets the minimum requirements of American National Standard for Information Sciences—Permanence of Paper for Printed Library Materials, ANSI/NISO Z39.48-1992.

Contents

Preface

Shirley Dawn Finn has been the engine behind this book, and finding her made everything possible. For seventy years she kept the faith, hoping that one day her brother's story would be told. I hope this will serve.

My father wrote a short memoir of his time in the service, in which he wrote: "Al and I both went missing, and they never found Al." Reading this as a young man, I was struck by Allan's having gone missing, and that he was never found. It seemed so little to say about a young man's sacrifice, especially since I knew the anguish that my grandmother went through during the time that my father was missing. I knew that if I did not do something to document this young man's service, the story of his sacrifice would just drift away into obscurity. So I resolved to find out what happened to Al, but first had to complete the manuscript about my father's service. By 2012 I had finished that work, and started to track down Allan Knepper. Finding his fate was actually a fairly easy task. I did an online search for Missing Air Crew Reports (MACR), and his name came up. I was able to obtain the MACR that pertained to his last action, and that gave me his serial number. With that information I could obtain his Individual Deceased Personnel File (IDPF) from the U.S. Army archives. That information (coming months later) gave me the names of his next of kin. I then did a search on Ancestry at the local library, and found the names of his siblings. His father, Jess, died in 1983, and his obituary included the fact that his sister, Shirley Dawn Knepper, lived in Lewiston (Allan's hometown). I focused my search on that area, and in researching the archives of the *Lewiston Montana Tribune* I found that Shirley Dawn Knepper (Finn) had in 2010 submitted a 1951 news clipping about her third-place award at that year's Blossom Festival

Parade in Lewiston Orchards. So then I had her married name and was able to locate her after a brief Internet search. My phone call to her on December 13, 2013 came as a surprise, but she told me that her faith had been strong all the years since Allan's loss and she felt that some information would eventually develop. She and I have become close friends, and the information about Allan that she had kept over the years was of inestimable help in the preparation of this book.

Special appreciation to William Gregory and Harold Harper, two P-38 fighter pilots from the 49th squadron, exemplars of courageous, selfless service. Thanks for your many contributions to this book, and most especially, thanks for your friendship.

To Robert Vrilakas, Jim Gregory, and Bob Riley, three fighter pilots who also served in North Africa—thanks, too, for your service, and for sharing your experiences and perspectives. It's a privilege to have heard your stories and to have come to know you.

The families of the young men who served with the 49th Fighter Squadron in the summer of 1943 have been of inestimable help in the preparation of this work. Special thanks to Rick and Carole Bitter, Art Taphorn, Gary Blount, Greg and Michelle (Boatman) Branch, Karl Boatman, Delana (Decker) Harrison, Tim Harris, Dawn and David Kilhefner, Bob Kocour, Dusty Lovera, Charlane Compton, Jeanette Richard, Jim and Steve Ritter, Karen Nickerson, and Hazel Trengove. Each has provided important material about their husbands, fathers, brothers, cousins, or uncles. This book could never have been written without their contributions, and their enthusiasm has lent real impetus to the project.

To all, it is my sincere hope that this effort will serve in some measure as a memorial to your loved ones, pilots who may have been unheralded and unappreciated outside of your families, but whose service and sacrifice ranks them among the war's many heroes.

Thanks to Mr. Bert Zimmerly Jr. Special recognition to the 49th Fighter Association for keeping the spirit of the squadron alive and relevant, and thanks to John Carter, Paul Skoskie, Ron Morrissette, Brian Reno, and Joe Onesty. Thanks also to the P-38 Association, and to John Stanaway. And thanks to Steve Blake for his contributions, support, and direction; to Shirley Burden at the Hanceville Library; to Kelly at the the

Natrona County High School; to the Lewis Clark State College library, to the Western History Center at Casper College, and to Wanda Wade at the Cheyenne Genealogical and Historical Society. And thanks to Kent Ramsey, a world-class photo historian, and to William Larkins, a world-class photo collector.

Among the many government and nonprofit agencies, museums, associations, and archives that contributed to this work, special recognition is due the Air Force Historical Research Agency. Their archive provided much of the organizational material that serves as the foundation for this book. And within AFHRA, special thanks to Maranda Gilmore, Lynn Gamma, Cathy Cox, Marcie Green, Tammy Horton, and Leeander Morris. Thanks, too, to Joshua Fennell and Joshua Frank of the Defense POW/MIA Accounting Agency, and to the contributors from the Army Air Forces Forum. The many technicians and librarians at the National Archives in College Park deserve thanks; the depth of knowledge among staff there is matched only by their interest in helping.

And the project would have never have taken flight without the contributions from the National Archives National Personnel Records Center in St. Louis.

Thanks also to those who have provided photographs from their private collections and archives, without which the work would have been diminished.

To Mr. Salvatore Fagone, my field associate in Sicily, I would like to express my sincere thanks for your passion for this effort, and for your dedication. Clearly you will be making many more significant contributions in the coming years, and it will be an honor to follow your successes.

I will be forever grateful to David Reisch, History Editor at Stackpole Books for agreeing to take on this project, and it is an honor to be included among the iconic works of military history published by Stackpole. And to Caroline McManus and Stephanie Otto and their editorial associates, I would like to express my sincere thanks for the exemplary edit that this work has received.

And finally, thanks to my family, for their patience and loving support.

INTRODUCTION

IN A RECENT INTERVIEW, WORLD WAR II FIGHTER PILOT WILLIAM Gregory was asked, "So you did not shoot anybody down, and no one shot you down, right?"—as though those two events could summarize the combat service of any pilot of that time and place. With an evaluating glance, and after making a mental entry about the questioner, "Greg" said, "That's right."

Over the long course of the war, most fighter pilots did not score an aerial victory, let alone become aces, and most were not downed in combat. And even pilots who did shoot down an enemy aircraft in combat often did not view that event as the defining moment of their combat careers. Harold Harper, who flew with the 49th Fighter Squadron alongside William Gregory, is credited with two aerial victories, but he himself claims only one and readily admits that he has no recollection of that action. But if you ask him, seventy years after the events, about "routine" combat operations in North Africa, or about living conditions on base, about the food or the effects of dysentery, or about his fellow pilots— those who survived combat and those who did not—he would have a full recollection and a ready answer.

While many spectacular and heroic episodes of aerial combat have been well served in literature and film, the wartime experiences of the vast majority of combat pilots, like those in the 49th Fighter Squadron, are largely unrecognized. In part, that may be because of the pilots' reticence. For many pilots, the thrill of flying and the fact of having survived combat were intensely personal and little shared. Few kept diaries or wrote memoirs. Even following combat, in the security of home and family, these pilots often kept silent about their experiences, leaving their loved ones to wonder if their service had been too mundane, or perhaps too horrific, to share. Fighter pilot Bob Vrilakas noted that "everybody in the military has a story," but he had been reluctant to relate his experiences until very late in life because he did not want to bore anyone.

This book reveals much of the *Sturm und Drang* of American combat flying, focusing on one P-38 fighter squadron during the hot summer of 1943 in North Africa. It gives a broad accounting of how these young men came to be part of an extraordinarily diverse cast of highly trained and lethal pilots. It explains how they were selected for pilot training, where they received their flight instruction, and what types of planes they flew. It follows the arrival of these newly minted second lieutenants to North Africa and records their reactions to the alien world in which they now lived, and which some would never leave.

Volunteers to a man, most of the 49th's cadre of fighter pilots had joined the Army Air Corps in the days immediately following the Japanese attack at Pearl Harbor. What follows includes many firsthand accounts by those men, all of whom are now quite aged and most of whom would describe their service as "just doing my job." Also included is a careful description of the context of their service—the military strategies adopted by President Roosevelt and his staff and implemented by General Eisenhower and his. It relates the state of war from the perspective of German pilots bent on resisting the Allied advances from myriad airfields in Sicily and Italy. And it describes how wrong a carefully planned mission can go, and how luck sometimes favors the prepared pilot.

As with any squadron, the pilots of the 49th were of different types, and the squadron quickly became a melting pot of ethnicities, cultures, backgrounds, and educations. Some were naturally aggressive; for them combat was a release of sorts. Others were surely less so. Some developed as leaders within the squadron. A few were natural fliers; for others flight was always a challenge. While few had planned a life in the military, all shared a commitment to their wingman and a willingness to stand up to their duty, to complete the dangerous task before them.

The following account explains how quickly any swagger or feeling of privilege fell away upon reporting to their new squadron and describes the final combat training they received from pilots who, after just a month of combat flying, were already considered seasoned veterans. It gives witness to the sometimes execrable living conditions, the sun and dust, the scorpions and the malaria. Importantly, it records the mutual dependence that developed among the pilots, their reliance on each other during a mission, on friends back on the ground, on ground crews and maintenance specialists, on the mission planners, and on the mission leaders.

In the early days of the war, the skies were lethal. A third of the flight cadets in their cohorts had already been killed in training accidents. About half of the pilots who reported for duty in North Africa during that time did not survive. Combat losses rose at an alarming rate, and squadrons were further weakened by losses during routine training flights between missions, and even by apparent suicides.

For these young men, it was a time of duty, of inevitable sacrifice, of coping with the unavoidable and constantly increasing physical and emotional stresses in the air and on the ground, of facing death and meting it out on every mission. It was hearing the near-constant drone of nearby aircraft, waking to a tap on the shoulder: "You're on." And for some fighter pilots, their tour became a starkly terrifying routine, fraught with anxiety, grief, and sometimes guilt.

The pilots lived in two different worlds. On missions against the formidable Luftwaffe, and in the face of withering flak, they had to forget about everything that had come before, even the losses, in order to concentrate on the task at hand. On good days, the pilots might reflect on a successful mission, quietly giving thanks that no one was lost. On other days, after other missions, the young men might find the living conditions especially harsh, or their dysentery worse. They might be plagued by thoughts of recent close calls or frustrated by incomplete or unsatisfactory missions. On these days, it would be difficult to cope with the now-empty cot next to them or to be civil to the even younger replacement pilot who would now occupy it.

Fear was a constant, and each man reached an accommodation to that fear in his own way, and within his own limits. As losses within the squadron mounted, so too did the grief felt by the men over missing friends and tentmates. Always there was the next mission, and yet despite all the flying, the end of their combat tour often seemed to be no closer.

This work will answer some of the questions long unasked and give to many a better understanding of the war and some men's role in it. In the spirit of truthfulness and full disclosure, the person who posed the myopic question to William Gregory was me. This book has become both my penance and my reward.

Chapter 1

GUMP

June 18, 1943

GUMP—A MNEMONIC DRILLED INTO HIS HEAD FROM FLIGHT SCHOOL— came to him as he brought his P-38 around for a landing back at his base at Telergma. GUMP: Gas, Undercarriage, Mixture, Prop—the last four things to check on final approach. As crappy as this day had been for 2nd Lt. Allan Knepper, especially considering how hopefully it had started and how eager for action he had been at takeoff, he wanted to make sure that he didn't make things worse with a lousy landing.

His excitement had been building since learning last night that he'd been assigned to today's mission. He hadn't slept much, reflecting that just a year earlier he had been flying Piper Cubs, teaching farm kids at a rural elementary school, and courting the coeds at Lewiston Normal in Idaho. Finally joining the squadron just nine days before, he'd spent fifty-nine days getting there—at each stage in his journey the conveyance got slower—transiting the United States by train, the Atlantic by convoy, and North Africa by narrow-gauge rail.

Lieutenant Knepper had been astonished by North Africa. The arid and stark landscape had an eerie familiarity to him, as he'd been raised in the dry hill country and canyonlands of Idaho. But the smells, the taste of the air, the rough villages, the odd mix of Moslem and French architecture, and the even stranger mix of nationalities—everything was alien to him. And the people, the local Arabs, both fascinated and repelled him. Nothing in his life could have prepared him for this, and he could not imagine ever becoming jaded by, let alone accustomed to, what was around him every day.

The 49th was hungry for replacement pilots: Since early May when it began its current posting in North Africa, the 49th had flown thirty-six combat missions and had already lost nine pilots—nearly a third of their cadre. And with the high number of sorties, its remaining pilots were steadily moving toward completion of their fifty-mission combat tours. More good pilots were needed. But the squadron was on a roll; in the ten days since Knepper had reported for duty, the squadron had not lost any pilots.

Lieutenant Knepper was up and dressed before the squadron clerk came around to his tent to wake him for the mission, with a curt "You're up, Lieutenant." Knepper made the short walk to the mess tent, greeting the other pilots with just a "Mornin'." Never very much inclined to talk, and with tension building in his chest, he preferred to listen to the quiet exchanges between the other pilots, the experienced ones. He'd seen his good friend Herman Kocour at breakfast, and knew that today would be Herman's first combat mission as well. Neither one having much of an appetite, they left ahead of the others and made their way to the equipment tent to collect parachutes, escape kits, and pistols. Catching a jeep ride to the flight line, they located their aircraft—Kocour to plane #43, Knepper, to #45.

With a wave and tight smile Knepper turned and began a quiet walk-around of his plane. The aircraft showed wear, and he knew that it had already seen a lot of combat. It was the favorite mount for Lieutenant Bob Riley, who had flown it on ten missions since early May. Four other 49th squadron pilots had also flown #45 into combat, and it had proven to be a very reliable and well-maintained aircraft.

Kocour had been assigned to aircraft #43—another well-used aircraft that had been flown by seven other pilots prior to this mission, including six sorties by the squadron commander, Captain Trollope. The aircraft had experienced mechanical issues recently and had been forced to return early on its two previous missions. On top of everything else he had to think about, Lieutenant Kocour also looked at his mount with some misgivings.[1]

While the crew chief attended to the aircraft, Knepper glanced around the hardstand to make sure no toolkits had been left, found a spot for a nervous nature break, and checked the direction of his nosewheel. Grabbing the retractable ladder on the rear of the gondola, he swung himself up to the left wing and eased into the cockpit. Wearing his bulky Mae West life jacket, his .45, and his parachute with its attached inflatable escape dinghy, he was grateful for his chief's help in getting settled.

His chief had been out earlier in the morning to make a more complete preflight check on his aircraft, and just before the lieutenant's arrival he'd started the engines and run them up to ensure that they were operating to standards.[2] He had knelt on the wing, helping Knepper to adjust his harness and crash belts, and scanned the instrument panel and engine switches. He was satisfied with what he saw, saying, "See you in a couple of hours, Lieutenant." The chief knew two things: that this was his pilot's first combat mission, and that he had delivered an aircraft that was ready for combat.

Pilots were greatly dependent on their crew chiefs for the maintenance of the aircraft, but the chiefs represented something else to the pilots. They were the last person the pilot would look in the eyes and speak to before each mission, and the first when he returned. The chief would know from the first glance at the aircraft and the first look into his pilot's eyes what sort of mission it had been.

As the chief dropped the canopy, Knepper engaged the safety lock and cranked the right window up. With a final wave, Knepper connected his headset and adjusted the throat mic before turning to the cockpit instruments.

By the book, there were twenty-five items to check. Although he had made a couple dozen flights in the P-38, he still took his time. He knew that more experienced pilots could complete these checks in just a few minutes, but for today, everything had to be just right. Most importantly, he checked the two things he'd had trouble remembering earlier in his training: setting the fuel selectors to reserve, and the cross-feed switch to OFF. He primed and energized first the left engine, then the right.

With both engines running smoothly, Knepper made sure the radio was on and tuned to the proper frequency. He glanced at the coolant settings, tested the gun sight light, and checked the fuel gauges. While keeping the engines at 1,400 rpm, he made a last check on fuel and hydraulic pressure.

Glancing back, he moved the yoke forward and back to check elevator movement, then checked the aileron and flap travel. One last check of the gauges.

With his plane fully prepared in its hardstand, Lieutenant Knepper waited for the telltale aileron waggle from the flight leader, knowing that he and his plane were equipped for this, his first combat mission. His engines were "galloping" at idle, the sound each P-38 pilot instantly recognized and would never forget. He was ready.

In checking the mission board the evening before, he had learned that he'd been assigned to Red flight, in number-two position as wingman to Capt. Henry Trollope, the squadron commander—a normal assignment for a new pilot's first combat flight. He knew that all of his fellow replacement pilots would undergo the same close scrutiny in their first few combat assignments, always being assigned as wingman to one of the squadron's more experienced pilots.

As Trollope's wingman, Knepper knew that his job would be to stay on his leader's wing no matter what. Head on a swivel, always knowing where the captain's wingtip was, covering Trollope's blind spot—his tail. He had done quite a lot of formation flying and was comfortable flying 4 feet away from another P-38 at 300 mph.

At 9:24 Captain Trollope flexed his ailerons and began moving from his hardstand to the flight line. Knepper, second in line for takeoff, eased his brakes and gave a bit of throttle to move from his own hardstand and take up formation behind Trollope. With a final sweep of the instruments, a last tug on his safety belt and harness, he ran the engines up to 2,300 rpm and, with the rest of the flight forming up behind him, Knepper pointed the plane for takeoff.

As Trollope's plane started rollout, Knepper brought his engines to 3,000 rpm, braked to keep the plane motionless, then released to start rolling. With a surge of power, it thundered down the runway. Airborne in fourteen seconds, he soon reached an airspeed of 130 mph. At this speed, he knew that if one engine failed, he could maintain control on just the remaining engine. He retracted his landing gear, switched fuel feed to a belly tank, and settled into position off Trollope's left wing.

Trollope eased his airspeed slightly to allow the others to catch up. As the squadron advanced to flight speed, assuming the standard "four-finger" configuration, Lieutenant Knepper had this thought: *Please don't let me screw this up . . .*

After a year of flight training, including a few weeks in North Africa doing combat training and a few days with the squadron learning its own unique set of procedures, Knepper's head told him he was ready for the mission. They'd been ordered to escort P-38s from their sister squadron, the 37th, on a dive-bombing mission to the Axis aerodrome at Milo, near Trapani, on the northwestern corner of Sicily. As escort, Knepper and his fellow 49th pilots would counter any attack by German or Italian fighters, giving the bomb-carrying aircraft of the 37th an unimpeded bomb run.

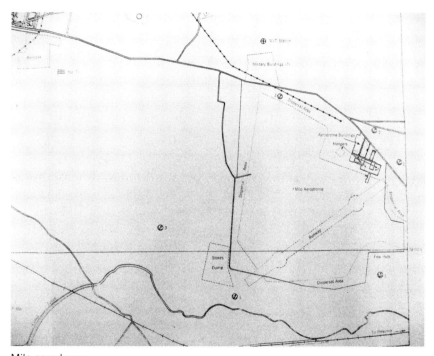

Milo aerodrome.

Milo was an important airfield for both the Italian and the German air forces in the summer of 1943 and had been used extensively in support of the failed Axis campaign in North Africa in the preceding year. The airfield was high on the list of priority targets for the Army Air Forces. Achieving air superiority over the Mediterranean Theater was the number-one priority for military planners, and knocking out German Air Force (GAF) assets, like aerodromes, was a critical part of the battle plan. Even before the Axis surrender in Tripoli in mid-May, the air force had sent bombing missions to Trapani/Milo. The airfield had been given a respite during the intensive Allied bombing campaign against the island of Pantelleria—Operation Corkscrew. But with Pantelleria's surrender on June 11, the Allied air forces had turned to Sicilian and Sardinian targets with fresh energy.

In mid-June, Milo was base of operations for Jagdgeschwader 77 (JG 77)—the German *Herz As* ("Ace of Hearts") command. For JG 77—one of the most storied, and perhaps the most experienced, of the German fighter commands—Trapani was their latest posting after having seen years of combat in Western Europe, Russia, and North Africa. Within JG 77 were some of the most experienced combat pilots the world would ever see. With two groups plus a headquarters flight operating out of Milo, and with extensive flak batteries, there was every reason to expect a strong German defense on this mission.[3]

Adding to Knepper's anxiety was the buzz that he'd picked up around camp regarding the German aircraft they were likely to encounter on this mission. The squadron referred to them as the "yellow-nosed squadron," and had first encountered them during the mission on May 19 when two of the 49th's pilots had been shot down. The "yellow-nosed squadron" was from JG 77—a German fighter wing based at Trapani that had been in combat since 1939, had thousands of sorties to its credit, with hundreds of air victories, and which never showed the slightest reluctance to engage American aircraft.[4]

Pilot William Gregory would later recount: "The yellow-nosed squadron—we knew about those; at least, some of us did. Neely, DeMoss, and myself always talked about them. It was an elite squadron. We could see those yellow noses on some of our early flights. We knew they were good.

Milo aerodrome, July 1943. Note dispersed aircraft.

We called them 'yellow-nosed kids,' and they were really good with the 109.[5] They were seasoned pilots, they had been flying for two years, and they had a lot of time in their airplane. They were the best of the best."[6]

Just three days earlier, the 49th squadron had escorted B-26s from the 320th Bomb Group on a bombing mission to Milo. On that mission, no enemy aircraft were engaged, but the Intelligence officer had cautioned them to be watchful for Axis flights. And even without enemy interceptors, they were advised that the 88mm flak could be intense. But with a bit of luck, the mission might catch a few GAF aircraft on the ground, and not encounter a swarm of enemy fighters already in flight.

Lieutenant Knepper's flight included fourteen aircraft: twelve for the mission, and two "spares" that accompanied the formation to the vicinity of the target, but would only be used if one or more of the primary pilots reported aircraft problems and were forced to return to base.

Lieutenant Kocour was flying number-two position in White flight to Lieutenant Neely. He and Knepper had known each other since the beginning of their flight training, permanently pinned to each other by the army's obsession with the alphabet. Kocour knew Lieutenant Neely was a good pilot and reckoned that he'd have to be at his best to stay with him.

Unknown to either Knepper or Kocour, three other North African fighter groups were also engaged in hard-hitting diversionary missions on this day, to targets on Sardinia. The P-38s of the 1st Fighter Group escorted B-26s on two bombing missions to the seaplane base at Olbia Harbor, while the 82nd Fighter Group sent thirty-six P-38s on a single bomber-escort mission to Golfo Aranci. And the 325th Fighter Group, flying P-40s, sent forty-four aircraft on a mid-morning counter-air-force dive-bombing and strafing sweep to Villacidro aerodrome in southern Sicily.[7]

The twelve P-38 aircraft of the 37th squadron, also based at Telergma, had taken off twenty minutes ahead of Knepper's formation. They were each carrying a single 500-pound general-purpose bomb, a weapon used primarily for demolition missions, and capable of inflicting considerable damage from the blast effect.

Cruising at 200 mph, the combined formation headed for Tunis on a northeastern bearing. They planned to overfly Tunis about an hour later, then drop to "the deck" for the remaining thirty-minute flight to the Sicilian coast in order to avoid German listening or radar detection. Just before reaching the coast, with its array of coastal guns and antiaircraft batteries, the formation would jump to 5,000 feet for the bomb approach.

Midway to Tunis, just thirty minutes into the flight, Captain Trollope signaled a problem with his aircraft. Evidently it was a mechanical problem, the sort of thing that occurred all too frequently with all the bomber and fighter squadrons. Peeling off from the formation, with Knepper still glued to his wingtip, Trollope retraced his route back to base at Telergma. The mission's spares, Lieutenants Deru and Church, filled in to complete the squadron formation.

With a disappointment that included more than a touch of anger and knowing that his aircraft was in perfect condition, Knepper had no choice but to follow his element leader back to base. Glancing over his shoulder as Kocour flew on and wishing him good hunting, he knew all too well the first rule of aerial combat, drilled into him over the prior six months: Never allow a fellow pilot to fly unescorted. An hour after takeoff, Trollope and Knepper were back at Telergma.

"Early returns" were a problem for the squadron, and during the summer of 1943, roughly 6 percent of all aircraft who took off for a combat mission were forced to return due to mechanical issues. On some missions, the number of early returns exceeded the number of "spares" that were available for the mission, resulting in fewer aircraft executing the mission, and with possibly less-favorable results.[8]

After landing and taxiing back to the hardstands, Knepper "sweated out" the return of the mission, along with Captain Trollope, the crew chiefs for the mission's pilots, squadron Intelligence officer, Capt. Howard Wilson, and squadron operations officer, Capt. Richard Decker.

It was an anxious wait. The combat risks were well understood by all. The entire squadron had worked hard in the intense desert heat to prepare the aircraft for this moment—taking the war to the Germans. They'd all heard the roar of the engines at takeoff, and everyone—armorers, mechanics, cooks, clerks, carpenters, medical assistants—were aware of the losses as they mounted. They'd been there many times before and knew that there was a strong likelihood that some of the fliers they saw that morning might not return from this mission. The chaplain hoped that it would not be his duty to write yet another letter to a family, or to clear a pilot's effects from his tent under the troubled eyes of his tentmates.

The wait was maybe hardest for the crew chiefs. Some had come to know their pilots, and in some cases had forged a solid regard, possibly even friendship. They'd grown an "internal clock," keeping time with the mission. With the combined formation formed up by 10:00 A.M., Neely would alert all pilots to prepare for combat. Pilots would turn drop-tank switches on, along with gun heaters and sight switches, and increase rpm and manifold pressure to maximum cruise. Still flying on-the-deck, by 10:30 the formation would be nearing the coast and forming up for the attack. A bit before 11:00 A.M. the P-38s would take less than a minute to make their jump to 5,000 feet; then, the bomb-laden P-38s from the

37th would, one by one, wing over to make the steep dive on the target. Flak would start to hit the formation, and the pilots would be working hard to maintain position. Over the target, flak now intense, bombs away. P-38s from the 49th would be holding position outside of flak range and reconnecting with the bombers as they emerged from the target. If the Germans were going to make a fight of it, their fighters would be hitting the bomber formation about now. By 11:30 A.M., the formation, or what might be left of it, would be headed to base, with the P-38s providing cover for any damaged bombers who were lagging behind.

Best expressed in the words of one North African crew chief, the anxious ritual repeated on every mission, on every base, and in every theater of the war:

> I busied my hands on the desert sands,
> In a heat that cracked my lips.
> Then man alive, they began to arrive
> In their battered and crippled ships.[9]

Ninety minutes after his own landing, Knepper and the waiting squadron spotted a lone returning P-38. Too early for the mission to return, the approaching aircraft had to be another early return. Lieutenant Kocour, with another mechanical problem, was forced to turn around just minutes before reaching the target. Apparently the mechanical problem that had plagued #43 had not yet been diagnosed, or it had been diagnosed but not corrected, or else other problems had developed on the seemingly snake-bit aircraft.

Another thirty minutes passed, and groups of aircraft began to appear. Just nine; two pilots were missing.

The returning pilots reported that the mission had been a success.[10] The 37th had dropped their bombs on target, including three direct hits on the aerodrome's administration building, and seven more within the target area. The formation had received intense flak, the Germans having concealed heavy 88mm flak and lighter 30- to 40mm guns in the woods near the edge of the aerodrome. As the flight turned for home, flak was everywhere.

Following standard procedures, the bomb-laden P-38s from the 37th squadron had left their escort just prior to reaching the target. No protection could be offered against flak, and there was no reason to increase the exposure of the escorts to the ground fire. The escorting P-38s—the 49th squadron—were still in the target area doing 90-degree cross-over turns, waiting for the dive-bombers to emerge from their dives. A maneuver requiring careful attention at any time, a cross-over made under flak attack, and while all pilots were also scanning the air for incoming enemy fighters, was especially challenging.[11]

Two flak bursts were seen close to 2nd Lt. George B. Church's plane. His aircraft was in a slight left turn just below 1st Lt. Bruce L. Campbell's P-38, which was in a bank to the right. Neither saw the other until just moments before they collided. Church's aircraft hit Campbell's, clipping off Campbell's rudder and part of his stabilizer, and lost one of its propellers. Church's aircraft spun into the sea. Campbell was able to right his aircraft for three or four seconds, allowing him to bail out. His aircraft hit the water near Church's, and he was taken captive, spending the duration of the war at a POW camp in Bavaria.[12]

It was a tough day for the squadron, and a tough lesson for Lieutenants Knepper and Kocour. The two missing men were experienced pilots who had arrived in North Africa in March and had begun combat flights in May. Two losses in one mission, particularly the loss of experienced pilots in a midair collision, were a blow. It must have also occurred to both Knepper and Kocour that Lieutenant Church was a "spare" on this mission, and that if either of them had been able to complete the mission, Lieutenant Church would surely not have been lost, and Lieutenant Campbell might very well also be safe. As these young replacement pilots soon learned, that was combat. A pilot was not responsible for mechanical problems that developed with his or any other aircraft.

This was not their day to fly. Not their day to fight. Not their day to die.

CHAPTER 2

Squadron Organization

THE UNIT TO WHICH KNEPPER AND KOCOUR HAD BEEN ASSIGNED, THE 49th Fighter Squadron, was one of three squadrons within the 14th Fighter Group. The other two squadrons, the 37th and 48th, also flew the P-38 fighter and operated from the same bases. Each squadron included enough men, materiel, and aircraft to operate semiautonomously for long periods of time without additional outside support, a critical factor, with the group and squadrons moving frequently to new bases as the battle line moved forward.

The army being what it was, the makeup of the fighter squadron was exactly specified, with separate tables of organization for twin-engine fighter and single-engine fighter squadrons.[1]

Divided into an Air Echelon and a Ground Echelon, a P-38 squadron included 38 officers and 278 enlisted men. The Air Echelon included that part of the squadron most directly involved with flight operations. In addition to the squadron commander, operations officer, and 24 combat pilots, each of the technical departments in the Air Echelon (Engineering, Communications, and Armament) were assigned a first lieutenant. Also included was a three-officer team in the Operations Department led by a captain, a two-officer team in the Intelligence Section, also led by a captain, and a flight surgeon who headed medical services for the squadron.

The Air Echelon also included ninety-six enlisted personnel who performed all the tasks essential for making sure the aircraft were mission-ready, including airplane and engine mechanics, armorers, inspectors, electrical specialists, propeller specialists, radio operators and repairmen, sheet-metal workers, supply staff, medical technicians, and clerks.

The Ground Echelon was led by a captain who functioned as adjutant/mess/transportation officer, two first lieutenants serving as statistical officer and administrative/technical supply officer, and a second lieutenant who assisted the armaments officer. Also within the Ground Echelon were the enlisted men—182 in total—who provided more-detailed maintenance for the aircraft, as well as mess functions, munitions workers, draftsmen, parachute repairmen, telephone technicians, painters, photography technicians, welders, refueling specialists, chauffeurs, surgical technicians, and more.

For administrative purposes, the squadron was organized into three "flights." Each flight included eight or nine aircraft, and each aircraft was assigned a crew chief, an assistant crew chief, and an armorer. Armament and radio teams were also assigned to each flight, under the supervision of a tech sergeant.

This cohort of thirty-four officers operated quite apart from the enlisted men in the squadron. The five-man tents that housed the officers were often located some distance from the enlisted men's quarters, although at this stage in the war, officers ate in the same mess tent as enlisted personnel.

In aggregate, each squadron operated with a combined total of 316 officers and men. The three squadrons, plus the administrative staff of the group headquarters, numbered close to 1,000 officers and men—a small, mobile, and responsive town, capable of self-support in most functions, and including hundreds of men who were assigned to their squadron for the duration of the war.

And seventy-five of the fastest, most performant aircraft the world had seen to that point—the Lockheed P-38 Lightning.

Aircraft Crews

Eighteen-hour days were not unusual for ground crews maintaining and servicing the P-38 that was entrusted to their care for as long as it would be flying.

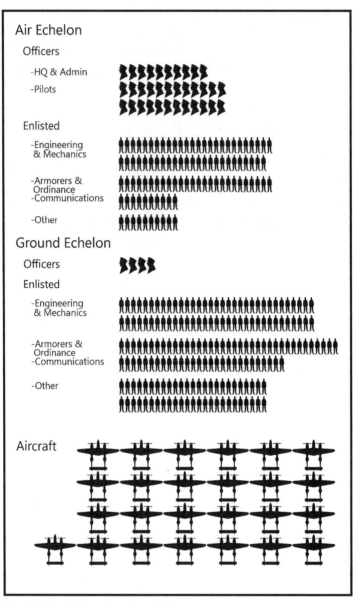

Air Echelon

Officers
- -HQ & Admin
- -Pilots

Enlisted
- -Engineering & Mechanics
- -Armorers & Ordinance
- -Communications
- -Other

Ground Echelon

Officers

Enlisted
- -Engineering & Mechanics
- -Armorers & Ordinance
- -Communications
- -Other

Aircraft

Twin-Engine Fighter Squadron Cohort.
RICHARDSON

For morning flights, the crews arrived before dawn, the crew chief starting each engine in turn to confirm that they were operating to standards. It was great news if both were operating well—the worst news if one "cut out" during preflight. In that case, the chief would tear open the cowling of the already-hot engine and begin swapping out spark plugs while his assistant ran back to the supply tent or begged a set of replacement plugs from one of the adjacent aircraft crews.

This job done, the engine was rechecked to verify the fix. Next was a quick cleanup of the cockpit, making sure the instruments, windshield, canopy, side windows, and mirror were clean. Fluids—both oil and fuel—were checked and topped off if necessary.

About now the oxygen jeep arrived. The radio was given a careful inspection by a corporal from the communication team. The undercarriage was checked and lubricated as needed. Covers from the pitot and relief tubes were removed and appropriate entries made on maintenance forms.

When the pilot arrived, the crew chief gave a short briefing of the condition of the aircraft and any quirks that may have arisen. With a wave, the pilot was off, carrying with him the chief's hopes for a successful mission and a safe return, and a special plea that the aircraft return in good shape, with nothing important blown off and without fresh bullet holes.

With the pilot's return, a quick debriefing took place to indicate how the plane was operating, identifying any obvious maintenance needs. Engines were again run up in a postflight inspection.

The crew next gave the aircraft an hour-long daily inspection, checking systems, equipment, and flight control services from front to rear. About this time, the armorers began to arrive to maintain and reload the machine guns and cannon for the next mission. If the mission would be escorting bombers, it meant hanging the external fuel tanks to the wing pods. If a dive-bombing mission, the chief might help the armorers in hanging the bombs.

More entries were made into maintenance forms and the aircraft was gassed up and secured until the next day's mission.

There was little doubt to whom the aircraft belonged: to the ground crew, on temporary loan each mission to the pilot. The pilot's name might have been stenciled in front of the cockpit, and perhaps the name of his best girl painted on the nose, but on each engine pod was also stenciled the name of the crew chief.[2]

The 14th Fighter Group was itself part of a vastly larger air force structure. Understanding how the 49th came to be in North Africa in the summer of 1943, the structure under which it operated, and appreciating the kinds of missions it flew, and why, requires consideration of the strategies, policies, and politics that so occupied Eisenhower, Roosevelt, and Churchill in the prior year. And those considerations are themselves rooted in the events of the years leading up to the United States' engagement in the war.

THE GERMAN MILITARY RESURGENCE

The Treaty of Versailles in June 1919 ended World War I and imposed many conditions considered onerous by Germany's leadership and its citizenry. Germany was required to make significant territorial concessions, pay reparations in the amount of $31 billion, and largely disarm and disband its military.

Following this "War to End All Wars," it was the intent of the victors to make the Reichswehr incapable of offensive action. In addition to the broad restrictions mentioned above, the treaty prohibited Germany from manufacturing or stockpiling military aircraft, forced German to surrender all aviation-related materials, and required that it disband its land-based and naval air forces.

For German leadership, and throughout the country, there was no peace with honor following their surrender. Though Germany had no choice but to accept the stringent conditions, the conditions were viewed as overly harsh, and Germany seethed with discontent for years following the end of hostilities. The inequity of the treaty was all the more intolerable for the Germans when they viewed the increasing military capabilities of their neighbors and former combatants. Making things worse, the German economy did not recover from the war—and the populace continued to pay the price of military defeat—for many years. These internal conditions created an environment ripe for discontent and gave life to the rise of nationalism within Germany in the 1930s. And with that emerging nationalism, Adolf Hitler rose to prominence.

The Treaty of Versailles did not forbid a military presence in Germany, but rather limited it severely. The treaty specified that the postwar German army could have a maximum strength of 100,000, and of this number, only 4,000 could be officers. Further, it required that the German General Staff—the core of military leadership for Germany—be dissolved.

Even a small army requires some level of leadership, and to this end the German forces reorganized to comply with the Versailles strictures, concurrently reviewing and revising their military policies. The new organization, the *Truppenamt* ("Troop Office"), completely revised German tactical and strategic doctrine. Over the next ten years, the group surreptitiously fostered the former Reichswehr, providing a new home for the core of the German General Staff. The formidable German Wehrmacht ultimately emerged as a result of the leadership of the Truppenamt.

Among the reforms introduced by the Nazi party, military rearmament became paramount. With the United States and Great Britain maintaining oversight of conditions in Germany, it was necessary for the German military redevelopment to be done surreptitiously.

The Strengthening Luftwaffe

By the mid-1930s, the need for both a strong tactical and a competent strategic air force in coming battles was accepted as truth by every military in the world. Military operations on the ground could only succeed under the protection of air superiority.

The first steps toward the Luftwaffe's formation were undertaken just months after Adolf Hitler came to power. Hermann Göring, a World War I ace with twenty-two victories, became national kommissar for aviation.

German military planners had for years taken advantage of a singular deficiency in the Treaty of Versailles: Aviation training on civilian planes was not prohibited. Maintaining the ruse that pilot trainees were going to fly with civilian airlines, such as Lufthansa, civil aviation schools in German operated only light trainers. To train pilots on the latest combat aircraft, Germany successfully engaged in a covert training program with the Soviet Union. At a secret base in Lipetsk, 200 miles south of Moscow, in western Russia, the German pilot cadets training program operated from 1924 to 1933, using Dutch, Russian, and German aircraft.

Emerging quietly and not yet openly from the strictures of Versailles, in 1933 Hitler ordered a tripling of the size of the army to 300,000 men, and directed the Air Ministry to build 1,000 warplanes. The Luftwaffe was "reborn" on May 15, 1933. Under Göring's leadership, it was one of the strongest, most doctrinally advanced, and most battle-experienced air forces in the world when World War II started four years later.

The buildup continued for two years in secret. In March 1935, Hitler publicly announced Nazi Germany's military expansion, in clear defiance of the Treaty of Versailles. The world became chillingly aware that the Nazis had 2,500 warplanes in its Luftwaffe and an army of 300,000 men in its Wehrmacht. Hitler felt confident enough to publicly announce that there would be compulsory military conscription in Nazi Germany, and that the army would be increased to 550,000 men.

In parallel, Japan was also very actively developing an inventory of military aircraft and trained pilots in the mid- to late 1930s. During the 1930s, the Japanese had a similar flight training program under way, without the need for secrecy. Starting in 1930, the Imperial Japanese Navy began a flying crew training program that was unequaled anywhere in the world.[3]

Tacticians and pilots in both Germany and Japan had the opportunity to experience combat prior to their engagement in World War II.

The German Luftwaffe formed the "Condor Legion," providing support to Francisco Franco's Falangists from 1936 to 1939 during the Spanish Civil War, significantly contributing to the defeat of the Republican forces. Experimenting with new doctrine and aircraft, the Condor Legion rotated key German pilot officers in and out of Spain, to both experience combat and contribute tactical ideas. Over 19,000 "volunteers" rotated through the Condor Legion, a number just low enough to ensure that Germany was not perceived as a combatant nation.[4]

German use of aircraft in close support of ground troops—the tactic that made blitzkrieg possible—was a concept that the Condor Legion developed in Spain. Additionally, Germany's latest aircraft were field-tested in combat, including the Messerschmitt Bf 109—widely known in America as the Me 109. The full range of the Luftwaffe's capabilities was tested in Spain, including its bomber force, reconnaissance, seaplanes, communication systems, and, very significantly, its antiaircraft battalions. Several months later, these veterans of the Spanish Civil War would be flying over Poland, Czechoslovakia, France, and the rest of Europe—an experienced, well-trained air force fighting for Hitler.

In the Pacific, Japanese aviators acquired important combat experience in the Second Sino-Japanese War, which commenced in July 1937. With the extensive flight training provided to aviators combined with two and a half years of direct combat experience in China, the Japanese navy began the Pacific War with arguably the best-trained and most experienced naval aviators in the world.[5]

By the late 1930s, the air forces of the United States and Great Britain were not remotely equivalent to those of Germany, Japan, or even Italy.

THE ERUPTION IN EUROPE

The year 1938 was a grim one in Europe. The interwar military buildup by the Nazis had reached its peak, and there was little doubt about Hitler's intentions. A false calm settled over Europe when British prime minister Neville Chamberlain acceded to the Munich Agreement in September of 1938, allowing German troops to occupy the Sudetenland, for the sake of "peace in our time."

Three months later Hitler's Wehrmacht occupied Czechoslovakia, and in May Germany concluded the "Pact of Steel" with Italy, laying the groundwork for the eventual "Axis" forces. In September, Poland fell to the German blitzkrieg. Britain, France, Australia, and New Zealand declared war on Germany.

The United States immediately declared its neutrality.

Over the next eight months the German army continued to devour Europe, invading and conquering Denmark, Norway, France, Belgium, Luxembourg, and the Netherlands, and the British were routed at Dunkirk. The Battle of Britain began in the late summer of 1940, Germany's attempt to secure air superiority over England preparatory to the planned Nazi invasion of England—Operation Sea Lion—later in the year.

With German war priorities in Europe clearly defined, the Middle East and North Africa then became additional objectives for the Axis forces. Italy invaded Egypt in September of 1940 and Greece in October. September also saw the finalization of the Tripartite Pact between Germany, Italy, and Japan. The Axis had formally become a reality.

As 1940 came to a close Great Britain faced the very real possibility that they would have to fight the German war machine alone and had begun to successfully contest the Italian army in North Africa. British success there would soon prompt Germany to dispatch Gen. Erwin Rommel and the "Afrika Korps" to the campaign in North Africa. Intense fighting between German and British armies began almost immediately, and by the end of March 1941 the British had been driven east to Egypt.

The military situation around the world continued to degrade at a remarkable rate. Along with these ferocious land battles in the North African deserts, early 1941 saw heavy German bombing in England, and British and German naval forces were locked in intense combat over a wide geographical range.

And in June of that year, the worst news: Germany had launched Operation Barbarossa—the invasion of the Soviet Union. The horrendous fighting there would ultimately lead to the slaughter of millions, and would become a determining factor in the conduct of war by the Allies, and on the locations where the Allies chose to do battle with the Axis forces. Axis advances toward the Volga and the oil-rich Caucasus would enrich German resources and could imperil the vital region between the Persian Gulf and Egypt. Britain greatly feared that a Russian collapse on the Eastern Front would allow Germany to increase its offensive actions in the West, leading almost certainly to a cross-Channel invasion by Germany onto British soil.

THE AMERICAN RESPONSE

American leadership, if not the American citizenry, had been moved to action by the events in Europe. As early as September 1939, following the fall of Poland, Roosevelt proclaimed a limited national emergency and authorized an increase to 227,000 men for the Regular Army and to 235,000 men for the National Guard.[6]

These German military successes in the spring of 1940 prompted further U.S. mobilization efforts. In May 1940 Roosevelt called for 50,000 new aircraft—an unimaginable increase—and a supplemental defense appropriation. Just one month later, a munitions program was put in place to procure all items needed to equip and maintain an army of 1.2 million, including the air corps, and creation of production facilities to support an army of over 4 million.

In September, the United States instituted military conscription—the draft—while continuing its neutrality.

With the equilibrium of the European continent thoroughly upset, invasion of Great Britain seemingly imminent, and the draft likely to take their sons for military service, the American public began to better understand the danger the country faced and to accept the need for heightened military preparedness.

Lend-Lease, the costly federal program to provide material for those nations already at war with the Axis, was started in September 1941. Lend-Lease helped to stimulate the U.S. military—industrial preparedness—and was especially important to the Soviet Union, then reeling under the German invasion of June 1941 and in desperate need of supplies and equipment.

In mid-1941, the main contribution of the United States to Great Britain and Russia was expected to be its industrial capacity. But while the American industrial base was already running at robust levels, it had its limitations, including the availability of manpower. Careful consideration was given to maintaining a balance between the manpower requirements of industry and those of the military. Lend-Lease was not without risks, costs, or unintended or unforeseen consequences for the U.S. military; for example, fewer aircraft became available for the U.S. Army Air Corps (USAAC), and this had the effect of retarding pilot training.

American aviation planners, notably Gen. Hap Arnold, recognized the importance of ramping up and then maintaining what would become very high levels of aircraft production. Significantly, where other nations stopped production lines to make modifications, or continued to manufacture models long obsolescent, Arnold ordered American factories to be left alone to ensure high production levels and established separate depots to modify and modernize older models.[7]

Industry responded. While German factories maintained a one-shift peacetime workweek until 1943, American plants ran around the clock, with a workforce that swelled with the employment of hundreds of thousands of women.

Army recruitment also responded well. Following Pearl Harbor, the army's ranks increased by an average of 300,000 men each month, reaching a total strength of almost 5.5 million soldiers by the end of 1942. The army's officer ranks also underwent a huge increase in the months after Pearl Harbor, reaching almost 400,000 officers by the end of the year.

THE EMERGENT ALLIED ARMED FORCES

With the Japanese attack at Pearl Harbor on December 7, 1941—an action for which the American people and most of the political and military leaders in the United States were unprepared—the United States clearly faced a new reality, and the pipe dream of neutrality disappeared.

Nerves were taut on the West Coast in the months immediately following the Japanese attack in Hawaii. In February 1942, reports of unidentified aircraft approaching California from the ocean resulted in the "Battle of Los Angeles," in which some 1,400 rounds of antiaircraft ammunition were fired at various "targets." The sightings were widely reported in the *Los Angeles Examiner* and *Los Angeles Times* newspapers, but never confirmed, and can now be attributed to the ambient tensions of the period.

Following Pearl Harbor, and in anticipation of the new aircraft and budget allocations, the War Department began creating ("constituting") aviation groups and squadrons. The 14th Pursuit Group, and its three pursuit squadrons (48th, 49th, 50th)—about which much will be reported in later combat actions—were constituted on November 20, 1940, and were activated at Hamilton Field, California, on January 15, 1941. 1st Lt. Troy Keith was named its interim commander. He was soon replaced in this position, but was again named CO in April of that year, and would eventually serve as commander during the invasions of North Africa, Sicily, and Italy, finally standing down on January 28, 1943. The group and its three squadrons were to serve in a variety of assignments, most notably under the North African Strategic Air Force during the invasion of Sicily in the summer of 1943.[8]

Peacetime mobilization—that period of time between Germany's invasion of Poland in September 1939 and Japan's raid on Oahu 828 days later—benefited the U.S. Army enormously. Within eight months after the United States' declaration of war, it had one-third more personnel than called for by early mobilization plans.

Equipment became the critical issue, and a massive effort was needed to meet the production goals announced by the president in January 1942: 60,000 airplanes in 1942, and unimaginably, 125,000 aircraft and 120,000 tanks in 1943.[9] The scale of required industrial production was fantastical and greatly exceeded the country's capacity to produce at that time. Despite this, aviation construction remained a top priority, and the final goals were only slightly reduced.

The costs associated with the mobilization were equally staggering. Prewar federal spending in 1938 was $83.0 billion; in 1942 it had more than quadrupled, to $375 billion, and the federal debt had soared to $845 billion. War planners were faced with one additional and critical problem: Assuming American industry could meet the production goals for aircraft, where were they going to get the pilots?

Before the war, General Arnold had established nine civilian Primary flight training schools, two AAC Basic flight training schools, and two AAC Advanced flight training schools. The number of trained pilots had jumped from 300 in 1938 to 30,000 in 1941 (plus 110,000 mechanics). On December 7, 1941, the USAAC had a running start and was in the war for the duration.[10]

Revamped Flight Training for the AAC

The U.S. Army Air Corps was given an impossible task: Its pilot training program had long been driven by demand, which in the late 1930s was at a nadir. In 1937 it graduated just 184 officers from advanced pilot training schools. All flight training was conducted at just three airfields located around San Antonio, and in the late 1930s the air corps was graduating on average two hundred pilots each year.

The events in Europe resulted in a slight uptick in the number of graduates in 1939, but the army continued to apply highly restrictive admission requirements. The pilot pipeline was still largely operating as it had in the early 1930s, and the army's pilot training program was itself due for a major overhaul in both policies and infrastructure. As recently as 1939, the army had graduated just 397 cadets from advanced flying schools and accepted just 11 percent of applicants who sat for the admission examination. The old-school system that had produced few pilots of exemplary quality would soon be required to produce highly qualified pilots by the tens of thousands.[11]

Faced with German, Italian, and Japanese militarism, in 1939 the AAC set a goal of training 4,500 pilots over the next twenty-four months—a 1,200 percent annual increase. But the demand for pilots continued to change, and by 1940 the new target was 7,000 pilot graduates each year.[12] Within two years, the demand had become a tidal wave.

The Army Air Corps sought to reinvent its training program, recognizing early that these targets could not be solely accomplished internally. It began contracting with private aviation schools around the country—initially with nine of the best civilian flying schools, and eventually expanding to ninety-nine schools.

The plan showed signs of early success. By 1940, only a year after admitting just 903 cadets to its training program, the army had 3,709 students in the flight program. The number of cadets increased to almost 17,000 by the end of 1941, and to 90,000 by the end of 1942. The types of flight personnel also expanded, with the army requiring nineteen different types of pilots, ranging from glider pilots to commanders of four-engine bombers. And the AAC demand was not just limited to pilots. Concurrent with the exponential growth in pilot production came a proportional growth in the production of officers in technical fields, including navigators, bombardiers, and specialists in communications, armament, weather, and radar.

The army also reaped the benefits of what could be considered a parallel program for flight training, Civilian Pilot Training (CPT)—an innovative aviation training initiative that was to have a profound effect on military pilot preparations for the coming fight. Seen as a part of the New Deal, the CPT program was not strictly oriented to training pilots for military service. It was believed that CPT would create an "air-mindedness" among American youth, resuscitate a depressed light aircraft industry, and give an economic boost to fixed-base operators who provided services such as flying lessons, charter flights, aircraft sales, maintenance, fuel, and supplies. In fact, military service was optional for students who completed the CPT program in its early years. It was designed around a partnership of academic institutions, private flight schools, and regional airports to provide ground school and flight instruction for qualified students.[13]

In 1939, thirteen schools with preexisting aeronautics programs were selected by CPT for a demonstration program, producing by year's end 330 qualified pilots. The imaginative program—not unlike the ones that had been in operation in Germany and Japan for many years—came at exactly the right time for the AAC. CPT expanded quickly, and by late 1940 it included over 450 schools, had trained 21,000 pilots, and had an enrollment of 15,000 flight students.[14]

In the three-year period from July 1, 1939, to June 30, 1942, CPT trained 125,762 pilots, including 13,094 flight instructors and 3,565 commercial pilots. Roughly half of the pilots trained transitioned to the U.S. Army Air Forces (USAAF) or U.S. Naval Reserve for additional flight training. Before Pearl Harbor, there was no legally binding requirement that graduates of the CPT enlist in the armed forces; it was intended to be a war-preparedness program.

Following the attack on Pearl Harbor, President Roosevelt directed the CPT to abandon its mission of supporting light aviation and to devote itself exclusively to preparing pilots for military service. As a sign of this refocusing, CPT was renamed the War Training Service. Graduates who had previously had the option of enrolling in army or navy flight programs now found this assignment compulsory. By June 1942 over 42,000 graduates of CPT were enrolled in the military flight training schools. These cadets achieved exceptionally high graduation rates; the "washout" rate for CPT-trained pilots was one-quarter that of cadets who did not participate in CPT.[15]

Some of the pilots who would serve in the 49th Fighter Squadron earned their wings by applying directly to the U.S. Army Air Corps for admission into the Flight Cadet Training Program, including Lieutenants Boatman, Kocour, and Harper. Others first completed the CPT and then entered the military flight training schools, including Lieutenants Gregory, Knepper, and Neely. But whether the applicants had never been in an aircraft before entering the AAC or had already earned their private pilot's license through CPT, all completed the same three-phase aviation training program that the army had established.

CIVILIAN PILOT TRAINING PROGRAM

Putting together a flight program under the CPT required a consortium of academic institutions, flight operators, and airport managers. Within the consortium, the college or university provided academic ground instruction, with students typically registering for a six-credit course in aeronautics or physics. The flight operators provided additional ground instructors, aircraft, and flight instructors, and were compensated only for trainees who "completed the flight instruction." The airports were required to meet Civil Aeronautics Administration (CAA) specifications for minimum length, width, and prevailing winds, to be located not more than 10 miles from the institution, and to offer appropriate ground facilities and supplies.

The program required cadet applicants to be U.S. citizens, between the ages of nineteen and twenty-six, and with no prior pilot certifications. At least two years of college were required, although current undergrads with one year were also accepted. Applicants were required to meet physical standards established by the CAA, and a parental consent was required for any student under the age of twenty-one.[16]

The CPT was offered in two sections: the private (preliminary) course and the restricted commercial (secondary) course. Only the best students from the preliminary course were permitted to continue into the secondary course. Student pilots who completed both courses were qualified to apply for the Aviation Cadet Program with the U.S. Army Air Corps. Significantly, applicants who were accepted for this military flight training were exempt from the first three months of preliminary training that was ordinarily required in the Regular Army training program.[17]

CPT INSTRUCTION

The CPT program in Lewiston, Idaho, where Allan Knepper took his flight training, was one of the largest flight training programs in the country in 1941. The program had started in late 1939 when the CAA approved the application submitted by the consortium of Lewiston Normal College, the Zimmerly Brothers Air Transport Company, and the Lewiston Airport. The *Lewiston Tribune* proudly reported on October 3 that Lewiston Normal had been allotted ten students by the CAA, joining the University of Idaho and the College of Idaho in the national program.

Owner Bert Zimmerly initially provided instruction through the CPT and later began training navy air cadets. At its peak, his program had twenty-five to thirty pilot instructors, plus a ground crew of twenty. By the end of 1943, the Zimmerly Air Transport School of Flying had trained over 1,500 pilots, more than any other training center in the United States.[18]

Zimmerly's academic partner, Lewiston Normal College, admitted thirty students each fall and spring term: twenty in the elementary courses, and ten in the secondary courses. Students paid the college a laboratory fee of up to $40, and the CAA paid the college an additional fee of $20 per student for ground school instruction. The CAA paid the flight operator $270 to $290 per student for the preliminary flight course. For the secondary course, which involved much larger and more costly aircraft, the flight operators received from $750 to $800 for each trainee who completed the course, the actual amount depending on the specific type of aircraft used for instruction.

PRELIMINARY COURSE

The preliminary course included both ground and flight instruction. The college provided a forty-eight-hour block of ground school, which was supplemented by a twenty-four-hour block of ground instruction at the airfield. Subjects in ground school included meteorology, navigation, civil air regulations, parachute theory, operation, and practice, the theory of flight, engines, instruments and radio.[19] At the airfield, ground instruction also included a thorough familiarization with the functioning of the airplane, its controls, and its instruments. Safety instruction was given regarding the principal hazards around the aircraft: dangers from propellers, ground handling during high winds, and operating the engine with no one in the cockpit.[20]

The students also got started in flight instruction, receiving between thirty-five and fifty hours of dual instruction in the air, and additional solo hours. Training was organized in three stages, commencing with eight hours of dual instruction, given in thirty-minute sessions, with six main elements of training:

- Proficiency in taxiing, including handling the aircraft into the wind, with a crosswind, in a downwind condition, and in gusty air;
- Takeoffs into the wind, with a crosswind and downwind;
- Air work, including developing proficiency in flying straight and level, gentle climbs and turns, flat gentle turns, 70-degree turns, and spirals and approaches for landings;
- Landings into the wind, with a crosswind, and downwind;
- Stalls and spins, with emphasis on approach and recovery; and
- Emergency situations, including forced landings.

The flying was done in a certified aircraft of not less than 50 horsepower (hp). In most cases, the aircraft used was the Piper Cub, a two-seater with an average cruising speed of 70 mph, a top speed of 90 mph, and a ceiling of 9,300 feet. The Cub was just 22 feet long and stood 80 inches high, with a wingspan of 35 feet. Holding twelve gallons of fuel, it had a range of just 190 miles.[21] Lilliputian though it might have been, by the war's end, 80 percent of all U.S. military pilots had received their initial flight training in Piper Cubs.[22]

After eight hours of dual instruction, and with the endorsement of the instructor, the student advanced to the second stage of instruction, primary solo, which consisted of five hours of solo flight and one hour of dual flight.

During primary solo, the student practiced the skills learned in dual instruction, with the exception of stalls, spins, and emergency landings. All takeoffs and landings were "into the wind" only, and all landings were without power. Initial solo flights were thirty minutes in duration, and a ten-minute check by the instructor was given after each flight. In addition, the student underwent a thirty-minute check after three hours of primary solo. By the end of primary solo instruction, the student had a minimum of fourteen flying hours.

The final stage of flight instruction—advanced solo—consisted of thirteen hours of solo flight and eight hours of dual instruction. The required learning outcomes in this phase of instruction were very well defined, with proficiency required in the following elements of flight: precision landings, including various types of approaches; stalls, spins, and slips; and power approaches and power landings.

A two-hour solo cross-country flight of 50 miles minimum distance, including two full-stop landings at different airports, was also required as the student neared completion of the program.

At the conclusion of these three phases of flight instruction, the student had a minimum of seventeen hours of dual instruction and eighteen hours of solo flight. The CPT program allowed for up to fifty hours of flight instruction, if needed.

SECONDARY COURSE

The secondary course was also in two parts: a 126-hour ground course, given jointly by the participating institution and the flight instructor contractor, and a 40- to 50-hour flight course.

The secondary ground course was much more thorough than that of the preliminary course and included instruction in power plants, aerodynamics, aircraft, and navigation. The flight instruction component of the secondary course was likewise very much more advanced than that of the preliminary course. The planes used were much more powerful, with engines of up to 225 hp. The aircraft most often used was the Fairchild M-62A, a low-winged sport and training plane with tandem seating.

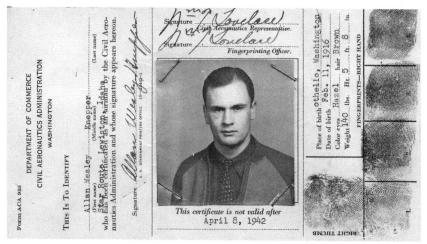

Knepper's CAA card.
FINN

The secondary flight course started with a complete review of the preliminary course and continued with additional instruction and practice in all forms of takeoffs, stalls, spins, loops, and other maneuvers. The length of the course provided the student with considerable practice and solo flying. At the conclusion of this course the student was given a flight test by a civil aeronautics inspector, and successful cadets received the Restricted Commercial Pilot Certificate.[23]

Lewiston's Allan Knepper was enrolled in the secondary class in September 1941. At that time, Lewiston Normal had thirty male students in the program: twenty in the elementary course and ten in the advanced. The airfield included four flight instructors, plus Zimmerly, and four ground instructors.[24]

At the end of his secondary program, Allan Knepper passed his certification flight and received his CAA card. Within a few short weeks he would present himself for acceptance into the U.S. Army Air Corps Pilot Training Program, beginning his long and arduous path toward becoming a combat pilot.

CHAPTER 3

Two Flyers for the Fray

LIEUTENANTS KNEPPER AND KOCOUR WERE SENT TO NORTH AFRICA AS replacement pilots, taking the places of other young men who had been killed in combat, had gone missing, had been reassigned to other flight duties, or had been captured. They came to the air corps from similar backgrounds, but by different routes. Born in the midst of wheat fields, growing up in small towns, graduating high school in the same year, and enlisting in the same month, these two men soon became part of what has come to be known as "the Pilot Factory."[1]

HERMAN KOCOUR

Herman Kocour was born on October 5, 1917, in Andale, Kansas, the fifth child in a family that would eventually include fourteen children. His parents, John and Emma, operated a leather and saddlery business in Andale, and later added a grocery store, with the leather business operating in the back of the store. With John's death in 1940, Emma and the children continued to operate the store. But when all five of her sons joined the service in the early days of the war, she was forced to sell the store, supporting herself and the children by taking in sewing and by boarding teachers in the home.[2]

Andale at that time was a very tight German community numbering 289, and the Kocours themselves probably originated in Bohemia.[3] Originally "Korzovce," Herman's grandfather changed the family name to Kocour when he became a U.S. citizen in 1878. Herman kept traces of that beginning in some of the phrases he sometimes used to express himself.

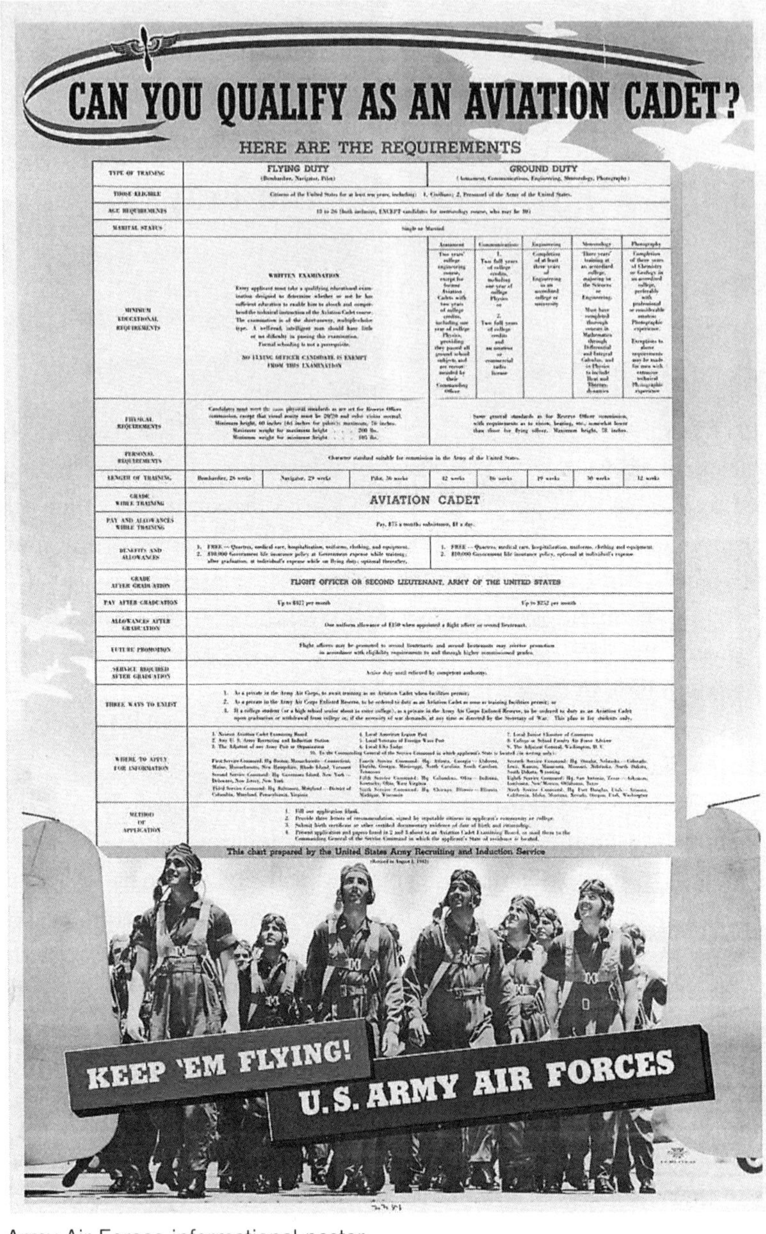

Army Air Forces informational poster.

Graduating from Andale High School in 1935, Kocour had no thought of college, and probably none of military service. He had worked in the family store through high school and continued working for his father after graduation.

With war approaching, Kocour began to consider in what way he would serve. Although he had never been in an airplane, when the U.S. Army Air Forces rescinded the requirement that applicants for pilot training have two years of college experience, he immediately applied to the Aviation Cadet Program.

ALLAN KNEPPER

Allan Knepper was born on February 11, 1916, in wheat country at Othello, Washington, to Jess and Stella Knepper. In 1930, the family moved to Lewiston, Idaho, population 10,584, where Allan grew up and completed his high school and college education.[4]

Knepper's graduation photo from Lewiston High School, 1935.
FINN

Allan was hard-wired for competition. Not satisfied with a second-place finish in the 1930 Lewiston-Clarkson Harvest Festival three-legged race, he entered and won the sack race.

He matriculated at the Lewiston Normal College, setting his sights on a career in education. He was active on campus during his two years at LNC, playing on the football team and acting in the school's dramatic programs. He was a member of the Intercollegiate Knights and chairman of the Student Body Athletic Committee. With three fellow students, he graduated from Lewiston Normal on March 11, 1938.

At the time, the primary mission of the college was to prepare teachers for serving in the region's many one-room, rural schools, and it was in just such a school that Allan got his start in the classroom.

He was hired at the rural elementary school in Summit, Idaho, located in the rich wheat field plateau overlooking the Clearwater River. He soon bought a '39 Plymouth Coupe for which he paid $700. Handsome, athletic, educated, and employed, he was doing alright for himself.

Summit Elementary School, 1942.
PEA

Allan Knepper, Lewiston Normal
graduate, 1938.
LEWIS CLARK STATE COLLEGE LIBRARY

Like everyone else in Lewiston, Knepper got his news from the hometown paper, the *Lewiston Tribune*. He had read of the building crisis in Europe and of tense relations in the Pacific. And like everyone else in the country, he was stunned to learn on that quiet Sunday morning that Pearl Harbor had been attacked and the United States was at war. Monday's *Tribune* headline read: "Dazed Lewiston Public Hears News of Attack: Citizens Slow to Get Full Import of First News from Honolulu; Sunday's Calm Broken." The copywriter's own shock is evident in the text:

> *A dazed, unbelieving Lewiston public on yesterday's peaceful Sabbath heard the first news that Japan had bombed United States Pacific ocean bases and hurled that tiny but militant island nation into war with America.*
>
> *Sunday's funny papers were being read. Homes were being set in order by late risers. Many people were enjoying the brilliant sunshine of the day and driving on nearby country roads; others were just eating breakfast.*
>
> *Shortly before 11 A.M., into this calm of an America at peace, broke the first news on radios that had been turned to favorite programs, some of them symphony music. Pearl Harbor had been bombed!*

Knepper would have read the *Tribune*'s editorial of December 12, writing that exactly reflected the emotional state of the country:

> *This has now become a world war whose magnitude strains the imag-*
> *ination of any man to comprehend. It is a war in which there can be*
> *no compromise, no deadlock, no half-way peace. The issue involved is*
> *so towering that civilization—civilization whose frontiers have been*
> *pushed back steadily by the armed might of the forces of fascism until*
> *the time has come at last for a final stand—must triumph or be blotted*
> *out for uncountable years.*
>
> *It is a war to the death. It is a worldwide war which will deter-*
> *mine whether the freeman's way of life shall perish from the face of*
> *this earth.*[5]

All the young men in the county knew that the stakes could not be higher, that war was upon them, and that they would be called to serve, to fight, and perhaps to die. War news was everywhere, and with it came the army's strident calls to arms.

Like the young man in the small Kansas town who would soon become his close friend, Allan Knepper felt the dread that had befallen the country, and knew that he would be a part of the conflict that awaited. But for Knepper, the path to service was clear—he knew he would fly.

Following his graduation from Lewiston Normal, Knepper had reenrolled to participate in its CPT aviation program. He had been the first CPT student in his class to solo, complete the secondary level of CPT during the fall of 1941, and qualify as a civilian pilot by the day the United States went to war. With his private pilot's license already in his pocket, Knepper applied to the Army Aviation Cadet Program shortly after the United States entered the war.

APPLYING TO THE AAF AVIATION CADET PROGRAM: REQUIREMENTS AND TESTING

In his book, *This Flying Game*, air force general Hap Arnold writes: "[I am] convinced that there is a 'flying type.'" He describes the person as

Recruiting ad from the *Lewiston Tribune*, December 12, 1941.

LEWISTON TRIBUNE, DEC. 12, 1941

being of "good moral fiber . . . honest, truthful, reliable," and possessing "the sine qua non, courage." "The frank, open-faced, pleasant-mannered, serious-minded, cooperatively inclined boy is the one who is wanted and the one who is selected nine times out of ten."[6]

More practically, the army's brochure, "Aviation Cadet Training for the AAF," recorded that "Mechanical aptitude, unusually quick reflexes, perfect physical coordination, and the ability to make rapid decisions are desirable in the applicant who wishes to become a pilot. A knowledge of mathematics and some experience in the field of the applied sciences are useful."[7]

Allan and Herman met the general physical requirements for acceptance into the Aviation Cadet Program. They were within the age limits (eighteen to twenty-six), within the height and weight specifications (60 to 76 inches tall, 105 to 200 pounds), had good vision and normal color vision, hearing, and blood pressure, and adequate teeth. And they were U.S. citizens.[8]

Submitting their applications from their homes in Idaho and Kansas to their respective Aviation Cadet Examining Boards, they would have included their birth certificates, accompanying affidavits that provided additional personal details (race, place of birth, weight and height, marital status, and education), and, "as evidence of good character," three letters of recommendations from non-family "reputable citizens."[9]

At their Examining Boards, they were given a preliminary medical examination, their medical history recorded, and immunizations noted. The physical exam went considerably beyond a normal enlistment examination. Vision and hearing were much more carefully evaluated. Candidates were tested to confirm "a stable equilibrium; a sound cardio-vascular system, a well-formed, well-adjusted, and coordinated physique; and an integrated and stable central nervous system." The army identified thirty-seven "disqualifying defects," including history of rheumatic fever, syphilis, kidney stones, malaria, asthma or hay fever, sleepwalking, fainting, amnesia, and more.[10] And a detailed eye examination was given, including color perception. They were also examined by the board to confirm that they possessed the personal and character traits "suitable to a person who may become a commissioned officer."

They then were administered the Aviation Cadet Qualifying Examination (ACQE), given by the air forces in lieu of the prior two-year college requirement. The test, AC-10-A, was designed to measure aptitude rather than specific technical information, formal education achievement, or specialized training. It identified applicants who were "sufficiently alert and intelligent to be capable of learning an air-crew assignment and who could measure up to the intellectual and leadership standards required of officers in the Army." It was the sole "mental" requirement for appointment as an aviation cadet.[11]

In relying exclusively on this test, the AAF had abandoned the extremely narrow application standards that had been in place in the late 1930s. "In time of war such factors as education and the social graces become secondary to the all-important question of whether the applicant can become a successful pilot, bombardier, or navigator. If he can, the Air Forces need him; if not, they cannot use him for air-crew training."[12]

This three-hour test was not a "pilot" test; rather, it was a "threshold test." A passing grade qualified the applicant to be considered for some type of aviation-related schooling and assignment. Successful cadets could eventually become pilots, navigators, or bombardiers; that assignment was made at the classification centers during their first weeks in the military. Reflecting the army way of doing things, the test protocol was carefully proscribed: what type of desk or table was to be used, how the applicant may be excused to visit the lavatory, what type of pencil to use, how to maintain control of the testing materials, and how to correctly grade the resultant answer sheet.[13]

The ACQE was three parts. The first part, broadly scoped, written, and timed, was the "mental" examination, which was designed to better ensure that individuals passing the test would possess those qualifications required for success in air-crew assignment, including vocabulary, reading comprehension, practical judgment, mathematics, alertness to recent developments, and mechanical comprehension. High scores in reading comprehension, mathematics, and judgment were strong indicators of an applicant's suitability for pilot training. Mathematics was the strongest indicator for suitability for navigator training, and those cadets who eventually became navigators had, on average, the highest test scores.[14]

The test takers themselves had different ideas about how the test scores were used, claiming:

> [T]he classification tests sorted cadets into three bins: pilots were chosen from those who gave quick and correct answers; bombardiers were chosen from those who gave quick and erroneous answers; navigators were those who gave slow and correct answers.[15]

The written examination included 150 questions, and three hours were allotted for completion. Ninety correct answers meant acceptance to the flight program.

The second part of the examination was a psychomotor test to measure hand-eye coordination, visual acuity, reflexes, and the ability to perform under pressure.

The third part of the test program was a psychological evaluation, which was in some ways the most difficult to administer. The candidate was interviewed, "during which the flight surgeon by means of skillful questioning of the candidate was able to obtain the desired information." The line of inquiry included family history and environment, personal achievements, mental stability, "sociality," and the applicant's philosophy of life—"the principles by which the individual lives." A score of 160 on the 200-point inquiry rated a passing score.[16]

In what the army must have considered an astonishing response for its call for pilots, over 122,000 applicants took the ACQE during the first three months of 1942. Knepper, Kocour, and 73,132 other applicants received a passing grade.[17] The "pipeline" of flight personnel was beginning to fill.

In early March,[18] Knepper and Kocour separately received letters from their Examining Boards, confirming that each had satisfied the mental, physical, and moral standards for enlistment in the U.S. Army.

Prior to February 1, 1942, successful applicants were not required to enlist in the U.S. Army Air Forces. Instead, they were admitted to the aviation program as aviation cadets. Cadets who did not successfully complete the flight training program were simply discharged from the service. After February 1, applicants were required to enlist in the U.S.

Army Air Forces and, if they failed to complete the flight training program, reverted to the rank of private and could be reassigned "according to the needs of the service."[19]

Knepper was instructed to report to Geiger Field for enlistment on March 19, 1942, at 9:30 A.M., and was advised that following his enlistment, he would be placed on furlough "to await appointment as an Aviation Cadet and shipment to a Replacement Center." During his furlough, he was paid in the grade of private, but would receive the pay of a cadet when his appointment was made.[20]

And so, on March 19, 102 days after the Japanese attack on Pearl Harbor, Mr. Allan W. Knepper reported to the recruiting officer at Geiger Field, together with his friends from the Lewiston area, Ralph Nichols and Leonard Richardson. He was given a second, more thorough physical examination, fingerprinted, and administered the Oath of Enlistment, becoming Pvt. Allan W. Knepper, U.S. Army serial number 19033105. At the age of twenty-six and a half, he was just short of the maximum age for acceptance into the pilot training program. As with all cadets, his enlistment was "for the duration, plus six months." His furlough began immediately, allowing him to complete the academic year at Summit and earning him pay in the grade of private.

Kocour, following a parallel path to the air corps, was directed to enlist in the U.S. Army on March 30, 1942. He was made to order for an aircraft cockpit: 5 foot, 9 inches tall, and 160 pounds, with hazel eyes and brown hair.[21] He quickly became known as "Koc" (pronounced *Coke*).

Lankier than Kocour, but still well suited to an airplane cockpit, Knepper was 5 foot 7 and weighed 138 pounds, and was called "Knep."

At the conclusion of their furlough, Allan and Herman were instructed to return, bringing a "sufficient amount of clothing (underwear, socks, etc.) to last at least a week." Upon reporting in, they would be assigned to the first stage of their aviation training: preflight.

U.S. Army Air Forces Aviation Training
During the war, any pilot who served in any capacity aboard any sort of aircraft quite likely received his training in the five-step U.S. Army Air Forces Training Program. Driven by the fantastic demand for trained

pilots, navigators, and bombardiers in the early 1940s, the program expanded to include almost one hundred flight training centers, each operated under a carefully controlled and uniform curriculum and a pro-scribed schedule.

The training process began with Preflight school, essentially a ground school that provided the same baseline training for all cadets, regardless of their eventual assignment. Importantly, Preflight also introduced cadets to life in the military.

During Preflight, cadets were given their future AAF assignments, and those selected for pilot training continued next to Primary flight school, where students first entered the cockpit and took to the air. For many of them, this would be their first time in an aircraft of any sort. In Primary, cadets learned the rudiments of flight and aircraft control, soloed, and continued classroom study. Roughly 25 percent of the cadet corps failed to complete Primary, and were "washed out." Many of these cadets would return to Preflight to be reclassified and assigned to a dif-ferent training program and subsequently receive their commissions as navigators or bombardiers.

Cadets who successfully completed Primary continued to Basic and Advanced flight schools, where more complicated flight maneuvers were learned, including formation flying. The final stage was Transition train-ing, where pilots were introduced to the specific aircraft they would fly in combat.

Each of the first four phases were nominally of ten weeks' dura-tion; however, the Preflight course could be lengthened or abbreviated depending on the demand for the flight specialties, space availability within subsequent courses, or to maintain an orderly flow of students.[22] Transition was normally of four to five weeks' duration, and the entire aviation training program, including transition, could be completed in forty-five weeks.

The flight training infrastructure became vast: The army operated six Preflight centers, fifty-six Primary airfields, thirty-one Basic airfields, ten Advanced single-engine schools, and twenty-two Advanced twin-engine schools. In less than a year, the army could take a young man from the fields, the classroom, the factory, the storefront, and make him the most feared warrior the world had ever known or could have imagined.

PREFLIGHT AT SANTA ANA ARMY AIR BASE

Knepper had been assigned to the Preflight center at Santa Ana Army Air Base (SAAAB) in Santa Ana, California. Knepper left Spokane on the "Pacific Electric" with his friends, Leonard Richardson and Ralph Nichols, who had enlisted in the AAF with him on March 19. The three were en route to Santa Ana, reporting to SAAAB on June 10, 1942.

In the interval between World War I and World War II, the AAF did not employ "ground schools." Instead, they relied chiefly upon high education requirements to ensure a sound background for aviation cadets, with military indoctrination being provided at the flying schools.

With the ramp-up to World War II, the huge expansion of the pilot training program entailed a lowering of educational requirements for flying recruits. The Preflight centers were instituted to guarantee a common level of academic background and to give newly recruited cadets the fundamentals of military discipline.[23] At the time of Kocour and Knepper's enlistment, the army's three centers were located at Santa Ana, Nashville, and San Antonio.

SAAAB was destined to become a huge training camp, but prior to the fall of 1941 the area was little more than bean and tomato fields. Transforming the site from bare dirt to a full training center took just 120 days. The result: 177 buildings were constructed, including 70 barracks, 4 classroom buildings, 10 administration buildings, mess halls, gasoline station, post office, theaters, chapels, a 151-bed hospital, and much more. A huge new city was built in just three months, and by the war's end, it had grown to more than 800 buildings, with a teaching and training contingent of 26,000. Although it was an air base, it was not equipped with a training airstrip; students received no flight instruction during Preflight.[24]

The demand for trained pilots by all branches of the service was enormous, and the rapid increase in aviation training is evident in the numbers of cadets processed through SAAAB. The first class of 2,601 cadets graduated on July 1, 1942, and by year's end, SAAAB had graduated 23,479 cadets. In 1943, the total was 57,895 cadets. At the end of the war, after the base was decommissioned, the SAAAB property eventually became the center of the city of Costa Mesa, California.[25]

The flying cadet program started immediately and moved quickly. Knepper, Richardson, and Nichols, along with hundreds of other cadets, were given another physical examination, issued the standard cadet "kit," and began their indoctrination into military life—the GI haircut, drill, mess, and guard duty. They were inoculated for smallpox, typhoid, tetanus, yellow fever, and cholera. And they marched. Everywhere.

In army fashion, they got right down to business. One cadet later recalled the commander's welcoming speech to the newly arrived cadets: "[H]e told us to look to the man on our right, the man on our left, the man in front of us, and the man behind us. He informed us that in one year one of these men would be dead—not from enemy action, but from [an] operational flying accident."[26]

Santa Ana gave many cadets their first inkling of the wide diversity in America at that time. Cadets came from all cultural, economic, and

Newly arrived aviation cadets, June 11, 1942. Ralph Nichols is at far right; Allan Knepper is third from right.

RICHARDSON

Cadets in fresh kit, June 11, 1942. Knepper is second from left, Leonard Richardson, fourth from left, Ralph Nichols, fifth from left.

Aviation Cadet Knepper.

Aviation Cadet Kocour.

educational backgrounds. Many were from large cities, and many from small towns. Religion was important for some, not so much for others. They shared an uncertainty about their futures, a concern for the families they had left behind, and a commitment to becoming pilots. The training program they had begun was not competitive—the army needed all the pilots it could get—and there were plenty of slots for anyone who could complete the program. The egalitarianism of the program, and the fact that all the cadets wore the same uniform, tended to minimize the differences that might have been initially apparent.

Cadets who passed the SAAAB physical began the "Classification" process—a weeklong battery of aptitude and physical tests to determine whether they were best suited for training as a pilot, navigator, or bombardier. These were tense days for the cadets. Young men who could only imagine themselves at the control of a powerful aircraft would be disappointed to learn that the army found them poor candidates for pilots and perhaps better suited as bombardiers or navigators.

In making assignments, the army also factored in the current demand for each category. In late 1942, with U.S. military efforts ramping up in the South Pacific, the demand for navigators capable of guiding aircraft from one small island to another was high, and many cadets who might have been good pilots found themselves assigned to the navigator track. The cadet's preferences were not considered; the arc of their service would be determined entirely by the army.

At Santa Ana, Knepper, together with his friends Richardson and Nichols, received the good news that they had received the "pilot" classification. Herman Kocour, assigned to the Preflight center at San Antonio, also received his pilot classification.

In the nine weeks following Classification, cadets underwent a rigorous program of classroom instruction, military indoctrination, and physical training. They were paid $75 per month, and $1 per day subsistence. As junior officers, cadets were addressed as "Mister" by all ranks. Aviation cadets wore the same uniform as army officers, lacking only the mohair cuff band of a full officer. The general-issue aviator's eagle emblem was replaced by a winged propeller insignia of the U.S. Army Air Forces.[27]

The Preflight curriculum—carefully designed, evaluated, and periodically assessed—was followed by all three flight centers in the country.[28] Cadets spent three and a half hours each day in academic instruction. Of the 160 classroom hours in Preflight, one-fourth was devoted to mathematics and physics. Math instruction stressed fundamentals and would have been familiar to former college students, including simple algebra, graphs, vector problems, and the use of scales. Physics instruction was related to fundamental laws of fluids and gases, heat and temperature, and the laws of motion, work, and energy. Nearly one-third of the classroom hours was devoted to developing proficiency in Morse Code; the minimum passing standard was six words per minute in aural sending and receiving and five words per minute in visual sending and receiving. Lecture topics also included maps and charts, aircraft identification, military customs and courtesies, communications, and chemical warfare defense.

Outside the classroom, cadets also spent an hour each day in basic military indoctrination and, throughout the nine-week program, were assigned twenty-six hours of infantry drill (marching). They spent an hour each day in physical training, which included mass calisthenics, supervised athletics, and competitive sports like volleyball, softball, touch football, boxing, wrestling, and track. Santa Ana had an excellent pool and pioneered in the administration of aquatic instruction, including swim tests, inflation of clothing, swimming through burning oil, and exercises in artificial respiration. Cadets learned to fire a .45 caliber pistol and attended first-aid classes that included instruction related to the various disease-carrying insects and foods that might be encountered abroad.

Off-hours were spent cleaning and polishing, doing KP duty, and in the evening, studying. George Loving, in his book *Woodbine Red Leader*, reported Preflight to be "a combination boot camp and officers' candidate school. The first priority, it seemed, was to instill discipline and whip us into shape physically. Concurrently, we studied the basic military skills required of commissioned officers, and attended classes to refresh our understanding of some basic academic subjects."[29]

At Santa Ana, cadet organization mirrored what they would experience as commissioned pilots. Cadets were assigned to squadrons, with four squadrons making a group and nine groups constituting a wing. Cadet officers were appointed from the rank of wing commander down through group commander, lieutenant, sergeant, and corporal.

Cadets marched to and from classes, and maintained military formality within the classrooms. At Santa Ana, retreat, formal guard mount, and the Sunday parade were emphasized, and inspections of the cadet's rooms took place on Saturday mornings.

The West Point ideal of military honor was adopted in theory at Santa Ana. Honor councils were organized, composed entirely of cadets, which reported conditions, made suggestions to base authority, and undertook indoctrination of the lower classmen. Discipline was rigorous and enforced in part through the use of "demerits." Accumulating sufficient demerits would warrant a variety of disciplinary measures: admonitions, reprimands, restrictions to limits, deprivation of privileges, punishment tours, or loss of leave. A punishment tour consisted of walking at attention for one hour, in uniform plus gloves, field belt, and bayonet scabbard.

Though they received no aircraft flight instruction, cadets spent ten hours training in a simple but effective simulator called a Link Trainer—more affectionately known as the "Blue Box."

Cadet pilot at the controls of a Link Trainer.

Link Trainer.

SAAAB cadets enjoying an afternoon's leave. Far left is Cadet Allan Knepper; far right is Cadet Leonard Richardson.

Knepper completed Preflight and was assigned to Primary flight school at the Morton Air Academy at Gary Field, Blythe, California, hard by the California–Arizona border, surrounded by baked desert landscape. Knepper's arc diverged from that of the two men with whom he had first joined the army, as his training would eventually take him to fighter training, while Nichols would train as a transport pilot. Although Richardson successfully soloed in Primary, he would later wash out of pilot school, become a navigator, and serve in the South Pacific Theater.

PRIMARY FLIGHT SCHOOL

Unlike the later stages of flight instruction, Primary pilot training was usually done by civilian pilot training schools under contract to the army, an arrangement made necessary by the impossibility of the army providing this preliminary level of instruction to the thousands of new pilots it required. These schools used training aircraft that were owned by the air force, but flight instructors were civilian employees. The air force paid the contract schools a fee for each graduate—initially $1,170—and furnished the airplanes, a cadre of supervisory personnel, textbooks, and the flying clothing for the students.

Cadets Allan Knepper and Herman Kocour first crossed paths at Gary Field. Assigned to Class 43-B, they were about to embark on their first real military aviation instruction—a ten-week program that would lead eventually to solo flights, cross-countries, and a private pilot's license. Upon arrival, they were issued the standard flight cadet kit: blue gabardine coveralls (silk-lined, with zippered front and big patch pockets), along with helmet, goggles, and a mechanic's cap.[30]

In at least one respect, how a cadet wore his gear was as important as what he wore. Newly arrived cadets, called "Dodos" until they soloed, were required to wear their goggles around their necks when not flying. After soloing, the cadets could demonstrate their new status by wearing their goggles atop their heads while on the ground and were also given a small set of wings to attach to their flight caps.

Like Preflight, the Primary program started fast and the pace never slackened. The cadet's routine was possibly even more circumscribed than it was during Preflight. Cadets awoke each day in time for the 5:45 A.M.

morning muster. After assembly, the men hurriedly returned to their barracks to wash and make their beds before marching to their 6:00 A.M. breakfast. After breakfast it was a march back to their barracks to prepare for inspection, then another march to their morning assignment. Those in the classroom had forty-five-minute classes in aircraft engines, navigation, theory of flight, and meteorology. Those students reporting to the flight line donned their flying suits, helmets, and goggles and prepared for their hour-long flight. When not in the air, the cadets studied and helped to park the planes.

After their morning program, it was another march to the barracks for an hour of physical training or military drill. Following lunch, the cadets who had been in the classroom in the morning reported to the flight line for flight instruction, and those who had already flown that day reported to the classroom. Cadets flew every day, and they also received regular hours in the Link Trainer—a valuable tool that simulated very closely the feel of flight. Cadets practiced navigation, altitude flying, spin recovery, how to "center the needle and ball" and maintain airspeed, and more. Following supper, the cadets studied, attended chapel, or played sports, then returned to their barracks for evening inspection, before "Taps" at 9:30 P.M.

One of the important features of army flight training was that at each level of training, the cadets were assigned to a single instructor, remaining with that instructor for the duration of that phase of the program. Knepper and Kocour were taught by instructor James Ciampolillo "Camp," the man who would be primarily responsible for deciding whether the cadets would proceed to Basic flight school or be washed out at Gary. Camp may well have used the traditional introduction for his flight cadets: "Mister, that's an airplane. I teach you to fly that."

The teaching sequence used in Primary was well-proven: explanation by the instructor of each new maneuver, followed by an actual demonstration by the instructor, and then supervised student performance, correction of student errors by the instructor, and then practice. Progress checks by supervisors were made at specified intervals, and final checks were given at the end of each stage of training. Every cadet received sixty to sixty-five hours of flight training, half of which would

Cadet Allan Knepper, no longer a "Dodo," shown with civilian flight instructor.
FINN

be hour-long solo flights. Cadets would make at least 175 landings while in Primary school.

Decisions were made quickly as to a cadet's suitability as a pilot. First to be eliminated were those cadets prone to airsickness or who exhibited poor coordination. Cadets who required repeated corrections for the same maneuver or who otherwise failed to show satisfactory progress were also washed out. The attrition rate could be as high as 40 percent, and during the course of the war more than 120,000 cadet pilots did not earn their flight wings. Cadets were washed out every day, and for some the decision was devastating.

The Primary course consisted of four phases:[31]

1. In the pre-solo phase students became familiar with the general operation of a light aircraft and achieved proficiency in preliminary plane-handling techniques: gentle, medium, and climbing turns; gliding, stalls, and spins; taxiing; takeoffs (including short-field and crosswind takeoffs); landings, including forced landings; and flying

in traffic. Cadets were taught to develop the habit of "looking into a turn"—turning the head and looking over the shoulder in the direction of the turn to prevent colliding with other planes. The greatest emphasis was placed on stalls and stall recovery, including all the different variations of conditions that can lead to or influence a stall.

2. The intermediate phase included the pilot's first solo. Cadets developed proficiency in precision control of the aircraft and learned to fly standard courses or patterns, including elementary figure eights, lazy eights, pylon eights, and chandelles. They also learned steep turns and maximum performance power glides, stalls and spins. And more hours were spent on forced landings and crosswind landings.

3. The third phase of instruction was termed the "accuracy" phase, where pilots were taught and practiced various landing approaches and landings.

4. The last block of instruction was the "acrobatic" phase, where the cadets learned to perform loops, Immelmann turns, slow rolls, half-rolls, and snap rolls. At various points in the course, detailed instruction was also given in the methods of bailing out of an aircraft, controlling descent, and avoiding obstacles.

Like thousands of other new cadet aviators, Knepper had flown a Piper J-3 Cub in CPT. That aircraft was powered by a 65 hp Lycoming engine and had a top speed of 85 mph and a ceiling of 9,300 feet. At Gary Field, Knepper and Kocour climbed into an open-cockpit Ryan PT-22 "Recruit"—a 160 hp, two-seat trainer with a maximum speed of 125 mph and a ceiling of over 15,000 feet. Nicknamed the "Maytag Messerschmitt" because of its sputtering engine sound and described as odd-looking and finicky to fly, the Ryan PT-22 was not as forgiving as the Cub and known for its demanding ground-handling characteristics.[32]

The instructor sat in the rear seat and communicated with the cadet through "Gosport tubes." *Dictated* would be a more apt term, as these systems were one-way only. Instructors could bark at the students, but

Knepper with a Ryan PT-22 trainer aircraft.

FINN

Herman Kocour shown in the front cock-pit of a PT-22.

KOCOUR

students could not reply. Since the forward and aft sticks were connected, the instructor could also express his displeasure by rattling the stick between the student's knees.

About Instruction

As with Preflight, discipline and adherence to proper military conduct were important realities at Gary Field. Infractions would result in a range of disciplinary actions, most commonly a walking tour.

Cadet pilots were issued the *Primary Flying Students' Manual*,[33] a 124-page document that provided graphical summaries, checklists, and cursory written instructions in all the flying maneuvers that would be taught during Primary. The manual also included:

- General Familiarity
    - Duties as a cadet
    - Equipment (flying suit, gloves, shoes, helmet, parachute)
- Principles of Flight
    - Thrust, Drag, Lift & Gravity
    - Control Surfaces (Ailerons, Elevators, Rudder)
- Understanding the PT-22
    - Power Plant
    - Fuel System
    - Flight Controls
- The Pilot's Checklist
    - Before engine start, during warm-up, and before takeoff
    - In flight
    - Before and after landing
- Airborne Traffic Rules

Great emphasis was placed on developing a "feel for flight." As William Mitchell notes in *From the Pilot Factory* (1942): "As any pilot knows, the relationship between stick and rudder is critical. This is especially true in a turn. Apply too much rudder and the airplane skids. Too much stick and the airplane slips. Apply the right amount of each and the turn is very smooth. It's a landmark moment when the student discovers how silky smooth the airplane will respond when the controls are well coordinated."

Roughly halfway through Primary, with thirty flying hours logged, cadets qualified for a civilian private pilot's license.

The Gosport, the cadet yearbook for Morton Air Academy, Gary Field, Class 43-B, described Knepper as follows: "Knepper the killer. His greatest trouble seems to be those biting flies. Mild and modest in manner, but watch him, fellows. The meekest-looking mule can kick the highest. We visualize medals on his tunic above that pair of silver wings." The entry for Kocour reads: "Ah! a sunflower son. Yes sir, the Kansas dust bowl, no less. This heat and dust hold no terrors for Herman—nor do the Ryans. A hot pilot, he is, who gets plenty of respect from his fellow classmen."

Knepper, left, in Ryan PT-22 (serial number 41-15437). This aircraft was crashed in a flying accident in September 1942 while Kocour and Knepper were students at Gary Field.

FINN

Kocour and Knepper completed their Primary flight instruction at the end of September 1942 and were assigned to the AAF Basic flight school at Gardner Field in Taft, California.

BASIC FLIGHT TRAINING

Unlike Primary, Basic flight training was done exclusively by AAF personnel, and cadets experienced a higher order of discipline in a more rigorous military setting. The relentless pace of the curriculum continued. By now, the routine was familiar: reveille, breakfast, inspection, three hours of ground school, drill, noon mess, PT and athletics, flying, Link training, then supper. There was plenty of marching in formation between each location, and then a return to the barracks to study and prepare for inspections, with an occasional lecture from 8:00 to 10:00 P.M.[34]

Cadets soldiered on with a new awareness of the danger involved in their training. As cadets moved from Primary to Basic, the enterprise became more deadly. Primary had a high elimination rate, but a relatively low casualty rate. In Basic, the "washout" rate was half that of Primary, but the mortality rate started to increase. As Samuel Hynes records in *Flights of Passage*: "Few airmen in Basic escaped seeing or knowing about somebody who died in a training accident. The grisly statistics . . . demonstrated that flying, even in the relatively benign early stages, was a highly dangerous occupation. Possibly during Primary, and certainly during Basic, the cold-blooded numbers took on visceral meaning."[35]

During Basic flight training, cadets received seventy hours of flight instruction. Pilots who had learned only the fundamentals of flight in Primary underwent a transformation into military pilots during this phase. Flying much more performant aircraft, cadets began to learn how to fly at night, by instruments, in formation, and cross-country from one point to another. And for the first time they operated an aircraft with a two-way radio and a two-pitch propeller.

It was during Basic instruction that it would be determined whether the cadet would continue on to single-engine or multi-engine Advanced flight school. Assignment was based on a number of factors, including the AAF's current requirements for fighter or multi-engine pilots, the student's flight abilities, and his size. And early in the war, the cadet's personal preference as to future assignment was considered.

A single-engine school would mean that the final combat assignment would be a single-engine fighter, observation, or air recon. Multi-engine could mean either a twin-engine fighter, a medium or heavy bomber, transport/cargo, or possibly a twin-engine recon. There was also the possibility that pilots who completed Advanced would be assigned as instructors.

Despite a growing optimism among the cadets, there still existed the real threat of elimination, and cadets had to catch on fast. But upon soloing in Basic, the cadet could be reasonably certain that he would complete Basic and be forwarded to Advanced training.

At Basic flight school, Knepper and Kocour flew the Vultee BT-13 "Valiant" aircraft—yet another step up in horsepower, capability, and performance. Whereas the PT-22 in Primary developed 160 hp and had a top speed of 125 mph and a ceiling of 15,000 feet, the Valiant was equipped with an engine almost three times more powerful, hitting 180 mph, with a ceiling of almost 22,000 feet. Weighing in at 4,500 pounds, the BT-13 began to approach the type of aircraft that these pilots would be flying in combat. It was altogether a much more complex aircraft than what the cadets had flown in Primary.[36]

Instruction at Gardner Field began with a review of fundamentals learned in Primary, including landings, stalls, spins, forced landings, and maneuvers. Next came further work in acrobatics, accuracy approaches, aerial navigation, strange field landings, instrument flying "under the hood," night landings, formation flying, and flying for long distances. When not flying, classroom instruction was given in military training.

Capt. Bob Norris provides a good account of preparing for a training flight in Basic in his memoirs, *The Dust Bowl to World War II*:

> *I met with [the instructor] at the aircraft for a preflight. We checked that nothing was loose in the baggage compartment that could move around and damage the controls, did the initial fuel check to make sure the fuel caps were on tight, walked around the aircraft to check for any damage, and climbed on board the front cockpit. We unlocked*

the controls, made sure the flaps were up and the trim set, and selected the fullest of the two 60-gallon tanks, keeping the balance between the two tanks within 10 gallons. If both tanks are full, you started on the right tank, checked all your controls, opened the moisture control, primed the engine, pumped the wobble pump to build up fuel pressure, adjusted the throttle, and energized the inertia starter.

After the engine start we checked oil pressure, radio on, propeller pitch to high rpm, uncaged the flight instruments, checked the brakes, performed S-turns to check for ground traffic, did a magneto check, rolled down 20 degrees of flaps using a hand crank, lined up with the runway, throttled forward slowly to full throttle. Once established in climb, you pull the throttle back about an inch, propeller pitch to low rpm, flaps up and continue the climb, level off and trim the elevator.[37]

Pilots were approved for solo flights in the BT-13 only when they could place their hands on each of the thirty-three controls and switches in the front cockpit while blindfolded.

On average, cadets flew about seventy hours in the BT-13, half of which were solo hours. Cadets would make 125 landings, would log 10 while practicing instrument flying, and would spend a dozen hours or more in the Link Trainer.[38] With the majority of the instruction in Basic devoted to instrument and formation flying, and day and night cross-country flying, little time was devoted to aerobatics. (In fact, the suitability of the BT-13 for aerobatic flight training was the subject of some debate by pilots who flew it.)[39]

Becoming adept at formation flying was critically important. In combat, aircraft flew in formations that permitted mutual defense, allowing pilots to cover each other's blind spots. Particularly for pilots who would fly bombers, a crew's survival absolutely depended on the pilot's ability to maintain formation.

But formation flying was an acquired skill, and it came easier to some pilots than it did to others. In training, three aircraft would form up at 6,000 feet, with one in the lead position, and the other two in "trail" position. Then the formation would shift to right echelon, with the second and third aircraft each positioning themselves behind and to the right of the aircraft ahead, and with each pilot making fine throttle adjustments to maintain position. From right echelon, the formation would shift to left echelon, then re-form in V-formation, and then back again to trail.

As Norris notes: "A number of the pilots were challenged; they would overcontrol, fighting to hold the proper formation position with wild burst of power, or by yanking the throttles back to idle to avoid chopping the lead's wing or trying to hold lateral position by using the rudders. They would end up all over the sky."[40]

Robert Vrilakas, a pilot with the 1st Fighter Group, reports that formation flying required a different form of flight control application, including cross-controls where the aircraft's rudder and ailerons are worked in opposite directions. The procedure, not aerodynamically sound, can lead to stalls or spins if not handled carefully. Pilots in formation flight made constant throttle adjustments. Sharp depth perception was critical.[41]

Future 49th Fighter Squadron pilot William Gregory recalls: "I always enjoyed flying formation. I had a friend from Texas, Harold F. Brown. It

Vultee BT-13.
U.S. AIR FORCE

Cadet Allan Knepper pictured before a BT-13 aircraft at AAFBFS, Gardner Field.

FINN

was dangerous to be in the same sky with him! Flying formation—he just never had a knack for it at all. He would have been great flying transport, but he never had a feel for flying fighters. He ended up getting killed."[42]

On December 4, 1942, ten weeks after arriving at Gardner Field, Knepper and Kocour completed their Basic pilot program and were assigned to Williams Field, at Chandler, Arizona, for their Advanced flight training.

Advanced Flight School

Knepper and Kocour, having completed Basic flight school, could be excused if they hit the main gates at Williams Field with a bit of attitude, with the conceit that they could handle a high-speed, high-performance aircraft with skill. Certainly, this had some validity. They entered Advanced with an awareness that they were nine weeks away from discarding forever their "cadet" status—nine weeks closer to earning their wings and receiving their commission as second lieutenants. If all went well, combat was in their future, in another twelve weeks or so, where they would confront the enemy over foreign soils, or above alien oceans.

The army did not yet share their conceit, and the instructors had their own attitude, considering that Advanced was "where the pig iron is taken and molded into the finished product."[43]

Advanced flying school prepared a cadet for the kind of single- or multi-engine airplane he was to fly in combat. Those who went to single-engine school flew AT-6s, learning aerial and ground gunnery and combat maneuvers, and working on increasing their skills in navigation and formation and instrument flying.[44] Cadets assigned to twin-engine school received the same number of flying hours but did not practice combat aerobatics or gunnery. Flying the AT-9 and AT-17 aircraft, they directed their efforts toward mastering the art of flying a multi-engine plane in formation and increasing their ability to fly on instruments at night.[45]

On occasion, depending on the demands of the AAF, Advanced graduates who had flown single-engine aircraft could be assigned to multi-engine aircraft during subsequent Transition training.[46] Shortly after arrival, Kocour and Knepper received their assignment to AT-9s and knew that in combat they would be assigned to twin-engine troop transports, twin-engine bombers, or twin-engine fighters.

The Curtis AT-9 "Jeep" was a significant step closer to the twin-engine fighters and bombers the pilots would fly in just a couple months' time. Equipped with two 295 hp engines, the AT-9 had a loaded weight of just over 3 tons, a maximum speed of 197 mph, a range of 750 miles, and a ceiling of 19,000 feet. It could be a challenging aircraft to fly, making it a suitable platform for teaching new pilots how to cope with the demanding flight characteristics of the current generation of high-performance, multi-engine fighters and bombers that were coming off American assembly lines in increasing numbers.

As they went deeper into Advanced, pilots also flew the Cessna AT-17 "Bobcat." Similar in size, weight, speed, and ceiling to the AT-9, the Bobcat could accommodate four passengers, making it possible for cadet pilots to join training flights as observers.

Advanced flight school was even more intense than Basic, with seventy to seventy-five flight hours in an aircraft that was yet again significantly more advanced than their previous planes. Half of the cadet's

AT-9 twin-engine Advanced flight school trainer.

program in Advanced was spent in ground school, athletics, or the drill that they had come to despise. Cadets became accustomed to eighteen- to twenty-hour days.

As noted in the class yearbook, *Silver Wings*: "We thought we had instruments and gadgets to worry about in a BT. What a shock we got when we looked at the Advanced trainers' dashboards and controls. They were twice as complicated as the BT and three times as many! But, like everything else, with hours of intense cockpit drill and practice, these too became familiar."[47]

Ground instruction also intensified. Instruction included weather, flight instrumentations, and flight planning. Thirty-two different courses were crammed into just eight weeks during Advanced.[48] Flight instruction was organized into five training phases: transition, instrument, navigation, formation, and aerobatics.[49]

The transition phase normally consisted of ten flight hours, during which time the cadet learned to handle the faster and heavier ship with its additional equipment, such as retractable landing gear, hydraulic flaps, and constant speed prop.[50] Instrument operation was a continuation and intensified the skill building started in Basic. Increasing emphasis was placed on formation flying, especially at high altitudes and using the close, three-plane V-formation.

Many of the pilots who were not assigned to single-engine fighters would ultimately be assigned to multi-engine bombers. For them, aerobatics was less important; vastly more critical was the ability to fly in close formation. And for those pilots who were assigned to multi-engine, but who would later be assigned to the twin-engine P-38, aerobatics training was largely left for the Transition phase.[51]

Pilots flew long cross-country flights, and night flights were included in the transition, navigation, and formation phases of Advanced. Higher-altitude flights were made to accustom cadets to the use of oxygen and the reactions of the plane in the lighter atmosphere.

The reality of war was never far away. Pilots recalled the introductory remarks of the commander at Santa Ana—that one in four cadets would be killed in training accidents.

Cadet Bob Norris recalls: "We flew extensive cross-country flights at night on instruments and honed our formation flying. We lost two of our pilots when they collided in midair during a solo formation flying session: it was a sober memorial service. Our instructor said, 'Get used to it; you will see death time and time again.'"[52]

As the weeks passed, cadets became more confident that they would complete this phase of training and be commissioned. Since graduation ceremonies were somewhat formal, and since the cadets knew that henceforth they would be expected to look like officers, new officers' uniforms were needed. A successful graduate qualified for a $150 uniform allotment, which Knepper spent at Herb Bland's Inc. in Phoenix on January 28, 1943, paying $55 for one blouse, $39 for two pair of slacks, and $18.50 for one shirt. His kit also included a full set of "Pinks and Greens"—the winter uniform of the AAF: a forest-green jacket with matching billed cap, gray gabardine trousers, tan shirt, tie, socks, and brown shoes. Also in his new kit were belts, socks, ties, hats, overcoats, various insignia— including his new second lieutenant's gold bar—just in time for the commencement ceremony at Williams Field on February 6.[53]

Ten months and seventeen days after starting the Aviation Cadet Program, Knepper and Kocour completed their Advanced training. On February 5, 1943, they were honorably discharged from the U.S. Army as enlisted men. The following day they were commissioned as second lieutenants, received their official "pilot's" rating and their new officer's serial numbers: O-737801 for Knepper, and O-737802 for Kocour. And with graduation, their pay increased to $291 per month.[54] Knepper was nearly twenty-seven years of age when he was commissioned, and Kocour was just six months younger. Both would be among the oldest replacement pilots when they reported overseas for their combat assignments.

Their successful completion of pilot training and their commissioning as officers were commendable, considering the odds. During the four-and-a-half-year period of January 1941 through August 1945, just over 190,000 cadets were awarded pilot wings. However, in that same period, over 130,000 "washed out" or were killed during training—a loss rate of approximately 40 percent due to accidents, academic or physical problems, and other causes.[55]

Here's ALLAN W. KNEPPER, an alumnus of Idaho's Lewiston State Normal, who used to teach school to kiddies and work in a lumber mill between times.

It's HERMAN J. KOCOUR, "Koc," the grocery man from Andale, Kansas. He'll show you a fast game of tennis.

Knepper and Kocour as seen in the Williams Field Class 43-B yearbook.
KOCOUR

2nd Lt. Allan W. "Knep" Knepper, April 1943.

FINN

Their new orders assigned them to active duty with AUS (Army of the United States), and included the requirement that each man "participate in regular and frequent aerial flights . . . while on inactive status." On the same day, the Supply Office at Williams Field issued their flyer's personal equipment.

The freshly commissioned second lieutenants received orders assigning them to the 329th Fighter Group at March Field and were placed on temporary duty (TD) at Glendale. Knepper left Chandler, Arizona, two days later, with a $22.70 army travel voucher in his pocket. He was headed for Glendale, most likely driving his 1939 Plymouth Coupe, and joined by Herman Kocour.

Upon arrival at Glendale they were assigned to the 337th Fighter Squadron of the 329th Fighter Group. They remained at Glendale for a couple of weeks, until the 337th was moved to Muroc, California, on March 1 for additional training at the gunnery range there.

Their flight training was not yet complete. They were assigned to a unit that flew P-38 aircraft, and since neither of them had ever sat in one, the next phase of their training, "Transition," would involve becom-

Shipping ticket issued to 2nd Lt. Allan Knepper by Sub-Depot Supply Office, Williams Field, February 6, 1943.

FINN

ing familiar with the type of plane they would soon fly in combat. This Transition training, which typically lasted about two months, was their last opportunity to prepare for battle before they deployed overseas.

TRANSITION TRAINING

The term *Transition* was generally applied to a pilot's introduction to unfamiliar, or more highly performant, aircraft. For this reason, a short period of Transition instruction was included in all phases of flight training. As has been seen, pilots who grew accustomed to the low-horsepower aircraft in Primary training were surprised by the complexity of the BT-13s, which themselves paled in comparison to the much more complicated and complex AT-9s in Advanced training.

In the early days of aviation, this transition to combat aircraft could be done in a few days. But with the ever-increasing complexity and specialization of combat aircraft, the length of the final Transition phase had been increased. For pilots completing Advanced flight school in January 1943, the transition phase of their training would take a full two months. The pilots viewed this training as critical: In their minds, it represented their last combat training (although in point of fact, they would undergo two additional courses in combat training after they arrived in the Mediterranean Theater of Operations).[56]

For pilots like Kocour and Knepper, the transition to P-38 aircraft was a more substantial undertaking than previous transitions to other training planes. They had to learn to fly an aircraft that, at first sight, was an unfathomably complex machine. More to the point, they needed to develop proficiency in all of the flying techniques that would be required in combat.

William Gray's article about P-38s in the August 16, 1943, issue of *Life* magazine addressed what could be a daunting transition for pilots:

> *Double controls [for twin engines] worried student pilots and bred the talk of "too much plane." The cockpit is about the size of a very deep bathtub fitted with a bus seat. In front on a black instrument panel are 21 clock-like dials, and the maze of other gadgets in the cockpit includes three dozen switches, 22 levers, five cranks, two plungers, half a dozen thumb buttons, and radio controls. One pilot peered into the cockpit and gasped, "It looks like a plumber and an electrician got together and had a nightmare."*[57]

Some pilots approached their introduction to the P-38 with trepidation. Early in its life the P-38 developed a reputation as a pilot killer; a high-speed dive was believed by some pilots to be a fatal maneuver. It was later determined that the problems associated with high-speed dives in the P-38 were due to the effects of "compressibility," and that all aircraft had problems in those speed ranges. But the P-38 was a pioneer in high-speed flight and was a target for early concern. Corrective measures were taken by the team at Lockheed, and the issue was effectively dealt with by a combination of aircraft redesign and changes in pilot operations.

There were a thousand ways to get into trouble while learning to fly a high-performance aircraft like the P-38. Six months earlier, in September 1942, a cohort of new second lieutenants, who would later become stalwarts of the 14th Fighter Group in North Africa, were doing Transition training at bases near San Francisco. A rash of accidents happened in the first days of their training. On September 5, Anthony Evans had a severe taxiing accident on one of his first training flights in a P-38, almost completely demolishing his plane. Future ace Marlow Leikness nearly destroyed his aircraft in a landing accident on September 14, Wallace Bland nearly destroyed his P-38 in a ground loop while taxiing on September 15, and on September 21, Robert Kuba had a forced landing due to engine failure on his aircraft.[58]

The worst accident for this cohort came on September 8. William Gregory recalled, in a 2014 interview, the loss of a close friend:

This was early training. We were at Mills Field—what today is San Francisco International. That was the place where I got my first flight in a P-38.

It was the second flight [September 8, 1942]. I remember [2nd Lt. William] Neely and I had just come back from an evening in San Francisco with a friend, Charley W. Stuart—he was our cadet commander, our number-one guy in the cadet class. There were three of us scheduled for a flight that afternoon, around 1:00. The instructor took off, and the cadet commander [Stuart]. It was my second flight; probably his second flight as well. And I could see as he was going down the runway that his right engine was smoking badly. He got off, and he got over the phone/electric [power] lines at the end of the runway. He got about 300 feet, and then went straight in—a big smoke.

So, on my second flight I had to take off right through that crash.

FLIGHT INSTRUCTION

At Muroc, the intense training pace continued, with four hours each of ground school and flight time each day, plus athletics and all the other time-consuming obligations. There was not enough sleep and little time for diversion (and Muroc being what it was, there was little diversion available anyway). Muroc was located in the Mojave Desert, adjacent to Rogers Dry Lake—an expanse of over 47 square miles of hardened silt and sediment. The U.S. Army first started using Muroc as a bombing and gunnery range in 1933. By mid-1941, the construction of Muroc Army Airfield began on the southwestern edge of the lakebed. An all-weather concrete runway, hangars, a tower, and a parking apron were added. The headquarters building, base hospital, and other structures were described as "marvels of tarpaper, wire, and wood." In addition to the P-38 pilots, Muroc also provided Transition training for B-24 and B-25 bomber crews. A tent city emerged to house the new trainees, and a housing area for married personnel, called the "Kerosene Flats," was added.[59] Sub-bases and auxiliaries to Muroc were located at nearby, and similarly arid, locations. Robert "Smoky" Vrilakas remembered Muroc in his memoirs:

Muroc Air Base was a perfect place to fly out of. It had a fairly long runway centered on the bed of a dry lake. There were no obstacles around the base, and the dry lakebed provided excellent terrain for a forced landing, if required. The desert surrounding it was practically uninhabited by people, and there was a lot of airspace available. The downside of excellent flying conditions was that living conditions were a bit primitive. Tar-paper shacks provided our living quarters and other buildings. They were hot and uncomfortable, but we were much too busy to notice.[60]

Robert was given this nickname while attending Red Bluff Union High School. He and some pals from his hometown of Proberta, the village from whence they bussed each day, had taken to gathering after classes in a shed behind the General Store. Smoking was part of their evening ritual, and Robert developed a fondness for cigars. His father burst in on them one evening, just in time to be enveloped by a smoke ring from Robert's cigar. Following the conversation that ensued, his classmates tagged him as "Smoky," and the nickname stuck through high school. He managed to give this nickname the slip when he first joined the army, but much later, after reporting for duty with his squadron in North Africa, Robert ran into a former high school pal, who called him "Smoky" within earshot of his squadron mates. From that point forward, Robert was known as "Smoky" to all his fellow pilots.

William Gregory, a P-38 pilot who later served with the 49th Fighter Squadron, remembers that Muroc would "occasionally receive heavy rains, even there in the desert, and the lake would fill up. And it was really helpful because it would smooth out the lake. Also there were just hundreds of birds that would come. Shellfish were buried in the dried mud, and when it rained they would come back up and the birds were everywhere."

Sgt. Tom Abberger, a radio technician with the 97th squadron, recorded: "[Muroc is] the last outpost of civilization. . . . The sand and wind are miserable. The numerous hard, flat expanses of dry lakebed make the area one huge landing ground. There are no trees, just sand, sagebrush, and jackrabbits."[61]

While Muroc was not Glendale, by a far cry, it was not without its charms. Shortly after the army first arrived at Muroc, Florence "Pancho" Barnes recognized an unmet opportunity and began supplying the army with fresh milk and pork from her newly purchased alfalfa farm close to the base. As the base expanded in the 1940s, she added a roadhouse restaurant and bar, catering to the pilots and officers. Within a few years, this grew into a 368-acre dude ranch called the Rancho Oro Verde. More commonly called the "Happy Bottom Riding Club," it included a motel, dance hall, swimming pool, horse corral and barns, and an airstrip with hangars and a tower, and above all, a reputation that became legendary.

Kocour's experience is characteristic of the Transition training program at Muroc. His instruction began with a thirty-minute flight in the familiar AT-9 on February 17. The next day, Kocour received a thirty-five-minute flight as a passenger in a "piggyback" P-38—an aircraft in which the radio had been removed from the rear of the cockpit, and a second cramped seat installed. The modified aircraft was a model P-38F—the latest high-performance upgrade to the P-38. The intent of the flight was to demonstrate to the transitioning pilot the latest P-38's capabilities.

Following three days of ground instruction, Kocour assumed the controls for the first time, with a fifty-minute flight on February 21. The aircraft he flew on that day, the RP-38E, was an early version of the P-38, one which did not incorporate all the latest Lockheed improvements, was not considered "combat-ready," and was used for training only. He would fly the RP version many times in March before perfecting the transition to the latest version of the P-38, the F model, in late March.

During training, the focus was on combat preparedness. The pilots flew their aircraft in detailed aerobatic, aerial bombing, and gunnery exercises, and in simulated individual combat. Navigation missions, instrument flying, and night flying were also included in the Transition training. And since one of the P-38's principal uses would be as a fighter escort for America's heavy bomber fleet, emphasis was placed on high-altitude, long-range operations and on developing the awareness and aggressiveness that would become important on later escort missions.

Official AAF reports would later confirm that "Unit as well as individual instruction was limited by the pressure of time during the first part of the war. Within the hours available, the greatest attention was paid to takeoff and assembly procedures, precision landings in quick succession, formation flying under varying conditions, and the execution of offensive and defensive tactics against air and surface forces. Along with these came instruction on how to maintain aircraft in the field, on procedures for movement to a new base, and on necessary administrative and housekeeping activities."[62]

While at Muroc, the pilots honed their ground targetry skills by making strafing runs and dive-bombing attacks on a most unusual target in the desert of south California. To give zest and incentive to the training, the army constructed a realistic 650-foot model of a Japanese heavy cruiser, officially referred to as the "T-799, Japanese Battleship, Plan No. 944/41, W-509-ENG 4239," but known to all pilots as the *Muroc Maru*. Built out of 4x4 lumber and chicken wire, then covered with tar paper and liberally coated with ground-up chicken feathers, it was the spitting image of an Imperial Japanese navy cruiser. Sand berms were added to give the appearance of a wake.[63]

Pilots and bombardiers hit this target with a vengeance. As a target it was such a success that the army made further improvements. Mounds of sand were skillfully packed around the ship to simulate ocean waves, the "Rising Sun" flying atop the aftermast. "The sun's reflection on the dry lake created a mirage that made the area appear [as if it were] underwater," explained a contemporary. "Then heat waves in the middle of the day caused the simulated ocean to shimmer so that the *Muroc Maru* actually appeared to move." The mock-up, riding the undulating billows of sand and heat haze, was strafed, high-bombed, and skip-bombed for years before it began to lose its realistic look.

The dangers of flight training continued. With new pilots flying dangerous combat maneuvers in still-unfamiliar high-performance aircraft, the level of risk remained high, the consequences, equally severe. The 20th Fighter Group was also doing Transition training at Muroc during the time Kocour and Knepper were training there with the 329th. On March 9, 1943, while the 20th was doing ground gunnery practice at Muroc, Lt. Alvah Miller flew into the ground and was killed. On the same day, while on the bombing range, two P-38s from the 20th collided in midair. One pilot was killed, while the second was able to bail out.[64]

The pilots continued their training with full knowledge not only of the risks they were currently operating under, but also with the understanding that combat was awaiting them, and that their adversaries would not be stationary targets, but well-trained and experienced Luftwaffe pilots, or seasoned Japanese aviators in the Dainippon Teikoku Rikugun Kōkūtai.

With three flights in February and twenty-two in March, Kocour completed his training at Muroc on March 26, having logged roughly fifty hours in the P-38.[65]

Following their stint at Muroc, for their final thirty days of training Knepper and Kocour were assigned to a Replacement Training Unit (RTU) at Santa Ana, not far from the SAAAB Reception Center where they had first reported for duty in June of 1942—just about where they had begun, but now with vastly different skill sets. The group to which Knepper and Kocour were assigned essentially served as a "reservoir" from which trained replacement pilots could be withdrawn for overseas assignments.

Working under instructors who were combat veterans of the North African Campaign, the pilots put in an additional thirty flight hours over these thirty days, including cross-country flights of up to four hours' duration. At Santa Ana, the pressure from the earlier training states relaxed considerably, and life was less formal than it had been at Williams Field or at Muroc. There was more leisure time, and pilots were usually free in the evening to partake of the Hollywood nightlife and other diversions. P-38 pilots were always accorded special treatment and known to the community as "Yippee pilots," a term derived from earlier models of the Lightning bearing the YP-38 designation.[66]

As they neared completion of their Transition training, the pilots began to expect that they'd soon be withdrawn from the RTU units and given deployment orders overseas to their assigned group in the combat areas.

P-38 pilots at the conclusion of Transition Training. 2nd Lt. Herman Kocour, rear, second from left. 2nd Lt. Allan Knepper, front, second from left.
KOCOUR

Operational Training Unit pilots who were assigned to the 14th Fighter Group in North Africa. Front: Richard Decker, Edgar Yarberry, William Gregory, William Neely, unknown. Back: Harry Vogelsong, Bruce Campbell, Henry L. Perry, Harold Harper. The fates of these nine pilots indicate the hazards they faced: Neely and Perry were killed in noncombat flights; Campbell and Decker were downed in the summer of 1943, with Campbell being taken as a POW and Decker rescued.

HARPER AND GREGORY COLLECTIONS

Previous graduates of the army's flight training program were more likely to be assigned to Operational Training Units, in which pilots undergoing Transition training would remain together throughout the training and be assigned to the same combat group and squadron at the completion of their training. This OTU system was required in the early days of the war to meet the urgent requirements for complete units in overseas combat theaters.

By January 1943, the overseas units were rapidly gaining in strength, and fewer complete cadres were required. But with the high rate of combat losses at this stage of the war, the demand for replacement pilots was high. Replacements were withdrawn from RTUs and assigned to overseas postings on an individual basis, rather than as cohorts. They received their final combat assignments only after they arrived in the combat theater to which they were posted.

Knepper and Kocour would have completed this transitional training in mid-April, 1943, thirteen months after their enlistment in the army.

While waiting for his final orders, and still not completely certain of his assignment, Knepper bought a "Locker Trunk Standard" for $4.90 on April 12, 1943. He was also issued other articles on April 13, 1943, in preparation for his departure overseas. At the same time he received a packet of sulfanilamide tablets and a first-aid packet.

Before going abroad, the army provided a checklist of things that the replacement pilots should consider doing before departure, including: executing a will; creating a power of attorney and having it notarized; arranging for life insurance and a pay allotment; and more.

Allan Knepper made arrangements for payment of his life insurance premium while he was abroad and gave instructions to his parents about how to make a claim in the event that he was killed. Allan, being young and confident and not wanting to overly alarm his parents, may have taken a flippant attitude in these conversations, but the message was hard for his parents, nonetheless. They had seen a transformation in their son over the past year, but still probably saw him as the considerate young man he had been before joining up.

EMBARKATION ORDERS

Second lieutenants Allan Knepper and Herman Kocour, along with fifty-nine other new replacement pilots, received orders on April 11, 1943, to report to the army aerodrome at Glendale. From there, after a train change in Los Angeles, they traveled cross-country to Orangeburg, New York.[67]

Up to this point, the P-38 pilots knew only that they would be moving soon to their combat assignments. Previously, pilots headed for the Pacific Theater had embarked through San Francisco, while an assignment to the European Theater would probably have involved embarkation from the East Coast. Alternatively, they could be assigned to a training squadron stateside.

SHIPPING TICKET

CONSIGNOR'S Vou. No. ....
CONSIGNEE'S Vou. No. ....
NUMBER OF SHEETS ....

CONSIGNOR: 332nd Fighter Squadron,
Army Airdrome,
Santa Ana, Calif.

DATE SHIPPED OR DELIVERED   April 13, 1943.

SHIP TO—   AUTHORITY OR REQ. NO.

TRANSPORTATION COST OF $........................ CHARGEABLE TO

P/A No. ....

QUANTITY		STOCK No.	ARTICLE	UNIT	UNIT COST	TOTAL COST
ORDERED	SHIPPED					
	2	ea.	Tent Shelter Half			
	10	ea.	Pins " "			
	2	ea.	Poles " "			
	1	ea.	Belt, Pistol			
	1	ea.	Pocket Magazine, Double Web			
	1	ea.	Suspenders			
	1	ea.	Bag, Canvas Field			
	1	ea.	Pouch, First Aid			
	3	ea.	Blankets			
	1	ea.	Can, Meat			
	1	ea.	Knife			
	1	ea.	Fork			
	1	ea.	Spoon			
	1	ea.	Canteen			
	1	ea.	Cover, Canteen			
	1	ea.	Cup			
	1	ea.	Bed Roll			

XXXXXXXXXXXXXXXXXXXXXXXXXXXXXXLAST ITEMXXXXXXXXXXXXXXXXXXXXXXXXXXXXXXXXXXXXXXXXX

I certify that the Articles listed hereon have not previously
been issued to me
_____(NAME   RANK   ORGANIZATION AND SERIAL NUMBER)

I certify that I have this date issued the items listed hereon
to the person who accomplished the foregoing certificate
_____
(RANK   ORGANIZATION)   (NAME)

ARTICLES listed in column "SHIPPED" have been received unless
otherwise noted in column "ORDERED"&
_____   (NAME   RANK)
(ORGANIZATION)

ARTICLES LISTED IN COLUMN "ORDERED" HAVE BEEN RECEIVED UNLESS OTHERWISE NOTED IN COLUMN "SHIPPED."   08—9929

_____   _____   _____
(NAME)   (RANK)   (ORGANIZATION)

Shipping ticket issued to 2nd Lt. Allan Knepper by 332nd Fighter Squadron,
April 13, 1943.

FINN

With these orders of April 11, the pilots knew their destination: east. And since all P-38 units to which they might be assigned as replacement pilots had been moved from England to North Africa in support of the Tunisian Campaign, the pilots were probably fairly certain that their destination would be North Africa as well.

Upon arrival in New York they were instructed to proceed to Camp Shanks, the New York port of embarkation. They were required to arrive at Camp Shanks not later than April 20 and were assigned to overseas shipment AFA-367-A. Their temporary mailing address would be APO 3868, c/o Postmaster, New York, New York. Upon arrival at their final overseas duty station and reporting to their combat squadron they would be given a new mailing address.

On April 19, while at Camp Shanks, Knepper completed a pay allotment, providing for a payment of $100 per month to be deducted from his salary and given to his father, Jess W. Knepper, commencing May 1. At the same time, he contracted for the purchase of a $25 Series E War Bond to be deducted from his pay monthly and sent to his father in Lewiston.

Camp Shanks, along with Camp Kilmer in New Jersey, was the U.S. Army's largest port of embarkation on the East Coast during World War II, shipping 1.3 million troops over to England and North Africa. To create Camp Shanks, the U.S. Army seized over 1,300 acres of tomato patch land in Orangeburg, New York, and evicted more than one hundred families. Camp Shanks was closed in July 1946 and the barracks converted into a veterans' housing complex.

Knepper and Kocour had come to know many of the pilots they were traveling with, having trained with them at various fields over the prior year, and a number of these pilots would eventually be assigned to the same fighter group as Knepper and Kocour.

IN TRANSIT

Knep and Koc boarded the vessel *Chateau Thierry* in New York on April 29,[68] joining 81 other officers, 1,273 enlisted men, and the regular crew of 253 sailors aboard, for what would be a two-week transit of the Atlantic. The *Chateau Thierry* had originally been conceived as a troop carrier to serve during World War I, but was not built until 1921. The ship had a length of 448 feet and a beam of 58 feet. It could minimally defend itself with a single 5-inch gun and four 3-inch guns, each suitable for either surface fire or antiaircraft defense and eight .50 caliber machine guns. With a maximum cruising speed of 15 knots, and with the extensive anti-submarine maneuvering that would be required, the transatlantic voyage would not be a fast one.

Art Ayotte was a crewman aboard the *Chateau* during the war, and his observations from the period provide in rich detail an understanding of what this Atlantic transit must have been like:[69]

Officers and enlisted were fairly well crammed aboard ship, though it must be said that the officers fared much better than enlisted. The Chateau had been built with four decks or levels of troop spaces in each hold. The upper tween-decks compartments had as few as four bunks in a stack, and these were likely where the officers were berthed. The lower tween-decks and upper troop hold were more likely to contain bunks stacked six high. In the deeper compartments of the lower hold, most compartments held bunks that were eight high or even twelve high.

Bunks were constructed of pipe frames 6 feet long and 2 feet wide, with a canvas bottom laced in place. There was a vertical space of 18 to 24 inches between bunks, and a passageway between stacks 24 to 30 inches wide.

Air handling aboard the Chateau was adequate for the top-most holds, but four decks down, the troop holds were fetid and stifling under the best of circumstances. As one of the ship's crew reported: "The moist and soggy stench in those holds was enough to make a hungry buzzard puke."

The ship served two meals a day while under way. The mess compartment extended the full 58-foot width of the ship, and was about 80 feet in length fore and aft, occupying about five thousand square feet.

Along the port side was a 6- or 8-foot-wide passageway, separated from the mess compartment by a sturdy wire mesh of the kind used in maximum-security prisons and zoos. Along the bottom of the mesh was a 5-inch-high fishplate. The troops lined up for meals in the passageway. As they waited outside the approximately 50 feet of wire mesh they could look into the mess hall and hear the clamor of steel trays and fighting gear [eating utensils]. The passage was filled with the humid, greasy smell of the food, the steam and the bodies of the packed troops. In rough weather this passageway became a river of vomit that sloshed from side to side with the rolling of the ship. At times it would surge over the fishplate and into the mess hall.

Once inside the mess hall, each man took a steel tray and utensils and passed from port to starboard along the serving line. Alternately struggling uphill and bracing themselves against the downhill slide as the ship rolled, each man would receive his rations. At the starboard end of the serving line, the men would turn toward the main portion of the mess hall and find a place to stand at a table. There were no seats.

As each diner finished, he took his tray to the garbage-grinder on the starboard side and dumped his food scraps and placed the tray in racks for the washing machine.

The *Chateau*, and its sea-weary passengers, arrived in Oran on May 12, 1943—fourteen days in transit.

Knepper wrote home: "I slept most of the time I was on the boat but got out once a day to see if we had moved. I didn't hardly think there was that much water . . . When we landed I thought my Spanish was going to be pretty useful, but I guess I'm going to have to learn French. They all speak French here but I haven't seen an Arab yet that couldn't beg in English ('Hello, Charley, give me chewing gum, thank you, OK, Joe')."[70]

REPORTING FOR DUTY

The pilots, including sixty-two first and second lieutenants, were immediately assigned to the Northwest African Training Command and instructed to report to its Fighter Training Center, Field #1, at Berrechid, Morocco.

Having just crossed the Atlantic and transited the Strait of Gibraltar, they would now travel 625 miles by primitive rail lines back to the west, crossing most of Algeria and half of Morocco. Countless times over those four days the passengers must have wondered why the navy had not just let them off in Morocco, instead of passing all the way into the Mediter-ranean Sea to Oran.

Knepper wrote to his family: "I just spent four days in a chain [-linked] car and feel thoroughly contaminated. The mosquitoes have about made a casualty of me too." In a chain-linked train, the individual cars are coupled together with chains and buffers. At the start, the cars lurch and jerk, and at slowdown crash together—all in all, a very uncom-fortable ride. This system, dating back to 1830, was relied on to a consid-erable extent by both the Axis forces during their occupation of North Africa and the Allied forces when it was liberated. Knepper added: "I've seen some awfully nice country, though, and can see why, now, the nasties wanted this country. I wouldn't mind having about 1,000 acres myself to raise cattle on—up in the mountains."[71]

A memoirist with the 82nd Fighter Group, making this same trek, reported: "This train passed through some of the most breathtaking scen-ery North Africa mountain ranges have to offer, at a slow-enough speed for everybody to get a second look."[72]

Arriving at Berrechid, 25 miles south of Casablanca, on May 18, the pilots found accommodations and prepared for the combat training they would receive at the Fighter Training Center (FTC), a component of the Northwest African Training Command (NATC).

Unbeknownst to these replacement pilots, this was a tense and exhilarating time for the fighter group to which they would soon be assigned. After a two-month stand-down following its costly battering during Operation Torch and the Tunisian Campaign, the 14th Fighter Group had been re-formed under the leadership of Col. Troy Keith, and with a core of experienced pilots who had just completed a tour with the 1st Fighter Group. The "new" 14th had trained extensively at Berrechid from February 18 to March 14, and just two weeks before Knep and Koc arrived, the 14th FG had completed its preparations and training, and had moved from Mediouna, French Morocco, to Telergma, Algeria. It was from Telergma that the 14th and its three fighter squadrons would reenter the war, flying its first missions as a "restarted" group on May 5.

The 14th's combat losses would mount quickly, and the replacement pilots who had just arrived at Berrechid would soon be needed. The pilots who were part of the 49th Fighter Squadron in early May would later welcome Kocour, Knepper, and the other replacements, and give them final combat training at Telergma—providing final confirmation of their competence as P-38 pilots before leading them into combat.

BERRECHID

The NATC provided brief but highly effective pre-combat flight training in combat aircraft by experts versed in the tactical methods and practices then in actual use at the front. A continuation of the fighter pilot's instruction, pilots receiving training at the FTC were just days away from their first combat mission. Every fighter pilot destined for the Mediterranean Theater of Operations (MTO) was required to spend a couple of weeks at Berrechid, studying aircraft and naval craft recognition, escape and evasion techniques, and the special procedures to be used when working with the army forces.[73]

Pilot George Loving comments on Berrechid in *Woodbine Red Leader*:

My new home was a four-man pyramidal tent, one of dozens beneath a line of lofty palm trees at the edge of the airfield. The terrain was barren except for scattered palms, and in the distance loomed the Atlas Mountains, more than 13,500 feet high, and beyond them the Sahara. Despite the blowing dust and sand, we kept the tent sides rolled up during the day to provide some relief from the July heat. While the daylight temperatures reached high levels, it was an arid heat, easier to tolerate than the humid kind, and since temperatures fell sharply at night, sleep was not a problem.

Pilots at Berrechid would occasionally visit nearby Casablanca, about which Loving recorded:

As we disembarked there was a great deal of excitement, this being the first foreign city most of us had ever visited. To us, Casablanca seemed to radiate an atmosphere of mystery and intrigued kindled by the strange attire of the Moroccans, (and) the exotic Moslem architecture. As we walked the streets and broad boulevards what struck me most forcefully was the extraordinary range of uniforms worn by officers and men of the army, navy, or air forces of Australia, Britain, Canada, France, India, South Africa, and the United States. These showed the Allied effort against the Germans and Italians.

Pilot Wayne Johnson recorded his recollections a bit less lyrically, but no less vividly:

What a god awful place. Beggars, whores, and every kind of terrible looking humans—solid milling crowds—I've never seen anything like it. I couldn't believe people could live like this. It was much worse than the movies. . . . What a hell hole—everything stinks and sand over everything. The people are supposed to be our allies but look sinister as hell.[74]

Johnson concurs with Loving in one aspect: "There are lots of interesting military though. English, French, Arabs, Indians, black and all shades of brown jabbering away in many different languages."

Aerial training at FTC consisted of twenty-five flight hours, but before that could begin, pilots were again tasked with additional classroom instruction, with particular emphasis on aircraft recognition. Pilots were taught to recognize, in an instant, every aircraft type they were likely to encounter—whether friendly or enemy—fighters, bombers, reconnaissance aircraft, trainers, or transports—Italian, German, French, British, or American.

Loving: "The approach to this formidable task was as simple as it was ingenious. A plain black silhouette of an airplane—either a front or rear view, side view, or overhead view—was flashed on a screen briefly for the group to observe, and whoever recognized it first called out the name. Initially the silhouette was flashed on for a few seconds, but as our skill increased the time was reduced to a fiftieth of a second. By the end of the course, we could identify almost all of the aircraft without error or hesitation."

The heat on the flight line could be ferocious. Pilots had to wear gloves if they had flights starting after mid-morning, or they would risk

Lambie   Kocour   Hanna   Herrall   Jennings
Korde   Highsmith   Hirsey   Vardel   Hill

Replacement pilots, Berrechid, Morocco, June 1943.
KOCOUR

getting painful burns from touching the wing surfaces or fuselage, which by that time had been baked to scorching in the hot African sun.

In a photo taken at Berrechid, Lt. Herman Kocour is shown with his fellow pilots, some of whom had been together since Primary training. All had done their Transition training with the 329th Fighter Group at Muroc and Santa Ana, had traveled together cross-country to New York, and shipped out on the *Chateau Thierry*. All received final combat training at Berrechid and, at the completion of their training, were assigned to the units indicated below.

Thomas F. Lambie	Herman Kocour	Harry T. Hanna
To:	To:	To:
NWA Photo Recon Wing	14th Fighter Group 49th Fighter Sq	14th Fighter Group 48th Fighter Sq (MIA/POW)

Erna G. Kord
To: Assignment
unknown

Robert L. Highsmith
To:
14th Fighter Group
37th Fighter Sq

Eugene V. Hersey
To:
NWA Photo Recon
Wing

Charles W. Herrall
To:
12th Bomber Command
14th Fighter Sq

Richard H. Jennings
To:
14th Fighter Group
48th Fighter Sq

Wilbur E. Vardel
To:
14th Fighter Group
49th Fighter Sq

James E. Hill
To: 12th AF, 3rd
Photo Grp Recon.
(probable)

Three of the pilots were assigned to the aerial reconnaissance groups with the North African Air Force. These pilots would fly the F-5 version of the P-38: identical in all respects to the combat version, but operating with cameras instead of guns.

On June 4, after eighteen days of combat training, Kocour and Knepper were released from duty with NATC at Berrechid and were assigned to the North African Strategic Air Force (NASAF) and instructed to report on or about June 5. Upon reporting there, each pilot's squadron assignment would be finalized, and they would be one important step closer to combat.

Their assignment to the NASAF answered a few questions for them: It confirmed that they would be flying combat P-38s and would not be in a reconnaissance squadron. And they had learned that the NASAF was responsible for strategic air operations, with primary emphasis on strategic bombing, so they knew that bomber escort would be their primary mission.

Turning in their mosquito bar, wool blankets, and mattress cover, the two friends began making their way to NASAF 5th Bomb Wing Headquarters in northern Algeria, 20 miles east of the old city of Constantine.

CHAPTER 4

America with No Choice Left

PRELUDE TO OPERATION TORCH

WELL BEFORE THE JAPANESE ATTACK ON PEARL HARBOR, THE UNITED States and Great Britain had begun planning for the eventual entry of the United States into the European war. By midsummer 1941, Anglo-American military planners had agreed on three strategic principles: that the main Allied efforts would be directed first against Germany, later against Japan; that the defeat of Germany would require an invasion in northwestern Europe; and that prior to an invasion, the German military capacity would have to be degraded through offensive actions in other regions under German control. At that time, North Africa was considered for military action, but not as a first priority.[1] Allied cooperative planning efforts intensified following the Japanese attack in early December 1941, but these three strategies remained unchanged.

American military planners, in particular, Gen. George Marshall, preferred an early invasion of the Continent because it provided the shortest route to the heart of Germany and would permit the United States to concentrate and maintain the largest combat force. It would also permit the bulk of British forces to be brought into action, and significantly, the Americans believed that conditions would allow the Allies to gain the necessary air superiority. If General Marshall and his associates in the U.S. military had had it their way, it is quite likely that North Africa would never have been invaded by the United States.

Plans continued in the direction of the American strategy, and by the end of 1941, tentative plans were in place for an invasion in northwestern Europe eighteen months later, in the fall of 1943, under the code name "Roundup." Germany's invasion of Russia, now at a high pitch, created doubt among the Allies about the ability of Russia to defend itself and the disastrous consequences for the Allies if it collapsed. Accordingly, a smaller, even earlier invasion on the Continent—code-named "Sledge-hammer"—was provisionally planned for just nine months later, in the fall of 1942, in order to drain German resources away from the Eastern Front. The buildup of forces needed to accomplish this cross-Channel strategy began under the code name "Bolero."

Within a few months, the AAF's preparations for the scheduled European invasion were well under way. In January 1942, three fighter groups (the 14th, 33rd, and 52nd) were activated in the United States, joining the already extant 1st Fighter Group. Two more followed in February 1942 (81st and 82nd Fighter Groups), two more in the late summer of 1942 (324th and 325th Fighter Groups), and a final group in October 1942 (the 350th).[2]

Initially the defense of the U.S. West Coast took priority for air force units, but following the decisive Japanese defeat at Midway in the Pacific, the U.S. Army Air Forces (USAAF) felt confident that the Japanese fleet had lost momentum and would not be a threat to the West Coast. Considering the lessened West Coast threat, and reflecting the current military priorities, plans were made in the spring of 1942 to release P-38 squadrons to Britain as part of Bolero. By mid-June 1942, the AAF was on the move, with the air and ground echelons of the 1st and 31st Fighter Groups embarking for the UK.

Bolero would require a huge production, training, and logistical effort for all branches of the military. For the AAF alone, final estimates were that a total of 3,266 aircraft would be needed by April 1943 to support the invasion then planned for the following fall.

P-38s for the fighter groups were initially set for delivery to England aboard ships. But with the development of reliable drop tanks, the ferry range of the P-38s increased to 2,200 miles, making it possible to fly the

Lightnings from Maine to Scotland, with intermediate stops at Labrador, Greenland, and Iceland. By August 1942, eighty-one P-38Fs of the 1st and 14th Fighter Groups had arrived in Great Britain, two squadrons remaining in Iceland to fly defensive patrols over the Atlantic. The 14th's ground echelon had sailed on the USS *West Point* in early August 1942, and arrived in Liverpool on August 17, 1942.[3]

That fall, the P-38 pilots continued combat training from bases in England, with particular emphasis on escorting high-altitude B-17s. Practice sweeps were made across the English Channel. But even as the buildup of forces in the UK accelerated, with pilots anticipating air battles over northern Europe, war planning continued. The military authorities in the United States and Great Britain became sharply divided on the proper strategy for countering the Germans in World War II.

When and where to first engage the Axis? American planners recognized that the U.S. military was not strong enough to mount a cross-Channel invasion in northern Europe, and join the fighting alongside the Brits in a North African Campaign, and still maintain a position in the Pacific. The Combined Chiefs of Staff were faced with the daunting challenge of assigning priorities for their limited resources.

President Roosevelt grew impatient. Once the United States formally entered the war, Roosevelt pressed for early military action against Germany. He was "determined to commit the Western Allies to action against the Germans before the end of the year, somehow and somewhere." He wanted to give the people of the United States the understanding that they were at war—a reality that was not fully appreciated given the safe distance between the United States and the war actions— and he wanted to "impress upon the Germans that they would have to face American power on their side of the Atlantic."[4]

The Brits were deeply skeptical about the prospect of taking on Germany via a cross-Channel invasion as early as 1943. Great Britain and its Commonwealth allies—France, Canada, Australia, and New Zealand— had been fighting Germany since the fall of 1939, effectively going it alone for eighteen months. British forces had suffered a stinging defeat at the hands of the Germans in France earlier in the war, at Dunkirk. The Brits were already engaged in fierce fighting against the Germans in Egypt and felt that the Allies had insufficient resources to mount a successful offensive as early as 1943 in northern Europe.

Part of their opposition lay in the fact that the United Kingdom would have to bear much of the military burden for such an attempt, since the American war effort was still gaining momentum.[5] Britain's military leaders recalled the desperate fighting against the Germans in World War I that had inflicted such heavy casualties on their forces. Most of the military planners had also confronted the Wehrmacht's formidable fighting power during the disastrous 1940 campaign in France, while the experiences of British forces in North Africa and Libya against Field Marshal Erwin Rommel had done nothing to diminish their respect for German military capabilities.

Apart from the potentially staggering human costs, Britain had deep concerns about military hardware, and the issue came down to boats. It was evident that the Allies did not have sufficient shipping to support the landings. Much of Allied shipping was dedicated to actions against the Japanese in early 1942, and with the Mediterranean unavailable for friendly convoys, Allied support of the beleaguered Egyptian campaign required shipping around Africa. Allied naval assets were simply insufficient for the invasion. Most significantly, the Allies did not have sufficient numbers of landing craft to transport troops to the beachheads.

It was estimated that at least 8,100 landing craft would be needed for the operation and would have to be available in mid-April 1943 to permit distribution and training. But navy demands in the Pacific and elsewhere made it likely that only half this number of landing craft would be available. Since the initial shock of an invasion force largely determines the success of establishing a viable beachhead, a half-strength invasion force was viewed as a poor way to start actions against *Festung Europa*. As late as May of 1943, just a few months before the proposed fall invasion, it was still being actively debated what kind of landing craft would be needed. The designs initially proposed appeared to be too small for the sea conditions likely to be encountered during the crossing.[6]

Historically, the Brits also showed a preference for peripheral campaigns, with subsequent direct attacks on the enemy only after they had been seriously weakened by attrition. This was typical of the British way of fighting wars and was "deeply imbedded in England's military tradition."[7]

Churchill began to argue strongly against beginning with a European landing, urging the Allies to first undertake an invasion of northern Africa. He believed that an Allied invasion of North Africa would prevent the Axis forces from penetrating further into French-held Morocco, Algiers, and Tunisia. A strong Allied presence there would help to secure British lines of communication through the Mediterranean, including air traffic from the western region of North Africa to the Suez. In the words of writer John Keegan, Churchill's firmly held position was "Germany First—but not quite yet."

The Brits made other compelling arguments for a North African landing. Resupply of British fighting forces in the deserts of Egypt was partially being accomplished via naval convoys through the Mediterranean, where they were vulnerable to Axis attack from the Gibraltar approaches all the way to Alexandria. A land operation in western Africa would challenge German supremacy in the region, might open Allied supply lines, and would provide a potential base for future land operations in the Mediterranean and southern Europe. And it would force the Germans and Italians to extend themselves beyond their capacity in reinforcing their trans-Mediterranean and southern front, potentially requiring them to withdraw some of their air assets from the Russian front. Additionally, the United States would also benefit from the ability to supply its operations in South Asia and the Philippines via the Mediterranean.

While this conversation was taking place, the Brits' Eighth Army lost a spectacular tank battle in Libya on June 13. Tobruk fell on June 21, and Rommel's army made a rapid advance toward Egypt and the Suez Canal. The Japanese made strong advances in Southeast Asia, the Philippines, and the Netherlands Indies. Allied shipping resources were degraded due to the stunning success of German U-boats. In the summer of 1942 the plight of the Soviet army seemed desperate, as Adolf Hitler's panzer divisions pushed ever onward toward Stalingrad and the Caucasus.

Perhaps the final point debated by the Combined Chiefs of Staff (CCS) was whether a North African operation would result in Spain abandoning its neutrality and joining the Axis forces. In that case, the Strait of Gibraltar could be closed, putting an end to the Allied forces' lines of communication and supply and worsening the Allied status in North Africa and elsewhere.

Despite the battle losses in Africa and logistical problems facing the Allies, Churchill and Roosevelt hoped to win the initiative against the Axis at relatively small cost, "[c]losing and tightening the ring around Germany, preparatory to a direct assault on northern Europe against the Germans."[8]

British resistance to Allied plans for operations in northern Europe hardened, and by July 8 the British War Cabinet confirmed their opposition to the cross-Channel invasion in 1943. Bolero was stalled.

At that point, in late July of 1942, Roosevelt did something that British prime minister Winston Churchill would never do during the entire course of World War II: He intervened and overruled his military advisers. Roosevelt gave his generals a direct order to support the British proposal for landings along the coast of French North Africa—code-named "Operation Torch."[9] D-Day for Torch was November 8, 1942.

AIR FORCES ORGANIZATION

While military planners on both sides of the Atlantic were answering the question of "where" and "when," AAF planners faced the prospect of an almost inconceivable increase in aviation hardware. They also faced the hard truth that the policies and command structure under which the AAF would manage and apply such a huge operation were ill-defined, unclear, and heavily contested internally. The air forces had become the victim of a very slow evolution.

At the conclusion of World War I, it was evident to all military planners that strong air forces would be critically important to any future armed conflict. U.S. brass came to this understanding quickly: American air forces had operated in Europe for just seven months during that war, but even this limited experience was enough to make the point convincingly. During the interwar years, aircraft development continued at a determined pace, with new aircraft types coming off the drawing boards and American runways at a regular rate. But the parallel development of aviation tactics and strategies advanced much more slowly, and with many internecine conflicts.

Army ground commanders viewed the application of airpower primarily in a tactical sense: in direct support of ground operations. This was best expressed in a 1919 position paper from U.S. Army HQ: "When the Infantry loses, the Army loses. It is therefore the role of the Air Service . . . to aid the chief Combatant, the Infantry."[10] Pilots and aviation strategists took a much different view. It was their position that the air forces should be considered on a par with ground forces, and that aviation assets should be free to pursue a number of useful missions during armed conflicts.

Foremost in the thinking of the U.S. Army Air Forces was the critical need to secure air superiority against their adversaries, and for this to happen, the air assets needed to be used in both tactical and strategic missions. For tactical missions, this meant close air support for ground troops, reconnaissance, interception of enemy aircraft, and interdiction of enemy ground and sea forces. For strategic missions, a priority was long-range missions against aerodromes and other enemy aviation assets— assets that must be degraded in order to reach a point of air superiority.

During the twenty years prior, with American air forces being part of the U.S. Army, the field manuals and other doctrinal regulations largely reflecting the thinking of army ground officers. Many aspects related to air forces were addressed imprecisely by army staff, including the hows and whys of close air support, air superiority, and maritime operations.

During this time, while the army and air forces thinkers were debating the proper role of aviation in combat, aircraft designs were making huge advances. In the early 1920s, the maximum airspeed of a production fighter aircraft was just 150 mph, with a maximum ceiling of almost 25,000 feet and a range of 310 miles. By 1935, aircraft performance had doubled, with planes reaching speeds of 317 mph, at sustained altitudes of over 31,000 feet and a range of 715 miles. By the time Germany invaded Poland, Lockheed's P-38 Lightning had boosted airspeed to an astonishing 414 mph, with a ceiling of almost 44,000 feet and a range of over 2,000 miles. Similar advances were seen in bomber-type aircraft, and in armaments.

Clearly, the military had been presented with vastly improved capabilities. With huge numbers of high-performance aircraft in the mobilization pipeline, there was tremendous pressure to develop corresponding doctrines governing the application of this new and formidable capability. Military planners struggled with two primary issues: How should they employ airpower, and under what organization and command structure would it operate? Judging from the tone of the debates between ground and air commanders, and the number of position papers, field manuals, and regulations that were issued in the period from 1920 to 1940,[11] it is evident that there was no clear consensus on either point.

Army ground commanders held to their view that the air forces should be supportive to ground operations and under the command structure of ground commanders. Aviation planners were equally adamant that the air forces had multiple roles, particularly control of the airspace and strategic bombing, and bridled at being under the direct operational control of ground commanders.

Aviation planners pointed to the great success seen in the British campaigns in Egypt and Libya against the Axis forces and General Rommel. The British doctrine called for a centralized control of air forces, co-equity between ground and air forces commanders, and air strikes en masse on ground targets of great importance.[12]

Finally, just six months before the planned invasion of North Africa, *Field Manual 31-35* was issued, and it was evident that the ground force commanders had once again won the argument. A few salient points from *FM 31-35*:

- Air forces were subordinated to the ground force needs, and to the local battle conditions.
- The air support commanders functioned under the army commander, and aircraft could be specifically allocated to the support of ground units.
- Target priorities would be set by army units on the ground.

The spirit of the manual is reflected in this statement: "The most important target at a particular time will usually be that target which constitutes the most serious threat to the operations of the supported ground force."[13]

AAF planners who had advocated for independent and largely strategic air forces had lost the debate, and the doctrine expressed in *FM 31-35* governed the AAF during the invasion of North Africa in the fall of 1942. As will be seen, those policies resulted in an ineffective use of air forces, which some would argue led to a tragic misuse of men and materiel.

TORCH AND THE TUNISIAN CAMPAIGN

Operation Torch was America's first large-scale combat against Axis forces. The landings on November 8, 1942, involved a huge contingent of British and American forces, establishing beachheads at five widely spaced locations in French Morocco and Algeria. A relatively short-duration battle, the invading forces were secure by November 16, and ground operations continued as the American forces immediately began moving east across North Africa, against stiffening German opposition.

The American invasion of North Africa carried tremendous import for Great Britain. Just three days after D-Day, with opposition crumbling, Prime Minister Churchill's speech in London included his now-famous statement: "The Germans have received back again that measure of fire and steel which they have so often meted out to others. Now this is not the end. It is not even the beginning of the end. But it is, perhaps, the end of the beginning."[14]

Torch was the first major operation of the war for the United States, and was unique in the demands it placed on close ground-air cooperation. This cooperative function was unfamiliar to the U.S. armed forces, whose only comparable experience was gained in the final months of World War I, more than twenty years earlier.

While ground operations proceeded well during Torch, and in the early days of fighting in what came to be called the North African Campaign, from the outset the AAF operations did not go well. The problem was not related to equipment or training, but rather in organization, leading to considerable friction among the Allies. Fundamental procedures regarding command and control of air assets had not been adequately addressed, and even the basic doctrines as to the application of airpower were still under considerable debate.[15]

It was becoming evident that military planners who had won the debate about who should control the air assets had gotten it wrong. Having the AAF controlled by ground task force commanders and the associated absence of unity of command prevented air planners from developing a coordinated air plan to support the entire theater of operations. While individual ground commanders agreed that gaining air superiority was essential, their overriding concern was the enemy troops directly in front of them, and they wanted air forces in their area to support them exclusively. None wanted to give up control over tactical air support for troops under their immediate responsibility.

According to the Air Force Historical Studies Agency, "The ground officers who had lain with their regiments in the hills around Tebourba had their own analysis of failure. They had seen their men dive-bombed continually, had seen this dive-bombing perfectly coordinated with tank and infantry attacks, had seen few friendly planes come to the rescue. Their favorite remedy became the uneconomical—and in the face of enemy air superiority, ineffective—air umbrella. Cries of 'Stuka' and parallel demands for umbrellas plagued the air commanders. Thenceforth the theory and practice of 'air support'—the term currently in use—were much mooted in Northwest Africa."[16]

As recognized in a 1953 Air Force study: After Operation Torch, "there followed many months of indecisive action in the course of which the earlier conception of air support, involving the lavish use of all available fighter aircraft as a defensive umbrella over the ground troops, was completely discredited. There were also examples of wholly unwise selection of targets for bombardment by ground officers."[17]

In effect, the "air umbrella" practice placed the air forces in a primarily defensive role. "Most Army officers had come to view the airplane as a defensive weapon. They were enthusiastic supporters of military aviation, but only as a tool for observation of opposing ground forces and for keeping the enemy's airpower off their backs. In the view of these officers, U.S. aircraft should be assigned to, and be controlled by, ground commanders down to division level or lower. Further, the aircraft should operate along and over a specific front."[18]

This doctrine was diametrically opposed to that employed so effectively by the Luftwaffe since 1939: the fundamental principle of fighter action is at all times and in all places to be on the offensive. "A fighter can only carry out [a] purely defensive task by taking the initiative in the offensive. He must never wait until he is attacked because he then loses the chance of acting. The words of Richtofen expressed during world War I . . . are still valid today. 'The fighter pilots have to rove in the area allotted to them in any way they like, and when they spot an enemy they attack and shoot him down; anything else is rubbish.'"[19]

The point was further reinforced in the writings of German general Hellmuth Felmy, a noted air force commander and strategist:

> *Ground forces fighting without air superiority on their side have no choice but to take such exceptional precautionary measures against intervention by enemy air forces that the freedom of action and the striking power they need to destroy the enemy on the ground are jeopardized to a dangerous degree.*
>
> *For this reason, the air force must be employed primarily against the enemy air forces until such time as air superiority has been achieved. The mobility inherent in an air force is its most valuable asset.*
>
> *The command of all the available air units must be concentrated in the hands of the air commander if their inherent elasticity and striking power is to be fully exploited in a decisive offensive.*[20]

In fairness to ground commanders, it should also be noted that the air force itself lacked the necessary experience, equipment, and tactics to perform well in a ground-support role. Close support bombers, like the A-20, proved to be vulnerable to ground fire, and pilots lacked adequate training in the tactics of strafing or dive-bombing. Applying U.S. air assets to a ground-support role proved to be a costly mistake. In pursuing its assigned mission of ground support, the American air forces did not degrade the offensive air assets of the German opposition, and the Allies were constantly confronted over the battle lines by proven aircraft piloted by officers with years of tactical combat experience. Allied pilots and aircraft were being lost in North Africa at a fearsome rate.

The result, seen in the early months of Operation Torch, was an overall failure to use the primary attributes of air forces—mobility and flexibility. Most significantly, its defensive employment prevented the air forces of the United States from gaining air superiority in North Africa—a well-accepted prerequisite for successful ground operations. In the winter of 1942–1943, the Luftwaffe controlled the skies in the Central Mediterranean.

At the beginning of 1943, when German aircraft were contesting the skies in North Africa, the ratio of losses per sortie for fighter aircraft was four times the average for the war, as high as 5 percent in February 1943. At this rate, a pilot would be lucky to survive twenty missions out of a fifty-mission tour. Later, as the Axis forces began to be attrited by Allied forces, the risk associated with combat operations decreased to the average observed for the war, about 1 percent. Ernie Pyle, famous World War II correspondent, noted: "[Fighter pilots] are the sponge that is absorbing the fury of the Luftwaffe over here. They are taking it, and taking it, and taking it."[21]

The 14th Fighter Group had been hard hit. Entering combat as part of the 12th Air Force during Operation Torch, the 14th Fighter Group had moved into northwest Africa in mid-November 1942, occupying the airfield at Tafaraoui, Algeria, initially with the primary mission of escorting heavy bombers in the coming campaign in Tunisia. Over the next two months, the group would move three times: first to Maison Blanche, then to Youks-les-Bains, and finally to Berteaux—all bases in northern Algeria, each move keeping the group close to the advancing battle line.[22]

By late January, after sixty-nine days of combat, the 14th had lost nineteen pilots killed due to enemy action, and five others were taken as POWs. Of the original fifty-four pilots who had arrived from England at the start of combat operations in North Africa, just thirty-eight remained.[23]

The inventory of aircraft had also taken a beating: Air forces commander Gen. Jimmy Doolittle was forced to move aircraft from one group to another in order to maintain combat-readiness. Instead of the seventy-five aircraft normally allocated to an AAF fighter group, just a dozen worn P-38s remained in the 14th. The 1st and 82nd Fighter Groups had suffered similarly high losses, and at times the combined strength of all three P-38 groups was as low as ninety aircraft.

For the 14th, the worst came on January 23. Sixteen aircraft of the 48th Fighter Squadron left their base at Berteaux, Algeria, at 0715 on a mission to strafe Rommel's forces near Medinine in Tunisia. Their route was hampered by ground fog, and when the formation emerged to clear air, it found itself directly over a new and unreported Axis aerodrome. Flak over the field was intense, and the German pilots were ready for a fight. Desperate, swirling combat ensued, and the 48th was badly mauled, losing five pilots and six aircraft, a terrible blow to the squadron.

The group's pilots assembled three days later for what has been referred to as a "big squadron powwow": "The pilots were angry after the mission of the 23rd . . . and made some pretty blunt statements regarding it."[24] Group commander Col. Thayer Olds, who had been the group's commander since April 1941, guiding them during their recent heavy losses, listened to the heated discussion. He decided to have the commanders of the 48th and 49th squadrons join him for a meeting with his superior, General Cannon, at the 12th Air Force headquarters in Constantine.

The meeting took place on January 27. To his credit, the general understood that the 14th had ceased to be an effective combat unit, and the next day the group was relieved of duty. Pilots who had completed their tours of duty were sent home; others were sent to other squadrons; staff officers and enlisted personnel were sent to the rear to rest and recuperate.

A similar fate awaited the 33rd Fighter Group. After flying many close air-support and ground-attack missions, it was down to just thirteen aircraft. Two weeks after the 14th stood down, the 33rd was also withdrawn from the theater for reconstitution.

AAF headquarters quickly began the process of reequipping and rebuilding the fighter groups in North Africa, including the 14th, but the extensive losses that began with Torch were symptomatic of a huge problem for air forces headquarters. This was in stark contrast to the experience of the Royal Air Force (RAF) in the eastern desert campaign against the Axis forces. This was due in part to the fact that the RAF was independent and co-equal to the British Army and Royal Navy; the partnership between General Montgomery's British Eighth Army with the RAF produced a high level of tactical and strategic successes.

Efforts to produce a similar organizational arrangement in the U.S. Army met with harsh resistance. Notably, Gen. George Patton—commander of ground forces in North Africa—complained that a "total lack of air cover for our units" in North Africa "has allowed the German Air Force to operate almost at will."[25] Vice Air Marshal Coningham, leader of RAF forces in the eastern desert, did not back down, questioning whether the complaints about American air cover might be a disguise for the possibility that Patton's II Corps was "not battle-worthy in terms of present operations." The fight was on, but the stakes were too high to permit the argument from becoming intractable.

As early as December 1942, just one month after launching the North African offensive, Eisenhower had become increasing frustrated with attempts to coordinate the efforts of the 12th Air Force with ground forces. He recognized the poor results and great sacrifices of the AAF and was cognizant that the coming Tunisian Campaign would rely even more on a strong and well-managed air force. In January he issued directions calling for a single air commander, and in an interim measure, Gen. Carl A. Spaatz was appointed air commander in chief of the Allied Air Forces.

Concurrent with this provisional appointment, President Roosevelt and Prime Minister Churchill met at Casablanca to discuss future operations, once North Africa had been secured. The reorganization of the air forces was of prime importance to the Allied leaders during the meeting in Casablanca, and a new unified command structure and functional organization was quickly adopted. The new organization was closely modeled after the RAF/Eighth Army experience in the eastern desert. The plan was designed to take fuller advantage of the primary attributes of air forces—flexibility, mobility, and concentration of airpower—through the establishment of centralized control of all airpower in the MTO.

A new administrative structure was created, the Mediterranean Air Command (MAC), with an implementation date of February 18, 1943. As if to emphasize the intent, British air chief marshal Sir Arthur

Tedder was named air commander in chief of MAC. The reorganization created five new commands under Tedder, including the North African Air Force (NAAF), which would include the great majority of American units then in North Africa. It was within NAAF that the functional reorganization became evident, most notably with the creation of the North African Tactical Air Force (NATAF) and the North African Strategic Air Force (NASAF).

Again in a nod to the tactical successes Britain had achieved in the eastern desert, NATAF's command was given to acting air marshal Sir Arthur Coningham. NATAF's air assets included shorter-range fighters, fighter-bombers, and light bombers—the sorts of aircraft that would be needed for tactical missions, including close air support.[26]

Coningham had paid his dues in the air. He flew with the New Zealand Expeditionary Force in Gallipoli during World War I, later joining the Royal Flying Corps, where he became an ace. Coming to Egypt in July 1941 and operating under extremely adverse conditions, Coningham's team achieved air superiority in the North African Campaign and was instrumental in halting the German offensive at El Alamein in July 1942. His threefold principles of air superiority, centralized command, and innovation in air tactics were well proven in North Africa, and it was hoped that he would bring the same success to the combined Allied tactical operations in the Mediterranean Theater.

Coningham immediately issued orders to abandon the use of air umbrellas and directed all air assets under his command to operate in a fully offensive mode at all times. He explained to his peers in the ground commands that an offensive approach put the enemy on the defensive and automatically protected ground troops.

And with the belief that American air forces had led the way in terms of aircraft and doctrine regarding strategic bombing, the command of NASAF was given to Maj. Gen. James Doolittle. NASAF's air assets included heavy and medium bombers for daylight operations, British bombers for night operations, supported by fighter groups operating P-40s, and three fighter groups equipped with P-38s—among them, the 14th Fighter Group and its three squadrons.[27]

Also created within NAAF were four additional units: The third major combined combat command created under MAC with this reorganization was the North African Coastal Air Force (NACAF) which like the NATAF, was equipped with a wide variety of medium and light bombers and fighters.[28] Its primary mission was air defense of North Africa, sea/air reconnaissance, antisubmarine operations, air protection of Allied shipping, and air interdiction of enemy shipping.

Four support commands were also included in the new MAC organizational structure:

The Northwest African Troop Carrier Command (NATCC) was equipped with C-47 aircraft and was responsible for delivery of troops and materiel to the war zone, including air drops of paratroops and the return of damaged equipment and injured personnel back to base.

The Northwest African Training Command (NATC) was to provide pre-combat flight training for new pilots and crews—both fighters and bombers. NATC provided brief but highly effective training prior to assignment to their final combat assignments.

The Northwest African Air Service Command (NAASC) was responsible for logistics and support functions.

In addition to these four main units, Northwest African Photo Reconnaissance Wing was responsible for providing air intelligence photographs to the NAAF military planners and was equipped primarily with fighter-type aircraft, in which guns had been replaced with cameras.

Also factoring into the reorganization of the air forces was the 9th Air Force, then based at Cairo. The origins of the 9th AF in the MTO date to June 1942, when twenty-four B-24s with hand-picked crews arrived in Egypt to support the desperate ground war then being waged by British and Axis forces in the eastern desert. Within six months, the 9th was equipped with 370 aircraft of all kinds, including heavy and medium bombers, transports, and three P-40 Fighter Groups, and had become an integral element in the campaign that led to the defeat of Axis forces in North Africa.

With the reorganization that led to the NAAF, some assets of the 9th AF were transferred to NATAF and NACAF, but the 9th still retained a powerful capability, which included B-25 medium bombers, and P-40 fighters. Air forces planners in the MTO assigned responsibility for the western Mediterranean to NASAF and for the eastern Mediterranean to the 9th Air Force, which conducted extensive strategic operations throughout the region, including during the coming campaign on Sicily. Later in the war, the 9th would be transferred to England to resume tactical operations.

This new structure appeared to clarify missions and responsibilities for Coningham and Doolittle, a clarity that was greatly in demand, but had been generally lacking.

The groundwork for a new set of AAF doctrines had been laid. The document that resulted—*Field Manual 100-20*, entitled "Command and Employment of Air Power," stated that "Land power and air power are co-equal and interdependent forces: neither is an auxiliary of the other." Mediterranean Theater commanders would exercise control of air forces through an air force commander and ground forces through a ground force commander. The directive assigned air superiority as the first priority for the air forces; second priority was air interdiction, and third was close support of ground troops.[29]

This new field manual would not be released for six months, but the new NAAF commanders were already implementing its key components. NASAF commanders, to whom all P-38 units reported, immediately issued new orders, stating: "The first objective is to gain air superiority," with a campaign against enemy radar installations, air forces, and airfields. The next mission was interdiction of enemy rear area movements and vehicles and troop concentrations.

The change in direction began to pay quick dividends, and by March the pendulum had begun to swing in the direction of the Allies. With the increased aircraft deliveries, new pilots, and a new set of doctrines and tactics, the combined Allied forces were beginning to outnumber the Axis air forces.

Included in the rebuilding effort was the 14th Fighter Group, newly reorganized under the command of Col. Troy Keith. A core of experienced pilots had been reassigned from the 1st Fighter Group to function as commanders, operations officers, and combat pilots of the 14th Group

Headquarters, and its three squadrons, the 37th, 48th, and 49th. Newly assigned pilots began to arrive from the States in the early spring of 1943, and by mid-April the group was approaching full strength, undergoing combat training under the guidance of the "old hands" from the 1st. They were a new group, operating under a new organization, with new aircraft and pilots, and with a fresh set of marching orders: Get and maintain air superiority. By early May, the group was ready to rejoin the fight.

Although the army's doctrinal debates had been conducted at a level far above the 49th Fighter Squadron, the conclusions reached at Casablanca, the subsequent reorganization of air assets, and the resultant development of the North African Strategic Air Force, were to have a profound impact on the missions the pilots of the 49th would fly for the rest of the war. It was the 49th, and all the other air force squadrons within the NAAF, that would undertake to master the learning curve associated with this new doctrine, and who would learn how costly the lessons would be.

CHAPTER 5

Meet the Group

In a Fighter Squadron the Fighting spirit must be predominant. It is aggressiveness; it is an understanding of the word "duty"; it is a man's pride in his work—whatever it may be—it is sacrifice; it is the ultimate conviction in a man's heart that he, as a man, has a job to complete before he can rest; and at present that job is winning this war.

—Maj. Marshall Cloke,
The Building of a Fighter Squadron

Replacement pilots Kocour, Hanna, Jennings, Highsmith, Vardel, and Knepper began the long rail journey eastward from Berrechid toward the Tunisian airfields that housed squadrons flying P-38s. Leaving on June 5, 1943, and boarding the same chain-cars that had brought them to Berrechid, their route took them on a northerly course through Morocco, passing through Casablanca, Rabat, Fez, and Taza. At Oujda they crossed the border into Algeria, trundling back to Oran, through the mountains toward Constantine and arriving at the headquarters of the 5th Bomb Wing at Chateaudun-du-Rhumel Airfield in northern Algeria on June 9.[1]

The replacement pilots received their final squadron assignments at Wing HQ. Catching transport from Chateaudun-du-Rhumel, the pilots made the 26-mile drive to their new base at Telergma.

Reporting to the 14th FG

Arriving at Telergma, Knepper and Kocour would have first reported to the group commander, Col. Troy Keith, and the group operations officer, Capt. Richard Decker. Being assigned to the 49th squadron, they would have next met the squadron commander, Captain Newman. They received their tent assignments, stowed their gear, and began meeting their tentmates and fellow pilots.

For the pilots who were already with the squadron, Knepper and Kocour's arrival caused no great stir. They were, on average, just eleven missions in to a fifty-mission tour of duty. In the prior six weeks, they had seen several of their close friends lost in combat, and their focus was on getting through the next few months with as few additional losses as possible. In any case, it would be at least ten days before the "newbies" were fully combat-ready, and a few flights after that to assess their performance in combat.

Typical of the war during this time period, commanders were changed often. The standard tour for fighter pilots was set at 150 combat flying hours and fifty combat sorties, and this rule applied to group and squadron commanders as well as combat pilots. Colonel Keith himself flew combat missions, and when finally relieved three months later, had fifty sorties and two air victories to his credit.[2]

Captain Newman had previously flown with the 1st Fighter Group before joining the effort to rebuild the 14th. He had just completed his fifty missions, with more than 200 hours in combat, and was relieved the day after Knepper and Kocour's arrival. He was replaced by the squadron's operations officer, Capt. Henry "Hugh" Trollope. Trollope was chosen from among men who were surely his equal in terms of combat flight expertise and combat experience. His promotion to the demanding job of squadron commander was in recognition of his strong performance in operations, and of his capacity for leadership. Trollope would, as a first task, work to continue the esprit within the cadre of pilots that Captain Newman had achieved.

Beyond that, the squadron commander had wide responsibilities. His decisions would inevitably cost some of his fellow pilots their lives—pilots with whom he had already flown many combat missions. Pilots whose lives he may have saved in combat, and who may have saved his. The squadron was his to shape. He would review his squadron staff and consult with the key department heads—Engineering, Communications, Armament, Operations, Medical, and Intelligence. He might reassign some of the men of his command, even down to the lowest ranks, based on their physical and mental qualifications, and their experience.

If Trollope had been inclined to gather the pilots and admin officers for a meeting after he was named squadron commander, he might have reflected on the combat they had already seen and on how he gauged the squadron's performance. He might have instituted new flight procedures or made changes to the squadron's flight tactics. He might have let the pilots know what his policy would be regarding rest leave. He would have reminded the new pilots that their flying would all be done in daylight, and that with no runway lights or instrument approaches, it would be impossible for them to land after dark. He would have reminded all of the importance of checking guns, engines, and radio right after take-off—and of the need to return to base immediately if any problems were found. He would have reminded them that an empty belly tank is full of explosive fuel vapors, and that if the tank did not release when the order comes in to drop, the pilot should turn around and go back, no matter how close to the target he was. And he would surely have confirmed to them that there was a lot of combat ahead as the Allies began the preparations for the next ground assault against the Axis forces.[3]

Concurrent with Captain Trollope's promotion to commander, Captain Decker transferred from Group to become the new operations officer for the 49th. This move was significant, since it was the operations officer who made combat flight assignments and decided who would be promoted to flight leaders. As operations officer, Captain Decker would serve as primary administrative officer on the ground and would himself fly a full combat tour of fifty missions. On base, he would assist the commander in developing and supervising the pilot's training program, including tactical instruction. It would be his responsibility to determine the qualifications of newly assigned flying personnel and recommend their assignment and training. Each week he would meet with the squadron's flight leaders to apprise them of anticipated operations for the following week, having first liaised with the group operations officer. And he would meet almost daily with the squadron engineering officer regarding the requirements and availability of aircraft for the following day's mission.

Like most of the other pilots who joined the squadron during its refitting in March, Trollope and Decker were just getting settled into their own combat roles, and now found themselves leaders of the squadron. While they knew their predecessors well, the learning curve in these new positions was steep, and both Trollope and Decker occasionally resorted to unconventional methods.

Captain Decker was very well-liked by his pilots and fellow officers. When vacancies developed through casualties or tour completions, it was Decker who decided which pilots would become flight leaders. Being named flight leader was important to the pilots, because it came with a promotion to captain, an increase in pay, and an opportunity for leadership. It was difficult to decide how these promotions would be made, since all of the pilots had arrived in theater at the same time, all had about the same number of flight hours, and all had about the same combat experience.

According to William Gregory, Decker had an unusual way of deciding who would receive the promotion: "It was kind of strange how

Decker handled that. He was the ops officer. When a slot came open, he said, 'Okay, we are gonna match for this,' because we were even, as far as experience and time. He would [say] 'Heads or tails.' I lost three times, and it [being assigned to flight leader] meant a promotion to captain, so it was a significant thing. But I made it pretty early—we had a lot of turnover, so it came around pretty fast. It was a fair way to do it, and I thought Decker handled it very well. Decker was a good guy—I always liked him a lot."[4]

In the brief thirty-four days since the squadron had restarted operations, the 49th had lost nine combat pilots out of their twenty-four-pilot cadre. Two, Lieutenants Bergerson and Green, had been lost on a dive-bombing mission to Milo aerodrome on the island of Sicily just four days previously. In the May–June period, the squadron lost more aircraft than it shot down. A tough reintroduction to combat.

There was no apparent pattern to the losses. Earlier in May, 2nd Lt. Burton Snyder had been lost on his first combat mission, and 2nd Lt. John Burton on his third. But very experienced pilots were also lost in the month prior to Knepper and Kocour's arrival, including 1st Lts. Albert Little and John Wolford. Wolford, downed on his eighty-third mission, was already a combat ace when he was reassigned to the 14th Fighter Group to assist in its rebuilding, having shot down five enemy aircraft with the 1st Fighter Group. While half of the losses had come at the hands of enemy aircraft, one-fourth had been the result of flak, and one-fourth due to crashes and aircraft failures.

Risk is determined by exposure and consequence: The probability of an event happening is related to exposure, and for pilots this obviously meant that the more sorties they flew, the greater their chances of being killed. Squadron losses were especially high during the early days of combat. Many years later, 49th pilot William Gregory recalled: "There were times where we were losing so many, you get to wonder how long . . . I think [Lt.] Knott did a study one time, and he figured that the luckiest of us would have maybe twenty more days, or something like that. At the rate we were going . . . Of course it doesn't work that way, because as you gain experience you become a better survivor. You think about [the odds of being killed]. You have to, because it's real."[5]

As it emerged from its rebuilding, the 14th FG reported seventeen pilots as missing in action during the month of May. Excepting Lieutenant Wolford, who was MIA on his eighty-third mission, the average number of sorties flown by the men who were lost was just under five.

The History of the 82nd Fighter Group records: "The Mediterranean was not a safe place for inexperienced P-38 pilots, and surviving their first few missions could be an accomplishment in itself. Of the twenty-one pilots assigned to the 95th squadron during the latter half of April, twelve eventually became casualties—nine of them during their first month."[6]

The 37th squadron reported similarly. In its summary report for 1943, over the first fourteen missions (May 5–25), the pilot losses per sortie was just over 4 percent, and the victory-to-loss ratio was almost even: 1.28 to 1. Over the next six months, covering 159 missions, the loss rate was reduced to .21 percent, and the victory-to-loss ratio increased to 13 to 1.[7]

Over a one year period commencing with the restart of the 14th Fighter Group on May 6, 1943, the Group would lose 83 pilots: 23 before they had completed their 4th combat mission. The overwhelming share of losses—81 percent—occurred in the first half of the pilots' combat tour. Pilots grew to understand that although the danger was inherent and unceasing, gaining combat experience was the best guarantor of survival.[8]

In the MTO, in the midst of the lead-in to Operation Husky, the number of sorties doubled between March and June, and Allied aircraft losses went from 117 to 256. During this period, the German air assets began to be degraded, but at a considerable cost. At the beginning of 1943, when German aircraft were contesting the skies in North Africa, the ratio of losses per sortie for fighter aircraft was four times the average for the war, as high as 5 percent in February 1943. But as the Axis forces began to be attrited by Allied forces, the risk associated with combat operations decreased to the average observed for the war, roughly 1 percent.

The lesson for the replacement pilots was stark: Losses were routine, expected, and largely unavoidable. The pilots learned quickly that these losses had to be taken in stride, insofar as possible, because the next combat mission was just around the corner, and would require their full concentration.

Trollope (left) and Keith.

Decker (right).

DELANA (SCOTT) HARRISON

The cohort of pilots at Telergma on the day Knep and Koc arrived were:[9]

Capt.	William G. Newman	Squadron Commander	Goose Egg, WY
Capt.	Richard E. Decker	Squadron Ops Officer	Coffeyville, KS
Capt.	Lloyd K. DeMoss	Flight Leaders	Shreveport, LA
Capt.	Mark C. Hageny		Hollywood, CA
Capt.	Henry D. Trollope		Dewey, OK
Capt.	Marlow J. Leikness		Fisher, MN

1Lt.	Wallace G. Bland	Combat Pilots	Hanceville, AL
1Lt.	Bruce L. Campbell		Belgrade, NE
1Lt.	Lewden M. Enslen		Springfield, MO
1Lt.	William J. Gregory		Hartsville, TN
1Lt.	Harold T. Harper		Bakersfield, CA
1Lt.	Carroll S. Knott		Bakersfield, CA
1Lt.	William D. Neely		Murfreesboro, TN
1Lt.	Wayne M. Manlove		Milton, IN
1Lt.	Robert B. Riley		Auburn, CA
2Lt.	Frederick J. Bitter		Butler, PA
2Lt.	Beryl E. Boatman		Okmulgee, OK
2Lt.	Sidney R. Booth		McKeesport, PA
2Lt.	George B. Church		Millington, MD
2Lt.	Aldo E. Deru		Rock Springs, WY
2Lt.	Kendall B. Dowis		Detroit, MI
2Lt.	Lothrop F. Ellis		Germantown, PA
2Lt.	George J. Ensslen Jr.		Germantown, PA
2Lt.	Anthony Evans		Akron, OH
2Lt.	Martin A. Foster Jr.		Harrisburg, PA
2Lt.	John B. Grant		Topeka, KS
2Lt.	John M. Harris		Yakima, WA
2Lt.	Walter L. Hoke		New Windsor, MD
2Lt.	Monroe Homer Jr.		Bakersfield, CA
2Lt.	Arthur S. Lovera		El Monte, CA
2Lt.	Harry H. Vogelsong		Toronto, OH
F/O	Charles W. Richard		Lake Charles, LA

During the next two weeks, other replacement pilots began to arrive:

2Lt.	Joseph F. Cobb	San Diego, CA
2Lt.	Eugene Churchill	Unknown

2Lt	Edward J. Hyland	Unknown
2Lt.	Raymond J. Kopecky	Unknown
2Lt.	Donald Leiter	Unknown
2Lt.	Louis D. Ogle	Pierce City, MO
2Lt	John D. Sandifer	Unknown
2Lt.	Wilbur E. Vardel	Canton, OH
2Lt.	William R. Palmer	Unknown

Most of the 49th's experienced pilots had been part of the original OTU—Operational Training Unit—that formed at Hamilton Field in California. These pilots had lived and trained together for over a year, and many had come to be close friends.

Many of the pilots might have considered that they had dodged fate in getting this far. Training accidents claimed many of their peers, and several of the 49th's combat pilots had close calls before ever leaving the States. Lieutenants Bland, Lovera, and Flight Officer Richard had each totaled a P-38 shortly after receiving their pilot's rating. Lieutenant Evans had destroyed *two* P-38s in the latter days of his training, and badly damaged a *third* in a takeoff accident. But the worst pre-combat record belonged to the group commander, Col. Troy Keith, who destroyed two aircraft and badly damaged two others in training accidents dating back to 1936.

With the addition of the new cohort of replacement pilots, the 49th squadron's thirty-eight-pilot roster actually exceeded the number speci-fied by the army's table of organization for a twin-engine fighter squad-ron. The higher staffing was undoubtedly due to the high losses that had been incurred by all fighter units in North Africa during the first half of 1943 and to the army's clear understanding of the unavoidable losses that would doubtless occur in the coming weeks.

Each squadron included a flight surgeon to oversee health care for all members of the squadron. For the 49th it was Capt. Lester L. Blount, his staff sergeant John Lawson, and seven other enlisted personnel, who treated over 1,000 patients during the summer of 1943. In addition to treating the normal colds, coughs, sprains, and broken bones, that sum-mer Captain Blount had to deal with a serious outbreak of intestinal disorder. An average of 62 officers and men were down with "intestinal disease" each month during June, July, and August, and a total of 250 pilot days were lost due to disorders.

"I'm not sure how sanitary the food was [on base]," Lieutenant Gregory noted. "We all got dysentery, and we all lost weight. I think I weighed 118 to 120 pounds, and we had a lot of stomach problems because of food." He believed that the pilots were showing signs of battle fatigue, due primarily to illness. "We had dysentery a lot, and it was just fatigue from the activity, and the poor food, and insufficient rest."

Blount was well-liked by the squadron, and could be counted on to provide a medicinal dose of fruit juice and ethyl alcohol to pilots returning from a particularly difficult mission.

Captain Blount and his team of enlisted assistants had also shown a readiness to provide medical care to the local populace. In April, as the squadron was making final preparations to return to combat, Captain Blount was photographed administering to the son of a local Moroccan tribesman.

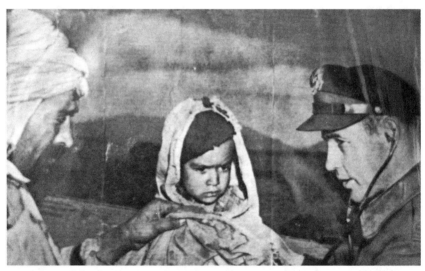

49th Squadron Flight Surgeon Capt. Lester Blount, here ministering to an ailing Arab child, often dispensed vitamins from his personal supply to residents of communities near the squadron's base.

CAPT. LESTER BLOUNT, *LUBBOCK AVALANCHE*, MAY 28, 1943. ORIGINALLY PUBLISHED IN THE *NEW YORK TIMES*, APRIL 28, 1943.

In the accompanying article Captain Blount was termed a "wizard of improvisation." With the help of Sgt. Lawson—an ex-gold miner from Nome—Blount directed the excavation of a large hillside dugout at one of their temporary bases, lining the walls with spent five-gallon fuel cans packed with rocks and sand to create a bomb-proof structure. Later, he crafted an autoclave out of an old P-38 belly tank which he used to sanitize surgical instruments.

Flight Surgeon Blount was also doing his best to ward off malaria. All squadron members were issued a "mosquito bar"—a cloth mesh that was hung above the cots—and everyone was required to take a daily dose of Atabrine, which had the disquieting side effect of yellowing the eyeballs and inducing a yellow cast to the men's skin.

The squadron medical staff kept a weather eye on another disease indigenous to North Africa: typhus, typically transmitted by lice, and thankfully not prevalent within the air force units. More troublesome was venereal disease, which was seemingly impossible to avoid, particularly after the squadrons were based for longer periods of time at bases situated near population centers.

Captain Blount would eventually serve under several group and squadron commanders, one of whom he was reportedly forced to "ground" because of a diagnosis of incipient polio. His diagnosis was later confirmed, though it did not lessen the withering dressing-down he would have received from the then still-robust commander.

Captain Blount, along with the squadron commander and the operations officer, had to be alert to signs of battle fatigue in the pilots. Blount recognized that the pilots' lives consisted of one type of stress being superimposed on another, and then on still another.

The business of flying ultra-higher-performance aircraft, laden with high-octane fuel and a half-ton of explosives, was inherently dangerous, even during routine training operations. Added to this was the strangeness that characterized North Africa at that time and the frequent change of locations to other more alien airfields. Worries about parents back home, new wives or newer children. Food was often poor, and rejuvenating sleep rare. Dysentery was common, and all pilots experienced significant weight loss. Physical fatigue increased with each passing day.

He also knew that the extent to which combat fatigue became debilitating could be influenced to a degree by the quality of squadron and group leadership, by the morale of the group, and by preventive or adaptive measures he could deliver.

Anxiety was a constant among the pilots, and naturally the fear of being injured or killed was the primary source of stress, a factor that became dangerously cumulative. Death became a more likely outcome with each mission: more flying resulted in greater exposure which led to increased risk of injury or death, until the point was reached where "possibility" becomes "probability." Added to this was the double load of grief and anxiety that resulted from losing a close friend in combat. And ultimately, all pilots came to the realization that future dangerous missions were limitless, necessary, and inescapable. In time, the combined effect could cause a pilot to question his motivation to remain in combat.

And the pilots were not immune to an understanding of consequence. Pilots helmed war machinery of great destructive capacity, and each knew that they were responsible for many deaths, including those of innocents. For some, the successful completion of a devastating mission brought great satisfaction in a job well done, a small step in ending the war. For others the uncomfortable recollection of a damaging dive-bomb attack or strafing run could be persistent.

Every pilot felt the stress, and the common refrain "Are you nervous in the service" became ubiquitous because of its underlying truth. Each man had his limit of tolerance to the physical and emotional stresses of combat. The fortunate pilot reached the end of his fifty-mission tour before reaching the end of his ability to withstand the stress. Other pilots—brave, adept, forthright—were not so lucky and began to show signs that they had reached a point beyond their capacity to cope.

Captain Blount was aware of the range of telltale signs of battle fatigue. Some symptoms were of a tactical nature: early returns from missions due to airplane problems that could not be verified on the ground, or being slow to engage the enemy in the air. Others became evident over time: transient fears that became entrenched as permanent anxiety, loss of appetite and unusual weight loss, heavy drinking, frequent sick calls where no illness could be found, depression, seclusion, forgetfulness, preoccupation, and increased irritability were among the most common manifestations of combat fatigue.

These signs could appear in any of the pilots to varying degrees, and it was the flight surgeon's job to assess the level of stress in each pilot and to both monitor their adaptation to the stress and assist them in their adaptations. As with the pilots, Blount's job was not without its own stress—it was his task to "keep them flying," and to insure that the tactical needs of the squadron were met. Sometimes this meant keeping a pilot on flight status despite their evident symptoms.[10]

And it was also true that some pilots were just not cut out for combat. In the month of May, despite its desperate shortage of pilots, the 14th Fighter Group transferred two new pilots—one after his first mission, and one after his second. There was little point in keeping a man in combat if he was ill-suited: he would create a more dangerous situation for all his fellow pilots.

Squadron flight surgeon Capt. Lester L. Blount administering to patients.
NATIONAL ARCHIVES

Future Nobel laureate John Steinbeck, serving as a correspondent during the war, filed a report from London during the early days of the Allied invasion of Sicily: "The men suffer from strain. It has been so long applied that they are probably not even conscious of it. It isn't fear, but it is something you can feel, a bubble that grows bigger and bigger in your mid-section. It puffs up against your lungs so that your breathing becomes short. Sitting around is bad."[11]

The five-man Intelligence Unit was under the direction of Capt. Howard Wilson, and included Asst. Intelligence Officer Lt. Royal Gilkey, a staff sergeant and a corporal who served as clerk—all as part of the Air Echelon. An additional sergeant was assigned to the Ground Echelon.

As Intelligence Officer for the squadron, Captain Wilson was responsible for making sure that ". . . the command is not surprised in any theater of operation." He participated in all mission briefings and provided specific combat intelligence for commanders and pilots. Beyond that, Captain Wilson also served as the counterintelligence officer and was responsible for camouflage and other passive protection measures. He was also responsible for communications security, censorship, and public relations.

Captain Wilson was tough on the men who worked for him because the information delivered through his office could determine the success of each combat mission and whether the squadron pilots would return or not return. When Lieutenant Gilkey first reported for duty, Captain Wilson told him "You make one slip, lieutenant, and I'll have your ass."—a message that would be hard to misinterpret.

The Intelligence Unit also delivered intelligence training to the pilots to assist them in making aerial assessments, and then debriefed returning pilots after each mission. This information might include the location and type of flak units, military facilities, enemy aircraft types and numbers, troop concentrations and movements, enemy naval activities and assets, and all too often pilot's accounts of squadron losses during combat missions. The data was prepared by the Intelligence Unit and forwarded to the Group Intelligence Office for furtherance.

Intelligence material was also incorporated into the squadron's Weekly Status and Operations Report (WSOR) that was prepared and submitted to the 12th AF Headquarters by Captain Trollope each week.

Capt. James Ritter, Adjutant,
49th Fighter Squadron.
RITTER FAMILY COLLECTION

The squadron adjutant was senior officer in the Ground Echelon. For the 49th Fighter Squadron, that man was Captain James Ritter of St. Mary's, Pennsylvania, Captain Ritter had been assigned to the 49th in its early days, and was with the squadron during its costly actions in the North African Campaign, during its rebuilding after having been taken off combat status, and during the Sicilian and Italian campaigns.

The adjutant functions much like the city manager of a small town, exercising authority over a wide range of squadron functions. Each morning Captain Ritter visited the Orderly Room and the flight line to review and take action on any urgent matter. He was responsible for reviewing and routing all incoming communications, and was charged with preparing and submitting all records and reports originating from the squadron headquarters.

The condition of the small tent city at Telergma that housed the Ground Echelon was his responsibilty, and he made daily inspections of the "barracks" area, the mess tent, kitchen, and supply area.

He was involved in any charges of dereliction amoung the enlisted ranks, and would twice-yearly assemble the enlisted personnel for a reading of the Articles of War. And he was the pay officer.

It would have fallen to Lieutenant Ritter to supervise the collection of the personal belongings of any squadron serviceman, officer or enlisted, who was killed or declared missing in action, and to prepare and forward the material to surviving family. Many of the pilots who were killed in combat had been with the squadron since its formation and were close friends of Captain Ritter. Collecting their belongings was a painful but necessary intrusion into their lives, and was surely the toughest part of his job with the squadron.[12]

The airfield at Telergma, built by the French colonial government prior to the war, was seized by American ground forces during the Tunisian Campaign. By mid-December 1942—six months before Koc and Knep's arrival—it had been improved to accommodate NASAF's heavy bombers. Most recently it had been a dual-purpose base, housing both bomber and fighter groups. These units had departed Telergma in March, and the 14th Fighter Group, with its three squadrons of P-38s, took over Telergma during the first week of May 1943.[13]

Hardly a garden spot, Telergma was a "windy, barren, rocky, cold place with some barren hills to the south." Fred Wolfe of the 82nd Fighter Group related his first impressions of Telergma when he arrived in January 1943: "It didn't look like much to us from the air, but it looked like less after we landed. You might think by the name Telergma that there was a town there, but there wasn't—just a little Arab village with a population of about 100. A more dirty and filthy place you'll never find anywhere in the world. There wasn't anything about Telergma that made you think of an air base except maybe the muddy strip of dirt that we landed on. Before the war the French had used it as an outpost for their Foreign Legion."[14]

Scorpions were abundant and aggressive. In what became a daily ritual, shoes, bedding, and personal gear in the tents had to be checked and cleared. The squadron learned that Algeria was also home to the full range of desert critters, including the Mediterranean recluse spider, the camel spider, and the Egyptian cobra.

Soon after they arrived, Kocour and Knepper were delivered this piece of bad news: the squadron had been informed just two days prior that there would be no mail for a month. As the American military forces

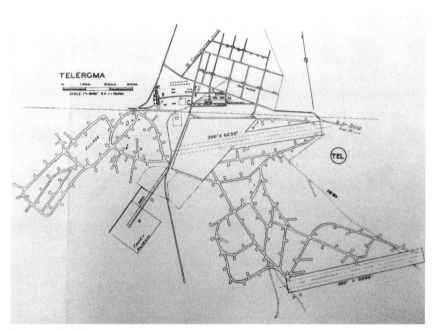

Telergma Airfield.
NATIONAL ARCHIVES

began the buildup in North Africa preparatory for an invasion into Sicily, every cubic foot of available cargo space was taken with supplies, munitions, fuel, and spare parts. As the squadron diarist recorded at the time: "This fact is important as all here are more concerned with mail than food." A telling statement, given the squadron's craving for better food.

The news was tough on the squadron's married pilots—Keith, Trollope, Bitter, Bland, Boatman, Booth, Hageny and Foster—and especially so for Lieutenant Colonel Keith and Lieutenants Bland and Boatman, whose wives were pregnant when the airman were posted abroad.

And outgoing mail would be limited to "V-mail," a system that involved writing a short note on a template, which was then photographed and returned home on film. This allowed the army to send up to 1,500 letters on one roll of film. Upon receipt, the film was developed and individual V-mails forwarded to the intended address. It was impersonal and unpopular, but it was all the servicemen had.[15]

When meeting their new CO and their ops officer, the new pilots would also have been given the squadron call signs—identifiers used when talking to controllers or other aircraft. The 49th call sign was "Hangman"; the 48th's was "Fried Fish." Each aircraft bore a two-digit number: aircraft of the 48th squadron were numbered 1 through 30; the 49th, 31 through 60, and the 37th, 61 through 90. This system allowed pilots and ground staff to readily know to which squadron a distant aircraft was assigned.[16] In practice, the pilot would open radio communications with, for example, "Hangman 47," instantly identifying him as being with the 14th Fighter Group, 49th Fighter Squadron, and that he was flying aircraft #47.

Pilots were housed in pyramidal canvas tents. Each tent measured 16 feet square, and stood 11 feet tall. When housing four pilots, each man had exactly 64 square feet to call his own. Drinking water and wash water came from Lyster Bags placed throughout the encampment. The mess was set up cafeteria-style, and slit trenches were dug for sanitary necessities. Officers and enlisted personnel alike were protective of their ration cards. With specific items rationed on a weekly, biweekly, or monthly basis, the ration cards provided minimal and utterly necessary comforts for the men who were enduring such challenging living conditions.

Captain Trollope, the 49th's new squadron commander, was not overly impressed with the preparedness of the replacement pilots, noting in the Weekly Status and Operations Report for June 20–26 that "Replacement pilots need considerable training in altitude formation and dive-bombing tactics." The problem of preparedness was apparently systemic, as Trollope's comments were echoed by his counterpart at the 37th, Maj. Paul Rudder: "Pilots are being sent out for combat without sufficient and adequate training. We have received pilots with only 15 hours in a P-38, no single-engine operation [training], no dive-bombing practice, no high-altitude formation and escort practice."[17]

Maj. Ernest Osher, commander of the 95th squadron (82nd FG), thought similarly, writing many years later: "I felt strongly that they needed initial indoctrination flights in a combat environment before being utilized on combat missions. We were not given any opportunity until late in my combat tour [late July, 1943] to fly new personnel on training missions. By utilizing them immediately on combat sorties when they arrived, we jeopardized some of our old hands as well as new pilots, and a considerable number, I feel, who could have been utilized effectively, were lost on initial missions."[18]

The commanders' counterparts in the South Pacific also had problems with replacements. In the same week that Trollope and Rudder were complaining to Wing about their new pilots, Maj. John Mitchell bluntly told the Bureau of Aeronautics: "New people coming out there [Guadalcanal] are miserably trained. They're afraid of the planes because they've heard unfavorable comments about them. When they've been kidded along a little, flown the planes and learned how stable they are, how well the pilot is protected, what a lot of damage can be dealt out with them—in other words, once they get in a flight—they're OK. It doesn't take very long for the ordinary American kid to catch on."[19]

Harold Harper, a pilot from the 49th, concurred: "The 49th received pilots who had never flown a plane larger than an AT-6. We had to check them out in P-38s and give them a few hours' training before sending into combat!"

Harper's fellow pilot William Gregory recalls: "I think everyone is unprepared for their first [combat] flight. The first flight is going to be exciting for the new pilot, and you don't have enough time, really, to train them when you are on the line. You are flying missions every day, or every other day, and you just can't take that much time [for training]. We always tried to give them one or two rides, but that is probably not enough. They were still not prepared. The only way to get prepared is to get in[to] combat. You have to do your best, and if you survive the first few missions, your chances actually improve. You learn fast in combat. You want to get [a new pilot] through his first mission."

It was clear that the AAF was pumping out pilots as quickly as they could, but with uneven flight training. It was left to the individual combat units—the squadrons—to bring these new pilots up to a level of proficiency that would allow them to participate in combat operations without undue danger to themselves or their fellow pilots. And so, despite a year of intensive pilot training, it was back to school for the new replacement pilots. Kocour and Knepper may have been vexed by this; after all, they had more than eighty hours in a P-38 during Transition training, and almost three hundred total flight hours. Additionally, they had logged many more hours at Berrechid. But realizing the lethality of the situation they were in, it's a good bet they applied themselves to squadron training.

Since the pilots would be escorting high-altitude B-17s on the majority of missions, high-altitude formation and escort training was a priority. Dive-bombing had not been part of the replacement pilots' training, so they loaded practice bombs and made dive-bombing runs on a nearby dry lake. Pilots were given a review of radio frequencies, takeoff and join-up procedures, fuel management, oxygen procedures, guns and gun sights, enemy-fighter tactics, and escape and evasion techniques.

Becoming proficient fliers soon qualified the replacement pilots for combat missions. Once airborne and in position their job was to fight, and engaging the enemy required a few critical last second preparations and a cool head. The instant the flight leader "called the break" to turn into oncoming enemy aircraft, the pilot had to drop external fuel tanks, and set gas switches to "main." He next increased his RPM and manifold pressure, turned on the gun heater switch and combat switch, and made sure his gun sight light was illuminated. In time, these preparations became rote. But new pilots had reportedly been lost when they failed to take any evasive action when "bounced" by enemy aircraft: one explanation was that they were so busy getting organized in the cockpit that they were shot down before they could take action.[20]

Beyond this additional tactical training, new pilots also needed operational training. Pilot William Colgan noted: "A new pilot's arrival in a multi-mission combat unit put him in a very time-compressed learning situation. He had to absorb all details of command/unit operational procedures and tactics and lessons of past combat, and learn the enemy and his weapons, the current situation, and maps and features of the enemy territory he would fly over." He also had to know the location of the "bomb line" to prevent cases of "friendly fire."[21]

This training, and the first few missions for the new replacement pilots, was crucial. In addition to their continued training, as commissioned officers, the new pilots would occasionally be assigned the job of censoring outgoing personal correspondence of the enlisted men. As Robert Vrilakas recalled, "It was a tedious and boring job, and one we didn't particularly like, since we felt we were put in the undesirable position of snooping into their personal life. Despite continual cautions from security officials, some of the letters would divulge our location or strengths and losses. When that occurred the scissors were applied, leaving gaping holes in the middle of a piece of correspondence. It was necessary, but had to have been disconcerting to the recipient of the letter."[22]

They might also be assigned to "slow-fly" an aircraft to break in a new replacement engine. When not flying or reviewing procedures, the pilots relaxed as best they could, writing V-mails, playing cards, or sharing endless conversations about flying, girlfriends, and home.

While getting settled at camp and completing their check rides, Knepper and Kocour would naturally have begun to anticipate their first combat mission, wondering with whom they would fly, on what sort of mission, and with what target. What would it be like to look down at an Italian naval vessel, an aerodrome on Sicily or Sardinia, or a large port complex? What would it be like to crisscross over a flight of fifty or more B-17 bombers, all flying in close formation? How would they react the first time an enemy aircraft put them in their sights?

While confident of their own skills and eager to get on with the work for which they had been trained, it would be understandable if their thoughts also turned, however briefly, to their own safety. Nonetheless, it would also be a fair assumption that after a year of training, they were ready to get after the job ahead, whether or not they were fully prepared.

Targeting the Axis

It can be postulated that by mid-1943 the defeat of the Axis forces, however costly, was inevitable. Allied forces had blunted the Japanese advances in the South Pacific. Guadalcanal had been retaken. The Soviet Union had won substantial victories against the Germans on the Eastern Front, even though the losses had been staggering to both sides. North Africa had been successfully invaded with Operation Torch and cleared of Axis forces in the subsequent Tunisian Campaign. At sea, the Battle of the Atlantic had been won, and the strategic bombing offensive from Great Britain, which would eventually have devastating effects, was beginning to show positive results.

The Axis forces knew that the Allies would use their recent successes in North Africa as a springboard for further advances, but the location of the expected offensives was hotly debated within the Third Reich, the Wehrmacht, and the Luftwaffe. Hitler was sure it would be the Balkans. Many German generals thought it would come at Sardinia, and still others thought that Italy itself would be invaded next. Mussolini thought it would be Sicily, but was given little audience. Field Marshal Kesselring thought Sicily most likely, and it was to him that the responsibility for the defense of Sicily ultimately fell.

Sicily, the largest island in the Mediterranean, sits between the tip of Tunisia and the Italian mainland—a natural stepping-stone for the Allied armies. A rough triangle in shape, Sicily measures 150 miles in the east-west direction, and is slightly larger than the state of Vermont. The terrain is mountainous, reaching the highest elevations at Mount Etna on the northeast corner of the island. Other than a narrow coastal band, the only extensive level ground is in the eastern and southeastern regions of the island. Because of its relatively small size, Axis aircraft could traverse the entire island in thirty minutes.

Well before the fall of Tripoli, Allied war planners had set their sights on Sicily for the next major offensive push against the Axis. And as part of the war plans that led up to Operation Husky—the invasion of Sicily—a carefully developed air plan had been put in place. NASAF's strategic plan for the Sicilian Campaign was weighted heavily toward degrading the Axis communication capability, including railroads and ports, and establishing air superiority in the region. As early as January, the 12th Air Force had delivered to NASAF a list of first, second, and third target priorities for Sicily, Sardinia, and southern Italy. The top-ten targets included the port at Palermo, the port and rail facilities at Messina, the port of Cagliari on Sardinia, and seven Axis aerodromes.[23]

The ports were given highest priority because they would be routes through which German troops and materiel would flow to reinforce defensive forces on Sicily, and from which Germans would most likely stage an eventual retreat from Sicily. The seven aerodromes included among the top-ten priority targets were of vital interest to Axis defenders and included the aerodrome complexes at Trapani, Sciacca, and Castelvetrano, in the western region of Sicily, and the aerodromes at Elmas, Decimomannu, and Villacidro, in the southern region of Sardinia.

A NAAF report issued in mid-May gave specific direction as to the conduct of the war against the Luftwaffe in the Mediterranean. It urged bombing concentrations of fighters on the ground wherever they could be found, dislocating fighter aerodrome installations and facilities, and bombing fighter aircraft and engine factories. It further identified the main GAF control center in Sicily—Sciacca—and sub-controls at Pantelleria, Bo Rizzo, and Catania. All would eventually be targeted repeatedly.[24]

The AAF was able to obtain astonishingly detailed intelligence from a captured German soldier, Adalbert Steininger, who had the two qualities most valued in a prisoner of war: an encyclopedic knowledge of a topic of vital interest to the Allies and a tendency toward volubility—a keen desire to share what he knew.[25] Steininger had been stationed at the GAF aerodrome at Comiso and had visited Catania, Trapani, and Marsala on several occasions. He had "an astonishing memory and powers of observation, and [had] been concerned with much actual construction." While he had little knowledge of current operational activity, he was well familiar with the location, construction, and purpose of a great many of the buildings and installations. He was able to pinpoint the location of water mains, power-supply systems, flight-control towers, command stations for both Italian and German forces, air-raid shelters, workshops and barracks, mess locations, and repair hangars. He even knew the location of Trapani's barbershop and shoemaker's shop.

The increased bombing activity on Sicily would be part of a broad ramping up of bombing activity throughout the Mediterranean Theater. These distributed attacks were designed to maintain enemy uncertainty as to where the next Allied landing would be. Attacks were staged as far as northern Italy by aircraft in the UK, and in Greece by aircraft based in the Middle East.

The 49th Fighter Squadron played its part in the Allied run-up to the Sicily invasion. During the month of May, it had flown eighteen combat missions to precisely the targets that NASAF had identified as critical to the MTO.

Mission Summary[26]
May 1943

Date	Mission Type	Target	Target Type	Target Location
6	B-25 escort	Antishipping	Naval	Sealanes off western Sicily
9	B-17 escort	Palermo	Port	Sicily
10	B-17 escort	Milo & Bo Rizzo	Aerodrome	Sicily
11	B-17 escort	Marsala	Port	Sicily
13	B-17 escort	Cagliari	Port and aerodrome	Sardinia
14	B-25 escort	Terranova	Port	Sardinia
18	B-17 escort	Messina	Port	Sicily
19	B-17 escort	Milo	Aerodrome	Sicily
21	B-17 escort	Castelvetrano	Aerodrome	Sicily
22	B-17 escort	Bo Rizzo	Aerodrome	Sicily
24	Dive-bomb/ strafe	Alghero	Port, seaplane base	Sardinia
24	Dive-bomb/ strafe	Arbatax	Port	Sardinia
25	Dive-bomb/ strafe	Milo	Aerodrome	Sicily
25	Dive-bomb/ strafe	Porto Scuso	Port	Sardinia
26	Dive-bomb/ strafe	Golfo Aranci	Port and RR	Sardinia
28	B-25 escort	Bo Rizzo	Aerodrome	Sicily
30	Dive-bomb/ strafe	Chilivani	RR and power plant	Sardinia
31	Dive-bomb	Pantelleria	Gun positions	Pantelleria

With Sicily decided upon, the next step lay in preparation for the invasion, and an important part of those preparations was the capture of the island of Pantelleria and the lesser nearby islands of Lampedusa, Limone, and Lampione. These islands lay squarely in the path of the invasion, midway between the tip of Tunisia and the southeastern beaches of Sicily. From these islands the Germans operated powerful radio direction finder stations that allowed the German Air Force (GAF) to track the movement of incoming American and British aircraft. At Pantelleria, a small island about 8 miles long and 5 miles wide, fifteen batteries of large guns posed a threat to Allied shipping, and a contingent of roughly eighty single-engine fighters was stationed at Pantelleria's airfield.[27]

Great Britain had wanted to occupy Pantelleria since late 1940, but before the Brits could act, the GAF had moved into Sicily, making the risks of assaulting Pantelleria too great. By the spring of 1943, the island appeared as impregnable as Corregidor in the Pacific. In planning for the invasion of Sicily, General Eisenhower had anticipated that the navy would be able to offer eight auxiliary aircraft carriers to provide air cover for the American assault. When in early February of 1942 it was learned that the carriers would not be available, AFHQ began to look hard at other ways to provide the needed air patrols.

Military planners recognized that Pantelleria could provide the bases they needed, and more. Its capture would remove a serious Axis threat to Allied air and naval operations during the Sicilian invasion; it could be used as a navigational aid for Allied aircraft and for bases for air-sea rescue launches, and it would eliminate the enemy radio direction finders and ship-watching stations which would increase the chances for a tactical surprise when the Allies launched their invasion of Sicily.

Eisenhower decided to seize Pantelleria, but without expending heavily in men or materiel. To obviate a full-scale assault, Eisenhower thought of making the operation "a sort of laboratory to determine the effect of concentrated heavy bombing on a defended coastline." He wished the Allied air forces "to concentrate everything" in blasting the island so that the damage to the garrison, its equipment, and morale,

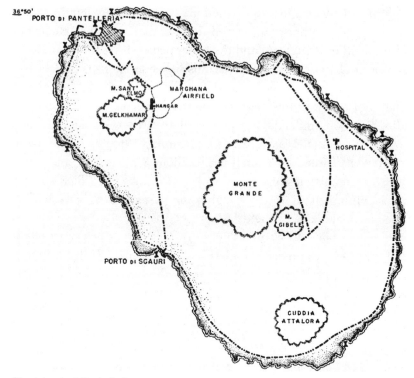

The island of Pantelleria.

AIR FORCE HISTORICAL RESEARCH AGENCY: W. F. CRAVEN AND J. L. CATE, EDS., *THE ARMY AIR FORCES IN WORLD WAR II, VOL. 2*

would be "so serious as to make the landing a rather simple affair." The attack was a further analogy to Corregidor, which had eventually succumbed to intensive Japanese artillery in 1942. Eisenhower wanted "to see whether the air can do the same thing."[28]

Eisenhower ordered the NAAF into action against Pantelleria, calling for a super-intensive aerial and naval bombardment, "with the idea of so terrorizing and paralyzing its defenders that it could be seized without the use of ground troops."[29]

From mid-May until mid-June, the Northwest African Air Forces launched over five thousand sorties against the island. Attacks by Allied medium bombers and fighters—as many as fifty missions per day—

quickly neutralized the port. B-17 heavy bombers with fighter escorts began attacks on June 1, focusing on the coastal gun positions. Bomber runs were immediately followed up by antipersonnel and strafing attacks. The sky was saturated with Allied aircraft—so many that planes had to circle the target area until it was their turn to attack.

All squadrons of the 14th Fighter Group flew often in both bomber-escort and dive-bombing missions, sometimes twice daily.

Mission Summary—49th Fighter Squadron[30]
May 31–June 9, 1943

Date	Mission Type	Target	Target type
May 31	Dive-bomb	Pantelleria	Gun positions
June 1	B-25 bomber escort	Terranova/ Sardinia	Port
2	Dive-bomb	Pantelleria	Gun positions
4	P-38 bomber escort	Milo/Sicily	Aerodrome
5	Dive-bomb	Pantelleria	Gun positions
6	Dive-bomb	Pantelleria	Gun positions
7	Dive-bomb	Pantelleria	Gun positions
8	Dive-bomb	Pantelleria	Gun positions
8	B-17 bomber escort	Pantelleria	Dock and town
9	B-17 bomber escort	Pantelleria	Dock and town
9	Dive-bomb	Pantelleria	Gun positions
10	Dive-bomb	Pantelleria	Gun positions
10	Dive-bomb	Pantelleria	Gun positions
11	B-26 bomber escort and dive-bombing	Pantelleria	Gun positions
11	B-26 bomber escort and dive-bombing	Pantelleria	White flags seen— no bomb drop

The Allied assault combined bomber attacks by B-17 Flying Fortresses with offshore naval shelling. American newspapers carried many accounts of the coordinated attack on Pantelleria—code-named "Corkscrew," and many pilots of the 49th squadron were cited: "Their flak is not accurate, said Lt. Col. Troy Keith of San Jose, Calif., a fighter commander who personally led his twin-tailed fighters in an afternoon smash at the island and came home without meeting a single enemy fighter." Lt. Mark Hageny added: "It was like watching a battle in a vacuum because the roar of our motors kept us from hearing anything. We couldn't see what (the Navy warships) were shooting at because the whole end of the island was covered with heavy brown dust clouds raised by the Fortress bombs. You actually could see the earth shake when those bombs hit." Lt. Robert Riley added: "Everybody practically had his ship over on its back so they could watch the show."[31]

On the last mission flown by the 49th against Pantelleria, William Gregory recalls that the pilots were advised during the preflight briefing that if they saw any white flags on the island, they should not drop their

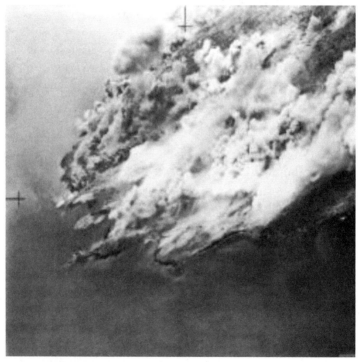

Strike photos. Allied combined assault on Pantelleria, May–June 1943.
NATIONAL ARCHIVES

bombs. "The weather was bad, but we did see the flags," he recalled, and the mission returned to base, jettisoning their bombs during the return.[32]

The British First Infantry Division had prepared for an amphibious assault on June 11, but as the first troops reached shore, enemy resistance ceased. The island was declared secured on June 13—the first strategic position the Allies had captured solely through the use of airpower.

Recognizing the inevitable, the islands of Lampedusa and Limone surrendered on June 13, and Lampione on the 14th. Operation Corkscrew became the first instance showcasing the power of intense air bombardment to induce surrender.[33] The action against Pantelleria allowed the 49th Fighter Squadron to gain invaluable experience in the techniques of dive-bombing and bomber escort, experience that would be put to good use in the bombing campaigns to follow.

Knepper and Kocour took no part in the campaign against Pantelleria; they had arrived at the squadron just two days before the island capitulated and hadn't had enough time to complete their combat flight training with the squadron. They could only watch the P-38s leave and return, and hear the stories of their new squadron mates over mess in the evening. And for the squadron, these eleven days of unimpeded action provided a respite from the heavy bombing escort duties of May and the heavy pilot losses that resulted from those missions.

With the surrender of Pantelleria, the way was clear to begin final preparations for the invasion of Sicily. NASAF again turned their attention to intensified strategic bombing, with Allied forces conducting missions deeper into Axis-held territory over a wide swath that included Sardinia, Sicily, and the Italian mainland. Bombing attacks on German and Italian airfields became particularly intense. After a two-day pause to regroup, rearm, and rest, NASAF conducted a large combined mission on June 15 to the aerodrome complexes in Sicily, targeting the airfields at Trapani/Milo, Bo Rizzo, Castelvetrano, Bocca di Falco, and Sciacca. The intent of these missions was to destroy aircraft on the ground and neutralize the ground assets and landing fields of the German air forces.

The attacks were devastatingly effective. NASAF bombers repeatedly caught large numbers of Axis aircraft on the ground. Hundreds were

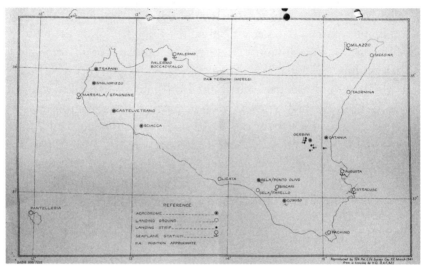

Axis airfields on Sicily.

AFHRA

destroyed by the Allied bombers. NATAF's tactical bombers were also busy, pounding the airfields on the western and central parts of the island.

The AAF began reequipping, repairing, and repositioning its bomber and fighter units for the coming invasion. Fighter units were moved farther forward, to bases closer to Sicily. The 49th Fighter Squadron was given notice to expect a move to their next base at El Bathan.

Hopscotching forward was certainly nothing new for the squadrons of the 14th Fighter Group. In the seven months since the group first arrived at Tafaraoui, Algeria in November 1942 in support of Operation Torch, it had already moved six times—roughly once a month. Its tenure at El Bathan was destined to be their shortest—just twenty days.

On July 3 at 0400 the squadron began the move to a newly constructed airfield at El Bathan. The pilots of the squadron were assigned a combat mission, taking off from Telergma at 1140 to escort B-17s to Cagliari and Chilivani. With the mission complete, the pilots landed at their new base. The advanced echelon arrived the next day, and by July 7 the remainder of the squadron had arrived. As a reward for a difficult move, the squadron was taken to Tunis and then Carthage for a swim in the Mediterranean Ocean.[34]

From that date forward, bombing attacks increasingly focused on Sicilian airfields and Axis communication with Italy, although beach defenses were left alone to preserve surprise as to exactly where the landings were to take place.

About El Bathan

The army had been actively looking for additional forward bases well before the Allies' defeat of German and Italian forces in North Africa. With each advance by ground forces, tactical bombers and fighters became further removed from the battle line. Air forces planners knew that with the collapse of Axis forces in North Africa, the next battle line would inevitably require overflight of the Mediterranean—further extending the flying time for tactical forces—wherever the next action might occur. Rearward bases resulted in less time-over-target and more difficulty in supporting ground troops. For strategic forces, like the 49th squadron, moving to bases located farther forward meant that more strategic targets could be reached, further degrading the war-making ability of the Axis forces.

In early March a directive was issued by air forces headquarters calling for the establishment of a welter of new air bases for central and eastern Tunisia, including thirteen forward fields for tactical air force units (NATAF) and fifteen fields for strategic units (NASAF) located in the region south and east of Constantine.[35] El Bathan was one site in eastern Tunisia under active consideration in May of that year. Unlike other airfields in Tunisia, El Bathan was not a captured German Air Force aerodrome. Rather, it was a "greenfield" location. The clay soil was dusty in dry weather, but muddy in wet weather. A new field destined for short service, its unpaved surface qualified it for "temporary use as a strategic dry-weather base for combat aircraft."[36]

The 14th Fighter Group was the first unit to occupy the base and stayed only from July 3, 1943, to July 25, 1943. Upon its departure, the base was used by the 320th Bomber Group (BG) until early November, and was then apparently abandoned.

Construction began on the El Bathan airfield in June by the Air Service Command, one of six concurrent airfield construction projects in the eastern Tunisia region. El Bathan had the most planned runways (three) and the longest runways (at 6,000 feet). It was scheduled for completion on July 5. The airfield was located 3.5 miles south of the village of Tebourba and about 15.5 miles from Tunis, along one of the major paved east-west roads in the region. The field was located just south of this main highway, on the gravel road to Attermine. Following standard army design, El Bathan was constructed to avoid presenting an easy target for enemy aircraft. Aircraft parking spaces (hardstands) were dispersed, as were housing, gasoline, and bomb-storage units, with roads and taxiways connecting the various facilities. Squadrons were sited separately at the base.[37]

The aircraft hardstands were located around the perimeter of the airstrips. A total of sixty-five hardstands were constructed, each at least 450 feet from the next hardstand, with a minimum of 150 feet from the taxiways, and with aircraft parking sites measuring 100 by 130 feet. The field would occupy a "footprint" of just less than two square miles, and within this site, all three squadrons of P-38 aircraft would operate: the 37th, 48th, and 49th Fighter Squadrons of the 14th Fighter Group— nominally, seventy-five fighter aircraft. Previously at Telergma, the 14th FG had briefly shared the field with the B-26 Marauders of the 17th Bomber Group. El Bathan would be the exclusive base for the P-38s of the 14th Fighter Group.

The bombers would not be far away: The 17th and 319th Bomber Groups were flying B-26 Marauders at this time in Djedeida, just 5 miles to the east; the 320th Bomber Group, also flying B-26s, was operating at Massicault, just 3 miles southeast. With a total of 192 B-26s based in such a small area, on a calm morning, the pilots of the 14th would be able to hear the engines of the B-26s warming up as they received their preflight briefing.[38]

A small village was located adjacent to the airfield on the west side, and a mosque on the eastern edge of the field. North of the village was an orchard and vineyard. Much of the perimeter was under cultivation in wheat. Army planners seemed to be concerned with local owners of the fields and crops. According to an aerodrome report at the time, "The wheat on this site will be harvested completely by June 25, after which the site would be plowed. A portion of the land is owned by M. Bianco, with residence at Attermine, and the remaining land is owned by the Bishop or Archbishop of Carthage."[39]

The army allocated six days for the construction of the airfield. The site included two wells: One 30-foot-deep well was located on a farm on the southern edge of the airfield. Equipped with a small pump, the well yielded clear but salty-tasting water. The second well, located a mile to the east, was also of masonry construction, in excellent condition, and was equipped with a nonfunctioning windmill.[40] As an advanced base intended for short-term use, the airfield would include no barracks, hospital buildings, support buildings, hangars, or workshops. There were no special provisions made for ammunition storage, and it was not equipped for night landings.

Leaving Telergma, the men of the fighter group reckoned they had gone from bad to worse. The airfield became known as the "Dust Bowl" by the men stationed there. The hot, dry winds constantly blew airborne dust into the tents, aircraft, and the support facilities.

Moving a twin-engine fighter group, complete with workshops, equipment, supplies, and over 1,000 men was a huge undertaking—one that the group had already performed on several occasions. Men assigned to the Air Echelon had it easy. Forming the advance team, this group flew to the new field in C-47s and readied the new airfield to receive the group's P-38s that would arrive at the end of the day's mission. The Ground Echelon was not so lucky—loading everything the group owned in 21 "deuce-and-a-half" (2-1/2 ton) trucks and 4 one-ton trailers.[41]

Master sergeant Lloyd Guenther, a crew chief with the 48th squadron, recounted his introduction to El Bathan:

It was a long drive [from Telergma to El Bathan], and hotter than Hades in this desert heat. By the time we got to where we were going, everyone had drunk up his canteen of water. The water supply for our new field was a dug well with a stone wall around it and a hand-cranked windless [sic] with a bucket. . . . The well was surrounded by water that missed the trough and was slobbered on the ground by the sheep. A muddy mess, mixed with plenty [of] sheep urine and manure that no doubt was seeping back into the mortared stone wall of the well. MPs stood guard around the well to prevent the thirsty men from drinking the water until it had been chlorinated for 30 minutes.[42]

Master sergeant Normal Schuller, also of the 48th squadron, recorded:

July 3: We left Telergma 4:00 this morning. Got here at El Bathan about 10:00. Covered a lot of battleground. Never had such a hellish ride—respirator and goggles. Roads torn to hell and a hell of a field here, and hot.

July 4: Never felt such heat. Must be 120 in the shade, and no shade . . . This place will be hell before long.[43]

The 14th had arrived at El Bathan in that miserable summer of 1943 just in time for the sirocco—a hot wind coming out of the Sahara, blowing at about the same time each day for weeks on end. Fred Wolfe with the 82nd Fighter Group wrote about coping with the strong Sahara winds: "All we could do was dampen a sheet or towel, lie down, and cover ourselves up with it. When the wind was over we'd get up and dust ourselves off."[44]

The sun was relentless. Men covered their backs with hydraulic oil as protection against sunburn. Aircraft were too hot to touch, and pilots would be wringing wet before their aircraft got off the ground. Starting their missions with damp clothing, pilots would suffer during high-altitude B-17 escort missions. Climbing as high as 30,000 feet, and losing 3 degrees of temperature for every 1,000 feet of altitude gain, resulted in below-freezing cockpit temperatures. On these missions, the ineffective cockpit heaters of the usually beloved P-38s were in for a round of rough cursing. Lieutenant Gregory reports: "It was just extremely cold, and our hands would get numb. Then when we returned to warmer air, the blood would start to flow again and our hands would just ache. I can remember the excruciating pain when our fingers started to thaw out."

The sun's intensity could lead to entirely unexpected consequences, according to Gregory: "Usually when we left in the morning we would have the flaps up on the tents to keep it open. One day, I guess I had been shaving early in the morning. I had this two-sided mirror; it fell on the ground by the side of my cot. During the day when the sun came up, the sun focused the rays on the cot, and it burned up my cot while I was off on the mission. [My tentmates said,] 'Hey, we had a little fire while you were gone.'"

And the heat also caused unexpected problems for the ground crews. "In this heat and humidity we had trouble with the guns freezing up on high-altitude bombing-escort missions . . . Sometimes the planes came home and the guns would be a solid mass of ice and frost from the cold upstairs and the humidity near the ground, condensing on them. We went to a special sperm oil, which kept the guns from freezing."[45]

The ground staff's war required endurance. "They did an extraordinary job under very difficult circumstances, which included having to do all their work outside, in fair weather and foul, because there were no hangars. On the job seven days a week, from early to late, their duties involved a lot of hard, dirty [work]. Unlike the pilots, they were overseas for the duration of the war, and they didn't have a lot to look forward to in terms of promotions, which were terribly slow for ground crewmen."[46]

The 49th would eventually fly twenty-six combat missions from El Bathan before being moved again in late July to a new base at Sainte-Marie du Zit, south of Tunis.

A Look at the Other Sides

The relative ease with which Pantelleria was taken, and especially noting the almost nonexistent resistance by Italian and German interceptors, prompts the question: What was the status of Axis airpower at this point of the war in the Mediterranean Theater? Historians Samuel W. Mitcham Jr. and Friedrich von Stauffenberg, in their authoritative work, *The Battle of Sicily: How the Allies Lost Their Chance for Total Victory*, note: "The Luftwaffe was having more than its share of difficulty in the months preceding the invasion of Sicily. From November 1942 through May 1943 the Luftwaffe had lost more than 2,440 aircraft in the

Mediterranean area. This figure represents over 40 percent of the forces on hand in November. During the same period, Allied strength was steadily increasing to a 2.5 to 1 advantage."[47]

For the German Air Force in the summer of 1943, three realities had become only too apparent: German industry could not keep up with the increasing demands for aircraft, either in numbers or design. It had not sufficiently ramped up to meet the replacement demands of a war fought on three fronts. And the Me 109 which had so dominated the air over Spain, Poland, and Russia had met its match in Great Britain in the Spitfire, and in North Africa, with the P-38. New, more highly performant German aircraft had been designed, but the manufacturing sector could not stop long enough to retool, and the new designs were late in making their appearance. As Adolf Galland, commandant of the Luftwaffe Fighter Corps, later wrote: "Our fighter production had fallen behind that of the Anglo-Americans in quantity as well as in quality of performance. We needed more powerful engines, longer range, more effective armaments, higher speed, better rate of climb, an adjustment of the ceiling . . . of our planes."[48]

Conversely, the American war industry was hitting full stride, out-producing Germany by a factor of two to one. The situation was especially galling for Galland, who wrote: "One of the guiding principles of fighting with an air force is the assembling of weight by numbers, of a numerical concentration at decisive spots. It was impossible to adhere to this principle because of the continuous expansion of the Eastern Front, and because of the urgent demands of the Army."

Germany was gradually losing the heart of its fighter corps. By the summer of 1943, German pilots had been flying in combat for four years, and knew they would continue to fly for the duration of the conflict. A prime example is German pilot Hans Joachim Marseille, who over the course of just one year flew in 388 combat sorties and shot down 158 Allied aircraft. Marseille was himself shot down in late September 1942, along with many of his peers who were also lost in combat.

These pilots were simply irreplaceable, given the conditions in Germany at the time. The German pilot training program could not keep up with the demands created by losses in the field. To rush replacement

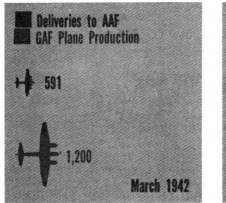

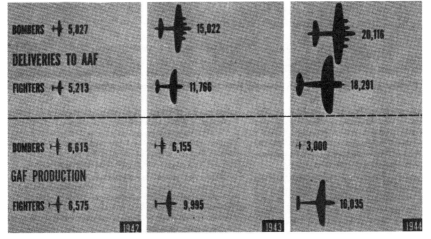

Comparative figures on fighter and bomber production of the GAF and AAF, by year.
IMPACT: THE ARMY AIR FORCES' CONFIDENTIAL PICTURE HISTORY OF WORLD WAR II, AIR FORCE
HISTORICAL FOUNDATION, 1980

pilots to the field, Germany had made large reductions in the amount
of flying time allocated to new students in training—down from
seventy-five hours in 1940 to just twenty-five hours in 1943. Any combat veteran from that period would flatly state that pilots with such
limited training would be only minimally competent and potentially
dangerous for their fellow pilots.

At the same time, American pilots were receiving almost three hundred total hours of flight training, eighty hours of Transition training in the P-38 before leaving the States, and additional combat training hours at bases in North Africa before making their first combat mission.[49]

The Germans had entered the war with the wrong mix of aircraft. The GAF fought the Battle of Britain with neither an effective strategic bomber, nor a sufficiently long-range fighter. The result was that the GAF lost the Battle of Britain and were not able to conduct an effective strategic-bombing campaign against the Allies in North Africa, particularly after the Allied air forces' mission had changed to a more aggressive, strategic mode.

Little support could be expected from the GAF headquarters, as Mitcham and von Stauffenberg note:

Goering's leadership of the Luftwaffe was by now all but nonexistent as he grew increasingly isolated from the top German leadership. He badly misunderstood the Luftwaffe's situation in Sicily. Rather than recognizing that its problems were due to inferior aircraft, reductions of aircraft deliveries, and inadequate pilot training, he leveled his criticism at the airmen themselves. In a communique to his forces on Sicily, Goering famously wrote: "I can only regard you with contempt. I want an immediate improvement and expect that all pilots will show an improvement in fighting spirit. If . . . not forthcoming, flying personnel from the commander down must expect to be remanded to the ranks and transferred to the Eastern Front to serve on the ground."[50]

According to Johannes Steinhoff, the British and American heavy bombardment of Sicilian airfields that began in mid-June had taken a heavy toll on enemy air forces.

The airfields had been ploughed up like arable [land] in autumn. [The Allies had been] laying their bomb carpets everywhere as though intending to destroy the place yard by yard. We were forced to pull out and were having to move our aircraft almost hourly, concealing ourselves in the stubble in between times. Then the whole area started blazing and the flames drove us out. . . . Both the Germans and the Americans learned that the bomb carpet was an extremely effective weapon when used against an airfield, and had a demoralizing effect on airfield personnel. Particularly effective were the smaller bombs that made only shallow bomb craters but released thousands of fragments, projected outwards at high velocity and close to the ground, shredding the outer skins of the German aircraft as though they were made of paper.[51]

For the German defenders, their archnemesis was the B-17. In later months, an Allied survey learned that a total of 1,100 enemy aircraft had been destroyed on the ground. On the key airfields at Gerbini and Catania were found the wreckages of 189 and 132 aircraft, respectively.

Steinhoff later recounted Galland's direction: "Up to now we've failed in our attacks against the Flying Fortresses [B-17s], the enemy's most effective weapon by far. The Reich Marshal [Göring] is angry about it, and rightly so. You must all concentrate on one thing and one thing only—shoot down bombers, forget about the fighters. The only thing that counts is the destruction of the bombers and the ten crew that each of them carries." The Reich Marshal also recognized the impossibility of operating an effective air defense above Sicily, but pressed Steinhoff and others to adopt fresh tactics, create new forms of combat.

Steinhoff shared Galland's awe over the B-17: "They flew in defensive boxes, a heavy defensive formation, and with all of their heavy .50 caliber machine guns they were dangerous to approach. We finally adopted the head-on attack . . . but only a few experts could do this successfully, and it took nerves of steel. Then you also had the long-range fighter escorts, which made life difficult."[52]

Sicily's air defense was assigned to two Luftwaffe Jagdgeschwader, equivalent to an American fighter wing. JG 77—known as the *Herz As* Fighter Wing—was nominally assigned to the western region of Sicily, and JG 53—*Pik As* ("Ace of Spades")—to the east. Like their American counterparts, each JG was made up of *Gruppen* (Fighter Groups) and *Jagdstaffel* (Fighter Squadrons) and was equipped with 120 to 125 fighter aircraft.[53]

NASAF's bombing campaign had reduced the normally strong Jagdgeschwaders to a level of minimal efficiency. Area responsibilities were no longer observed, and the commander of air forces on Sicily was forced to shuttle aircraft around Sicily in order to provide some level of protection against the Allied "heavies."

On July 10, 1943, D-Day for the invasion of Sicily, Allied forces had an inventory of roughly 5,000 first-line aircraft of all types, operated by trained and experienced crews. Even the most generous count of the opposition's assets credited the Germans and Italians with no more than 1,250 aircraft, few of which were operational. The GAF based in Sicily and Sardinia had suffered such attrition through Allied bombing that it could launch just 128 Me 109 and Fw 190 [Focke-Wulf] fighters.[54]

It was Steinhoff's great lament that the nature of air battles had changed. The duel in the air—the classic dogfight—was becoming rare. "Nothing was left of the strange attraction that drew us almost compulsively to aerial combat, first over the English Channel and then in Russia. The chivalry associated with the duel in the air, the readiness to accept challenge again and again, had given way to a sense of vulnerability, and the pleasure we had once taken in fighting a sporting battle against equal odds had long since become a thing of the past. . . . . The strategic bombers, with their frightful capacity of self-defense, came increasingly to dictate the nature of air battles."[55]

Steinhoff and others pled their cases to superiors, with no good result. His commander, when confronted by Steinhoff with the reality of the overwhelming Allied airpower, retorted with a croak of laughter: "For heaven's sake, who in fighters today still bothers about relative strengths? When I tell you that the Allies have about five thousand aircraft against our three hundred and fifty, you'll be able to calculate the enormous number of chances you have of shooting them down."

While greatly overmatched, the GAF was far from toothless. The 49th's frequent opposition in western Sicily, JG 77, was led by German pilots of exceptional experience and ability. Oberstlt. Steinhoff, the JG

77 commander, would be credited with 176 aerial victories, including 6 bomber kills, in nearly 1,000 combat sorties, while being shot down himself 12 times in combat. Steinhoff's friend Siegfried Freytag was credited with 102 aerial victories, including 2 solo victories over four-engine bombers. And by midsummer 1943, Maximillian Volke already had 35 aerial victories to his credit.[56]

Steinhoff later wrote: "Admittedly our opponents had succeeded in (smashing our airfields), but we were still flying and still inflicting losses on them, which in turn compelled them to carry out further attacks against our airfields. However the British and the Americans possess such ample resources that they had no need to husband them; they would be unlikely to rest until they had either destroyed us or driven us out."[57]

The commanders of the Luftwaffe on Sicily had come to a point of utter desperation. "There was nothing now to recall the dashing, stylish fighter pilot with his yellow scarf and his imaginatively modified uniform. Our outward appearance accurately reflected the pass to which we had come: crumpled, filthy, oil-stained trousers, ancient, greasy life jackets, emaciated and in many cases unshaven faces. Everything was dusty brown—earth, clothes, faces, airplanes. There are the hardships of victory, hardships which in Russia and North Africa we cheerfully shrugged off and which, on occasion, we had not even noticed, so elated had we been by our sense of superiority. And there are the hardships of defeat, hardships of dirt and dishonor which feed on morale, impair the fighting spirit and only serve to engender fresh defeats. This, we had been taught, was the hour of the born military commander, the hour when he would jerk his men out of their state of depression, give them a purpose, inspire them with new elan and lead them boldly to death or glory against the foe. But to all of us here, engaged in the routine task of fighting in the heat and dirt, that concept was a highly dubious one. It was a relic of the First World War, if not of the days of cavalry charges, and was utterly useless in the situation in which we now found ourselves. The war in the air is a technological war which cannot be won by a technologically inferior fighting force, however high its morale or dauntless its resolution. There was a point our field marshals had failed to grasp and it was also the reason why the Reichmarschall could think only in terms of bravery and cowardice and why, to his mind, a fighter arm which had lost its superiority could be nothing other than cowardly."[58]

FLAK

In the wake of the widespread destruction of the Luftwaffe's aviation assets, the German flak capability became of increasing importance, and continued to pose a very serious threat to Allied warplanes. This was even becoming evident in the German homeland, where the Luftwaffe could no longer be depended upon to provide broad area defenses for its forces in the field, or for its cities, factories, and other strategic assets. Though the flak units were subordinate to the Luftwaffe for administration, operationally they were controlled by the army to which they were attached in the field.[59]

The most effective, and certainly the most respected, antiaircraft gun used by Axis forces against fighter-bombers was the 20mm Flakvierling 38. Its four-barrel design was first introduced in late 1940 and continued in widespread use throughout the war. It was a feared aircraft-killer that was used widely in the Mediterranean Theater. This gun had a range of just over 7,000 feet, and could fire up to 1,800 rounds per minute. Against dive-bombing or strafing aircraft, it was terribly effective.

A normal detachment for a single-barrel 20mm gun was a crew of six. For the four-barreled 20mm Vierling, three more loaders and three more ammunition men were required, making a crew of twelve. Pilots could see the incoming orange tracer rounds and the blankets of blue-white aerial bursts of this automatic-weapon fire. Less evident were the machine-gun and small-arms fire, the accuracy of which often became evident only after landing, when the pilot's crew chief pointed out shell holes in the aircraft.

Also very widely used was the German Flak 30, of which Germany produced over 144,000 during the period 1934–1945. Operated by a crew of seven, this single-barreled gun would fire up to 180 rounds per minute, with an effective range of just over 7,000 feet. The Flak 38, with an increased firing rate, was introduced later in the war.[60]

Against higher-flying aircraft, the German 88mm cannon was more effective, and greatly feared. Capable of firing a 20-pound shell to over 49,000 feet, it was most often deployed in defending highly valued assets. Pilots saw the orange fireballs and black greasy smoke of the 88s as they neared the target of bomber-escort missions—what P-38 pilot Jim Graham of the 1st Fighter Group referred to as "Ping-Pong balls rising up from the ground at you."

The shells fired by the antiaircraft guns exploded without striking solid objects. Timing devices were programmed into the aiming of the projectiles. The 88mm shells were made up of explosives encased in steel jackets. When detonated, the jackets would explode, sending out a mushroom of steel fragments. The principle was similar to that of firing a shotgun. The Germans fitted their 88mm guns in batteries of four.[61] Like all German antiaircraft artillery, it was also highly effective against ground targets during army ground operations.

As an example of flak deployment in Sicily, the Hermann Göring Division (panzer) included a flak regiment, which normally included

88mm flak establishes a pattern against incoming B-26 bombers.
NATIONAL ARCHIVES

four battalions in the field. Each battalion could contain up to four light batteries, with each battery equipped with twelve guns (most often operating in groups of three guns)—which meant close to two hundred guns available for antiaircraft fire.[62]

The air offensive against the Luftwaffe and the Italian Air Force had been extremely effective, but as will be shown in later chapters, the Axis forces were still capable of a stiff defense, albeit with far less frequency. As the Allies continued preparation for the next ground action against the Axis forces in the Mediterranean, German pilots, and German ground fire, continued to exact a costly toll of Allied aircraft.

CHAPTER 6

Meet the Pilots

THE COMPOSITION OF A SQUADRON WAS CONSTANTLY IN FLUX, WITH some pilots completing their tour of duty and returning home, while others lost their lives in combat missions or were downed and taken captive, with eager new replacement pilots stepping forward to fill the ranks. What follows is a snapshot of one part of the 49th Fighter Squadron, introducing a handful of the pilots who fought the German Luftwaffe during the summer of 1943.

Although not officially part of the squadron, the first man introduced here was the commander of the 14th Fighter Group, the man who directed all squadrons, including the 49th.

Col. Troy Keith
Commander
14th Fighter Group

Troy and his twin brother Roy were born in Arkansas in 1912. Joining the Arkansas National Guard in 1932, by 1935 he was working as an airplane mechanic in Little Rock. He was accepted into the Aviation Cadet Program, and attended flight schools from October '35 to June '37. Commissioned as a second lieutenant in the Army Air Corps Reserve, on June 10, 1937, his commission in the regular Army Air Corps came in August 1939, and he was promoted to first lieutenant in September 1940.

Lieutenant Keith's reputation as a "hot pilot" had gotten off to a good start. In 1936 he was forced to bail out of a P-12B bi-plane when he blacked out due to lack of oxygen, but not before setting an unofficial speed record.

In 1939 he was christened the "Human Meteor" by newspapers around the country in recognition of an incident that could well have proven fatal. While flying at 28,000 feet, Lieutenant Keith's aircraft went into a nearly 4-mile dive when he blacked out due to a failure of his oxygen system. Regaining consciousness at 9,000 ft., Lieutenant Keith was able to land the plane despite a buckled wing. It was unofficially estimated that he might have attained an airspeed of 670 miles per hour, a new army flight record.[1]

In November 1940 he finished first in the prestigious Frank Luke Memorial Trophy competition, flying a P-40 in an army event that rated a pilot's marksmanship in aerial and fixed target firing, and on bombing.

A few months later, with the war approaching, the 14th Fighter Group was activated on January 15, 1941 and 1st Lt. Troy Keith, age 30, was named as its first provisional commander. He relinquished command to Col. Thayer Olds in April 1941, who commanded the group during its embarkation to England in July–August 1942, and during its initial operations escorting bombers to targets in France. The group fought in the North African Campaign from November 1942 to late January 1943. Then-Captain Keith flew many combat missions during these operations and is credited with two aerial victories in January. In late January, having suffered tremendous losses in combat, the 14th was withdrawn from combat operations. During the rebuilding period, Keith resumed command and was charged with reequipping and retraining the group in preparation for the Allies advance into Sicily. He was promoted to major in March.

Lt. Troy Keith.
DAVID KILHEFNER

Col. Troy Keith, Commander, 14th Fighter Group.

NATIONAL ARCHIVES

14th Fighter Group leadership, with visitor. This photograph, taken in May 1943 shortly after the 14th FG's "combat restart" after a three-month reorganization show, from left to right, Lt. Col. Troy Keith (Group Commander), leading American World War I ace Eddie Rickenbacker, Maj. Clarence L. Tinker Jr. (Group Operations Officer), and early P-38 ace Maj. Joel Owens (Deputy Group Commander/Executive Officer). Major Tinker's father, Gen. Clarence Tinker, was killed while leading a B-24 bomber attack during the Battle of Midway in June 1942. His son, Maj. Tinker, was killed along with three other pilots on May 18th, 1943, while leading a combined formation from the 37th and 48th squadron on a bomber-escort mission to Messina.

STANAWAY

Pilot Troy Keith with his P-38 aircraft. It was Colonel Keith's responsibility to manage the men and equipment of three fighter squadrons, including over 1,200 men.
DAVID KILHEFNER

Capt. Henry "Hugh" Trollope
Commander
49th Fighter Squadron

Also a twin, Henry Trollope was reared on a ranch in Goose Egg, Wyoming, the son of Harry and Beulah Trollope, pioneering Wyoming citizens. While he signed all official documents as "Henry," he went by his middle name, Hugh.

The Trollope twins got their early education on the ranch. Their mother hired a teacher, providing him with room and board and a place to hold classes. When Hugh and his brother Harry were ready for high school, their mother moved with them to Casper so they could attend Natrona County High School. Nothing is known about Hugh's academics, but he and Harry were well-known athletes, competing on both high school football and boxing teams. Both graduated in 1936, and attended the University of Wyoming, where they continued their boxing careers.

In the Montana–Wyoming AAU Boxing Tournament, held on August 6, 1936, Hugh won the Class B light-heavyweight title, and Harry won the Class B middleweight title. Hugh played halfback at the University of Wyoming. Sometime during their college days, Harry injured his leg severely enough to disqualify him from military service.

While at UW, Hugh Trollope earned his private pilot's license through the CPT program, and entered the Army Air Corps Aviation Cadet Program in the fall of 1940. His Primary flight training was done at Mira Loma Academy, where he survived a training crash in his PT-13B in late December 1940. He completed Basic flight training at Moffett Field, his Advanced at Stockton, and was commissioned on July 12, 1941. Trollope flew with the 49th Fighter Squadron at its rebirth in North Africa in the spring of 1943, and when the commander of the 49th squadron, William G. Newman, completed his combat tours on June 10, 1943, Trollope was named its new commander. He served in this post until succeeded by B. E. Mackenzie on September 21, 1943, having commanded the squadron during the entire run-up and execution of Operation Husky.

Squadron commanders had relatively short tours at this stage in the war, because they were subject to the same fifty-mission rule as the rest of the combat pilots. As has been seen, with combat missions coming daily—sometimes twice daily—a combat tour could be completed in three months. In the period of 1941 through 1943, the squadron was led by ten different commanders. Fifty missions meant a return to stateside, a short leave, and reassignment.

During his combat tour, Trollope named his plane "Maggie," after his wife, Margaret. She remained in Casper while Hugh was abroad, working at the Casper Air Base.[2]

Capt. Richard Decker
Operations Officer
49th Fighter Squadron

Capt. Richard Decker was born in Oberlin, Kansas, on October 8, 1918. He was raised and educated in Coffeyville, Kansas, and graduated from Coffeyville Junior College. He also attended the Colorado School of Mines and the University of Arizona.[3]

For Captain Decker, there had only ever been one future: "In junior high, we were assigned the task of writing a paper on what we wanted to do when we grew up. There was no doubt in my mind. . . Airplanes had fascinated me. I even wore a pilots helmet in the winter time. I was going to be an airplane pilot." By his sophomore year of high school, he was accompanying a neighbor in his Curtis Robin three-seat high-wing monoplane on barnstorming trips to county rodeos and fairs, given the job of selling rides and helping passengers in and out of the aircraft.

His interest in military flying was piqued when he attended the National Air Races at Mines Field in 1936. By 1939 he had begun taking flight lessons, selling his car to pay for them. His father and his sister both became pilots about the same time, with Decker serving as his father's entirely unauthorized flight instructor.

Decker entered the Army Air Corps in 1940 as a flying cadet, completed flight training at Kelly Field, San Antonio, Texas, in 1941, and was commissioned a second lieutenant in 1941. In 1942, he was assigned to the 78th Fighter Group and was sent overseas to England along

Flight Cadet Decker, Advanced flight training, Kelly Field.

DELANA (SCOTT) HARRISON

with other members of the group in late 1942. Shortly after arriving in England, Decker and his fellow pilots were reassigned to North Africa, part of the rebuilding effort for fighter squadrons that had suffered such high losses in the early days of combat. Upon arrival, the 78th was dismantled, with pilots, ground personnel, and aircraft becoming the new 14th Fighter Group. Initially serving with group, Decker joined the 49th Fighter Squadron as operations officer when Captain Trollope assumed command on June 10, 1943.

Captain Decker and Lieutenant Harper later confirmed a story about Lieutenants Gregory and Neely that occurred after Advanced flight training, while the pilots were being introduced to the P-38. Captain Decker supervised taxi training for the new pilots by riding on the wing of the P-38 with the pilot at the controls and the window open. One day, after having certified both Gregory and Neely, Decker asked Gregory to drive him out to his aircraft in the pilot's jeep. He was astonished to hear that Lieutenant Gregory couldn't drive. He then asked

Capt. Richard Decker, right.
DELANA (SCOTT) HARRISON

Telergma, June 1943. Decker is shown with aircraft #36, an aircraft flown primarily by Lieutenant Neely.
DELANA (SCOTT) HARRISON

Lieutenant Neely for a lift: "Was I ever surprised when I checked . . . he couldn't drive either. They were both from Tennessee and turned out to be exceptional pilots."

Decker also reported a second surprising incident with Lieutenant Neely: "In late December (while in England) we received some P-38s and began flying camera gunnery passes against another plane. On one flight Lt. Neely was setting off to my side and not making passes. I called on the radio, but got not answer. Then I saw this white stuff coming from the window of his plane. As he began making passes at my plane, nothing more happened. (Later) I questioned him on the ground, and was told how he always became ill flying. He had lasted this long, and knew how to overcome the problem, so nothing was said to the others. You could certainly admire him for his determination."

As operations officer, Decker divided the pilots into two "teams" for scheduling. He led Team One and Captain Trollope led Team Two. As Decker noted: "This way the same pilots flew together all the time and became used to how the others flew and what to expect from them. It also make it easier for me, as I only had to step out of my tent and yell 'Team One' or 'Team Two' for briefings, as all officers' tents were nearby."

Decker had a field phone in his tent. Calls came in from the group operations officer for mission information, and in turn he would relay the type of mission to the squadron engineering officer.[4]

Lt. Frederick James Bitter
49th Fighter Squadron

Frederick James "Jim" Bitter was born on February 26, 1917, in Butler, Pennsylvania, and graduated from Butler High School. He was a solid athlete, lettering in both swimming and football in high school, and playing semiprofessional football for the Butler Cubs Football Team. Lieutenant Bitter was one of the pilots who came to North Africa in early 1943 to rebuild the devastated 14th Fighter Group. He named his aircraft "Mary Jane,"[5] after the girl he married in September 1942.

The P-38 pilots looked for diversion on days when they were not assigned to a mission and appreciated getting away from the airfield and its near-constant bustle and noise. Fellow pilot Harold Harper relates a story about bird hunting with Lieutenant Bitter in the mountains south of their base. "I used to shoot these nice partridge. Good eating. I'd fry them up with butter. We picked up these rifles, two nice Mauser rifles. Bitter picked up a rifle, and shot it, and said, 'Hey, Harper, I can't hit anything with this thing.' I said, 'What's the matter?' He said, 'I dunno.' So I took the bolt out, and looked down the barrel, and it was bent . . . the bullet went out, but couldn't hit nothing."

Lieutenant Bitter was credited with one probable and one damaged enemy aircraft during his tour of duty in North Africa.

Jim Bitter (back row, second from left) in his football days.
RICK BITTER

Jim Bitter in North Africa,
summer of 1943.
NATIONAL ARCHIVES

Lt. Wallace Grady Bland
49th Fighter Squadron

Born in Hanceville, Alabama, Wallace Bland had graduated from St. Bernard College and the University of Alabama, and had practiced law briefly before enlisting in the Army Air Corps on September 26, 1941.[6] Tall among his fellow cadets, at 6 feet, Wallace Bland completed all of his flight training in Texas: Primary was at Perrin Field, Basic at Corsicana, and Advanced at Moore Field in Mission, Texas. He was commissioned on April 30, 1942.

He was assigned to the 83rd Fighter Squadron, 78th Fighter Group at Hamilton Field, California, and shipped out with the 78th when it was assigned to England as part of Operation Bolero.

He found himself in North Africa in the early spring of 1943 when the 78th moved to Casablanca and was reconstituted as the 14th Fighter Group.

Aviation Cadet Wallace Bland
ART TAPHORN

Lieutenant Bland had married Carolyn Smith shortly after his commissioning, and they were expecting their first child when his unit left the States for England. Their daughter Carolyn Jessica was born on March 18, shortly after Lieutenant Bland had been assigned to the 49th Fighter Squadron and while he was busy with high-altitude escort training exercises and preparing for the group's move forward to the airfield at Telergma. By the time his daughter was six weeks old Lieutenant Bland and his fellow pilots in the 49th were in combat, facing the Luftwaffe in the waning days of the North African Campaign. His eagerness for combat could have been attributed in part to his desire to complete his combat tour and return home to meet his daughter.

Lt. Beryl Boatman
49th Fighter Squadron

Born December 28, 1921, Beryl Boatman was one of seven children born into a sharecropping family in the dusty eastern Oklahoma town of Henryetta, a town that was later to adopt the motto "a legacy of legends, cowboys and heroes." The town was bisected by Coal Creek, a testament to the many coal mines in the area.

Beryl's parents had schooled only to the eighth grade, but instilled in their children the importance of a solid education. Beryl graduated from Okmulgee High School in 1939, and began taking classes at the local junior college.

He enlisted in the Oklahoma National Guard (Reserve) while still in high school. Activated in the fall of 1940, he received regular promotions and by the spring of 1942 he was a staff sergeant posted to the 45th Division at Camp Barkeley in Abilene, Texas.

Early in 1942 Staff Sergeant Boatman applied for and was accepted into the Aviation Cadet Program. Completing the Advance flight school at Luke Field, he earned his wings and was commissioned on December 3, 1942.

Beryl and his brother married sisters: Beryl, to Margaret Louise Miller, and Samuel, to Nellie Virginia Miller, of West Virginia. Beryl and Margaret Louise had a son, Ronald, who was born after Beryl's departure for England.[7]

Margaret Louise delivered their son Ron on June 1, 1943. Half a

Aviation Cadet Beryl Boatman.
MICHELE BRANCH

Lt. Beryl Boatman with his P-38.
MICHELE BRANCH

world away and unaware that he had just become a father, Lieutenant Boatman's day was to be eventful in other ways: in the morning, the group was visited by Prime Minister Winston Churchill, General Doolittle, and several other British and American military leaders. After a brief address by the prime minister, Lieutenant Boatman and 23 other pilots from the 49th squadron were off on a five-hour mission escorting B-25 bombers to the Axis airfield at Terranova, Sardinia, a mission marked by intense and accurate heavy caliber flak from the German and Italian defenders. Lieutenant Boatman returned safely from this, his ninth combat mission, and would not learn of his son's birth for another six weeks.

Lt. Anthony "Tony" Evans
49th Fighter Squadron

Lt. Anthony Evans was born in 1919 and lived in Marion, Ohio. He graduated St. Mary's High School in 1936 and briefly attended Akron University before joining the Army Air Corps Aviation Cadet Program on January 20, 1942.

Tony Evans completed his Primary flight training at Oxnard, his Basic school at Merced, and his Advanced flight training at Victorville.[8] While based at Hamilton with other members of the 78th Fighter Group, Lieutenant Evans stacked up a P-38 during training.

Harold Harper was a good friend of Tony Evans and recalled an event that occurred when the 78th Fighter Group—later to become the 14th Fighter Group—were ferrying new aircraft on the long flight from England to North Africa.

"Tony could not get his engine started when the formation took off. We were following a B-25 this time, which was providing navigation. When you take off you gotta go, and when we took off we heard Tony call, saying 'I can't get my engine started! Wait! Wait! Wait!' But we kept on going, and pretty soon we were 15–20 minutes gone already, and we heard him say 'I'm airborne—what's your heading?' So we gave him our heading. We could hear him call every once in a while, but he never did catch up with us.

Lt. Tony Evans, by his good friend Harold Harper upon Evans's return from a combat mission. As evidenced by the markings on his aircraft, this photo was taken when Evans was well into his combat tour.

LT. COL. HAROLD HARPER (RET.)

Lt. Anthony Evans, upon completion of fifty combat missions, North Africa, 1943.

NATIONAL ARCHIVES

49th Fighter Squadron Lieutenants Anthony Evans, Wayne Manlove, Lloyd DeMoss, Marlow Leikness, and Carroll Knott, showing tally board in which they are credited with nineteen of the squadron's twenty-seven victories over enemy fighters. North Africa, summer 1943.

NATIONAL ARCHIVES

"We got into Casablanca, and we heard a call way out there somewhere. I called in and said that I had plenty of fuel. I called Tony and asked for his altitude and heading. I made the reciprocal of the heading, and it wasn't too long when I found him."[9]

Lieutenant Evans shot down his first enemy aircraft during the mission of June 20, 1943, and would later become an "ace."

Lt. Martin Aloysius Foster Jr.
49th Fighter Squadron

Lt. Martin Foster was born in Wilkes-Barre and lived in Harrisburg, Pennsylvania. He attended William Penn High School and was an outstanding athlete, competing in basketball and swimming. He also participated in music and dramatics.[10] In 1938 he competed in the sixteenth YMCA International/National Swimming and Diving Championship in Detroit, placing fourth in the 400-yard freestyle relay. After graduating high school, Foster found work as a claims adjuster for the State Auto Insurance Company.

He was accepted into the Aviation Cadet Program and enlisted on March 10, 1942, at Harrisburg, Pennsylvania. He completed his Advanced flight training at Luke Field and was commissioned on December 3, 1942. He was assigned to the 331st Fighter Squadron at San Diego for Transition training in the P-38, and was with the 78th Fighter Group when it moved to England at the end of 1942. Like other members of the 78th, he was reassigned to the 14th Fighter Group when it was "restarted" in early 1943 in North Africa.

Martin and his wife Faye Stewart were married just before he was sent abroad in late 1942. At the time he was posted abroad, his father, Martin Sr., wrote a poem that was published by the *Harrisburg Telegraph* on May 14, 1943, "eloquently setting forth a dad's pride in his son," part of which read:

> *The "Blue Star" in the window,*
> *Was taken down to-day*
> *And a "Silver One" replaced it*
> *When our Pilot went away.*
>
> *Don't know where they're going to send him,*
> *But I'm warning "Hun" and "Jap"*
> *Don't tangle with this pilot,*
> *Or they never will come back.*

Lt. William James "Greg" Gregory
49th Fighter Squadron

Known to all as "Greg," Lt. William James Gregory was born in a rural area outside of Hartsville, Tennessee, in 1920, graduating from Trousdale County High School in 1938. His family was rich in character, but materially poor. He had done well in high school, and hoped to continue to college, but the expense made it impossible. Then his high school principal intervened and secured Gregory a job at Middle Tennessee State College. Gregory worked his way through college, and in the spring of 1941 joined the CPT program.[11] Greg recalls: "At MTS we had two Piper Cubs and two instructors, and they could accommodate about twenty students. I got into it in the spring of 1941. This was the preliminary training program—small fifty-horsepower airplanes, two-seaters, tandem seats." He got "really hooked" on flying.

In the fall of 1941 he had a tough choice: to continue with the Advanced program of CPT at Knoxville or to accept an admission to the AAC Aviation Cadet Program. "I was twenty-one, and the draft was on," says Greg. "And at that time, it was not a matter of if, but when we would be at war. And so I spent a week at home, trying to decide which way to go. I finally decided to take the Aviation Cadet Program." He enlisted in the Army Air Corps just after his twenty-first birthday.

Aviation Cadet William James Gregory.
COL. WILLIAM GREGORY (RET.)

He completed Primary flight school at Garner Field at Uvalde, Texas, on December 7, 1941. "We were going seven days a week starting at that point. There was a lot of pressure to get us finished. [Garner] was a brand-new field, and as a matter of fact, when we arrived there the barracks were not completely finished. We lived in the Kincaid Hotel for about a week. I thought, boy, this is all right. We were having steaks at night, but that didn't last. About a week later we were in the barracks. We were lucky because we did not have an upper class until we got to Randolph (i.e., no hazing.)"

Basic flight training was at Randolph Field, and Advanced at Moore Field. Greg completed the course at Moore Field in April, with class 42-E. "There were eighty-two of us in that class, and they sent us all to fighters— P-38s. And we trained there until October, and then went to England." Transition training was done at Hamilton Field in San Francisco.

Greg recalls: "I remember on my very first mission I saw tracers coming at me. A 109 was on my tail. I got to thinking later that I was seeing all these tracers but there were four times that many rounds that I didn't see. I managed to get out of that situation, but there were tracers coming at me and across the wings—it was an exciting moment for sure."[12]

P-38 pilot Lt. William James "Greg" Gregory.

COL. WILLIAM GREGORY (RET.)

Gregory (second from right) with his P-38 and ground crew.

COL. WILLIAM GREGORY (RET.)

49th Fighter Squadron pilots Bland, Neely, Gregory, and DeMoss.

COL. WILLIAM GREGORY (RET.)

Unmarried while abroad, his friend and fellow pilot Lloyd DeMoss once showed him a photo of a young lady. "I told him, 'Boy, you are crazy not to go out with that girl.' She was the most beautiful girl I had ever seen."

"That girl" was Helen, who was to figure prominently in Greg's life later on.

Lt. Harold Harper
49th Fighter Squadron

Born in 1921 in Bakersfield, California, Lt. Harold Harper graduated from Bakersfield College in 1941. Sharing an uncertain future with the other young men in Bakersfield, Harper took a job driving a school bus on the twisty mountain roads after college, waiting for international events to help him decide on his path.

Harper recalls: "Minter Field, about fifteen miles out of Bakersfield, was a Basic flying school, and you would see these BTs and PTs flying around, and I thought, that was for me. But at that time you needed two years of college, and had to be twenty years old. I wasn't twenty years old until December 5, so I got a job out at Bell Ridge Oil Company, making $160 to $170 a month. Pretty good money for a kid—for anybody back

Telergma, Summer 1943. Harold Harper with crew chief Sgt. Michael Whiteford. Before a mission.
LT. COL. HAROLD HARPER (RET.)

then. December 5 was a Friday, and I was working at nights. I came home, and turned twenty years old. December 7, the war started, so I went right down on Monday, 'cause I had the qualifications, and they took me right in."[13]

Harper made his first flight in an airplane on February 26, 1942, while at Primary flight school at Sequoia Field in Visalia. He relates some words of wisdom he received from his instructor at Sequoia, Hunter Warlow: "Harper, there is one thing you wanna do: Keep your head out of the cockpit. Look around." This proved to be solid advice when Harold reported for combat duty.

Flying both Stearman PT-17s and Ryan PT-22s, he completed Primary on April 20 and reported to Lemoore Field for Basic flight school. He completed Basic on June 12 and continued to Advanced flight training at Victorville. While there, he trained in twin-engine AT-9s and AT-17s, completed the program on August 20, and received his commission on August 27, 1942.

At that time, pilots could request what types of aircraft they preferred to fly, and at Victorville he volunteered for P-38 training. "Yeah, I didn't want any goddamn bomber. . . . I talked to Knott and Homer, and said, 'They want P-38 pilots, let's sign up for it,' and they did." They were immediately sent to Hamilton Field for Transition training to P-38s. "Carroll Knott was just at the age where [he] could still get into flight school, twenty-six and a half. He was the old man of the whole outfit. He was older than Decker and all the rest of them. He married my niece. He knew her when we were cadets."

Harper, Knott, Homer, and others began training in P-38s on September 8, assigned to the 83rd Fighter Squadron of the 78th Fighter Group. The first flight was from Mills Field (now San Francisco International Airport), where they slept and took their meals in a hangar. "After checking out with a few hours of flight time, we were sent back to Hamilton Field to continue training flights while standing alert with the P-38, ready to go in the event an unidentified aircraft were sighted entering the United States." In early November of 1942, the 78th received orders for overseas duty. At that time, Harper had 92 flight hours in a P-38 and a total of 307 flying hours since starting Primary flight school.

All the men of the group were sent by train to Camp Kilmer, New Jersey, for transport to England. Harper recalls: "We departed the United States in November aboard the *Queen Elizabeth*, carrying 20,000 troops. We crossed the Atlantic Ocean unescorted, [because] its 30-knot speed was capable of escaping German U-boats. The pilots were given a stateroom with twelve men to a room, and the crew chiefs and other enlisted men were bunked four deep below the deck. The trip took us five days, disembarking at Edinburgh, Scotland. From here the 78th Fighter Group was sent to an air base near Goxhill, England, to begin acquiring P-38 aircraft for combat. These aircraft were first sent from the United States to Lanford Lodge at Belfast, Ireland, for final assembly."

The 78th pilots were flown to Lanford Lodge in Belfast to ferry the P-38s to Goxhill, and then return by C-47 to Belfast to ferry more P-38s. Harold's brother, Weston, was also a pilot, assigned to transport duties with a C-47. One day, loading onto a C-47 for the return flight to Ireland, Harold was surprised to see his brother in the pilot's seat. "Neither of us knew that we were both overseas at the same time," says Harper.

In early 1943 the 78th began the move to North Africa. On February 16, 1943, the group departed from Land's End, England, for the five-and-a-half-hour flight to Cazes, Casablanca, Morocco. Harper later returned to Ireland to fly an F-4 P-38 reconnaissance plane back to Casablanca. On March 28, the pilots flew from Cazes to Mediouna, where they did various types of training flights: squadron formation, ground gunnery, bomber altitude flying, squadron formation, altitude flying, and formation flying.

"Newly arrived pilots were sent to Marrakesh to re-form the 14th Fighter Group," says Harper, "whose pilots were being sent back to the States after enduring terrific combat duty. I was assigned to the 49th Fighter Squadron, and with a few days' training flights, we were sent to a combat airfield at Telergma, south of Constantine, Algeria." The pilots left Mediouna on May 5 and flew to their new base at Telergma. The 49th's first combat assignment was the next day, and it proved to be a brutal introduction to combat. Harper was assigned to this antishipping mission to Egadi Island, Sicily. Flying back, and without being briefed prior to the mission, the formation made a strafing run over Bizerte, where Lieutenant Moore was lost to ground fire. Harper had his right tire shot out by ground fire.

Quoting Harper: "The B-25s dropped their bombs on some fishing boats, I think. We flew around in a circle and we could see bombs dropping. They never hit anything, and they took off back to their base. The leader never did tell us, because I thought we were going to follow the bombers back. But no, we flew up the coast several miles, one hundred miles or so, and came in right over an airfield. I didn't even have my gun sight on or nothing. We weren't ready for strafing, and that's when Moore got shot down, on his first mission. I looked over my left wing and here is a ball of fire. He either got shot down or ran into something. He should not have taken us up there without telling us ahead of time that after we lead the B-25s, we are going to go in and do some strafing. That's when I got my tire shot out."

Harper remembers: "In old movies the gallant fighter pilots were rationed to a two-ounce glass of spirits, either brandy or whiskey, after returning from a mission. But in our times in combat, never was this ration awaiting us. A cup of coffee and a doughnut was sometimes provided us at interrogations after the missions. It seems that the cold beer and whiskey for us was short-stopped in Oran or Algeria."

Harper recounts an experience with Colonel Keith: "While at Telergma an Arab chieftain came riding into our compound on a white horse, demanding payment for our use of the landing strip. If payment wasn't received he would graze his sheep and camels on the field. Our CO, Col. Troy Keith, replied that he would send up a P-38 and strafe any animal on the airstrip. He then sent an airplane up to make a few passes over the runway. The Arab thought better than to put his animals on the airstrip."

Harper's never missed a chance to get away from the airfield on days he was not flying, and his adventures off the field sometimes took a strange turn: "As I say, we used to get a jeep and we'd go out all over. One time I took a prisoner of war with me—an Italian guy. We fired machine guns. Oh yeah, we had a helluva time. Threw hand grenades. Oh shit, we were crazy."

Harper had some special commendations for the ground crews: "Nothing much has been said about the men who kept the planes flying and cared for the pilots. The crew chiefs and their assistants—the armorer, fueling personnel, and other enlisted men—were ever on the job, preparing the P-38s for their next mission. My crew chief, Michael Whiteford, was such a dedicated person that he built his sleeping quarters next to his aircraft. I say this because he let me fly his aircraft, and never once did I have to abort a mission because of mechanical problems."

Through the end of 1943, Harper, Knott, and Homer were seemingly inseparable. Flight schools, transport to England, transit to North Africa, tentmates, combat flying together, rest camp together. Harper recounts: "All three of us went to flight school together—all three flight schools, all through training, and all through combat. I made good friends in the squadron. Carroll Knott and I went to rest camp together. Oh, we had a helluva time there. We always did, no matter what we did.

"He would always follow me too. We had rest camp in the Atlas Mountains. There was a beautiful stream coming down. He was a fisherman, and I was a fisherman. Trout fishermen. So we checked out two trout rods, tackle and all that stuff, and we went out. Clear water—beautiful creek. The trout were wary. I said, 'Hey, I did this when I was a kid and had a .22.' They had some Springfield rifles at the rest camp, because they had wild pigs there. We went back and checked out two rifles and ammunition. And we'd sneak up and shoot at the fish. We just stunned them. We picked up forty or fifty—enough to feed the guys."

While in North Africa, Harper shared a five-man tent with his friends Homer and Knott, plus Lts. Wayne Manlove and Tony Evans.

Still a bachelor during his combat tour, Harper had a sweetheart at home. He had known Miss Elinor Pyles since his freshman year of high school, and the two exchanged letters and V-mail while Harper was abroad. Due to censorship, there was little that Harold could tell Elinor about where he was or what he was doing, but he told her what he could about camp life. Harper used to write Elinor (who later became his wife): "'Well, we are in our tent cooking eggs, and I killed some partridge today,' and she said, 'That is all you ever said in your letters—that you were cooking something.'"

Lt. John M. Harris
49th Fighter Squadron

John Harris was born in 1918 to a ranching family in Toppenish, Washington. He graduated from Yakima High School and had one year of college at the University of Washington before joining the Army Air Corps. He started pilot training on his birthday, April 27, 1942, completed his training, and was commissioned on October 30, 1942.

Among his many missions, on June 22, 1943 he was assigned to escort the king of England on a flight back to the UK from Tripoli.[14]

Harris would later have nose art added to his aircraft—a picture of Hitler in mid-jump with a lightning bolt striking him in the posterior. Speaking about the early days of his assignment in North Africa, Harris would later report: "The lack of something to do gets me down more than

Lt. John M. Harris upon completion of Advance Flight Training, Luke Field.
TIM HARRIS

Lt. John Harris, North Africa, 1943.
TIM HARRIS

anything. Sometimes I sit on the ground for three or four days in a row and 'sweat out' the return of the gang sent up. Once in a while the squadron gets together over a keg of beer which helps to break the monotony. A lot of us play chess and some 'eager beaver' is always starting a volleyball game. But in spite of all this a day on the ground is a long day."

Lt. Arthur S. Lovera
49th Fighter Squadron

Art Lovera was born June 8, 1919, in Montana, attended high school in Butte, and enrolled at Montana State University. He played football in both high school and college.[15]

Art enlisted in the Army Air Corps on January 29, 1942, after two years at MSU. He completed Primary flight school at King City, California, and Basic flight school at Chico Army Flying School, class 42-H. Lovera had many close calls while in combat, and a few that occurred while on non-combat missions. On January 23, 1943, he crashed on takeoff while with the 78th Fighter Group in Scotland. Apparently a jinxed airplane, the same ship was totaled in a noncombat crash later in the year, in North Africa.

Harold Harper also recalls: "Oh, Lou! He crash-landed there in North Africa. We were on a practice mission over the desert, and the

Art Lovera at Montana State University.
"THE MONTANAN," YEARBOOK OF MONTANA
STATE UNIVERSITY, 1939.

damn leader was leading them around too long, and Lou ran out of fuel. They almost run me out of fuel too, keeping me up too damn long."

Lt. Charles W. Richard
49th Fighter Squadron

Lt. Charles W. Richard was born on February 19, 1922, in Lake Charles, Louisiana. Like his future squadron mate, William Gregory, he grew up in simple surroundings.[16] His home in Lake Charles had no indoor bathroom, only an outhouse. The family maintained a garden, had chickens, pigs, a milk cow, and later, a horse. He had a bicycle, and when the street was finally paved, he graduated to roller skates. His father bought a Model T for hunting and fishing, and Lieutenant Richard learned to drive it at age twelve.

Richard graduated from Landry Memorial High School and had one year at John McNeese Junior College. He was an avid hunter and fisherman, and enjoyed a good cigar. He joined the Army Air Corps on September 28, 1940, and was first sent to Barksdale Field in Shreveport, and

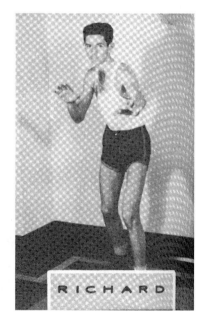

Charles Richard at McNeese Junior College.
"THE LOG," YEARBOOK OF MCNEESE COLLEGE, 1940

Charles W. Richard.

RICHARD FAMILY COLLECTION

from there to Scott Field. After Basic training, Richard was tabbed to be an enlisted radio operator. He completed a radio course at Scott Field in Illinois, and was then transferred to Kelly Field at San Antonio, where he worked in the control tower. After a few months at Kelly, he was transferred to Albuquerque to open a control tower there.

He applied for, and was accepted into, the Army Air Corps Aviation Cadet Program. After Primary school at Hemet, California, and Basic at Bakersfield, he completed Advanced flight school at Luke Field.

P-38 pilots during Transition training. Charles Richard is top row, fifth from left.

KOCOUR

Seasoned combat pilots of the 49th. Rear, from left: Frederick Bitter, Carroll S. Knott, Anthony Evans, Harold T. Harper, and Wayne M. Manlove. Front, from left: Marlow J. Leikness, Richard E. Decker, William J. Gregory, and Lloyd K. DeMoss.

COL. HAROLD T. HARPER (RET.)

Assigned to the 78th Fighter Group, he completed his Transition training and shipped out for England in November of 1942. Like many of his fellow pilots, he was reassigned to the 14th Fighter Group and was part of the cadre that "restarted" the 14th in the spring of 1943.

Unlike his fellow pilots, Charles Richard was not a commissioned officer. His rank was that of flight officer. In early 1942, the U.S. Army Air Corps had reduced the entrance qualifications for pilot applicants. Where two years of college had formerly been required, by May the regulations stipulated that completion of high school was sufficient to qualify for admission to the Aviation Cadet Program. In July, President Roosevelt acted to create a new rank—akin to a navy warrant officer. The flight officers actually received a higher pay than their commissioned counterparts, and they were not required to perform other functions on base that fell to commissioned officers, such as mail censoring.

CHAPTER 7

Bomber Escort

June 20, 1943

WITH NO MISSIONS SCHEDULED FOR THE SQUADRON ON THE DAY AFTER what should have been their first combat sortie, Knepper and Kocour had the day to think about the loss of two fellow pilots. Though they had been carefully trained for precisely the type of action that would now face them almost daily, the events of the previous day would have added a starkness to the camp, and a sharpness to their perceptions.

Stopping by the operations tent after evening mess, Knepper and Kocour learned that they were scheduled for the next day's mission. Details of the mission would come the next morning at the preflight briefing. What they knew was that it would be large mission—all of the squadron's pilots were assigned—including the newly installed squadron commander, Captain Trollope, and Captain Decker, the operations officer. An all-squadron mission could only mean bomber escort. The new pilots would have reflected on what type of bomber they would be escorting, since the tactics used varied depending on the bomber type.

It would all be new to them; although they had seen many bombers in the air throughout their training, they had had no live practice with any of the three bombers that the squadron would be escorting routinely: the B-25 Mitchell, the B-26 Marauder, and the B-17 Flying Fortress.

B-25C [123] "Mitchell"	B-17F [456] "Flying Fortress"	Martin B-26B [789] "Marauder"
	Aircraft silhouettes are to scale	
Crew: 5 Pilot, co-pilot, bombardier, radio-operator, gunner	Crew: 10 Pilot, co-pilot, navigator, bombardier, engineer, radio operator, 4 gunners	Crew: 7 Pilot, co-pilot, bombardier, navigator, 3 gunners
Classed as Medium bomber	Classed as Heavy bomber	Classed as Medium bomber
Length: 52' 11"	Length: 74' 9"	Length: 58' 3"
Wingspan: 67' 7"	Wingspan: 103' 10"	Wingspan: 71'
Height: 15' 9"	Height: 19'1"	Height: 21' 6"
Weight: 34,000 lbs. (max load)	Weight: 56,500 lbs.	Weight: 38,200 lbs
Bomb Load: 5,200 lbs (max)	Bomb Load: 20,800 lbs	Bomb Load: 8,000 lbs
Armament 6 x .50-cal machine guns	Armament: 11 x .50-cal machine guns	Armament: 11 x 50-cal machine guns
Maximum Speed: 284 mph	Maximum Speed: 325 mph	Maximum Speed: 282 mph
Cruise Speed: 233 mph	Cruise Speed: 200 mph	Cruise Speed: 214 mph
Range: 2,900 miles	Range: 2880 miles	Range: 2,850
Service Ceiling: 24,000 ft.	Service Ceiling: 37,500 ft.	Service Ceiling: 21,700
Rate of Climb: 909 ft./min.	Rate of Climb: 360 ft./min.	Rate of Climb: 1220 ft./min.
Production Cost:	Production Cost:	Production Cost:
In 1943: $109,670 [10]	In 1943: $204,370 [11]	In 1943: $156,333[12]
In 2014 equivalent: $1,534,893	In 2014 equivalent: $2,860,273	In 2014 equivalent: $2,187,968

B-25

The North American B-25 Mitchell was an American-built, twin-engine medium bomber manufactured by North American Aviation at its plants in Kansas and California. In addition to equipping many American groups, it was flown by Dutch, British, Chinese, Russian, and Australian bomb groups in every theater of World War II. Named in honor of Gen. Billy Mitchell, a pioneer of U.S. military aviation, nearly ten thousand B-25s were built during the war.

B-25s in formation.

NATIONAL ARCHIVES

B-25s in low-level formation flight over North Africa. Note the low-level flight typical of the B-25 in its approach to target.

High-angle view of B-25s of the 12th AAF.

North Africa, B-25s in flight.

NATIONAL ARCHIVES

B-26

The Martin B-26 Marauder was a World War II twin-engine medium bomber built by the Glenn L. Martin Company in Baltimore. The aircraft received a harsh welcome by pilots, who termed it the "Widowmaker" due to the early model's high incidence of accidents during takeoffs and landings. It had a number of other colorful nicknames, including "Flying Coffin," "B-Dash-Crash," and the "Flying Prostitute," the latter earned because the aircraft's short wings provided "no visible means of support."

Operational safety improved with aircraft design modifications and crew retraining. By the end of the war, over five thousand aircraft had been delivered to the air forces, and the Marauder had achieved the lowest loss rate of any USAAF bomber.

B-26 Marauder on a bombing mission over Rome.

9th Air Force B-26s over Belgium.

B-17

The Boeing B-17 Flying Fortress was a four-engine heavy bomber aircraft developed in the 1930s in order to operationalize the army's philosophy that a daylight precision bomber would be essential for future strategic air warfare. In all theaters of the war, it was a potent, high-altitude, long-range bomber. Bristling with thirteen .50 caliber machine guns, the B-17 could defend itself against fighter attack and was capable of staying aloft even with extensive battle damage. First flown in 1935, production reached nearly thirteen thousand by the war's end.

Boeing B-17 from the 381st Bomb Group in flight over Europe.
NATIONAL ARCHIVES

B-17s under attack during a bomb run over Europe.

B-17 in attack formation, encountering heavy flak.

ESCORTING BOMBERS

As the war continued beyond the Mediterranean, and into 1944 and 1945, strategic bombing missions became of such long duration that escorts—even the long-range P-38s—could not accompany the bombers for the entire mission. Handoffs were arranged, with one formation of escorts taking the bombers partway to the target, another taking over for the escort in the target vicinity, and a third formation to protect the bombers as they returned to their bases.

But in combat operations in the Mediterranean Theater in midsummer 1943, strategic bombing missions planned by AAF headquarters created the perfect match of escort and bombers. P-38s had sufficient range, with extra fuel drop tanks, to accompany bombers for their entire mission throughout the theater.

Bomber-escort tactics were very much influenced by the type of bomber being escorted, and Army Air Corps field manuals attempted to provide some direction regarding fighter escort. In April 1942 the War Department issued *FM 1-15*, "Tactics and Technique of Air Fighting," in which the authors primarily addressed fighter tactics for the performance of defensive operations.

> *In the direct defense of other aviation forces, pursuit provides security by escort. . . . Single-seater pursuit forces . . . normally operate above and to the rear of the defended formation from positions that guard vulnerable sectors and that facilitate immediate counterattack against any enemy force endeavoring to launch a direct attack on the defended formation. Distance from the supported force will be influenced by relative speeds, escort strength, and visibility conditions. Forces in special support counterattack immediately when hostile fighters make direct attacks on the defended formation.[13]*

Although the field manual went to considerable lengths to describe what should be done in a variety of combat situations, it did not say how these tactics should be undertaken. For this reason, much responsibility in refining bomber-escort tactics fell to group and squadron commanders. "The squadrons of the group should be so trained that in the normal methods of air attack the squadrons automatically take proper position to furnish appropriate assault, support, and reserve forces. Radio and visual signals are kept at a minimum. Indoctrination (i.e., pilot training) is the only dependable method of control in the heat of combat."[14]

In fairness to the authors of *FM 1-15*, it should be noted that this important field manual was released in April of 1942, at the very onset of American involvement in World War II. At that time, and during the preceding months when the manual was being researched and written, little direct combat information from the field was available on which to base recommendations for tactics and techniques for the technologically advanced fighters and bombers in its arsenal. The manual contains, therefore, the best theoretical practices for combat tactics as envisioned in mid-1942.

Within six months of the release of *FM 1-15*, the AAF had received substantial combat experience as a result of operations against the Axis forces from bases in England, and in the course of Operation Torch and the succeeding Tunisian Campaign, and this new experience was reflected in the tactics and formations adopted by bomb and fighter groups.

As seen above, the escort aircraft engaged enemy aircraft only after an assault had been made on the bombers being escorted. This policy did not espouse aggressive initiation of combat by the escorting forces—a policy that would change substantially as the air war moved north.

Dick Catledge, a pilot with the 1st Fighter Group, was unenthusiastic about the defensive posture of the fighter escorts:

[I]t was frustrating to have enemy fighters make a firing pass at us, or the bombers, and then dive away safely, and we couldn't give chase! The P-38 had four machine guns, and a 20mm cannon, all were in the nose of the gondola, and all fired straight ahead. The enemy fighters were very much afraid to see the nose of a P-38 coming in their direction because of the awesome firepower, and in many cases, this was our salvation. Often, all a P-38 pilot had to do was start a turn toward an incoming fighter, and he would break off the attack.[15]

Bob Vrilakas, another combat pilot with the 1st Fighter Group, had similar thoughts:

It was often not only nerve-wracking but frustration to see enemy fighters loitering at a safe distance hoping for an opportunity to attack the bombers uncontested. So, while enemy fighters flew at a safe distance and searched for a specific position of our fighter defense that would give them the opportunity to make a quick pass at a bomber without facing our fire, we responded with our own tactical maneuvering. It required our constant weaving over the bombers, with flights crossing in opposite direction to each other. The enemy fighters always had altitude and in-the-sun advantage, which aided them in making a quick pass at high speed and then a return to a safe position at minimum risk. If there was a straggler among the fighters or if we were in a vulnerable position their attack would be directed at one of us.[16]

Catledge and Vrilakas also felt strongly that keeping the four-ship flight together at all times was unproductive and cumbersome.

Vrilakas wrote: "Both Dick Catledge and I felt that we could more effectively provide bomber protection by breaking the flights into two elements over the target area—a Flight leader and his wingman, and an Element leader and his wingman. This provided much more fighter maneuverability, more effective individual firepower, and more continual coverage of the bombers. The flight of 4 was unwieldy when attacked and in any melee of size ended up in flights of 2 anyway."

Catledge continued to press his case with the squadron, and even took his argument to the Group Headquarters. That is as far as he got with his tactical suggestions: he was told that the four-ship formation was the way the Army Air Corps had set it up and there wouldn't' be any changes.[17]

During combat in the Spanish Civil War, Luftwaffe tactician Werner Mölders had developed a "finger-four" formation to compensate for cockpit view limitations of fighter aircraft. This formation was based on two mutually supporting pairs of aircraft, with the positions of the number-two and number-four aircraft providing good fields of vision for their four-ship flight. The formation was subsequently adopted by both the RAF and the USAAF, and remains the standard basic flight formation to this day.

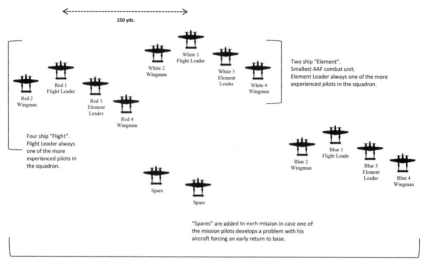

Standard configuration for a P-38 combat squadron consisting of 12 aircraft arranged in three "flights," four aircraft per flight. Each flight consists of two "elements," and each element consisting of two aircraft. The Flight Commander and Element Leaders were always chosen from the more experienced pilots in the squadron.

STANDARDIZATION BOARD, ONTARIO ARMY AIR FIELD, SOP, 3 MARCH 1945

The element leaders in fighter formations were the "shooters," primarily responsible for engaging enemy aircraft. Their wingmen acted as "spotters," and protected their element leader from rear attack. And despite the cardinal tactical rule for airmen flying in number-two or four position—never to leave their element leader—that rule was sometimes broken, and sometimes for fair reason. The flight leader's aerobatic maneuvers might be more abrupt than his wingman could follow, or the wingman might be presented with a target he could not ignore.

Replacement pilots were always positioned as wingman on a flight leader. After a few missions, he would transition to the number-four position, and after a few more solid missions, he might be chosen as element leader. Only the most experienced pilots were made flight leader, a position that included promotion to captain's rank.

With few exceptions, the 14th Fighter Group assigned aircraft from two squadrons on bomber-escort missions, each squadron typically providing twelve aircraft. One squadron would be assigned to lead the escort mission, and one individual within that squadron would serve as overall mission leader. In radio communications, pilots would first identify their squadron by call sign, then their position within the squadron by flight and aircraft number. For example, "Hangman Blue Leader" or "Fried Fish Red 3."

Unlike the long-range missions that characterized strategic bombing attacks later in the war, the flight time of bombing missions in the Mediterranean Theater permitted the escort fighters to accompany the bombers for the entire mission, with each squadron assigned to a specific defensive zone in the overall formation.

5TH WING DOCTRINE

The B-17 heavy bombers employed in long-range strategic missions operated within NASAF's 5th Bomb Wing, which also included three P-38 fighter groups, the 1st, 14th and 82nd, and one group of P-40 fighter aircraft, the 325th, to provide defensive cover for the B-17s against attack by enemy aircraft. Coordinating operations involving vastly different types of aircraft was a priority for the wing, which provided much more specific and certainly more succinct instructions to both the fighter and bomber groups than was offered in *FM 1-15*.

With regard to P-38 escort procedures, the wing instructed:

In escorting high-altitude bombardment, the P-38 fighters of this Wing have adopted a formation of elements of two airplanes, flights of two elements, and squadrons of three flights each, flying in line abreast. The fighters maintain what might be classed as a medium-close cover flying above the bombers at from 1,500 feet to 3,000 feet. Minimum cruising speed . . . is used, and whenever there is danger of over-running the bombers, a 360-degree in-place turn is made (each flight making its turn in-place, either to right or left as the leader decides).

About ten minutes from the target area the fighters [increase their speed], necessitating a greater number of in-place turns, making the fighters at all times a moving target and yet keeping them over the bomber formation.

When the target is reached, the fighters [increase speed further].
As the bombers turn on to their bombing run, the fighters assume an
up-sun position (keeping the sun behind their aircraft and making it
more difficult to be seen by attacking enemy aircraft), [retaining this
position] as the bombers emerge from the flak area, and are alert for
any stragglers which may have been crippled by flak, whom they will
proceed to defend against enemy fighter attack.[18]

Field manuals aside, the main combat tactics used by fighters of
both sides were the same: Keep airspeed high by attacking from a higher
altitude, dive out of the sun to prevent detection by enemy aircraft, move
into a position behind the target, fire, then split away in a diving roll to
escape other enemy aircraft that might be trailing.

B-17 bombers in formation, with P-38 escorts flying cover.
NATIONAL ARCHIVES

When escorting bombers, "bogeys" (unidentified aircraft, presumably hostile) were called in by the "clock" system and relative altitude using the bomber formation as the point of reference. For instance: "This is Hangman Red Leader. Bogeys at one o'clock high." The first sentence identifies the escort squadron ("Hangman" was the 49th squadron call sign) and element (Red Flight). The second sentence advises that the bogeys are at one o'clock from the bomber formation and at a higher altitude.

Even with throttles retarded, fighter aircraft operated at higher speeds than most of the bombers they escorted. In order to maintain combat airspeeds while keeping in contact with the bombers, it was often necessary for the escorting fighters to orbit or weave over and around the bombers. And spotting incoming aircraft early, before an attack was launched, was critically important. Since early in flight training, pilots were admonished to "keep your heads out of the cockpit" and to constantly scan the air for bogeys.

Harold Harper relates: "I am convinced that most guys who got shot down never saw the airplane that shot them down. They did not look around. We always used a silk scarf. That was from World War I, but we had silk scarfs because if we wore shirts and looked around, you'd wear your skin off. I still have my silk scarf."[19]

Fellow 48th squadron pilot Maurice Nickle related: "My first mission was a high-level escort mission. I believe there were thirty-two P-38s escorting about forty-eight B-17s into Austria. It was quite a sight to see; the P-38s were scissoring back and forth over and above the B-17s. . . . As they entered their approach to the target area there was a solid alley of black puffs of antiaircraft explosions. The P-38s stayed outside of this "alley," and then we came back over the B-17s that came through after the bombing run. Several blew up in the alley and several were damaged. The main body of P-38s escorted the main body of B-17s that went through intact and still in formation. Then some of the P-38s in two's or four's were separated off to escort damaged B-17s back to Italy."[20]

The optimum tactical formation for bombers was developed by Gen. Curtis LeMay: a staggered three-element combat box formation, with eighteen bombers in the "box." This arrangement was compact, but still maneuverable, and was based on a three-aircraft element. In the early months of the war, each flight carried a bombsight in the lead ship, and all planes made their bomb drop when the leader dropped. Later, as bombers began to concentrate on pinpoint targets, a bombsight was carried in every element, and three aircraft dropped off one bombsight.[21]

Types of Cover

There were several types of escort cover for a formation of bombers, including close cover, medium cover, top cover, area cover, and roving cover. Not all types of cover were included on each mission. The type of cover, and the number of fighters required, depended on the number of bombers, the type of bombers, the target, and the anticipated enemy interception. The fighter's mandate was to remain with the bombers and to conserve fuel. Unnecessary maneuvering and excessive fuel consumption during the approach to the target were to be avoided, because the first action taken by fighters in responding to enemy aircraft was to jettison external fuel tanks. While the fighter's performance increased without these tanks, their range was decreased, making it less likely that they would be able to complete the escort mission and possibly jeopardizing their ability to reach base before exhausting their fuel supply.

Dropped tanks also sent a clear signal to the bombers being escorted. Bomber pilot Robert Davila records: "What frightened me every time so that the hair stood [on end] was if our fighter escort suddenly threw off [their tanks]. . . . I then knew that German fighters were nearby."[22]

Close cover for heavy bombers usually meant that one squadron was assigned to each of the flanks, one squadron ahead, and one squadron astern.[23] Top cover fighters flew 4,000 to 8,000 feet above the bomber force, weaving as necessary to maintain position over the bombers and escorting close cover, and 10 miles into the sun in anticipation of the normal fighter strategy of diving out of the sun's glare. Maj. Thomas McGuire, writing in 1944, provides extensive details on flying cover:

> German aircraft did not always have sufficient numbers to attempt
> a real interception—breaking the bomber formation. Most often the
> GAF would make attacks on the bomber formation singly or in pairs,
> from altitude. In a typical attack, an enemy aircraft at altitude would

do a half-roll and make an overhead pass, diving through the bomber formation, clearing away to the side, and then returning to altitude. The only possible counter-tactic is to break up the P-38 top cover into flights and drive off the attacks as they are begun; there can be no general movement of the squadron, for the scattered distribution of the enemy fighters and the impossibility of anticipation leave no alternative but to check each pass as soon as possible after the enemy pilot has committed himself.

The above also holds true to some extent for the close cover. While a number of the enemy will attack from above, there will be others attacking from beneath, particularly against B-24s. At such times the close cover will move down somewhat and will break up into flights to ward off the single passes.

A favorite target for enemy fighters is the "target of opportunity." Leaving the target area, damaged bombers or escorting fighters may begin to struggle and lag. A crippled aircraft is no match for five or six eager E/A [enemy aircraft], and the best way to forestall such attacks is for the squadron leader to assign flights to each of the stragglers within range of his cover.

B-17s versus B-25/B-26 Escort Missions

The B-17 could carry a tremendous bomb load—up to 8,000 pounds. But it had a low cruising speed—just 160 mph in level flight, and 130 to 140 mph while climbing with a full bomb load. And its rate of climb was the slowest of all the strategic bombers—just 360 feet per minute. This meant that a climb to its normal bombing altitude, 24,000 feet, would require just over an hour. In practice, this meant that the bombers were in climb mode almost the entire flight in to the target, which also required the fighter escort to stay with them. This long, slow climb rendered the bomber formation and its escort more visible to enemy radar sightings, more obvious for enemy fighter sweeps, and extended the time when the formation was within range of the flak batteries that would be overflown during the mission.

Lt. Harold Harper did not like B-17 escort missions. "Slow. You had to weave. You pick them up right off their base, after they had formed up. You'd pick them up and climb all the way to the IP [initial point], up to 24,000, 24,500 feet. Slow—140 mph. And the same way coming back." Harper was much happier with B-25 and B-26 escort missions. "They would take off and fly on the deck, till they got to their IP, and then they would pour the coal to them, and you had to pour the coal to yours to keep up with them, they'd get up to 12,000 and drop their bombs and down they'd go again."[24] Harper's preference for escorting B-25s and B-26s was shared by his fellow pilot, Lt. William Gregory: "The B-17s would do a slow climb all the way to the target. They were trying to get altitude all the way."[25]

FROM THE PERSPECTIVE OF THE BOMBER PILOTS

Much has been written about the gratitude bomber crews felt toward their fighter escorts. Excerpts from the history of the 321st Bombardment Group—a group often escorted by fighters of the 14th Fighter Group—are illustrative:

> It might be [helpful] to note here the feeling we have for the peashooters [fighters], and the boys who fly them. We lean slightly toward the P-38s. On a mission we seldom see them in the vicinity of the target. They are off in parts unknown, raising hell. And although we seldom see our fighters, we also rarely see any enemy planes. The boys tie into them before they get to us . . . so they do their job well and we can't complain. On a recent raid I saw two P-38s in the immediate vicinity of the target. They were hot after an Me 109 that had come in a little too close to us. He never got quite close enough. They got him. And some of my crew saw him crash and blow up.
>
> Bradley, the boy who hit the water off the coast of Sicily on the same raid, is now back here. It seems that a couple of P-38 boys stayed with him, circling over him until help came from Malta. It's boys who do things like that who, I believe, deserve the DFC [Distinguished Flying Cross].[26]

CHANGING TACTICS

The tactics employed by the Allied air forces in escorting bombers were initially much different than those espoused by their German counterparts. As expressed previously by General Galland, commandant of the Luftwaffe, the GAF's preferred method of defense was a strong offense. Keeping fighters tied to the bomber formation was anathema to the German way of operations. Naturally, the ability to adopt this philosophy is greatly determined by the extent to which an air force enjoys air superiority. While conditions may have permitted this approach for the German Air Force in Spain and in the earlier days of their combat in North Africa, the attrition caused by superior numbers of Allied fighters forced the Luftwaffe to adopt other tactics by mid-1943.

By the time the invasion of Italy was well under way, and General Doolittle had been put in charge of the 8th Air Force Fighter Command in England, the Allied air force supremacy had become a tidal wave. Galland felt that the Allied advantage in aircraft approached two hundred to one. This overwhelming numerical advantage, coupled with the newer, more performant P-38 and P-51 aircraft, permitted a change in bomber-escort tactics in the European Theater of Operations.

During the North African Campaign, the door to General Doolittle's office held a sign asserting "The mission of the fighters is to protect the bombers." As the Air Force approached air supremacy, the sign was changed to "The mission of the fighters is to destroy the Luftwaffe."[27]

In the words of a fighter pilot:

> *But we all know what to do: attack on sight, per Maj. Gen. Jimmy Doolittle's welcome directive when he took over the Eighth Air Force Fighter Command. Before that, fighters had been required to stay with the bombers they were escorting until they were attacked, which gave the Luftwaffe the initiative. Now we were more effective. Our number of victories had increased and, more important, fewer bombers were lost. Nobody is worried about enemy fighters, just the anti-aircraft batteries. I want—all fighter pilots want—to engage enemy fighters.*[28]

MISSION TO BO RIZZO

On the morning of June 20, the sun had just crested the low foothills 4 miles to the east when the squadron clerk woke the men at 0500. After a quick and uninspiring breakfast, the squadron pilots began to form up at the Operations tent for the morning briefing, sharing a bit of quiet conversation while waiting for the administrative team to begin the briefing. It looked to be a good day to fly.

The briefing got started with Group Intelligence Officer Howard Wilson referring to a large easel-mounted photograph. Bo Rizzo, also referred to as "Chinisia" by the local Sicilians, was easily identified by all the pilots who had flown missions to it previously, but it was all new for the recent replacement pilots, Knepper and Kocour included. Captain Wilson advised that the 49th Fighter Squadron would be escorting a formation of twenty-three B-26s from the 320th Bomb Group. He confirmed that the B-26s would be taking off from their base at Montesquieu Airfield, 125 miles to the southwest, beginning at 0652. The 49th's P-38s would be wheels-up from their base at Telergma at 0635, and would rendezvous with the bomber formation at Montesquieu at 0720. The combined formation would then fly on an east-northeast heading for the 270-mile flight to the Sicilian coast, with the P-38s providing top cover. Captain Wilson concluded with an assessment of fighter opposition that the escorting P-38s should expect on the mission and what type and intensity of flak was likely.

The pilots listened nonchalantly, but each was thinking about the mission—fuel supply versus target distance. Estimated time in the air. Who's on my wing, target flak. And the one constant—enemy aircraft.

Following the intelligence briefing, Captain Decker, operations officer, went over all the tactical issues involved in the mission, including how high the top cover would operate, timing points, and compass headings. Meteorology was next, and the briefing officer advised that the conditions were expected to be "CAVU"—ceilings and visibility unlimited.

The mission leader, Lieutenant Leikness, would confirm engine start time, flight positions, and call numbers. Last thing: watch sync. "Check your watches. It is exactly 5 . . . and . . . 45 . . . now! Good luck." New pilots were sometimes surprised at the informality of the briefings. At this point in the war, there was no "squadron office"; briefings were stand-up and brief—quite different from the more formal briefings the folks at home were seeing on film.

Typical Telergma briefing for the 14th Fighter Group at the Operations tent. Maj. Bernard Muldoon of the 48th Fighter Squadron is leading the mission pilots in synchronizing their watches. Aircraft #10, rear, is from the 48th squadron. The mission being briefed in this photograph was to Pantelleria in early June 1943.

NATIONAL ARCHIVES

With the briefing concluded, the pilots returned to the supply tent to pick up their mission gear: pistol, life jacket, helmet, oxygen mask, and parachute. Lieutenant Gregory carried a canteen of water, and on two occasions dropped the canteen to bomber crews who had ditched in the Mediterranean.

In later months, pilots would be issued a survival vest that included emergency rations, flares, a first-aid kit, and other equipment, but in the summer of '43, pilots were pretty much on their own if they were downed. Each carried a .45 and had been given a silk escape map and a small gold coin that might help them barter their freedom from the locals if they were shot down over enemy-held territory. (Harper's and Gregory's coins had already been stolen—Gregory's while he was in the shower.)

Forty pounds heavier, the pilots now made their way to the waiting jeeps for the short trip to the flight line. This combined bomber/fighter mission was carefully timed to coincide with two similar missions being done concurrently by the 319th and the 17th Bomb Groups—all B-26 missions, and all targeting airfields in the northwest sector of Sicily.[29] The 319th, under escort by P-38s from the 37th and 48th Fighter Squadrons, would take off at 0700 from their base at Sedrata to bomb the aerodrome at Trapani/Milo, just 10 miles north of Bo Rizzo. The 17th Bomb Group, also based at Sedrata, would send thirty-six B-26s under the escort of fifty P-38s from the 1st Fighter Group on a bombing mission to the Castelvetrano aerodrome, 20 miles to the south. In all, there would be 82 medium and heavy bombers in the stream, with 101 fighter escorts.

Despite the large combined formation, the mission was minuscule compared to raids being conducted by the 8th Air Force in northern Europe as part of the Combined Bomber Offensive. A few days earlier, Cologne, Germany, was targeted by more than 1,000 bombers. The next night, Essen was hit with a similar force. A few days after this day's mission, Bremen would be hit by 960 bombers. The scope and tonnage of these missions was astonishing and reflects the huge number of strategic targets in Germany for the Allied bomber forces.

Since all pilots from the 49th squadron were included in the mission, it would be organized as two separate squadrons of twelve aircraft each. Five of the pilots assigned to this mission were brand-new replacements: Kocour, Knepper, Cobb, Hyland, and Ogle. And three—Cobb, Hyland, and Ogle—had only reported to the squadron the day before.

Knepper flew in the first squadron of twelve aircraft, flying number-two position to Trollope in the Red flight. Kocour flew in the second squadron of twelve planes, flying number-two position to Bland in the White flight. Reaching his airplane and seeing the crew chief readying the aircraft for the mission, Knepper slid into the cockpit and began the preflight routine that was becoming more familiar to him. Only slightly less anxious than two days prior when his mission was aborted, Knepper again had the same thought: "Please, let everything go right today."

Takeoff and rendezvous with the bombers went to plan, and the combined formation of forty-seven aircraft set a heading for the Sicilian coast. En route, three bombers developed problems and returned to base. Lieutenant Homer's P-38 developed a mechanical problem, and his place in the mission was taken by Lieutenant Hyland. Homer, along with Lt. Ogle, a spare not required for the mission, returned to base.

The bombers escorted by the 49th Fighter Squadron "jumped up" to their bombing altitude of 16,000 feet as they approached the target. The bombers made their drop at 0855—22 tons of fragmentation bombs, designed to destroy or damage any aircraft or equipment on the ground at the Bo Rizzo aerodrome. The bombs landed on the north end and on the dispersal area on the west side of the aerodrome, destroying eleven enemy aircraft parked in protective revetments.

The Axis threw up "barrage-type" flak—medium in caliber, but intense. It created a flak envelope, 2,000 to 3,000 feet in depth, centered right on the bombers' altitude. Yet despite the intensity of the flak, none of the B-26s were hit.

Ten miles to the north, and at exactly the same time, the 319th Bomb Group with its escort of P-38s from the 37th and 48th Fighter Squadrons also made its attack. That mission also reported moderate to intense flak; twelve bombers were hit by flak, and one crewman was killed. Two of the escorting P-38s were also hit by flak but were able to return to base. Enemy aircraft also jumped the bomber formation, both on the approach and while over the target. The P-38s fought them off, with no losses.

Twenty miles to the south, the 17th Bomb Group with P-38 escorts met very determined resistance, both on the approach to the target and after withdrawing, with the German interceptors seeming to be eager for combat. Twelve German fighters jumped the formation before it even reached the Sicilian coast, and another fifteen attacked shortly after the bombers had completed their drop. In the swirling dogfights that ensued in both of these encounters, three American P-38 pilots went missing, and nine GAF Me 109s were shot down.

The B-26s veered left after the bomb drop and headed for the coast. As they exited the target area, in the vicinity of Marettimo Island, the formation was jumped by twenty-five German Me 109 and Fw 190 aircraft, attacking out of the sun from altitude, and eager to take on the "Injuns" of the American Air Force.[30] The mission report for the 320th noted: "Last plane this formation reports that escort accompanied formation over target above and to the rear, and was seen to be heavily engaged with enemy aircraft as this formation left coast of Sicily."[31]

Gregory remembers: "On this day the enemy aircraft seemed fairly eager and came quite a ways out to meet us and managed to make one pass at the bombers, with very little results. We noticed quite a few stooging around as we hit the enemy coast, but no one bothered with them until they got pretty close or started for the bombers. We were not attacked until we started leaving the enemy coast, but at this time a great number started to make simultaneous attacks. Lieutenant Bland saw the first attack coming and started the break, but was unable to call it, as he had no radio."

Flying on Bland's right hand, Gregory called the break, and all twelve fighters in his formation broke around to face the German interceptors, and then broke again as the GAF planes pressed their attack.

The German fighters managed to get in very close on one or two of their passes. Captain Decker later reported: "My wingman, Lt. Manlove, and I went after the 109s. (In going after one) I put everything to the firewall and was in a steep climb when the turbo charger blew out on my right engine. I shut down the engine, feathered the prop and expected to return to base on a single engine. It wasn't long before the coolant light come on for the left engine." He feathered that prop and prepared to ditch. "On the glide down I rolled down both side windows and released the canopy. Luck was with me for I landed in the trough and touched down so smooth I actually skipped on the water. Just before the nose started digging in, a swell caught my right wing tip and I did a ground loop on the water." Not having had any training in either ditching or sea survival, and a bit woozy from a blow to the head he received in the ditching, he had a fair degree of difficulty in jettisoning his 'chute and deploying his inflatable dinghy before his damaged P-38 slipped away beneath him.

The melee above Decker continued, with the P-38s continuing to engage the enemy interceptors and protecting the bomber formation. Pilots Manlove and Evans each shot down an Me 109, and Gregory, Boatman, and Bland each had a probable kill. Kocour, flying as Bland's wingman, would have been in on the chase to confirm the "probable."

Capt. Richard Decker, upon receipt of the Distinguished Flying Cross.
NATIONAL ARCHIVES

The bombers continued their escape, with the 49th's P-38s continuing to fight off the enemy attackers. Decker's four-plane flight included pilots Richard, Manlove, and Boatman. As Decker's plane hit the water, these three pilots circled his location, recorded the coordinates, and provided cover against the superior numbers of German aircraft that were still pressing their attack. Finally, thirty minutes after his downing, the cover pilots were running low on fuel and were forced to return to their base in Tunisia. Captain Trollope, with Lieutenant Knepper on his wing, heard of Decker's loss and attempted to locate him, but was not successful. Gregory reported that the radios were not operating well that day, and the rest of the squadron was unable to give any close support to Captain Decker because they had lost sight of him.

The 49th's P-38s returned to base at 1050, and four hours later, a new mission formed up to recommence the search. Eight P-38s, piloted by Trollope, Richard, Bland, Manlove, Gregory, Grant, Lovera, and Hoke, took off from Telergma at 1415. The pilots relocated Decker, just to the west of Egadi Island, waving a distress flag. He appeared to be uninjured, and Trollope contacted the air-sea rescue service to request a pickup. But due to the lateness of the hour, the rescue could not be effected.

The next day, June 21, a second rescue mission was launched by the 49th at 0550. Led by Lieutenant Gregory, it included pilots Foster, Leikness, and DeMoss in the first flight, with Lovera, Homer, Neely, and Boatman in the second. Decker was again sighted in his dinghy at 0745, having spent the night in open water. Food and water were tied to a life vest and dropped to Decker. One of the P-38s was sent back to secure aid from the air-sea rescue service, while the remaining seven aircraft maintained patrol over Decker. Fuel again became an issue for the patrol, and planes were relayed back to friendly bases to refuel. A single-engine floatplane, a British "Walrus," was led back to Decker's location, landed, and brought Decker aboard. He was taken to the 97th General Hospital in Tunis, in good condition. Decker's rescuers returned to base at 1510—a ten-and-a-half-hour mission, and the end of a grueling two days.

On his return, Decker took some ribbing from his friends in the squadron. Harper remembers: "Goddammit, Decker, if I'da been with you, I wouldn't have let you do that. Lieutenant Knott saw Decker get shot down, and this was Decker's story: We were in this flight, and my turbo blew up. And Knott said, Yeah, that guy who was right on your tail is the one who blew it up."[32]

Leaving their aircraft, the pilots returned to their squadron area to drop off their parachutes, revolvers, and life jackets. Debriefings were conducted by the S-2 (squadron Intelligence) officer who made notations and compiled reports. The debriefings were even more casual than the mission briefings. They were not mandatory, and a return pilot with little to add, or one who was naturally reticent, could give them a skip. William Gregory remembers: "We were debriefed by the Intelligence officer. It was sort of an individual thing—the guys that wanted to say a lot sought out the Intelligence officer. I seldom ever did."[33] Doubtless on this day, with as much activity as there had been surrounding the squadron's operations officer, the debriefing was robust. In fact, Captain Decker had most likely been shot down by one of the "yellow-nosed kids" from the JG 77 based at Trapani.

According to Gregory, "This [the rescue] was quite an achievement, in that a pilot was rescued from right under the nose of the enemy."[34] Lieutenant Boatman and Flight Officer Richard earned the Distinguished Flying Cross as a result of their valor and extraordinary achievement in the mission to Bo Rizzo, and the subsequent rescue of Decker. Col. Troy Keith, commander of the 14th Fighter Group, also recommended Gregory for the Distinguished Flying Cross for this mission, citing:

As the squadron was leaving the target area it was aggressively attacked by over twenty-five Me 109s and Fw 190s. In the violent combat that followed Captain Decker was shot up and an Me 109 was closing in on his crippled P-38. Captain Gregory immediately saw this 109 and broke into the enemy aircraft head-on, closing to a range of 50 yards, and giving him a burst of machine-gun and cannon fire which set the engine on fire and probably destroyed it. By this action, Captain Gregory undoubtedly saved his fellow officer's life, because Captain Decker was later able to crash-land his plane safely and was rescued by a plane escorted by P-38s, which Captain Gregory was leading. The flying skill, devotion to a crippled comrade, and fighting spirit of Captain Gregory as a combat pilot have reflected great credit to himself and the Armed Forces of the United States.[35]

The new replacement pilots—Kocour, Knepper, Ogle, Cobb, and Hyland—had run straight into a steep learning curve on their first combat sortie. Within two days, their squadron had lost two pilots and seen their operations officer shot down and subsequently rescued. Apart from what they learned in the air, these new pilots had learned that pilots will not quickly abandon a downed comrade so long as any hope persists. Duty and loyalty—annealed in combat—became inseparable realities for the pilots of the 49th.

CHAPTER 8

Losses Mount and the Mission to Palermo

THE MISSIONS OF JUNE 24 CAME OFF WITH CONSIDERABLE CONSTERNA-
tion for NASAF's fighter groups.

The 1st Fighter Group nearly emptied its squadrons in sending fifty-
two P-38s to escort B-26s from the 319th Bomb Group on a bombing
mission to Chilivani, on the island of Sardinia. Eight of its aircraft had
to return early due to mechanical issues. And after rendezvousing with
the bombers at Sedrata, twenty-three of the remaining P-38s lost contact with the formation, could not reestablish contact, and were forced to
return to base. The remaining escorts continued with the mission, only
to be jumped by a large number of enemy aircraft as the bombers were
exiting the target. In the words of the group report, "A general dogfight
ensued." At the end of the skirmish, eight enemy Me 109s were shot
down, with another four probables. But the 1st lost three of its own pilots
in the melee. The escorts, on return to base, must have wondered what
evil genie it had failed to appease before that day's mission.

The 14th Fighter Group, sending thirty-six P-38s from the 37th,
48th, and 49th squadrons on a bomber-escort mission to Alghero on Sardinia, also had problems on this day's mission. Failing to rendezvous with
their assigned bomber formation at Montesquieu, the formation encountered instead an entirely different bomb group and proceeded to escort
them to a mission to Chilivani! Only the 82nd Fighter Group, escorting
B-25s from the 321st Bomb Group to Olbia, were able to complete their
mission without confusion, and ultimately with success.

The 14th took a couple of days off to regroup following its strange mission, before returning to regular operations again on June 28. As this was happening, the army issued its biennial report from the chief of staff, reviewing where America stood after two years of war. Citing from the report:[1]

Reviewing briefly the military situation as we find it on July 1, 1943, it will be remembered that our entry into war was marked by a succession of serious reverses, at Pearl Harbor, in the Philippines, and through the Malaysian Archipelago. It was a time for calm courage and stout resolution on the part of the people of the United States. With our Pacific fleet crippled and the Philippines overwhelmed at the outset, we were forced to watch the enemy progressively engulf our resistance to his advances. One year ago the German offensive in Russia was sweeping through the Donetz Basin, jeopardizing the whole of south Russia and the Caucasus and ominously menacing the Allied positions in the Middle East, particularly the oil supply at Abadan on which the naval forces in the eastern Mediterranean, the Indian Ocean, and Australia depended, in addition to the air and ground motor requirements in those theaters. Rommel's Afrika Korps with selected Italian troops had the British with their backs to Cairo, threatening the lifeline of the British Empire. Our successes in the Coral Sea and at Midway and the repulse of the Japanese forces in the Aleutians had not prevented the Japanese from carving out a vast empire from which they threatened India, Australia, and our position in the Pacific. Just a year ago also the ability of the United States to transport its power in supplies, munitions, and troops across the Atlantic was being challenged by submarines which in a single month had sunk 700,000 gross tons of shipping.

July 1, 1943, finds the United States Army and Navy united against the Axis powers in purpose and in operation, a unity shared when the occasion demands by the British Commonwealth of Nations, the Chinese, Dutch, French, and other fighting elements among our friends and supporters. Across the Atlantic the enemy has been driven from North Africa, and Europe has been encircled by a constantly growing military power. The Russian Army, engaging two-thirds of the German ground forces and one-third of the German air fleet in deadly and exhausting combat, has dispelled the legend of the invincibility of the German Panzer divisions.

The British Isles are stronger than ever before and a new France is arising from the ashes of 1940. Strategically the enemy in Europe has been reduced to the defensive and the blockade is complete. In the Pacific the Japanese are being steadily ejected or rather eliminated from their conquered territory. The Aleutians are about to be cleared of all tracks and traces of the enemy. In the south and southwest Pacific two facts are plainly evident to the Japanese command, as well as to the world at large: Our progress may seem slow but it is steady and determined, and it has been accompanied by a terrific destruction of enemy planes and surface vessels. This attrition must present an appalling problem for the enemy high command. Whatever satisfaction they may draw from the fanatical sacrifice of their soldiers with whom our forces come in contact, the destruction of their airpower and shipping continues on an increasing and truly remarkable scale.

In brief, the strength of the enemy is steadily declining, while the combined power of the United Nations is rapidly increasing, more rapidly with each succeeding month. There can be but one result, and every resource we possess is being employed to hasten the hour of victory without undue sacrifice of the lives of our men.

Several new pilots had been assigned to the 49th after Knepper and Kocour reported on June 9, and these new pilots were also given additional flight instruction by the squadron. Following a final "check ride" by the squadron's pilots, the replacement pilots would be ready for assignment to combat sorties. It was the squadron's way of ensuring that the pilots would be capable of contributing to the success of their missions without increasing the hazards for their fellow pilots.

Harold Harper recalls: "I checked out quite a few guys. We would take them up and fly in formation, do some low-level stuff. Maybe practice dive-bombing. We would take up two or three at a time."[2]

On June 26, Lt. William Neely was conducting a check ride for newly reported pilots Kopecky, Leiter, Vardel, and Churchill. His tentmate and good friend Lieutenant Gregory had given Neely a ride down to the flight line for the mission. In this check ride, Neely was taking the role of a GAF pilot, working through maneuvers to see how well the new pilots would perform. Neely went into a steep dive from approximately 35,000 feet and attempted to pull out at 4,000 when his right wing reportedly failed. The plane continued in level flight for a short distance and then went into a spin and crashed on a steep hillside, just 3 to 4 miles from base.[3]

Gregory hurried to the crash site just as Neely's body was being brought down the hillside. Neely was Greg's best friend in the squadron. They'd trained together since college, joined the squadron together, and had flown many of the same missions. They were both highly qualified pilots and well respected within the squadron. With all the tough combat losses that the squadron was experiencing, it was especially hard to lose a pilot as well liked and as capable as Lieutenant Neely was.[4]

The question arises: What empowers combat pilots to continue flying almost daily, after repeatedly losing close friends in combat? One partial answer might be that the losses often occur at a remove; fellow pilots may not learn of a friend's loss until hours later, after returning to base. And even when the loss is seen firsthand, it is somewhat in the abstract, most often "missing in action," not "killed in action." No sound is attached to it; the pilot himself is rarely seen. The only sign of his loss is the crash of his aircraft on land, or a splash at sea, a loss somehow made less personal. The world moving at 400 mph permits little real-time reflection. For the most part, they simply were not there anymore—their bunks were empty, their places at mess, vacant. Not minimizing the loss, but possibly the horror, one might maintain hopes of a capture, or if not that, an honorable death.

Except for Neely. His death was intensely personal, and deeply felt by all who knew him. Neely's loss brought the weight of the war onto the men of the squadron more directly and unavoidably.

Following the harrowing mission on June 20 to Bo Rizzo in which Decker was shot down, and after the tough loss of Neely, the new pilots continued learning hard lessons about combat in North Africa. Knepper next flew on June 28—a mission to escort a formation of twenty-five B-26s from the 320th Bomb Group in an attack on the landing ground and dispersal areas at Millis on Sardinia. The mission would include thirty-six P-38s: twelve from each of the 14th's three squadrons. On this mission, Knepper was flying as spare, with Harris.[5] On the same day, the 14th would fly a second bomber-escort mission, sending twelve P-38s from both the 48th and 49th squadrons, augmented with a large escort of forty-four P-40s from the 325th Fighter Group. The B-26s were from the 17th Bomb Group, and were targeting a second important Axis airfield on Sardinia: Decimomannu aerodrome, located just 52 miles southeast of Millis. Lieutenant Kocour was assigned to the mission, again flying number-two position to Lieutenant Bland.

The P-38s assigned to the first mission were off at 1045: the 37th squadron off first, followed five minutes later by those of the 48th, and again five minutes later by those of the 49th. Aircraft assigned to the second mission started just a few minutes later. It was a stirring sight at Telergma: sixty high-performance P-38s taking off in just over a half-hour.

Knepper's formation of P-38s made their rendezvous with the B-26s at 1130, setting a slightly northwest course before turning back to the east, toward Sardinia. Flight distance to the target would be 329 miles. Flying initially "on the deck," the formation would climb to its bombing height of 10,000 feet when 15 miles away from the target. Forty-five minutes into Knepper's mission, Trollope's aircraft peeled away from the formation and returned to base, probably with a mechanical issue. His place in the formation was taken by Harris. A short while later, and per normal procedure, as the formation neared the target the flight leader released Knepper back to base, as it appeared that he would not be required for this mission.

With Harris in Trollope's position, the mission continued with a successful bomb drop: Nineteen aircraft were parked at the aerodrome, and fourteen were probably destroyed. As the bombers headed for home, a sudden coordinated barrage of heavy flak began to hit the bombing formation. Two B-26s were downed by flak, and ten others damaged. Then the formation was jumped by twenty-five to thirty

Macchi 202s and Me 109s. In the aerial combat that ensued, DeMoss shot down two Me 109s, and Lieutenant Harris shot down one enemy aircraft and is credited with another as "probable." Two other enemy fighters were downed by pilots of the other escorting squadrons, plus two more probables. Two P-38s, one with an engine shot out and the other with the tip of its right wing shot off, joined the bomber formation for protection while the formation returned to base. All of this action occurred in just thirteen minutes following the bomb drop. In its summary report for the mission, the 320th noted: "The escort provided by P-38s of the 14th Fighter Group was excellent."

In comparison to the tough enemy resistance encountered in the squadron's morning action, Lieutenant Kocours's mission later in the day was a milk run. Just thirty minutes after the morning mission had released their bomb loads at Millis, Lieutenant Kocour's formation of B-26s made their drop on Decimomannu. Bomb coverage was very good—three strips of bombs were laid across the runways at Decimomannu, and six fires were observed in dispersal area on the south part of the field. Twenty enemy aircraft were seen at a lower altitude, but they did not attempt to engage the bomber force. Flak was inconsequential, and no bombers were lost. The escorting P-38s returned to Telergma at 1450.

The squadron diary records that after the day's missions, all pilots and the squadron commander drove the 24 miles to the American section of the communal Cementary at Constantine, Algeria, to attend the burial services for Lieutenant Neely. A military funeral was given, and the lieutenant was buried in the American section of the cemetery, with squadron chaplain Frank Robinson presiding. This was a ceremony that, despite the high losses incurred by the squadron, was rarely held. Most of the pilots who were lost in combat were killed or declared MIA over open water or hostile territory, and no burial was possible.

In conformance with his father's request that Lt. Neely's remains should not be repatriated to the U.S., but rather they should remain with his fallen comrades in North Africa, in March 1944 Lt. Neely was reinterred at the American Cemetery in Constantine, Algeria, and in September 1948 was again reinterred at the permanent U.S. Military Cemetery near Carthage, Tunisia.

North African American Cemetery in Carthage, Tunisia.

AMERICAN BATTLE MONUMENTS COMMISSION

JUNE 30, 1943

D-Day for the invasion of Sicily was fast approaching, evidenced by the ramp-up of missions targeting Axis air forces and facilities. NASAF planned five bombing missions for June 30, involving B-17s, B-25s, and B-26s from seven bomb groups hitting targets on western Sicily.[6] The attacks would be nearly simultaneous, targeting the city of Palermo and the airfields at Palermo, Sciacca, Bo Rizzo, and Trapani/Milo—a broadly based attack on the Luftwaffe that could pay big benefits in securing air superiority over Sicily.

In checking the flight board on the evening of June 29, Knepper learned that he was assigned to the next day's mission to Palermo, escorting a combined force of B-17s from the 2nd and 301st Bomb Groups. The 49th squadron led the escort contingent and would contribute twelve P-38s for the mission. The 37th and 48th squadrons would also each contribute twelve aircraft for the mission. The 49th would take off first at 1000, with aircraft from the 37th and 48th joining them ten minutes later.

A big day for the strategic bomber forces, the four other missions planned for that day included the following:

The 99th Bomb Group would send twenty-one B-17s on a mission to the Axis airfield at Bocca di Falco—the air base located on the western edge of the city of Palermo. This mission would be escorted by twelve P-38s from the 37th squadron, and twelve from the 48th.[7]

Bocca di Falco had been the home to the Regia Aeronautica (Italian Royal Air Force), as well as the headquarters of the Italian 4th Aerial Zone. Italian-made S-79, S-84, and Ca 314 medium bombers had been based there following the German evacuation of Tunisia. During May, the aircraft of the 13th and 37th Gruppos had moved from Bocca di Falco to bases in Italy, partially in response to the heavy Allied bombing campaign and its emphasis on Axis airfields.[8] The Intelligence Section of NAAF had estimated in a May 13 report that Bocca di Falco held thirty-eight German single-engine fighters. These were not in evidence on June 30.

B-25s from the 310th and 321st Bomb Groups would attack the airfield at Sciacca, about 40 miles south of Palermo, in an effort to destroy German fighters based there at the time. A large mission, it was composed of thirty-six B-25s from the 310th, and an equal number from the 321st. Escort was provided by twenty-four P-38s from the 82nd Fighter Group from their base at Souk el Arba, Algeria.

B-26s from the 17th would attack the airfield at Bo Rizzo, an airfield located on the extreme western coast of Sicily, 40 miles west of Palermo. Escorted by fifty-four P-38s of the 1st FG from their base at Mateur, Tunisia, it appears from the escort's mission report that General Doolittle joined this mission as an observer. At that time, Bo Rizzo was the home of the 17th Gruppo, with Macchi 202 "Thunderbolt" fighter aircraft, and the 21st Gruppo CT operating MC 200. The 202 was the most performant Italian fighter, and was considered equal to the P-38 and probably superior to the P-40.

Twenty-eight B-26s from the 319th BG would attack Trapani/Milo airfield, escorted by a force of forty-four P-40s of the 325th FG based at

Mateur, Tunisia. Trapani had long been a stronghold for the Luftwaffe, and on June 30, German fighters continued to operate from it.

MISSION TO PALERMO

Palermo had been getting quite a lot of attention from NASAF since the Axis defeat in Tunisia. Earlier in the year, the Intelligence Section of the 12th Air Force listed Palermo, its airfield at Bocca di Falco, and the Cuba Barracks as their number-two priority target. The port of Palermo was a destroyer and submarine base, a leading commercial port, and a shipbuilding center. Prior to the fall of Tripoli, cargo was delivered via the port of Messina by rail to Palermo, then transshipped to resupply German troops in North Africa. The Italian Air Force also operated a seaplane base from the harbor at Palermo, one of the largest fuel depots on Sicily was located in the city, and it was home to the only iron foundry on the island of Sicily. The military targets also included an important ordnance factory, as well as an arsenal capable of repairing and refitting naval guns.[9]

This would not be the Allies' first visit to Palermo. On May 9—Mother's Day—a bombing raid to Palermo was described in the combat diary of W. Harold Plunkett:[10]

Sunday, May 9, 1943: This was a bad day, and also the first real mission where I got shot at. It was Mother's Day, and it was our first target that was not a military target. Our mission was to destroy the city of Palermo, Sicily. The intention was to destroy the morale of the people so they would be willing to surrender the Island of Sicily to the Allies. The Red Cross said that we killed over 18,000 people that day.

Tuesday, May 11, 1943: The International Red Cross has declared Palermo, Sicily, would be an open city for three days. That meant for three days we were not supposed to bother that city while they buried their dead.

Most of the Italian Air Force assets had been moved from Palermo to bases in Italy in response to heavy Allied bombing. At the end of June, the Italian air forces based at Palermo included only the 66th Gruppo, operating the Ca 312 and 313 light bombers. No fighters were based at Palermo at the time of the bombing mission on June 30, though this fact may not have been known to the Allied mission planners.

With the 49th squadron leading the escort mission, Knepper would fly number-two position to Lieutenant DeMoss, in Captain Trollope's four-ship flight. Knepper may have felt a sharper excitement for this mission, his first escorting B-17 Flying Fortresses. Until now, both Knep and Koc had been limited to B-26 escort duties. Unbeknownst to Kocour, his first B-17 escort mission lay just ahead, and he would fly three in the first week of July alone.

The B-17s were able to throw up a ferocious defense, but it is also true that they were magnets for GAF interceptors and flak. Since restarting operations on May 5, the 49th Fighter Squadron had escorted these heavy bombers on twelve missions, and had been intercepted by GAF fighters eight times. The Germans had lost seven aircraft in aerial combat against the 49th, but had shot down six of the 49th's pilots.[11] This was a frightful record, and pilots approached these escort missions with apprehension, knowing chances were quite good that one of them could go down on this day.

But with recent missions an encouraging pattern had emerged that would not have been lost on NASAF's fighter pilots: With the heavy NASAF bombing of airfields that commenced after the fall of Pantelleria, GAF fighters were much less inclined to engage the B-17 formations. In the four most recent B-17 escort missions, the Axis fighters had appeared just once, with no losses. It was beginning to appear that the Germans had lost either the capacity to resist the fierce B-17 Flying Fortress or the appetite for taking on the task.

Flak was another matter. As the German air assets waned, increased emphasis was placed on flak, and at times it could be ferocious.

ABOUT FLAK

In the wake of the widespread destruction of the Luftwaffe's aviation assets, the German flak capability became of increasing importance and continued to pose a very serious threat to Allied warplanes. This was even becoming evident in the German homeland, where the Luftwaffe could no longer be depended upon to provide broad area defenses for its forces in the field, or for its cities, factories, and other strategic assets. Though the flak units were subordinate to the Luftwaffe for administration, operationally they were controlled by the army to which they were attached in the field.

In order to create better theater intelligence, the AAF had established criteria for pilots to use in their post-mission briefings. The flak encountered on a mission was carefully recorded so that future missions could be apprised of what might be waiting for them.

Pilots were asked to categorize the type of flak, referring to the caliber of flak that they encountered:

- heavy, from 88mm cannon;
- medium or moderate flak, from 20mm cannon; or
- light, from machine guns.

At the altitudes from which B-17s operated, they would be most concerned about heavy 88mm flak over the target, but they'd be exposed to medium or light flak as they made their hour-long climb to the drop zone.

Pilots were also asked to assess the amount of flak.

- "Slight" meant widely scattered smoke puffs.
- "Moderate" meant many scattered smoke puffs.
- "Intense" meant that the sky was full of puffs, as if they "could walk on it."

Finally, the pilots were asked to make an assessment of the accuracy of the flak:

- "As to altitude," meaning, whether the flak had zeroed in on the altitude of the formation.
- "As to deflection," meaning, how accurate was the aiming of the flak.

The worst flak situation, encountered often during the air war over Sicily, was "heavy, intense, and accurate."[12]

Germany invested heavily in research, production, training, and the development of operating practices for its flak units. The captured German document, "German Training Regulations for AA [Antiaircraft] Flak," discussed the "Ways and Forms of Attack" by enemy (Allied) aircraft, identifying sixteen different types of attacks that should be expected. In addition to the obvious attack modes, the Luftwaffe distinguished between day, dusk, and night attacks, glide attacks as opposed to dive-bombing attacks, and concentric attacks as opposed to sector attacks.[13]

HEAVY FLAK

The weapon most often associated with the term "heavy flak" is the 88mm cannon—arguably the most famous artillery piece of World War II. It was originally developed in 1934 as a secret prewar collaboration between the German Krupp and the Swedish Bofors armament manufacturers, with research and production conducted in Sweden in order to circumvent the limitations imposed by the Versailles Treaty. Like the Luftwaffe, flak units were first deployed during the Spanish Civil War as part of the Condor Legion. At the start of German offensives in northern Europe, the flak units were well equipped and well trained.

The 88 fired a nearly 21-pound shell to an altitude well beyond the practical limits of Allied fighters and bombers, and could fire fifteen rounds per minute with a trained crew. The shells fired by the antiaircraft guns exploded without striking solid objects. Rather, timing devices were built into the projectiles, making it possible to "tune" the explosive charges for a specific altitude. The 88's shells were made of explosives encased in steel jackets. On reaching the preset altitude, the shells exploded, sending out a mushroom of steel fragments. The principle was similar to that of firing a shotgun.

As an example of flak deployment in Sicily, the Hermann Göring Division (panzer) included a flak regiment, which normally included four battalions in the field. Each battalion could include up to four light batteries, with each battery equipped with twelve guns, most often operating in groups of three guns—close to two hundred guns available for antiaircraft fire. It could be towed, permanently mounted on a flak tower, placed on a railcar, and was even installed on the German Tiger tank. It was ineffective at altitudes under 3,000 feet and was of relatively little concern to fighter dive-bombing missions, where the target approach was "on the deck." For Allied bombers, the 88 was greatly feared.

MEDIUM AND LIGHT ANTIAIRCRAFT (AA)

Germany had seven different forms of light and medium AA guns, with maximum vertical ranges of 9,000 to 15,000 feet, but effective ranges against aircraft of about 4,000 feet. The 30/38 Flakvierling was widely used, the 30 with a firing rate of 120 rounds per minute, and the fearsome four-barreled Flak 38 firing up to 800 rounds per minute. This feared aircraft-killer was widely used in the Mediterranean Theater. It was these lighter AA guns that were the greatest danger to lower-flying fighter

U.S. naval antiaircraft fire directed at incoming enemy aircraft. Official caption: "Some enemy air activity and what we did about it."
NATIONAL ARCHIVES

aircraft on sweeps, dive-bombing, or strafing missions. Accepted as the standard army gun in 1939, the 30/38 Flak was not only the primary German light antiaircraft gun, but by far the most numerously produced German artillery piece, with more than 140,000 produced during the war years.

Approaching Palermo

After Knepper's formation rendezvoused with the bombers, it was a slow crawl to the target. The straight-line flight distance to Palermo from Telergma is just over 400 miles, but with the time required for form-up and rendezvous, it took the slow-moving B-17s almost three hours to reach

Aerial view of the Palermo docks under attack, March 22, 1943.
NATIONAL ARCHIVES

NAAF precision bombing, March 3, 1943.
NATIONAL ARCHIVES

the target. Reaching their bombing altitude of 26,000 feet, the bombers completed their drop at 1300 and turned for home.

Ellis and Boatman had both developed mechanical problems with their aircraft and returned to base. Their places were taken by Grant and Cobb, who were flying "spares" for this mission.

It proved to be a good mission for Knepper to gain experience in escorting B-17s, because it was the closest thing to a "milk run" that the 49th had experienced since the campaign against Pantelleria. It was certainly not without risk, as the formation was met with flak from heavy guns in the vicinity of the target. Fortunately, it was not accurate, and only "slight to moderate" in intensity.

According to the bomb group mission report: "The 301st and the 2nd attacked the barracks, stores, and some unidentified military compound buildings in the city. The target was well covered and there was considerable damage in the surrounding residential area of the city. Unlike the Mother's Day raid on May 9th, there was a nominal amount of inaccurate flak and not one enemy fighter sighted, perhaps because of the twenty-four escorting P-38s of the 14th Fighter Group."[14]

While the escorting P-38s were over the target, a considerable amount of smoke and dust was observed from the nearby aerodrome at Bocca di Falco. When he saw this, Lieutenant Knepper knew that the attack on Bocca di Falco was also under way. In fact, that mission had made its drop just twenty minutes earlier. Like Knepper's mission, no enemy aircraft were encountered.

All thirty-six aircraft from the 14th Fighter Group—the escort team for both missions—arrived back to their base at Telergma at 1500.

CHAPTER 9

The P-38 Fighter Interceptor

DEVELOPMENT

IN THE LATE 1930S THE WRIGHT FIELD PURSUIT PROJECTS OFFICE WAS the center for testing aviation technology and developing new military aircraft. In February 1937, with the crisis in Europe deepening, it issued requests for proposals for a single-engine fighter and a twin-engine fighter. Seven aircraft manufacturers were invited to participate, including Bell, Boeing, Curtiss, and Douglas.

The requirements for the new aircraft were clearly specified: minimum top speed of 360 mph; an operating ceiling of at least 20,000 feet, and a climb rate that would allow the aircraft to reach its ceiling in less than six minutes. Cannon armament was also specified, since the primary function of these new airplanes was high-altitude interception of hostile aircraft, specifically bombers. The aircraft had to be equipped with tricycle-type landing gear to facilitate ground handling, and the aircraft engines had to be able to operate at full throttle for at least one hour.

An airframe with these advanced specifications was needed by the Army Air Forces in order to keep pace with the rapidly advancing combat aircraft capabilities of Germany and Japan. To put these requirements into perspective, two fighters previously evaluated by the army in 1937 had maximum speeds of 313 mph. The new aircraft would represent a quantum leap forward in airplane design and performance.

The proposals submitted by Bell for the single-engine aircraft, and that of Lockheed for the twin-engine aircraft, were accepted.[1] Bell's design led to the P-39 Airacobra. Operating most effectively below

12,000 feet, the P-39 proved to be a useful ground-attack aircraft that was used widely by the Allied air forces.

Lockheed's design led to the P-38 Lightning. Developed by noted aviation designers Hall Hubbard and Kelly Johnson, the proposed aircraft was so well received that an army contract was issued in June 1937. Although the amount of the army contract was just $163,000, Lockheed actually spent $761,000 to fulfill it—a testimony to their faith in the design and their commitment to get the aircraft into testing. Lockheed's prototype was one of the world's fastest aircraft when it first flew in early 1939, and became the first fighter to fly faster than 400 mph. It was destined to be the only U.S. fighter to remain in production throughout World War II.

Lockheed had originally dubbed the aircraft Atalanta, from Greek mythology, in keeping with the company tradition of naming planes after mythological and celestial figures: Atalanta—Greek goddess of the hunt. But initial orders for the P-38 went to Britain, whose RAF dubbed it the "Lightning," and the name stuck. In his technical report "Assessing the Lockheed P-38 Lightning," Dr. Carlo Kopp noted a further extraordinary feature of the Lockheed aircraft:

> The P-38 excelled in that design parameter which is pivotal to fighting a strategic air war, its combat radius in excess of 700 NM [nautical miles] had no equivalent in either camp. The Lightning's combat radius was exploited repeatedly and surprisingly, the Lightning repeatedly succeeded in catching its opponents off guard. Both in the Pacific and the Mediterranean, the P-38 provided long-range escort for heavy bombers, long-range fighter sweeps deep into hostile airspace and interdiction of surface targets.[2]

DESIGN

The muscle of the twin-engine P-38 was provided by the new Allison V-12 engines mated to a new GE-developed turbocharger that provided enhanced performance at higher altitudes. This power plant enabled the Lightning to easily meet the army specifications. Among many innovations, the engines were "counter-rotating," meaning the left engine rotated in the opposite direction from the right. This had the effect of negating torque—a troublesome attribute of single-engine aircraft or multi-engine aircraft that did not counter-rotate.

The cockpit, nosewheel, guns, and ammunition were all contained in a central pod (nacelle), and the engines were mounted in mid-wing nacelles extending back into tail booms joined by a horizontal tail and twin rudders. The cockpit was equipped with a jettisonable top cover and crank-down side windows. The windshield was a single slab of armored glass, and the pilot was protected by a steel plate forward and multiple rear plates. Responding to the army requirement for heavy armament, the P-38 was fitted with one 37mm cannon (later downgraded to a 20mm caliber) and a battery of four 12.7mm Browning machine guns, all mounted in the nose.

The Lightning was a heavy machine, categorized as a fighter but achieving the same weight class as lighter bombing platforms of her time. Yet even with its impressive size, it met the army's specification of 400 mph top speed, and remained one of the fastest fighters through the mid-war period. Its long flight duration allowed it to outrange any single-seat fighter during the early war years.

A P-38 test pilot summed up the war bird's legacy: "[T]his comfortable old cluck would fly like hell, fight like a wasp upstairs, and land like a butterfly."[3]

PRODUCTION, DELIVERY, AND VARIANTS

The army's initial order for P-38 aircraft in September 1939 was intended to allow the army and Lockheed to refine the design and give the Army Air Forces experience with handling this new type of aircraft.

In the spring of 1940, President Roosevelt issued his call for fifty thousand new aircraft. At that time, the P-38 was already far along the development curve and the most readily available design. It was formally accepted into service in August of 1940, with serial production of the initial model—the P-38E—beginning in September.

Deliveries of the P-38G model—the first fully combat-capable version, commenced in August 1942, and by November Lightnings were operating from bases in North Africa and in the Southwest Pacific. It was this variant that was flown by the 14th Fighter Group in the summer of 1943, although it was also common for each squadron to hold two or three of the older F models in their arsenal.

Development of other highly performant aircraft continued, ultimately leading to the P-47 Thunderbolt and the P-51 Mustang, but by the time these new aircraft were introduced, the P-38 had already been in combat service for two and a half years.

By war's end, just over ten thousand P-38s, in all variants, were produced. Roughly one out of eight P-38s initially produced were either used for photo reconnaissance or were modified for that purpose after delivery to the army. These photo reconnaissance variants, termed F-4s or F-5s, saw widespread service throughout the war, commencing in late 1942.

P-38G SPECIFICATIONS[4]

Maximum speed: 345 mph at 5,000 feet—400 mph at 25,000 feet.

Range on internal tanks: 850 miles (at 219 mph cruising speed and at 10,000 feet).

Range using drop tanks: 1,750 miles (using two 125-gallon drop tanks).

Time to climb to 10,000 feet (combat load): 3 minutes, 42 seconds.

Time to climb to 20,000 feet (combat load): 8 minutes, 30 seconds.

Service ceiling: 39,000 feet.

Weight empty: 12,200 pounds.

Weight with normal load: 15,800 pounds.

Wingspan: 52 feet.

Length: 37 feet, 10 inches.

Height: 9 feet, 10 inches.

Armament: One 20-mm Hispano M1 cannon with 150 rounds; four 0.50 Colt-Browning MG 53-2 machine guns with 500 rounds per gun.

Bomb load: Two 325-, 500-, or 1,000-pound bombs.

Features and Description

Unlike other fighters of the era, the P-38 did not use a central "joystick" for flight controls. Rather, it used a control wheel, called a yoke. This design innovation was required because the wing taper of the P-38 necessitated the use of small ailerons; in addition, the large movement of the aileron needed to initiate roll in the aircraft required more muscle at the controls than could be achieved with a stick. Radio and gun buttons were also located on the yoke, as was the drop-tank/bomb-drop button.

Clustering all the armament in the nose was unlike the typical style of most other U.S. aircraft, which used monocoque fuselage design and wing-mounted guns. Wing-mounted guns required that the trajectories be set up to crisscross at one or more points in a "convergence zone." This was a limitation for these types of aircraft, since they could only bring their maximum firepower to bear on a single point, Typically 100–250 yards ahead of the aircraft.

Pattern convergence was not an issue for the nose-mounted guns of the P-38, permitting pilots to commence firing earlier, reliably hitting targets up to 1,000 yards ahead of the aircraft.

The guns and cannon were set to fire concurrently: The rate of fire for the cannon was about 650 rounds per minute, and 850 rounds per minute for each of the four .50-inch machine guns. This gave the P-38 a ferocious combined rate of fire of over 4,000 rounds per minute, with one out of six rounds a 20mm cannon shell. The magazine sizes limited the duration of fire: The cannons had a sustained duration of fire of about fourteen seconds, and the machine guns, about thirty-five seconds. It should be noted that pilots fired in bursts, rather than sustained firing, because the buildup of heat in the guns could cause malfunction and contributed to early gun-barrel wear.

Nose armament of the Lockheed P-38 Lightning.

NATIONAL ARCHIVES

The P-38 in Flight

The P-38 was an exceptionally aerobatic aircraft. With the exception of dives, mentioned below, there were no restrictions on maneuvers: Immelmanns, high-speed Split S turns, and a variety of high-performance loops, rolls, and figure eight aerobatics could all be executed easily. It was a very able aircraft "in the vertical," both ascending and descending very quickly, making it an excellent platform for dive-bombing and strafing, and then climbing back up. It had an excellent rate of climb, and an exceptional "zoom rate"—a brief steep upward movement following horizontal acceleration. It could easily change direction while executing vertical maneuvers, and it was a very stable gun platform. The Lightning was also very maneuverable at low altitudes, due in part to the counter-rotating props and the elimination of engine torque.

Operational Advantages

The P-38 offered many exceptional operational advantages over other aircraft of the era—both Allied and Axis:

- The P-38 was unusually quiet for a fighter, the exhaust muffled by the turbo-superchargers.

- The P-38 was the only multi-engine fighter in operation during the war, and this new dimension gave the Lightning a great advantage during ground-attack missions. Single-engine airplanes equipped with liquid-cooled engines were quite vulnerable to ground fire; even a small nick in the coolant lines could cause the engine to seize in just a few minutes. And in flight, single-engine pilots had to be on high alert for any sign of engine failure—every ping, miss, or stutter could have severe consequences. The added insurance of a second engine made it possible for many P-38 pilots to safely return to base after losing an engine.

During the first eighteen months after America's entry in the war, the P-38 was the fastest and most performant aircraft in wide usage. No World War II fighter had as much available horsepower at altitudes of 25,000 feet and above as the P-38.

The strategic air war in the Mediterranean Theater depended on the P-38's exceptionally long range—up to 1,750 miles—in order to provide fighter protection deep into enemy territory. And it was capable of long-distance independent fighter sweeps to conduct dive-bombing and strafing missions. It was also possible for the P-38 to trade range for payload, carrying a bomber's load of armaments on shorter missions. It had no equivalent among other Allied aircraft, or in the Luftwaffe.

The P-38 handled well both on the ground and in the air, making it less fatiguing for the pilot. And with the engines placed to the side and the cockpit placed forward, visibility was excellent.

It was an excellent fighter/interceptor whose versatility and ruggedness were legendary. Properly equipped, it could be used in any theater of the war and could be applied to a wide range of missions: it could sink a ship,

Capt. William Hoelle inspecting damage to his P-38, sustained when he hit a telephone pole on a low-level pass.

NATIONAL ARCHIVES

dive-bomb tanks, radar installations, or gun positions, strafe troop concentrations or tanks, and destroy even hardened ground emplacements.

Finally, the P-38 could take a lot of punishment and still stay in the air. In one noteworthy example in the 49th squadron, Capt. William Hoelle's P-38 clipped a telephone pole at 300 miles per hour. Flipped on its back by the impact, Hoelle was able to right his plane and return to base.

The aircraft that would later be assigned to Lieutenant Knepper in North Africa came off the assembly line at the Lockheed plant in Burbank just as Knepper was entering the halfway point of his Basic flight training, on November 6, 1942. It was originally destined for the 8th Air Force operating out of England, but when Operation Roundup was canceled and Operation Torch decided upon, the aircraft was redirected to the 12th Air Force in North Africa. It was flown to the port of Newark, disassembled, and packed for shipment to Europe.

It was a P-38G model, serial number 42-12961. With one exception, Lieutenant Knepper would fly this aircraft on all of his future combat missions, although as the aircraft was being test-hopped in Burbank, Knepper still didn't know whether he would complete the flight program and receive his wings or wash out and return to the enlisted ranks.

Operational Disadvantages

For all of its outstanding design and operational features, the P-38 was not without its flaws:

- The Lightning's most crucial limitation was in high-speed dives. The problem was not a lack of speed, but rather an excess of it. In a steep, high-speed dive, airflow over parts of its frame reached near supersonic velocity, causing a form of turbulence known as "compressibility" that could lock the flight controls and induce extreme vibration. In air combat this meant that P-38 pilots had to avoid extreme dives. One of the German fighters' favorite tactics was to make head-on attacks against the bombers, followed by tight rolls and high-speed dive-aways. The Lightnings could not follow. The diving problem also deprived Lightning pilots of their own otherwise useful escape maneuver.

In May 1943 the Army Air Forces Proving Ground Command issued a report on the "Tactical Suitability of the P-38G Type Airplane as Compared to the P-38F." In that report, the authors noted that the "general maneuverability of this aircraft is probably the lowest of any type of current fighter aircraft." Due to its size and design, the P-38's ability to roll—rotation of the aircraft around the front-to-back axis—was inferior to that of single-engine planes, and it was not as nimble in dogfights.

It was also expensive to produce. Lockheed had never expected to mass-produce the P-38 design and did not engineer it for fast or easy assembly, low-cost operation, or easy maintenance. Coming later in the war, the P-51 fighter had just one engine to maintain and was easier to manufacture and maintain. In 1943 the P-38 had a price tag of $106,000 compared to $59,000 for the P-51.[5]

Unrelated to the aircraft, pilot training was inadequate in some aspects of operation, due very much to the haste with which new pilots had to be trained and dispatched to combat squadrons. Many new replacement pilots had as little as twenty hours of flying time on the P-38, with little or no air-to-air gunner training, and were especially lacking in deflection shooting skills.

The P-38 was a particularly cold aircraft, because the pilot sat in a pod separated from the engines. With no conductive warming effect, and only an inadequate heating system to channel warmth from the nacelles, pilots suffered in their aptly dubbed "airborne ice wagons." And with ground temperatures in North Africa extreme, pilots operating from Tunisia or Sicily could not add additional clothing to combat lower temperatures at altitude. Pilot Robert "Smoky" Vrilakas of the 1st Fighter Group reports trying to stay warm by wrapping his legs in pages taken from the *Stars and Stripes* newspaper.

THE GERMAN VIEW OF THE P-38

The German Air Force was of two views regarding the performance and capabilities of the P-38. The head of the Luftwaffe's Fighter Section, General der Jagdflieger Adolf Galland, was unimpressed with the P-38, declaring "it had similar shortcomings in combat to our Bf 110; our fighters were clearly superior to it."[6]

The head of the GAF in Sicily prior to and during Operation Husky felt much differently. Oberstleutnant Johannes Steinhoff recorded:

> *Our old Messerschmitts were still, perhaps, a little faster. But pilots who had fought them said that the Lightnings were capable of appreciably tighter turns and that they would be on your tail before you knew what was happening. The six machine guns mounted in the nose supposedly produced a concentration of fire from which there was no escape. Certainly the effect was reminiscent of a watering can when one of these dangerous apparitions started firing tracer, and it was essential to prevent them maneuvering into a position from which they could bring their guns to bear.*[7]

Queried after the war about which of the Allied fighters he encountered was the most difficult to handle with a good pilot at the controls, Steinhoff responded: "The Lightning. It was fast, low-profiled, and a fantastic fighter, and a real danger when it was above you. It was only vulnerable if you were behind it, a little below and closing fast, or turning into it, but on the attack it was a tremendous aircraft."[8]

MISSIONS

It soon became apparent that the P-38 was capable of undertaking many different kinds of missions.

In aerial combat, early in the war the P-38 was the only U.S. fighter capable of engaging the Bf 109G and Fw 190A on equal terms.

On bomber-escort missions—the majority of missions flown in the MTO by P-38s—P-38s could escort bombers to targets far beyond the range of P-40s or Spitfires based in North Africa.

P-38s flew dive-bombing and strafing ground-attack missions in the MTO, inflicting heavy damage on the German and Italian air, sea, and land convoys attempting to reinforce the theater.

The P-38 design had the flexibility to carry a wide variety of weapons, including torpedoes, bombs, and later, rockets.

CONCLUSION

Gen. Jimmy Doolittle, who led the Raid on Tokyo in the spring of 1942 and later commanded the North African Strategic Air Force, was a great fan of the P-38. He flew a P-38 himself during the Normandy Invasion and declared it to be "the sweetest-flying plane in sky."[9]

As a World War II fighter, the Lightning's legacy is unmatched. In all theaters of operation, P-38s equipped a total of twenty-seven fighter groups and ten reconnaissance groups. At any one time in the war more than two thousand P-38s were stationed around the world, combat-ready.

In the European Theater, the P-38 was found to be less suitable for high-altitude escort duty than the P-51 Mustang. It was gradually withdrawn from combat service with the 8th Air Force, but was still widely used for high-altitude reconnaissance.

The P-38 became the model for combat aircraft of the future, which utilized speed, altitude capability, and firepower to defeat more maneuverable opponents.[10]

CHAPTER 10

Attacks on Sardinia

Chilivani
July 3, 1943

STAGING AN INDIVIDUAL BOMBING MISSION DURING THE WAR WAS A complex venture; a coordinated attack involving several bomber and fighter groups was immensely more so, from target selection right through to preparation of the aircraft, pilot briefing, coordinated takeoffs and rendezvous, and the mission itself. With careful planning, and with well-trained and professional ground staff and pilots, the missions came off with a very high rate of success.

But as seen in previous chapters, complex operations like bombing raids could go wrong in many different ways. Weather, including ground haze, was a bigger factor than most contemporaries realize. And communications were, by today's standards, primitive. Radar was not widely available, and the multi-engine aircraft—both bombers and fighters— had hundreds of electrical, hydraulic, and mechanical systems that could go wrong. And then there was always the human element.

Beyond the explicable factors that could complicate or even threaten a mission, there were the unfathomable events that were impossible to anticipate.

Following the extensive NASAF missions on June 30, NAAF's bomb groups had a rare three-day hiatus until their next missions to the German aerodromes on Sicily and Sardinia. Three days with no missions gave the bomb and fighter groups time to repair damaged aircraft, stockpile munitions, and rest the flight crews for the intense mission schedule that lay ahead—a campaign that all personnel knew was coming, and for which there were strong intimations about the likely location of the Allied landings.

The Allied air forces continued to move men and equipment to advanced bases. Troop-carrier squadrons, flying the workhorse C-47, would be tasked with delivering airborne troops to their drop zones on the island, and having them positioned forward reduced the flight time to the drop points. Dive-bombing units, flying A-36 Apaches, also moved forward, giving these tactical bombers shorter flights to the likely beachheads and more residence time over the battle line. Reconnaissance aircraft also moved to bases closer to Sicily.

The North African Air Force was well positioned, fully provisioned, and poised for the major air operations that would come soon.

The missions scheduled for this date reflected the evolving NASAF bombing strategy of concentrated attacks on a single target or region. On June 28, NASAF had sent multiple missions to airfields in Sardinia. On June 30, five bombing missions had hit the airfields in northwestern Sicily. Later in July, the target would shift to Gerbini. On this day, it was back to Sardinia.

The intent of these attacks was threefold: Axis air forces based in Sardinia could potentially support the German defense of Sicily during the British-American invasion and could contest the hard-won air superiority over Sicily. Catching German fighters on the ground, or forcing them to come up to fight, would lessen the impact they might have on D-Day. And further destruction of ground facilities would reduce the effectiveness of the German air operations, a benefit that could possibly accrue during action after Sicily. And finally, a multi-target mission to Sardinia would keep German HQ uncertain about the location of the coming inevitable invasion: Would it be Sicily? Possibly Sardinia? Mainland Italy? Or even Greece? The uncertainty required Germany to continue to maintain defensive forces in many widely spaced locations, reducing the capabilities of each of these defensive forces.

On another "Big Day," twenty-two missions would be flown by the nine bomb groups and four fighter groups within NASAF.

The attacks began the night before, when night-bombing Welling-tons attacked the port facility at Olbia on Sardinia, as well as the German base at Trapani—a base located on Sicily but near enough to Sardinia to provide fighter interception. Today's mission for the NASAF's B-17s, B-25s, and B-26s targeted five separate airfields on Sardinia; light bomb-ers from NATAF would hit the area around Marsala and the airfields at Sciacca and Trapani; and B-25s from the 9th Air Force would target the airfield at Comiso.

The Axis forces ringed Sardinia with highly effective radar and radio direction finder (RDF) systems as part of their air defenses for the important aerodromes at Chilivani and Millis, and the ports at Cagliari and Olbia. As noted in a contemporaneous German report: "Most pen-etrations [of Sardinian airspace by the Allied air forces] were detected in good time by the 'Pula' station on the southern coast of the island."[1] An effective strike against the installations at Pula and Alghero would increase the chances of catching German and Italian aircraft on the ground when NASAF's bombers made their attacks later in the day, and so the bombing missions were preceded by fighter strikes against the radar stations at Pula and Alghero.

In the first antiradar sweep, the 1st FG sent just six P-38s to strafe the radar station at Alghero, southeast of Chilivani aerodrome. Taking off at 0920, the mission was relatively uneventful but successful. It encoun-tered no enemy aircraft, and minimal flak. The 1st repeated this same fighter sweep later in the day, with seven P-38s again strafing the radar station at Alghero.

A much larger formation of twenty-two P-40s from the 325th FG took off at 0955 to attack the radar and RDF stations at Pula on the southern point of the island. The strafing attack successfully destroyed two radar towers, two homing towers, an RDF station, and defensive gun emplacements, but lost one of their pilots in a midair collision with one of his fellow pilots.[2]

NASAF assigned the B-17 and B-25 groups to attack the airfields at Chilivani, Monserrato, and Alghero. The B-26s were set to hit the Sardinian airfields at Millis and Capoterra.

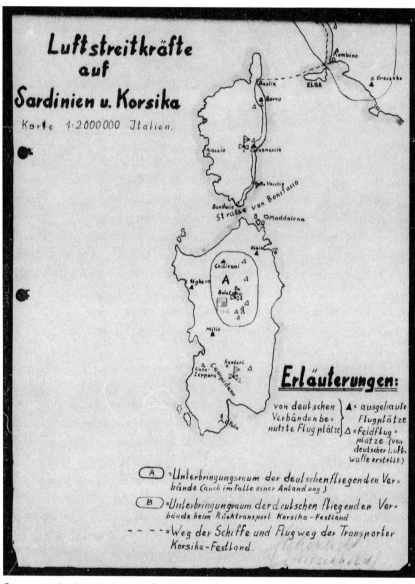

German radar installations on Sardinia.

As the fighters from the 1st and 325th Fighter Groups were taking off for their antiradar sweeps, other units from widely dispersed airfields in Tunisia and Algeria began to take off and form up, bombers and fighters rendezvousing before making the turn to the island of Sardinia.

At 0915 the 17th Bomb Group sent thirty-two B-26s to attack Millis Aerodrome, with an escort of thirty-six P-38s from the 1st FG.

An hour later, the 319th BG sent a formation of twenty-four B-26s to bomb Capoterra, with an escort of twenty-four P-40s from the 325th FG. At about the same time, the 321st BG sent thirty-six B-25s to bomb Alghero, with an escort of forty-two P-38s from the 82nd FG.

At 1040, thirty-six B-25s from the 310th BG took off on a bombing mission to Millis, with thirty-six P-38s from the 82nd FG escorting.

Medium bomber attacks concluded when twenty-five B-26s from the 320th BG took off on a second mission to Capoterra, with cover provided by thirteen P-38s from the 1st FG, and twenty-four P-40s from the 325th FG.

All of the heavy bomb groups, flying B-17 Flying Fortresses, were assigned targets on Sardinia.

The 2nd and 301st Bomb Groups, flying in a combined mission, and escorted by twenty-three P-38s from the 48th and 49th Fighter Squadrons, targeted the aerodrome at Chilivani. The 97th and 99th Bomb Groups, also flying in a combined mission, targeted the aerodrome at Monserrato, located near Cagliari, with an escort consisting of P-38s from the 37th, 48th, and 49th Fighter Squadrons.[3]

In the first mission of the day for the 49th Fighter Squadron, the twelve escorting P-38s assigned to cover the mission to Chilivani took off at 1140. The approach to Chilivani was uneventful. The defensive flak over the target was slight, and inaccurate. And it appeared that the early strikes against the radar installations on the island were very effective. On reaching Chilivani, the bombers reported catching thirty-nine enemy aircraft on the ground, a perfect scenario for the carpet-bombing techniques of the two formations of heavy bombers. Perfect except for one new twist that had been added to the mission: On this mission a new bombardment system was being tested by the bomb groups. They planned to overfly the target in waves, with the lead plane of each wave using the C-1 automatic pilot mechanism.

Under normal circumstances, the bombardier would instruct the pilot verbally over the intercom or send instructions via an instrument on the pilot's instrument panel, with the pilot controlling the attitude, speed, and direction of the bomber. The bombardier would make his drop when the pilot had correctly positioned the aircraft, per the bombardier's instructions. In order to operate under the autopilot, the bombsight is mated to the autopilot, giving the bombardier direct control over the aircraft during the final minutes of the bomb run. Once the lead ship had made its drop, the other aircraft in the formation would make theirs in synchrony.

On this day's mission, in the final minutes of the approach to target, the autopilot failed on the lead ship. The bomber's pilots had to respond quickly, taking back control of the aircraft and attempting to bring the formation into position for the drop. They were only partially successful. Roughly half of the 2nd's bombs fell on the target, with only a few of the enemy aircraft parked there "possibly damaged." The bombers of the 301st fared little better, their bombs falling to the north and west dispersal areas of the enemy aerodrome.

Exiting the target area, the bomber formation was intercepted by five Me 109s. Captain Leikness's four-ship flight engaged the German aircraft, with Leikness shooting down one, and Lieutenant Harper getting a "probable." The fighters returned safely to base at 1530.

Gremlins were also at work on the second Fortress mission of the day. The combined formation of B-17s from the 97th and 99th Bomb Groups with their escorting P-38s made their approach to the aerodrome at Monserrato at 25,000 feet. Lieutenant Kocour was included in this mission, again flying as Lieutenant Bland's wingman. Due to heavy haze and poor visibility, the bombers were not able to identify the target and did not drop their munitions. All bombers returned to their bases still carrying their bomb loads, with the exception of two bombers who jettisoned their bombs earlier. The escorting P-38s returned to base, still carrying their extra belly tanks. This mission counted as a combat sortie for the pilots, but the squadron reported the results as "Nil."

On their return, the P-38s of the 14th FG landed at their new airfield—El Bathan—their squadron having begun the move the night before the mission.

QUICKENING PACE OF PRE-INVASION MISSIONS

The pilots had a number of clues that the invasion of Sicily was at hand. The movement to forward bases, the rushed maintenance on all aircraft to ensure their readiness, the stockpiling of bombs and ammunition—all pointed to an action coming soon. And, confirming that secrecy was very difficult to maintain given the enormous buildup, pilots began to talk about the enormous amount of Allied shipping seen at Bizerte Harbor, just south of the coast of Sicily.

With the invasion obviously close at hand, and with the GAF no longer very much in evidence, the pilots of the 49th Fighter Squadron may have wondered what sort of missions they would be flying in the coming days. More strategic bombing escort duty? If so, to what targets? And they may also have wondered to what extent they would be assigned tactical missions. At this time and place in the war, they might be excused if they did not see a distinction between the two.

STRATEGIC OR TACTICAL?

"Strategic engagement"—actions taken to systematically degrade the capacity of a combatant to wage war—had little meaning until the development of national air forces. Militaries had plenty of munitions, but lacked the means of delivering them accurately to targets deep within the opponent's territory.

The development of increasingly capable aircraft changed all that, and quickly. Within a few short years of the beginning of powered aviation, aircraft were already being used for military applications. While primarily tasked with tactical support of ground troops, and for observation, aircraft were soon adapted to carry bombs. And it soon became clear that bombers could be used in a strategic sense, more or less independent of ground operations.[4]

Germany undertook a program of strategic bombing in the early months of World War I, commencing with an attack on August 6, 1914, by a German zeppelin on the city of Liege in Belgium. England's first foray into strategic bombing came in the fall of 1914, targeting the German zeppelin bases in Cologne and Dusseldorf. Within the first month of the war, Germany had formed a special air unit to conduct bombing missions over London, and in early 1915 launched the first extended campaigns of strategic bombing.

Strategic bombing in World War I had no significant impact; the most extensive bombing conducted by the Germans against Britain amounted to no more than 300 tons of munitions dropped. Despite this, the important foundation for strategic bombing had been laid, leading military planners on both sides to understand its potential importance in any future conflict.[5]

The initial intent of strategic bombing, and in particular, the bombing of cities, was to create terror among the citizenry of the opposing country and to destroy the enemy's morale. It was soon evident that the use of strategic bombing had a second and potentially more direct effect on the conduct of the war: The targets of strategic airpower came to include the sources of the enemy's war-making potential—important industries, power plants, oil facilities, and communication centers, such as ports and rail yards—hence developing the parallel intentions of strategic bombing: to degrade a country's ability to conduct war, and to simultaneously degrade its willingness to conduct war.

In the Mediterranean Theater, a disconnect developed between the doctrine of strategic bombing and the practicalities of military operations in the theater. In Europe, thousands of significant strategic targets fell within the range of Allied bombers. These conditions did not exist in the MTO, where there were relatively few suitable strategic targets. For operational purposes, the Mediterranean Theater was one enormous tactical area. The highest-priority targets identified by air force mission planners—railroad marshalling centers and ports—were arguably strategic, but the primary purpose of bombing missions to these targets was to interrupt the flow of men and materiel to the battlefront—clearly a tactical objective.

As early as January, the Combined Chiefs of Staff issued a memorandum setting forth bombardment objectives for North Africa. First priority was assigned to "furtherance of operations for the eviction of Axis forces from Africa"; that is, tactical missions in support of ground forces.[6]

By early 1943, a looser definition of "strategic" had evolved, with AAF planners assigning bomber forces to targets that had little to do with Germany's war-making capacity and more to do with near-term threats to the army's ground forces. The mission of the air forces medium and heavy bombers, at least as applied to the Mediterranean Theater, was quickly morphing into something that was arguably neither strategic nor tactical in nature.

A major retrospective prepared by the Office of Air Force History after the war notes:

> *The organization of the North African Air Forces bespoke a distinction between tactical and strategic operations which in the broader context of the war may prove misleading, however useful it may have been for the Mediterranean theater in 1943. . . . [T]he function of NAAF was almost exclusively tactical in nature; in other words, that its mission was one of cooperation in land and amphibious operations. That cooperation might be direct or indirect; it might be delivered by the relatively short-range planes of Tactical Air Force, or, as in strikes against enemy transportation in Italy, by the longer-range aircraft of Strategic Air Force. But in any case, its purpose was to further the advance of our land and sea forces in accordance with plans for the occupation of specific geographical areas, and thus it differed basically from efforts to strike directly at the enemy's capacity to wage war.[7]*

During the run-up to Operation Husky, the vast majority of targets selected for NASAF and for the 9th Air Force operating from Egypt were directed at the Axis transportation and air force assets. These targets were selected because their continued operation directly and immediately threatened ground and naval operations in the theater. In that sense, they were operating in a manner that was decidedly more tactical than strategic.

During the period of May–August 1943, the 14th Fighter Group escorted NASAF bombers and conducted their own dive-bombing and strafing missions against the following target mix:[8]

Target	Percentage of Missions
GAF Aerodromes	36
Pantelleria Island	24
Antishipping	11
Ports and Naval Infrastructure	11
Targets of Opportunity	10
Bridges, Railroads, Tunnels, Dams	3
Search and Rescue	3
Factories, Dams	2

The clear focus of these missions was on tactical targets, and of all the missions flown by the 14th during this period, only 5 percent could be considered anything other than tactical. The weight of the air force was brought against targets that could threaten Allied ground forces during the invasion of Sicily.

The targeting of GAF aerodromes was meant to establish Allied air superiority over the battlefront. The reduction of Pantelleria Island was meant to remove the possible threat of German air and naval actions against Allied shipping in the Mediterranean, and most specifically, to the Sicilian invasion force. Targeting shipping and ports was meant to interrupt the supply of munitions and materiel to the Axis forces, and the targeting of bridges, railroads, and tunnels was required in order to hamper the movement of troops and materiel on Sicily prior to and during the invasion. It is also noteworthy that the attacks on these tactical targets were undertaken with close cooperation between NASAF and NATAF. Like the previous joint operations at Kasserine Pass, it was evident that the functional distinction between NATAF and NASAF did not preclude them from conducting effective combined operations.

American air forces bombing in the Mediterranean during this period was strategic in name only, and since strategic forces were being applied in a tactical sense, it is useful to consider the doctrine that governed the Allied tactical air forces at this time in the war. This doctrine, and the associated policies and strategies that would govern the use of the vastly expanded Allied air forces at this time in the war, were anything but clear.

Because of the necessary interplay of these three factors, their shifting nature, and the changes in the world environment in which the air forces operated, American army planners had great difficulty in developing concrete plans. Having been the focus of discussions for nearly twenty years, the development of a sound set of principles governing the use of the air forces continued to be an intractable problem. Even into the early war years, as American airplanes and airmen headed for Europe and North Africa, operating doctrine was still unspecified, even though its critical importance was widely recognized. And at the heart of the uncertain debate were two interrelated missions: tactical and strategic air operations.

In the 1920s and early '30s, the primary debate went like this: Ground commanders viewed air forces as extensions of artillery and considered their primary purpose to be direct support of ground operations; air commanders concurred that the air assets could fulfill an important role in ground support, but also had a critical strategic mission that should be independent of ground support. Additionally, while the two groups agreed that adequate ground support was a key function of the air forces, there was no agreement as to who should have ultimate control over the air assets that fulfilled that role. Ground commanders believed that the unit on the ground should dictate missions, while air commanders felt equally strongly that the assets should be controlled by the U.S. Army Air Corps.

Aviation commanders also wrestled with defining strategic targets. In the 1920s, these targets were largely military in nature. By the mid-1930s, the target list had expanded to include surface vessels, submarines, and power plants. And by the early 1940s, the list had further expanded to include oil and electric power industries. The debate continued for decades, with field manuals issued irregularly that attempted to codify the accepted policies, strategies, and doctrines.

In 1935 the army issued *FM 31-35*, "Employment of the Air Forces of the Army," which remained in effect when the European war erupted in 1939. That manual defined the general mission of airpower as comprising "the air operations required for carrying out the Army mission." Although the document recognized the separate tactical and strategic missions for airpower, it treated much more carefully air activities "in immediate support of the ground forces." At least for a time, ground commanders had won the debate. The field manual noted: "When war broke out, strategic bombing as a highly significant aspect of airpower had barely achieved recognition in official doctrine, and no realistic body of principles governing the use of this weapon had yet been worked out."[9]

The AAF doctrine was put to the test during the invasion of North Africa, and in the early days of the Tunisian Campaign that followed. The heavy combat losses incurred over the winter of 1942–1943 demonstrated clearly that *FM 31-35* had gotten it wrong.[10]

The glaring unsuitability of the American doctrine was especially evident when compared to the brilliant successes of the British air forces in the eastern desert during the same period. There, the air arm operated independently from, but in close cooperation with, the British Eighth Army ground forces. RAF air marshal Sir Arthur Coningham had developed and perfected three important principles: establishing air superiority as first priority, centralizing the command of air operations and making it co-equal with that of ground operations, and employing innovative tactics when supporting ground operations.

Questions related to tactical use of the air forces were complicated further in the reorganization that led to NAAF and NATAF, because the resulting amalgam included both British and American air units. Eisenhower's preferences were soon made clear when he named General Coningham as commander of the tactical forces—NATAF. Issues that related to the American doctrine contained in *FM 31-35* were essentially, and practically, swept aside. The new operating principles were laid out in a pamphlet, authored by Coningham but issued by Field Marshal Bernard Montgomery, stating in part:

The greatest asset of airpower is its flexibility. . . . So long as this is realized, then the whole weight of the available airpower can be used in selected areas in turn. This concentrated use of the air striking force is a battle-winning factor of the first importance. It follows that control of the available airpower must be centralized and command must be exercised through Air Force channels.

Nothing could be more fatal to successful results than to dissipate the air resources into small packets placed under command of army formation commanders, with each packet working on its own plan. The soldier must not expect, or wish, to exercise direct command over air striking forces.[11]

In a presentation to Eisenhower and other Allied senior officers on February 16, 1943, the day before he took command of the tactical air operation, Air Vice Marshal Coningham commented: "The Army has one battle to fight—the land battle. The Air [Force] has two. It has first of all to beat the enemy air, so that it may go into the land battle against the enemy land forces with the maximum possible hitting power." He declared: "An air force on the offense automatically protect[s] the ground forces."[12]

Two days later, wasting no time in implementing the same principles that had been so effective for the RAF and the British Eighth Army, he issued a general operational directive prioritizing the objectives for NATAF: attaining air superiority, air interdiction of enemy assets behind the battle line, and air support of ground troops.[13]

ATTAINING AIR SUPERIORITY

By the late spring of 1943, NAAF was beginning to make significant progress in achieving superiority in the air. German and Italian aircraft were destroyed in the air when they attempted to intercept Allied bombing missions, and they were caught on the ground by medium and heavy bombers, and in dive-bombing missions by fighter aircraft. Of equal importance, the Axis aerodromes were targeted massively and repeatedly in order to deprive the Axis of its support facilities. The enemy was forced to transfer their planes from the Mediterranean islands, and from the Italian mainland, to remoter locations from which they could not so readily interfere with Allied ground efforts.[14]

This target selection was not undertaken piecemeal; actual target selection for missions prior to and during Operation Husky had been completed by the Intelligence Section of the 12th Air Force in February of 1943. The top ten targets on the S-2's First Priority List were aerodromes (seven), rail centers (one), and ports (two). Overall, aerodromes accounted for 61 percent of the First Priority targets. The first-, second-, and third-priority targets included forty-six individual aerodromes or landing ground, which were reflected repeatedly in the missions assigned to the 14th Fighter Group.[15]

As will be seen, the objective of attaining air superiority was largely met by the end of June 1943, although even as late as D-Day on the day of the invasion of Sicily, the GAF was able to launch over one hundred sorties against invading ground forces.

INTERDICTION

Interdiction missions are air attacks that destroy, neutralize, or delay the enemy's assets before they can be used in battle. Coningham recognized early on in the eastern desert that effective interdiction can have a profound effect on ground operations. Friendly ground forces advance much more quickly if the enemy is denied food, ammunition, or reinforcements.

Air interdiction missions, sometimes referred to as "deep air support," do not directly support ground operations and do not require close communication or coordination with ground units. Interdiction missions typically attack ground targets that are not in close proximity to friendly ground forces, and may be performed hundreds of miles from the battlefront. The early AAF missions against Sicilian ports would certainly qualify as interdiction, since they were intended to impede the flow of troops and materiel from mainland Italy to Sicily prior to the Allied invasion.

Further, the intense bombing campaign against German and Italian airfields in the days prior to the invasion was clearly interdiction. At that time, the battle line had not yet been established, but the destruction of these airfields was intended to reduce the capacity of Axis forces, so as to prevent air attacks during the invasion. U.S. Air Force historians later noted: "[T]he function of airpower . . . was to interfere constantly with Axis supply lines—to isolate the theater of war. The great contribution of the strategic air force in Africa was its vigorous participation in this campaign to deny supplies and reinforcements to the enemy. The only real distinction made between tactical targets and the targets assigned to strategic bombers was one of range."[16]

On D-Day of Operation Husky, air interdiction would "isolate the battlefield" with direct attacks on enemy units and ancillary targets, like railroad lines, bridges, truck convoys, and roads. Bombers could be used for interdiction strikes, because they could operate from altitude. In more purely tactical operations—that is, in providing close air support to ground troops—their slower speed, larger silhouettes, and less-responsive flight characteristics made them ready targets for ground gunners and enemy aircraft.

CLOSE AIR SUPPORT

Close air support missions—air actions against hostile targets in close proximity to friendly forces—require detailed integration of each air mission with the fire and movement of those forces. And as was learned during Husky, integration with naval bombardment forces was also required. They are the most difficult to control and execute, and carry the greatest risk to the pilot.[17]

Combat results using light bombers in close air support missions were mixed. Even in the successful German offensives in 1939 and 1940, it became clear that the ground-support aircraft, the feared Stuka dive-bomber, was vulnerable to the higher speed and guns of fighters, and to general ground fire. And the first American encounters with German forces in North Africa revealed the flaws in low-level bombardment tactics against the highly effective German light antiaircraft artillery. Despite these realities, providing close air support was essential to the combined air-ground effort.

Missions very close to the battle line were particularly challenging for the pilots, because they increased the risk of Allied losses by friendly fire—a true nightmare for AAF pilots. An effective control system had been developed by the British in the deserts of North Africa, and was later used in Europe. The Americans developed their own system for command and control of close air support aircraft used during Husky—a system that was ineffective in the early days of the invasion. Military historian B. Michael Bechthold notes: "Most support seems to have been directed at predetermined targets at a reasonable distance from the ground troops, and real 'close air' support for attacks was provided by the rather more precise creeping barrages from artillery developed in the Great War."[18]

The distinctions between tactical and strategic evaporated in the week leading up to the invasion of Sicily, when NASAF was temporarily put under the administrative control of NATAF. The transfer of strategic forces to tactical control was later confirmed in *FM 100-20*: "When the action is vital and decisive, the strategic air force may be joined with the tactical air force and assigned tactical air force objectives. Although nowhere directly stated, the clear intention of the directive was that strategic aircraft, when participating in a tactical program, should pass under the control of the joint air-ground headquarters—that is, of the tactical air force."[19]

The importance of the extreme versatility of the P-38 Lightning now became apparent: As the invasion of Sicily approached, NASAF fighter pilots flew bomber-escort missions to attack Axis aerodromes, interdiction missions against radar installations, ports, and rail centers, and during the invasion itself, missions that could only be described as close air support.

CHAPTER 11

When Things Go Wrong

The Gerbini Mission

JULY 5, 1943, WAS A DAY OF HEAVY ACTION FOR ALLIED FORCES IN ALL theaters and in all branches of service.[1] In the Pacific, navy planes and B-24s from the 13th Air Force bombed targets in the Solomon Islands; Marines prepared for an amphibious landing there; and B-25s of the American 5th Air Force hit targets in New Guinea. In the Mediterranean Theater, ground forces were making final preparations for the next assault against Germany, and much of the action fell to the air forces. Wellington night bombers attacked airfields on Sicily and Sardinia, and light and medium bombers hit the large aerodrome at Sciacca and the airfields at Trapani, Comiso, and Biscari. Bombers from the 9th AF, operating in the eastern Mediterranean, made strong attacks against the Messina, Sciacca, and Biscari airfields. Catania was also hit by heavy bombers from the RAF.

As for the fighters, the medium and heavy bombers of NASAF, the target was Gerbini.

ABOUT GERBINI

Sicily's terrain provided limited areas for locating aerodromes. The island has been compared to a "jagged arrow-head with the broken point to the West."[2] Roughly laced with mountains reaching over 3,000 feet, and with only a narrow, low coastal belt, most of the airfields were clustered in three areas: the eastern group between Catania and Gerbini, the southeastern group at Comiso-Biscari-Ponte Olivo, and the western group in the vicinity of Castelvetrano. Of these, the best equipped was in the Catania-Gerbini area.[3]

Located 14 miles west of Catania, the main aerodrome at Gerbini was an all-weather field with paved runways and taxiways, plus associated hangars, administrative buildings, fuel and ammunition dumps, and personnel housing. The airfield complex encompassed a series of flat agricultural fields that were also used for runways and parking areas. These associated fields came to be referred to as numbered "landing grounds." Initially numbering nine, these satellite fields were increased to twelve in the days leading to the invasion, with more and more German aircraft seeking relief from the relentless Allied bombing that was targeting aerodromes throughout the island.[4]

Because of the excellent reconnaissance capability within NASAF, air planners knew quite a lot about the facilities at Gerbini, including

Gerbini main aerodrome, surrounded by level agricultural fields used as Luftwaffe landing grounds during the summer of 1943.
AIR FORCE HISTORICAL RESEARCH AGENCY

aircraft shelters and protective earthen revetments, hangars, barracks, fuel dumps, and other key support components.

The commander of Luftwaffe forces on Sicily had a modest opinion of the Gerbini complex: "The complex of airfields was an ideal target for the Fortresses (B-17s) with their carpet-bombing technique. Just now the whole plain around Gerbini was covered with aircraft. Not far from our landing strip were a fighter-bomber group equipped with Focke-Wulfs and one wing each from the 51st and 53rd Fighter Groups, all of them dispersed under sparse cover of the olive trees."[5]

Earlier in the year, the AAF mission planners assigned a lower priority to the airfield complex at Gerbini. But Gruppos II and III of the JG 53 fighter "Ace of Spades" wing remained an effective force at Gerbini, as well as a still-robust fighter-bomber wing flying Fw 190s. And Gerbini had become the assembly point for German air assets relocating from other fields to avoid the Allied bombing campaign. Neutralizing Gerbini would reduce the incidence of air attacks by German defenders during the invasion of Sicily.

Allied planners were taking a longer view of Gerbini. Its main aerodrome was suitable for use by heavy bombers and was a short distance from the important port at Messina and other targets in the south of Italy. Securing this base early in the coming invasion would permit a deeper penetration of these bombers into Italy.

The GAF, though far from subdued, had been pushed around during the prior four weeks. While still able to mount effective defensive efforts, and never to be underestimated, the Luftwaffe heads knew they were up against it in the defense of Sicily. Gerbini had risen to the top of the Allied target list, and on this day, every bomber and fighter group in NASAF was assigned a mission there. And while Gerbini came late in the run-up to the invasion of Sicily, when the attacks commenced they were performed with an intensity that had only been matched previously by the campaign against Pantelleria.

In just seven days, July 5 through 12, thirty-six bomber missions were launched against Gerbini by NASAF, and more by medium bombers of the 9th AF. On this day, July 5, every bomber and fighter group within NASAF was assigned a mission there.

NEW ASSIGNMENT

Unbeknownst to the pilots of the 14th Fighter Group, a brief but important reorganization of air forces was about to take place. It had long been agreed by Allied military planners that during the invasion of Sicily—Operation Husky—the North African Strategic Air Force (NASAF) would be temporarily assigned to the North African Tactical Air Force (NATAF).

In making this change, the planners were granting the authority to NATAF to develop specific tactical missions for execution by NASAF, including specific targets. On paper, NASAF would shift into a tactical mode. In reality, the missions that would be flown by NASAF during the invasion of Sicily differed significantly only for a four-day period, commencing with the invasion. With the invasion secured, the role of the 14th FG in particular shifted back to what might be considered more conventionally "strategic," although it is now seen that the operations of the 14th during this period would more properly be described as "interdiction."

During the month of May 1943, when the 14th first "restarted" operations, the missions flown were roughly one-third dive-bombing and strafing and two-thirds bomber escort. The same pattern of missions held true for the month of June.

In the ten days immediately preceding the invasion of Sicily, July 1 through 10, the mix of missions shifted appreciably. No dive-bombing missions were flown by the 49th squadron during this period; they were assigned exclusively to bomber-escort missions. And the converse was true during the four-day period after D-Day: The 49th flew only dive-bombing and strafing missions. Then from July 14 onward, the missions flown by the 49th reverted back to predominantly bomber escort.

THE MISSIONS

The 14th Fighter Group was assigned two escort missions on this day.

The first mission of the day was set for takeoff at 0915. Twenty-five P-38s would escort B-17s to the Gerbini complex, attacking specifically landing grounds #1, #4, and #5, located northwest of the main aerodrome. The 49th would contribute twelve aircraft and would be joined by thirteen P-38s from the 48th squadron.[6] The mission was expecting heavy resistance from the Luftwaffe units at Gerbini. Just the day before on a bombing mission to Gerbini, the 319th Bomb Group had been met with fifty German and Italian interceptors. In the ensuing battle, sixteen enemy fighters had been shot down, but two B-26s were lost, one of which was piloted by the group commander.

In an effort to keep the Axis forces off guard, NASAF dispatched two squadrons of P-40s from the 325th Fighter Group on early-morning missions against the German radar installations at Marsala and two more squadrons to the Wurzburg radar station at Licata.

Lieutenants Bitter and Homer returned to base twenty minutes after takeoff with an apparent aircraft issue. Lieutenant Grant also returned at

German Wurzburg radar site.
NATIONAL ARCHIVES

1030, also probably due to an aircraft issue. Spares, Lieutenants Foster and Knott, filled in for this mission, and were joined by Lieutenant Baker from the 48th squadron to complete the twelve-ship formation.

Lieutenant Knepper was again flying number-two position to Lieutenant Bland, with his good friend Herman Kocour flying close behind in the number-four position. Half of the pilots making up this formation were new replacement pilots, with just a handful of combat missions between them.

On this mission, the route took the combined fighter/bomber formation over Lampedusa and Malta before it turned north to the Sicilian coastline. An unusually circuitous course, this route may have been dictated by the other bombing missions that were attacking Gerbini on this date; there simply may have been too many bombers in the queue to permit a direct flight from the rendezvous point to the target.

As the formation overflew the German airfield at Chiaramonte, it became apparent that the missions' circuitous route, coupled with the additional maneuvering the P-38s were required to perform in order to remain with the lumbering B-17s, had led to a too-high fuel consumption for the fighter escorts. Just 40 miles south of their target, and with fourteen enemy aircraft in sight and preparing for an attack on the bomber formation, the escorting P-38s were forced to return to base.

The B-17s roared forward unescorted to the target at Gerbini and made their drop at 1125. In fact, the turnaround came too late for four of the P-38s. Lieutenants Bland, Knepper, Kocour, and Foster had to stop at the Allied base at El Djem to refuel, arriving back to their base at El Bathan at 1630. The turnaround over Chiaramonte was unavoidable—continuing on would have meant that all twenty-four of the escorting P-38s would have had to ditch in the Mediterranean on the way back to base. Still, it would be understandable if the pilots sharply regretted having to leave the bombers unprotected.

On this mission, Kocour earned his first air medal—five combat missions. The occasion probably went unnoticed by the young second lieutenant, and even if he had realized the milestone, he probably would have paid it little attention. With fifty combat missions needed to complete a combat tour, he had forty-five more to go before he could return home. Had he mentioned anything to the more experienced pilots, they would surely have hooted at him.

Close on the heels of the first attack, a formation of B-25 Mitchell medium bombers from the 321st Bomb Group, with P-38 escorts from the 82nd Fighter Group, was scheduled to attack landing ground #1 at Gerbini. But due to poor visibility and haze, #1 was overflown by one of the bomb squadrons, and bombs were dropped instead on the main Gerbini aerodrome.

The strange day continued for the 14th Fighter Group. In the second mission of the day, the 37th squadron escorted B-17s from the 2nd Bomb Group to attack Gerbini landing ground #6, 10 miles southeast of the main aerodrome. As the formation neared the target in a heavy haze, the P-38 escorts spotted a group of single-engine fighters approaching, seeming to parallel the bomber formation. The aircraft causing them such concern were in fact friendly Spitfires based at Malta that were also assigned as fighter escorts for the mission—a fact no one had mentioned during the 37th's preflight briefing.

The Intelligence officer for the 37th, Capt. John McCarthy, would later note: "Several Spitfires approached bombers near Sicily in menacing fashion and P-38s dropped tanks and were just about ready to shoot when they recognized planes as Spits. Pilots claim Spits made them very uneasy, as groups of several Spit planes would be off to one side, and impossible to tell whether or not they were enemy aircraft. At times some of the Spits flew altogether too close to the formation and were lucky they were not shot."[7]

Following standard practice, the P-38s had dropped their external fuel tanks in preparation for what they believed to be an imminent attack on the bomber formation by German Me 109s. Moments later they discovered that the single-engine aircraft were in fact friendlies. Too late, the P-38s had jettisoned their fuel supply, leaving them with scant fuel to continue as an effective escort for the mission. But the flyers' luck held: "All in all, the resistance offered by the enemy was quite weak, as the fighters were scarce and the slight to moderate flak was only fairly accurate."[8]

The mission continued, with the B-17s making their drop of 20-pound fragmentation bombs at 1435. The target was well covered, and fires were observed in the area for 40 miles. At the time the bombers made their drop, the 37th reported much smoke and several fires in the Gerbini satellite field areas—all remnants of bombing missions already completed by the Allies earlier in the day.

Other NASAF missions reported similarly light opposition by the Luftwaffe. The 1st Fighter Group, escorting B-26s on two separate missions to Gerbini, reported no enemy aircraft opposition on either mission.[9]

The Luftwaffe, with limited resources, were picking their fights carefully, and it was against one of these Gerbini missions that the Luftwaffe chose to make a stand. The 99th Bomb Group, flying B-17s and scheduled to make their drop just after the 49th's first mission of the day, was confronted by an estimated one hundred enemy aircraft which made "persistent aggressive and determined attacks from all angles, singly and in groups, in a furious attempt to break up the bomber formation."[10] Returning the fire with devastating effect, the 99th successfully penetrated the enemy defenses and covered the target area completely, destroying twenty aircraft on the ground, plus hangars, fuel supplies, and ammunition dumps.

During the running air battle with enemy fighters, the gunners on the B-17s shot down thirty-eight fighters, with eleven more probables. In total, the bombers alone accounted for the destruction of seventy Axis aircraft on this single mission and rendered the Gerbini airfield unusable. For this effort, the group was awarded a rare Unit Citation by the North African Air Force (NAAF).[11]

FROM THE GAF SIDE

Oberstlt. Steinhoff recorded the events of the day in his memoirs:[12] Starting this day at Trapani, on the northwestern tip of Sicily, he took off at first light with twenty or so Me 109s from JG 77 to fly the 135 miles to Gerbini, joining JG 53 as part of the GAF's efforts to shore up the eastern sector on the island. Temporarily combining assets from JG 53 and 77 would give Steinhoff a total force of some thirty-eight fighters. Shortly after his arrival at Gerbini, he was advised that the German airfield at Comiso, 50 miles to the south, had been attacked by NATAF's medium bombers. Refueling immediately, his wing was ordered to "cockpit readiness," awaiting the German direction finders' report on any new approaching Allied aircraft.

Shortly thereafter: "Odysseus One, Comiso bombed—pantechnicons flying north, very high.[13] Watch out for Spitfire escort." The planes Steinhoff refers to were probably the B-17s from the 99th Bomber Group, mentioned above. B-17s were fearsome engines of war; their bombardment could utterly destroy an aerodrome and everything on it, and their armaments made it nearly impossible to shoot them down. All aircraft from the GAF headquarters squadron and both fighter wings scrambled to engage the approaching Allied bombing mission. The German interceptors were spotted by the bomber escorts, and the Spitfires

Strike photograph taken June 13 during a bombing raid by B-24s of the 9th Air Force on the landing ground complex at Gerbini. Included here to illustrate the surroundings and bomb patterns, note the Axis aircraft in the lower right corner, taxiing into the fields to avoid bomb damage.

immediately attacked. A wild melee soon developed, with the Allied fighters giving more than they received.

On this mission, while attacking the escorting Spitfires, Steinhoff was shot down, crash-landing just south of Mount Etna.[14] But by 1400 he had been collected by his squadron and was back in the air, flying a small "Storch" recovery aircraft, headed back to the Gerbini complex. "We were probably about 30 miles from Gerbini. The plain with its fields of yellow stubble extended to the horizon. Conditions were hazy and the air shimmered in the heat."[15] His flying companion in the Storch shouted, "They're attacking Gerbini!" Steinhoff had run into the 2nd Bomb Group and its escorts of P-38s from the 37th squadron, and Spitfires from Malta. The bombers made their drop on Gerbini at 1435.

Strike photograph taken June 9 during a bombing raid by 9th Air Force B-24s on the landing ground complex at Gerbini, included here to illustrate the smoke patterns arising from damage to GAF planes on the ground.

NATIONAL ARCHIVES

The missions of this date were just the beginning—there was no lessening of the tremendous effort the North African Air Force expended against Axis airfields. On the next day, NASAF forces and bombers from the 9th Air Force hit Gerbini again, while NATAF bombers hit the airfields at Biscari, Sciacca, Trapani, and Comiso. NACAF continued sea patrols and convoy protection.

Four groups of B-17s, five groups of mediums of the North African Air Force, and five groups of B-24s of the 9th Air Force operated almost continuously—a seemingly endless stream of bombers and fighter escorts, largely unencumbered with Axis air force interceptors.

By D-Day, July 10, the main aerodrome at Gerbini had been rendered unserviceable, along with satellites 1, 4, 5, 6, 7, 8, and 12. Comiso and Bocca di Falco were also destroyed, and Castelvetrano was abandoned.

The effects of this Allied bombing blitz on the German air defenders were devastating. Col. T. Christ, chief of the German Air Staff, stated: "All the aerodromes, operational airfields, and landing grounds in Sicily were so destroyed in continuous attacks by massed forces that it was only possible to get this or that airfield in running order for a short time by mobilizing all available forces, including those of the German and Italian armies." The German and Italian antiaircraft batteries shot down many aircraft, but they were unable to halt the massive air attacks.[16]

In his memoir, German general Adolf Galland reports: "Our pilots were exhausted to a terrifying degree. From North Africa and Malta the American and British air fleets took us in a pincer movement and the grip became tighter every day. The Luftwaffe was burning up in the southern theater of the war."[17]

CHAPTER 12

Bombs at Their Fingertips

ARMY DOCTOR BRENDAN PHIBBS WAS ONCE AN EYEWITNESS TO AN Allied dive-bombing attack developed against opposing forces:

Air strikes on the way; we watch from a top window as (Allied fighter-bombers) dip in and out of clouds through suddenly erupting strings of Christmas-tree lights [flak], before one speck turns over and drops toward earth in the damnedest sight of the Second World War, the dive-bomber attack, the speck snarling, screaming, dropping faster than a stone until it's clearly doomed to smash into the earth, then, past the limits of belief, an impossible flattening beyond houses and trees, an upward arch that makes the eyes hurt, and, as the speck hurtles away, WHOOM, the earth erupts five hundred feet up in swirling black smoke. More specks snarl, dive, scream, two squadrons, eight of them, leaving congealing, combining, whirling pillars of black smoke, lifting trees, houses, vehicles, and, we devoutly hope, bits of Germans. We yell and pound each other's backs. Gods from the clouds; this is how you do it![1]

While dive-bombing could be effective and devastating, it was always a high-risk undertaking. When done right, the combined effect of effective piloting, a good aircraft, and the bomb itself created what would later be described two generations later as a "smart bomb"—a munition carefully guided to its impact point.

As with many tactical innovations in military aviation, dive-bombing has its roots in World War I, when a Royal Flying Corps pilot sank a munitions barge by dive-bombing on the Western Front in 1917. In the decade preceding World War II, the U.S. Navy made significant advances in the art and science of dive-bombing. In early practice, the aircraft was put into a vertical or near-vertical dive at an altitude of 15,000 to 20,000 feet and aimed directly at the target. Bomb release usually took place at about 3,000 feet, after which the aircraft made a high-g dive recovery to a level flight attitude. Dive-bombing was found to be especially suited for use against small, slow-moving targets such as tanks and ships, and is recognized as being one of the most accurate and destructive forms of air attack.[2]

In subsequent developments, nations who would later become Axis allies made substantial improvements in the methods and tactics of dive-bombing. Japan's invasion of China during the 1930s proved the value of the dive-bomber as a weapon, and this experience enabled Japan to enter World War II with superbly prepared dive-bombing squadrons. The Spanish Civil War was a testing ground for the Germans, Italians, and Russians, where the Junkers JU 87 (Stuka) proved its worth in Spain in action against ground targets and as an antiship weapon.

As the value of dive-bombing became apparent to aviators and tacticians, and as combat aircraft become more performant, the dive-bombing techniques and practices evolved, with attacks and bomb release sometimes coming from much lower altitudes. For groups flying the P-38, by 1943 the dive-bombing techniques had considerably evolved. On bombing missions to known targets, as opposed to targets of opportunity, the formation would approach the target at a low altitude, always much less than 100 feet, in order to avoid enemy radar detection and guarantee surprise. Prop wash on over-water approaches would leave rippling wakes on the surface of the sea.

Nearing the target, the flight leader would drop his external fuel tank, signaling the rest of the squadron to drop their tanks and begin moving from an echelon ("four-finger") formation to an in-line, trailing formation. Within one minute the formation would climb to 5,000 feet, pilots scanning for bogeys and double-checking that their bomb release was armed. With the target in view, the flight leader would bank over to start his dive, the remaining aircraft following at suitable intervals. The aircraft would then dive toward the target, reaching speeds approaching 400 mph, and in many cases, pilots would also fire all guns in their approach. The bomb would be released at 300 feet, and the pilot would pull out of the dive to either return to base or begin a strafing run.

It was standard practice in the 49th Fighter Squadron for the attacking formation to leave the target area immediately; there was no going back around for a strafing run, no turnaround to see how well the target had been covered.

Most of the 49th's dive-bombing assignments had come in the roughly two-week period between May 24 and June 11, with Pantelleria the most frequent target and the 1,000-pound general purpose bomb the most common munition.

Date	Dive-Bombing Target
24 May	Railroad bridge at Arbatax (500-lb. bomb)
25 May	Seaplane base, factory, and docks at Alghero, Sardinia (500-lb. bomb)
25 May	Docks at Portovesme (1,000-lb. bomb)
25 May	Hangars and admin buildings at Milo (500 lbs.)
26 May	Ships and RR yards at Golfo Aranci (1,000 lbs.)
30 May	RR and power station at Chilivani (1,000 lbs.)
31 May	Gun positions at Pantelleria (1,000 lbs.)
2 June	Gun positions at Pantelleria (1,000 lbs.)
5 June	Gun positions at Pantelleria (1,000 lbs.)
6 June	Gun positions at Pantelleria (1,000 lbs.)
7 June	Gun positions at Pantelleria (1,000 lbs.)
8 June	Gun positions at Pantelleria (1,000 lbs.)
9 June	Gun positions at Pantelleria (1,000 lbs.)
10 June	Gun positions at Pantelleria (500 or 1,000 lbs.)
10 June	Gun positions at Pantelleria (1,000 lbs.)

Bombing and strafing were used effectively on a wide range of targets, including transportation and supply, ammo, bomb and fuel dumps, warehouses, communications, power plants, and other facilities that helped move men and materiel to combat units. On "target of opportunity" sweeps, little was off limits; vehicles, armor, half-tracks, staff cars, motorcycles, troop concentrations, and railroads were favored targets.

AAF planners gave the highest priority to railroads and rail center targets, which appear repeatedly in target lists. In the target list prepared for the bombing campaign in Sicily in advance of the Allied landings, the railroad junction at Fiumetorto, Sicily, was ranked first, even ahead of major port facilities and aerodromes.[3]

Why the importance of targeting railroads? In literature citing history's "greatest weapons of war," among such arms as crossbows, machine guns, and atomic bombs, is also found "railroads." Every major country involved in World War II had extensive rail systems supporting the war. In North Africa, the German Air Force targeted Allied military trains as a priority. On Sicily, with a relatively crude road system, railways were crucial to the movement of troops and supplies to defensive positions.

Both Axis and Allied armies recognized the importance and vulnerability of rail systems, and trains were often heavily defended. Antiaircraft

Train-mounted antiaircraft flak units.

SA-IMAGE

batteries were installed at all important rail junctions, and individual trains were equipped with the most advanced antiaircraft equipment available, some housed in carefully concealed "bait" cars. Some of the roughest air gun-fighting of the war would be between airplanes and trains.[4]

Pilot Harold Harper of the 49th recalled: "The strafing shown in the missions in Europe is not like what we were doing in our time in the 49th. We were mainly after airdromes, trucks, tanks, and airplanes. I remember dive-bombing a train station in Sardinia after the bombers we escorted over the stations didn't hit the target. Four of our planes were sent over to dive-bomb, and I was one of the four. I always fired my machine guns during the dive if no other plane was ahead of me in the dive."[5]

FLYING THE AIRCRAFT IN DIVE-BOMBING MISSIONS

Dive-bombing required highly advanced flying skills. The attack may have taken a minute or less, but many things happened during that brief interval. The aircraft itself was in a high-speed, near-vertical dive, the target may have been in motion, and many forces were acting on the bomb after its release, including its momentum and the effects of air resistance, wind, and gravity. Flying the airplane smoothly in a dive, while making proper allowances and corrections to the aircraft's position, was the key to effective dive-bombing.[6]

By 1943, experience had shown that the best approach was what came to be referred to as a "normal" dive-bomb attack, with a dive angle of 65 degrees. The army-issued pilot training manual for the P-38 included an important admonition: no negative accelerations above 3.5 g's.[7] But there is little doubt that pilots routinely exceeded these limits on dive-bombing missions. Pilot Jim Graham of the 1st Fighter Group reports sometimes "going gray" during a pullout from a dive-bombing or strafing run[8]—a progressive loss of vision that may start with a loss of peripheral vision, followed by a smaller vision field, and then an overall dimming of vision. In extreme cases, pilots could black out from the negative g's, with results that could be catastrophic.

Careful piloting did not end with the bomb drop. Following too close behind a fellow pilot who had just released his bomb could be deadly. Nathaniel G. Raley, a pilot in the 48th Fighter Squadron, recalls: "You don't want to get too close to the plane that's ahead of you in case there's a secondary explosion. In other words, if they hit an ammo dump or something like this, everything is going to go up, and you don't want to be caught with that. And also, you don't want to be caught with just the blast of his bomb. And so you'd come down. And then as soon as [you'd] done your dirty work, there was a strong urge to get out of there."[9]

On one dive-bombing mission to a German airfield, Harold Harper had just dropped his bomb when he was hit by a terrific explosion. His aircraft was flipped onto its back, at 400 mph and just 100 feet elevation. He flipped it back, not knowing if the concussion was from the bomb dropped by the pilot in front of him, or if it was his own bomb... "When I got back to base they said, 'Hey, Lieutenant, you got a hole in your horizontal stabilizer.' And the hole was eighteen inches across. So a bomb fragment got me—I got too low."[10]

Damage to Lieutenant Harper's horizontal stabilizer caused by ground explosion during low level strafing mission.

LT. COL. HAROLD HARPER (RET.)

And even after he released his munition, the pilot had to continue to be aware of the bomb's position. Charles Everard Dills, flying with the 27th Fighter-Bomber Group, recounts a dive-bombing mission to an Axis-held port. "We went straight down on a ship at a dock. I wanted to do a good job, so I probably stayed in the dive a little longer than I should have. After I dropped my bombs, I looked out and got ready to pull out of the dive, and there was a 500-pound bomb sitting there, right in my way. I can still see the lettering on the bomb, '536 pounds GP' [General Purpose]. I had to continue straight down until it passed me before I dared pull out!"[11]

Properly executed, dive-bombing attacks could be done with astonishing precision. The photo below shows the results of a March 1945 raid by aircraft of the 14th Fighter Group on the Radovljica railroad bridge in Yugoslavia—a target that was probably less than 10 yards wide.

Dive-bombing results on the Radovljica railroad bridge by P-38s of the 14th Fighter Group, April 5, 1945.

NATIONAL ARCHIVES

The P-38 proved itself well suited for dive-bombing missions. Despite the fact that the army had developed and deployed specialized dive-bombing aircraft, notably the A-20 Havoc and the A-36 Apache, P-38s flew far more combat sorties and dropped more tonnage of bombs than either. And, reflecting the relationship between exposure and risk, four times more P-38s were lost in combat than A-20s and A-36s combined.[12]

While the dive-bombing pilots were part of a well-coordinated team, the attack itself was a solitary enterprise. Pilot Frederic Arnold recounts:

I had smelled the gunpowder that seeped into the cockpit, but I had never heard my guns fire. On dive-bombing runs, I saw the explosions made by the bombs dropped ahead of me, I saw the faint shock wave that preceded the explosions, but I'd never heard the sound. The mushrooming black-and-white clouds rising from the target, the flak bursting off my wingtip, tracers from my guns pouring into enemy aircraft, incendiaries and cannon shells finding their marks—all were silent pictures to me.[13]

Flying the Aircraft in Strafing Missions

There are compelling arguments that low-level ground attacks were the most dangerous and difficult-to-perform missions flown by fighter pilots, and in many instances, extremely effective. As in dive-bombing, strong piloting skills were required in air-to-ground strafing attacks. "Fly the airplane right" is the first requirement in successful air-to-ground combat.[14]

Air-to-ground gunnery instruction was part of each pilot's training in either their Advanced pilot training program or during Transition training. In this instruction, the training involved preset patterns and approaches, with windsocks, smoke pots, and other ground aids. But in contrast to dive-bombing, there is no "normal" in air-to-ground combat.

After arriving in the combat theater, the pilots learned additional tactical methods, including varying approaches and dive angles. And significantly, experienced combat pilots mentored new replacement pilots on the value of maneuvers that had been forbidden in gunner school.

A P-38 in low-level gunnery practice.

Replacement pilots learned that every mission brought new conditions that had to be considered in determining how the attack would be made:

- Winds near ground level were always challenging. Operating in crosswinds required the pilots to bank or crab into the wind to maintain targeting.
- Headwinds flattened the dive, and tailwinds could increase the steepness of the dive.
- Clouds, topography, and even trees could provide limited cover for an attacking aircraft and delay detection by ground forces, but they could also make the strafing run more difficult.
- Many aircraft returned with damage resulting from hitting man-made structures or natural features during a run. Buildings,

bridges, radio towers, cables, and barrage balloons all had to be flown around, possibly delaying target identification.

In later years, air-to-ground combat was sensationalized in media and film. In many films, aircraft were depicted as descending slowly and menacingly, their engines loud and high-pitched, with little surprise involved. Bullets hit the ground short of the target and "walked" toward the target in uniform parallel lines, as wide as a roadbed. Those images bear little relation to the reality of ground attack. As practiced by the 14th FG, pilots controlled their aircraft so that fire was delivered with high accuracy, at a designated target—"pinpoint fire," not "walking fire." And this accuracy was made possible by correctly flying the aircraft to bring guns to bear on targets. Accurate fire was not attributable to the guns, but rather to good piloting.

Strafing passes were made at a relatively steep angle, since foxholes and dug-in equipment could be hard to reach with flat passes. Mid-pass maneuvering to bring the aircraft to bear on a target, or to change to a different target, was rarely desirable, and when undertaken, "resulted in some of the most violent, max-performance of all fighter flying in order to get the plane's guns in position to hit the enemy."[15] Against trains and other moving targets, passes were not made by set dive angle, speed, or direction. When a target was seen, "you went from where you were and put your guns on it."[16] Getting there quickly, before the enemy could take cover, before operators and passengers could get out and escape, was the primary tactic, rather than taking time to fly a particular type of pass. As "Pappy" Boyington, commander of the famed "Black Sheep Squadron," noted: "High-speed runs are essential. Speed will reduce the number of rounds which can be delivered and will diminish the opportunity for observation, but it must be maintained."[17]

The P-38 was equipped with one 20mm cannon with 150 rounds, and four .50-inch machine guns with 500 rounds per gun, all mounted in the nose of the aircraft. Armorers included tracer rounds with armor-piercing incendiary rounds (API) in the machine-gun magazines, which provided valuable information to the pilots during an attack. The visible trajectory of the red tracers confirmed whether or not the pilot was on target, and could indicate if one or more machine guns were becoming worn or burned out. The loading of tracers was variable; some squadrons preferred a one-to-five mix of tracer to API; Harold Harper of the 49th Fighter Squadron recalls that the ammunition loading was one tracer, two high-explosive shells, and one incendiary.

Lt. Ward Kuentzel with armorer Cpl. Howard Schaffner, 82nd Fighter Group, based at Souk el Arba, Algeria.

NATIONAL ARCHIVES

In air-to-ground gunnery, a P-38 could complete a strafing run in just over five seconds. Short bursts of one or two seconds were quite normal. Longer bursts could overheat and burn out a gun barrel. In a five-second pass, the pilot would have time for just two bursts, at most. The P-38's single 20mm cannon fired at 650 rounds per minute (11 rounds per second). In a combined five seconds of firing, the pilot would deliver 55 rounds of cannon fire—about one-third of his magazine. The P-38's .50 caliber machine guns fired at 850 rounds per minute (14 rounds per second). With all four guns firing for a combined five seconds, the pilot would deliver 280 rounds of machine-gun fire—about half of his magazines.

While the time-of-fire is brief, the concentration of guns in the nose of the P-38 was devastating. They were all fired in unison, and the pattern of the .50 caliber guns and 20mm cannon on impact was about 1 yard wide. This clustering resulted in enormous impact energy and destructive power, and was particularly effective against relatively hard targets, such as port facilities, radar stations, locomotives, and railcars. Just a few shots were needed to destroy a target—what veteran Army Air Corps pilot William Colgan refers to as a "touch" of fire.

The 5th Wing, for whom the 14th FG flew, had very specific instructions regarding ground attack:

> Ground attacks should be made from minimum altitude using all cover available. Attacks on roads and columns are never made at an angle of less than 45 degrees. In string or in line abreast, the "front" will cross the column at a minimum of exposure to themselves and yet cover the whole target. If attacking in a front, the ships at line abreast cover the whole target. If attacking in string, each man takes an area adjacent to that which has been attacked by the ship before him. The air force will be the loser to the ground force being attacked if the element of surprise is eliminated, as they are exposed for too long a time. Crossing a column at right angles or near-right angles lessens the period of exposure, and yet the target can be completely covered.[18]

Beyond this general direction, each group and even individual squadrons in the MTO developed unique tactics, approaches, and variations that had shown good results in prior missions, but always with three points of general agreement: First, accomplish the mission while holding losses as low as possible. Second, undertake the mission with extreme aggressiveness. As Colgan records: "Timid war fighting will get you killed." P-38 pilot Curry, when asked by his crew chief why he never came home with any ammo, replied, "When they are shooting at you, you just want to shoot back." He also quipped that "'temper' made up for 'bravery,'" confessing that he had plenty of temper.[19] And third, that inclement weather may cause a mission to be aborted, but that enemy opposition never would.

In general, the 14th Fighter Group flew two types of missions that included air-to-ground attacks: In the first type, against preselected known targets, missions were ordered, preplanned, and pre-briefed carefully. Munitions were carefully selected for the specific target, approaches were discussed and set, and tactics were well explained. In the second type—fighter sweeps, armed reconnaissance, or on missions tasked with attacking "targets of opportunity"—detailed briefings may not have included the same level of intelligence information. For this reason, flight leaders were required to exercise some flexibility in judgment and tactics in order to inflict the maximum damage to the enemy without taking undue risks.

The USAF-produced documentary, *Thunderbolt*, posited that "every man is his own general," meaning that squadron leaders and individual pilots had to make quick decisions in light of ground and air conditions. "Generalship" related to the ability of a pilot to change attack geometries and techniques based on his specific situation; to make a nearly instant assessment of what was on the ground and in the air and to judge just how far the squadron could press in and still safely pull out. The pilot might determine that the particular situation in front of him would prevent an optimum approach and that he might have to begin firing his guns farther away from the target than desired, achieving the most effective fire possible for the situation.

A good example of a combined dive-bombing/strafing mission was flown by the P-38s of the 49th squadron on May 24, 1943—a busy day for the 14th Fighter Group, putting up five separate missions to targets on the island of Sardinia.[20] Lt. William J. Gregory—"Greg" to all—was included in the fighter sweep and dive-bombing mission by the 49th

P-38 in a strafing attack.

squadron to the rail yards and harbor at Alghero on the island of Sardinia. This was the first dive-bombing mission for the squadron since its restart in early May and would bring the aircraft right to the deck over what was expected to be a well-defended target. On May 15, in preparation for the mission, some of the squadron pilots had done dive-bombing practice near base. The squadron was on edge about the mission; it had been scheduled and then postponed a couple of times previously, and the men were eager to get on with it.

An eight-aircraft mission, the formation took off from Telergma just after noon and flew right on the deck to northwestern Sardinia. Reaching the target area at 1400, the formation "zoomed up" to 5,000 feet, moved into a trail formation, and started their dive to the target. Releasing relatively high—from 2,000 feet—the formation made a strafing pass over the harbor as it returned to base.

Gregory recounts: "[W]e had been briefed that there was a harbor there, and that if we came out of our dive in good position, we could make a strafing run on appropriate targets."[21] Greg made his dive, and found himself lined up on a floatplane. He gave it a long burst, and it went up in flames. He then saw that he was lined up on a second floatplane, and he gave it a burst. As he flew over it, he saw that it had also gone up in smoke and flames. He said the mission was surprising because there was no flak. He thought this odd, since it was an important rail yard in Sardinia, and it had a floatplane base next to it. The dive-bombing was successful, and a total of four of the twelve seaplanes located at the harbor were destroyed. The seaplanes destroyed appeared to be the very large three-engine Savoia-Marchetti S.66s.

On missions involving armed reconnaissance, or "targets of opportunity," the flight leader would often adjust altitude during mission. Some terrain permitted reconnaissance from 5,000 feet. Other terrain, such as areas that were heavily treed, would need to be seen from a lower altitude. Rarely were these types of missions flown above 5,000 feet, and this altitude put the formation well within the reach of German automatic ground fire.

CHAPTER 13

Approaching Air Rule

FOLLOWING THE GERBINI RAID ON JULY 5, AND FOR THE NEXT FEW days, the pilots of the 14th Fighter Group witnessed firsthand the result of the overwhelming air domination achieved by the Allies in the Mediterranean Theater. With German aerodromes continuing to be almost daily targets for NASAF medium and heavy bomber attacks, the 14th's three squadrons were up often to provide bomber-escort protection. But these missions differed from many previous raids on German airfields in one important respect: Few enemy fighters were seen, and fewer still engaged. And on some missions, they were missing entirely.

Beginning on July 6, a huge formation of forty-four P-38s consisting of aircraft from all three of the 14th Fighter Group squadrons escorted 36 B-17s back to the Gerbini satellite fields. The 88mm flak was intense, but inaccurate. The 49th squadron, leading the combined formation, and including Lieutenant Kocour, saw just ten enemy aircraft, and they did not engage the bomber formation.

On July 8, another formation of forty-eight P-38s from all squadrons of the 14th escorted 48 B-25s of the 321st Bomb Group to the #6 landing field at Gerbini. Lieutenant Kocour was also assigned to this mission, which saw extensive flak from the time the squadron crossed the Sicilian coastline at Licata until the target was reached and the opposite coast was left behind. But no enemy aircraft.

Returning from the mission, B-25s from the 445th Bomb Squadron took a wrong turn and almost overflew Malta. That navigation error allowed pilot Col. Bailey Cook, to glimpse a portion of the invasion fleet that had been assembling near Tunisia:

We could see the largest collection of boats of all sizes I have ever imagined! Its size is almost unbelievable. . . . Boats line up and scattered around for as far as the eye could see. Just before we got to the Tunisian coast we passed right between two more convoys—big ones—in fact I don't think I've ever seen a herd of cows with as many cows in it as that convoy had boats! [1]

In an early-morning mission on July 9, the 49th sent up twenty-four P-38s to escort twenty-six B-17s from the 2nd Bomb Group and an equal number from the 301st to the airfield at Biscari. Over the target, the air cover over this large bomber formation was supplemented by a contingent of thirty-six Malta-based Spitfires. Kocour and Knepper were both assigned to the mission, but Knepper's aircraft apparently failed to start, and Kocour's developed a mechanical problem, forcing an early return. On this mission, the 49th's mission history reports: "Not a single E/A [enemy aircraft] was seen. The most unusual observation on this mission was the complete absence of flak, both from the target area and other adjacent areas from the shore inland." This was a sign that not only had the GAF abandoned the field, but that they no longer considered it worthy of a defense.

A bombing mission begun shortly after this early mission involved B-17s attacking the airfield at Sciacca, under the watchful escort of the 37th and 48th squadrons. On this mission, German aircraft made an attempt at interception, and one was shot down. On a late-afternoon mission that same day, July 9, the 48th and 49th squadrons teamed up to escort B-25s to attack military barracks at Caltanissetta. The 40th's mission history reports: "Not a single enemy aircraft was seen." NASAF fighter pilots might well have considered the game fairly won, at least with respect to the enemy fighter opposition. The air plan that had been laid out by Army Air Forces HQ, in combination with an overwhelming numerical advantage, had worked.

On May 13, 1943, the very day that the last German surrendered in Tunisia, the Allied headquarters moved immediately into the final preparations for Operation Husky. By late May, a companion air plan had been finalized that dealt with the general policies to be followed in the application of airpower and with the specific missions of the various components of the NAAF. Issued as "NAAF Air Planning Memorandum No. 2," and entitled "Procedures for Detailed Planning and Action Necessary to Mount Operation Husky," the plan identified nine principal goals for the air forces, the first of which was "the destruction or neutralization of the enemy air forces within range of the operation"—i.e., maintain and expand air superiority.

The air plan identified four phases of operation for the Sicilian Campaign, with Phase I consisting of preparatory operations—"softening up." During the period from mid-May to July 3, targets would be "the main German airdromes in Sicily, Sardinia, and southern Italy, together with submarine bases, communications lines, and industrial plants. Apart from the airdromes, the more important targets would be Naples, Messina, and Palermo."[2] In the latter part of the preliminary phase, from July 3 through 9, "Allied air forces were to step up their offensive against the enemy air force with the objective of rendering it impotent to offer serious opposition to the projected landings. German, rather than Italian-occupied, landing dromes were to be given primary attention."

The North African Air Force, including all Strategic, Tactical, and Coastal Air Force assets, would carry the lion's share of the responsibility for supporting air operations. It would provide close air support for the assault forces, launch the paratroop attacks, degrade enemy air forces within range of the invasion area, interdict Axis reinforcements behind the front lines, protect naval operations and the assault convoys, attack naval forces, and protect captured areas in Sicily against air attack.

In the months since the first landings in North Africa, and most particularly in the few weeks since the Germans had been forced from Tunisia, the Allied forces had assembled a tremendous air capability. As the combined invasion convoys steamed toward Sicily on the night of July 9–10, the Allied air forces numbered approximately 4,900 operational aircraft of all types, divided among 146 American and some 113 British squadrons. American air assets made up most of the bomber and air-transport aircraft, and about one-third of the fighter contingent. The

RAF provided the majority of the single- and twin-engine fighters and coastal aircraft, and the entire night bomber force.[3]

The missions flown by NASAF in the final days leading up to Husky well reflect the targets identified by the air plan, and the paucity of enemy opposition attests to the effectiveness with which the plan had been carried out. NAAF gave instructions that all groups and squadrons were to be brought up to and maintained at full strength, that all equipment be overhauled and made serviceable, that new groups and squadrons were to be fully trained, and that sufficient stocks of bombs, small-arms ammunition, gasoline, etc., were to be established in the vicinity of the operations bases to cover the period from D minus 7 (July 3) to D plus 14 (July 24).

One squadron clerk noted in his July 2 mission report: "The planes have been getting special attention the past two days. The guns on all the planes have been tested. Everyone has the feeling that they will get quite a workout very soon."[4]

Importantly, the army realized that the disembarkation of ground troops on D-Day could not be accomplished rapidly enough to ensure the security of the beachhead. In order to isolate the battlefield for the invading forces, it would be necessary to interdict the enemy's movements from the interior toward the assault area. Because of the island's terrain, enemy movements would be by road, largely from the Axis concentration area around Gela. That interdiction was in the eyes of North African Air Force (NAAF) planners, best accomplished by NASAF fighter-bombers. Accordingly, two groups of P-38s from NASAF—the 1st and the 14th—were transferred to reinforce two groups of A-36 light bombers of NATAF. The three P-38 groups were assigned to the eastern region of Sicily, and the A-36 groups were tasked with the western and central areas. Both were to launch combat missions every 30 minutes throughout the day beginning at first light, and were ordered to attack all enemy troop movements.

This heightened air activity did little to confirm to the Axis leadership that Sicily was next. By the end of June 1943, there was little consensus among German military authorities as to the most likely site of the next Allied attack. Greece was the option most favored by Hitler. And the Allies appeared to be showing interest in a landing at Sardinia. In a famous Allied deception—"Operation Mincemeat"—faked invasion documents were attached to a British corpse which was "discovered" after being intentionally placed ashore on a Spanish coast. This subterfuge led Hitler to order the diversion of German reinforcements to Sardinia and Corsica.

But the only target that made any sense given the preceding efforts in North Africa was Sicily. As Churchill allegedly remarked: "Anyone but a bloody fool would know it was Sicily."

THE OPERATION HUSKY PLAN

Decided at the Casablanca conference late in January 1943 by President Roosevelt, Prime Minister Churchill, and the Combined Chiefs of Staff (CCS), the invasion of Sicily was designed to "intensify pressure on Italy, divert German forces from the Eastern Front, and cement the Allied hold on the Mediterranean." General Eisenhower was designated supreme commander, and General Alexander, his deputy, was placed in command of ground operations.[5]

The final plan for the invasion of Sicily—Operation Husky—had been approved by the CCS in mid-May 1943 and was to be a combined land, sea, and air operation concentrating British and American troops on the southern and southeastern coastline. The plan called for eight simultaneous seaborne assaults to be made along approximately 100 miles of coastline. The British Eighth Army under the command of General Montgomery was to land on the southeastern coast. The American troops were divided into three assault forces, with landings planned for the Bay of Gela.[6]

Nearly a half-million American, British, and Canadian ground troops would be used in the offensive, and nobody expected an easy victory. Sicily, a mountainous, rugged country, offered every advantage to the defender, thought to number about 350,000 troops easily reinforced from Italy across the narrow Strait of Messina. The Allied invasion of Sicily was to be the greatest amphibious operation yet attempted, and was to remain the greatest in World War II in terms of initial assault. There were to be more than 3,200 vessels in the vast armada, of which 1,700 were required to carry American men and cargo. In the first week alone, the United States would need to land over 132,000 men, 25,000 vehicles, and over 500 tanks.[7]

Allied air planners adopted a very conservative approach, insisting that no question remain of air superiority on D-Day. "During the assault period the primary aim of the air forces was to insure that the enemy did not interfere with ground or naval operations from the air. Until mastery of the air was achieved, the bomber effort was to be concentrated for the achievement of this end."[8] Arguably, "mastery of the air" had been well secured by D-Day, and bomber forces could have been released from missions targeting the GAF, instead focusing on interdiction missions targeting Axis ground forces in the vicinity of the invasion beaches. In fact, NAAF had been so successful in neutralizing air opposition prior to the commencement of the land battle that after D-Day, the scale of attacks on airfields was reduced to just 21 percent of the total bomber effort.

The bomber forces were not especially nimble and could not be easily re-tasked. A twelve-hour notification was required before attacks by medium and heavy bombers could be executed. Nonetheless, anticipating that air mastery would be soon secured, the air plan had included a list of known pivotal defense positions and other easily definable targets in the assault areas, in case the bombers could be released to conduct missions in the immediate vicinity of the land operations. Each target was assigned a code number, and target maps were prepared and distributed by NAAF.

The air plan also anticipated that the light-bomber force within the North African Tactical Air Force (NATAF) would be called upon for close air support missions during the invasion. Specifically, "light bombers were to furnish close cooperation with the land forces . . . when enemy air had ceased to be a factor in the operations, enemy ground forces were to be attacked by offensive sweeps."[9]

The German and Italian air forces opposing them were estimated to have between 1,500 and 1,600 aircraft based in Sicily, Sardinia, Italy, and southern France. Eliminating noncombat aircraft and assuming that the serviceability of Axis aircraft was not above 50 percent, Allied air forces outnumbered their Axis adversaries by at least four to one.

Enemy airfields were the primary targets for both the Tactical and Strategic Air Forces during the run-up to Husky. The raids of June 30 against Palermo, Sciacca, Bo Rizzo, and Trapani had devastated the airfields, causing GAF and Italian aircraft to relocate to more easterly airfields and the remaining bomber forces to leave Sicily altogether for safer bases in Italy.

During the first week of July, the shorter-range aircraft of NATAF targeted the western and central portion of the island, with NASAF's longer-range aircraft targeting the east, most particularly the airfields at Gerbini and Catania. The Sciacca landing grounds—located close to the planned landing beaches—were attacked nine times from July 3 through 9. Milo/Trapani was hit four times, and additional missions were flown against Bo Rizzo and Castelvetrano on Sicily, and Villacidro and Pabillonis on Sardinia.

The bombing blitz by NAAF yielded precisely the intended effect: Many of the Sicilian aerodromes were rendered unserviceable. Gerbini's main aerodrome, and seven of its satellite landing grounds, were reported as unusable, as were the large aerodromes at Comiso and Bocca di Falco. Castelvetrano appeared to have been abandoned by D-Day.

The intense bombing campaign also caused the Luftwaffe to defend its bases, with a resulting spike in the number of enemy aircraft destroyed in air combat. In the week before the invasion, 139 enemy fighters were destroyed in the air. Combined with the heavy losses of aircraft that were caught on the ground, the destruction of German aircraft dealt the Luftwaffe a blow from which it never fully recovered, and which was to have great significance to Germany's defensive capabilities later in the war.

By D-Day, July 10, 1943, the Allied air forces had clearly achieved air superiority over Sicily, perhaps attaining air supremacy.

AIR RECONNAISSANCE OF THE BATTLE AREA

Leading up to D-Day, Allied planners were well supported by aerial intelligence gathered by the Northwest African Photo Reconnaissance Wing. NWAPR units, flying camera-equipped P-38 aircraft, flew 130 pre-D-Day missions, starting in late March. Almost 200,000 aerial photographs were obtained, with 100 percent coverage of the island of Sicily. By D-Day, 1,400 photo mosaics had been produced. As the invasion neared, army ground force planners required more detailed images of landing beaches, cities, airfields, drop zones, and objectives for the airborne troops. A detailed 1:5,000 relief model of the beaches was prepared.[10]

Some areas of Sicily were overflown and photographed at ten-day intervals, others, at five-day intervals. Enemy airfields and naval forces received careful attention in the period leading up to D-Day: The twenty-six major Axis airfields were photographed twice daily, as were the Sicilian ports and the Strait of Messina—the likely points where Axis reinforcements would enter Sicily.

As D-Day approached, photo intelligence provided details on troop dispositions and strength, locations of artillery, and secondary defensive positions. By D-Day, the Allied planners were completely informed of the disposition of enemy troops, and the likely routes that would be used to reinforce Axis defensive positions along the invasion beaches. Intelligence analysts were able to estimate how quickly German units could reinforce the beaches, based on their transport capabilities and the available roads.

The disposition of Axis forces immediately prior to D-Day is shown in the following map. The intense bombing campaign had convinced the Italian commander of forces on Sicily that it would be the invasion site, and he guessed correctly that the invasion would come ashore on the

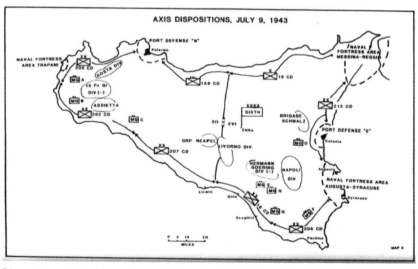

Disposition of Axis forces immediately prior to Allied invasion, July 9, 1943.
NATIONAL ARCHIVES

southern beaches. The Italian Livorno and Napoli divisions were positioned on either flank of Germany's Hermann Göring Division, which had moved into position from southern Italy just three weeks earlier. The intense counterattacks that developed against American troops on D-Day came from the well-equipped and battle-tested Livorno and Göring divisions. The Napoli division was directed against the British landing farther to the east.[11]

Aerial reconnaissance—both photographic and visual—on D-Day was also carefully planned. The 111th Tactical Reconnaissance Squadron flew twenty-seven missions on D-Day, providing dawn-to-dusk coverage for the most critical day of the operation. Particular emphasis was placed on the road networks leading from the inland regions to the beachhead, and on roads and junctions between major towns. Landing beaches and the areas immediately proximal were photographed. Upland regions—the locations of German reinforcements—and coastal roads were covered repeatedly.

German and Italian forces that would likely reinforce their coastal defenses on D-Day were known to be based in the Enna-Caltanissetta region, and it was well known that the reinforcing forces would have to use two main roads leading to the invasion beaches: the southern roads from Canicatti and Piazza Armerina. It was also known that reinforcing and/or retreating forces were likely to use the Vizzini-Caltagirone road, and the road leading to the invasion beaches from Ragusa.

Communications among the various army units, photo reconnaissance units, and NASAF and NATAF command centers were occasionally difficult. Following the actual landings, requests for new overflights could be processed within two hours, and for urgent taskings, the attacking air units could be airborne within three hours of the request. But processing and disseminating the results of these urgent overflights reduced the overall value of tactical recon missions on the day of the invasion. Rather more success was had by AAF tactical units in conducting pre-planned assaults on targets that had been identified during the planning phase of Operation Husky.

As H-Hour approached, Allied commands were at least adequately informed of the precise location and strengths of all opposing forces.

Interdiction missions had been preplanned, and the combined British-American air forces were poised for the attack.

D-DAY ON SICILY

On the bright, sunny afternoon of July 8, the ships and landing craft of the Allied landing forces swarmed out of the harbor and into the dark blue of the Mediterranean, headed for the Tunisian Channel and the Sicilian coastline. To war correspondent Ernie Pyle, aboard an Allied ship, the armada standing on the horizon was a sight he would never forget. It "resembled a distant city. It covered half the skyline, and the dull-colored camouflage ships stood indistinctly against the curve of the dark water, like a solid formation of uncountable structures blending together. Even to be part of it was frightening."[12] Described by AAF reconnaissance pilots, the sea was "black with ships," including more than three thousand cruisers, destroyers, cargo vessels, landing barges for tanks and infantry, and huge passenger ships that in peacetime had been luxury liners.

The *Lewiston Morning Tribune*, Allan Knepper's hometown newspaper, included a report on July 12 that described the scene. As reported by reconnaissance pilot Lt. Col. Frank L. Dunn, "the whole thing spread

Visualization of the invasion armada during Operation Husky.
NATIONAL ARCHIVES

out before me as I came in yesterday afternoon about six miles up in the air. Our ships were the greatest collection of naval strength I have ever seen. And there seemed to be thousands of landing craft with the noses firmly planted on the beach. . . . There was considerable smoke on the southern coast and the roads leading to it. Warships were firing at the shore . . . Looking over the entire island I must have seen hundreds of fires with one chain stretching from east to west, right across the middle. They appeared to be airports, but it was impossible to tell definitely."[13]

2nd Lt. Marion Legendre was also on scene: "There were many medium-size ships in the first group and behind them large landing craft. Destroyers and cruisers were grouped all around on the outside for protection. It was an amazing sight—just like a cluster of islands in the sea."[14]

Even the troopship USS *Chateau Thierry* was on hand—the vessel that had recently brought pilots Kocour, Knepper, and hundreds of other air force officers and enlisted replacements to North Africa. Stationed just outside the main assault armada, it began landing troops late in the day and into the night. She remained off Sicily for two days, firing to aid in turning back German air attacks and taking on board Italian and German captives for transport to POW camps already waiting in North Africa.

The invasion began in the early hours of July 10, 1943. As recorded by the Mission Diary of the 49th Fighter Squadron:[15]

The invasion of Sicily began at 0800 hrs. on this date. The event was very much looked forward to by all of us, and the time was most opportune, as the moon and weather were very favorable. The American troops made landings from Licata to Religione Pointe. U.S. airborne troops were dropped behind Licata, some by gliders, others by parachute, their mission to consolidate the port, cut communications, and occupy adjoining territory. Other units were landed along the beaches to the eastward and are advancing in a north and easterly direction, to make contact with British forces landing on the eastern side of the island, which will move inland and northward. British forces [Canadian] will make their landing from Religione Pointe, around the S.E. tip of the Island, to Cape San Panagia north of Syracuse. British airborne troops will be landed back of

Syracuse, their mission to occupy the port, cut communications, and occupy adjacent territory.

All of our fighters and bomber strength was sent as support. And as soon as the progress of the ground forces permits, airfields shall be used by the Air Forces.

Apart from targets in the immediate vicinity of the landings, the great majority of AAF targets on D-Day were contained within a corridor extending 50 miles by 70 miles within the eastern part of Sicily. It was within this corridor that German defensive units were already positioned, and where reinforcements would transit on their way to the battle line. And it was to this sector that most of the missions for the 14th Fighter Group would be flown, with particular emphasis on "targets of opportunity"—that is, truck convoys, troop columns, tanks, artillery pieces, antiaircraft guns, trucks, and staff cars.

All fighter groups and squadrons within NASAF were flying on this day. NASAF Bomb Groups were assigned a range of interdiction missions: The B-17 "heavies" of the 2nd, 99th, and 301st Bomb Groups delivered an attack in three waves against the Gerbini aerodrome and its satellites, rendering the fields unserviceable. The B-17s of the 97th Bomb Group also flew an early mission against the German headquarters at Caltanissetta. B-25s were in action against the aerodromes at Sciacca and Trapani. In the Sciacca mission, the escorting P-40s of the 325th FG had their hands full, encountering intense and accurate flak, of both light and heavy caliber, during the mission. And the Luftwaffe was up, sending a large formation of Me 109s against the attacking bombers. Three of the attacking aircraft were shot down.

Enemy aircraft also gave battle in the late-afternoon mission at Trapani, losing three aircraft. Antiaircraft fire was also reportedly very intense and accurate. In a final mission of the day, B-25s of the 321st BG also flew an interdiction mission against the barracks at Palazzolo Town, hoping to keep reinforcements from reaching the battle lines to the south. B-26s flew an early mission against Caltagirone, the headquarters of the Hermann Göring Division, and the assembly point for many of the Axis forces in the eastern region of Sicily. And, importantly, the

B-26s of the 320th BG were assigned a late-afternoon interdiction mission to Vizzini. Off at 1439, and making their drop at 1640, the mission reported poor results in an operation that could have had a telling effect on the Axis counterattack that came on D-Day +1. The bombs of the first squadron dropped east of the target, and the second squadron could not identify the target and did not drop. Among all the bombing missions of that day, this mission was surely an opportunity lost.

In accord with the earlier agreement struck with NATAF, NASAF fighter-bombers were assigned fighter sweep missions to the southeastern region of Sicily.[16] For the 14th Fighter Group, seven missions were scheduled for July 10, each involving a formation of twelve P-38 aircraft. All three fighter squadrons contributed to these missions. Similarly, all three squadrons of the 1st Fighter Group, also flying P-38s, flew a total of eight missions on this day, all dive-bombing "targets of opportunity" missions to the same areas as the 14th aircraft would fly.

The 82nd Fighter Group flew three large missions on this day, sending not less than twenty-four aircraft on each mission, which included a bomber escort and two large fighter sweeps. By the end of this day, NASAF's P-38s would fly 829 sorties.

Opposing the Allied onslaught on this day were the remnants of the Luftwaffe on Sicily, including the greatly weakened but still dangerous JG 53 and JG 77.

The squadrons of JG 53 had exacted a steep toll against Allied air forces in the run-up to D-Day, accounting for 186 downed Allied aircraft since May. It was led by pilots who had achieved impressive results since early actions in 1939, including Ofw. Herbert Rollwage with 47 kills, Oblt. Hans Roehrig with 73, Ofw. Gunther Seeger with 37, Oflt. Fritz Dinger with 64, and Hptm. Friedrich-Karl Muller with 118.

JG 77 was equally menacing, having accounted for 132 downed Allied aircraft over the same brief period. It was led by airmen with equally impressive combat experience, including Hptm. Siegfried Freytag with 98 kills, Oflt. Heinz-Edgar Berres with 50, Maj. Johannes Steinhoff with 160, and Maj. Kurt Ubben with 108.

By the end of this day, pilots of JG 53 and JG 77 would shoot down 16 Allied aircraft.

For pilots Knepper and Kocour—both assigned to today's mission—there was an emerging awareness that for fighter pilots at this time and place, a "normal" combat mission could only be loosely defined. They had each, by this time, flown a half-dozen missions, and their experiences already spanned a broad spectrum. Two of their fellow pilots were lost on their first mission, and their squadron operations officer was shot down on their second. The next couple of missions had been milk runs, with no enemy aircraft encountered and minimal flak. The missions to Chilivani and Monserrato were at best ineffective, and on the escort mission to Gerbini, the fighters had had to turn back just before reaching the target, leaving the bombers to fend for themselves. While NASAF was operating at a very high level of success overall, at times the squadrons felt snake-bit. Today's mission did not involve bomber escorts, but rather dive-bombing and strafing—a new sort of mission, to critical targets, on the most important day of the war so far.

The first mission of the day for the 14th Fighter Group was given to the 37th Fighter Squadron. Taking off at 0530, a flight of twelve P-38s were assigned to dive-bomb targets of opportunity in the region north of Ragusa. By the time the 37th was airborne, the Allied paratroop attack had begun, American and British troops were already coming ashore, and the German and Italian defenders on Sicily had already moved into action. Within hours of becoming aware of the invasion, the commander of Italian defensive forces had ordered his Livorno division and two independent units to counterattack the landing force at Gela from the northwest. The Hermann Göring panzer division, though somewhat delayed while its commander awaited approval from headquarters, was moving by dawn in the direction of the landing forces at Gela and Scoglitti, with a planned attack from the east. Within a 30-mile coastal band ranging from Agrigento to the southeastern tip of Sicily, all Axis units were alert, and many were moving along the few Sicilian roads toward the landing beaches.

By 0700, the 37th squadron had overflown the massive Allied flotilla, crossed the Sicilian coastline, and sighted the enemy forces. It made an effective dive-bombing attack on a line of trucks moving south near Santo Pietro. Upon return to base, the pilots reported seeing twenty vehicles

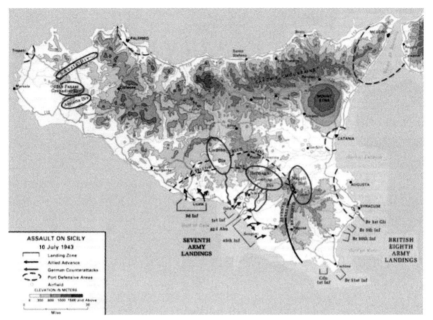

Allied assault on Axis-held Sicily, July 10, 1943. Showing location of German and Italian reinforcements and their lines of communication to the assault beaches.

on the road going south near Cap di San Pietro and about fifty vehicles, including tanks, trucks, and motorcycles moving south toward Comiso aerodrome below Vizzini. The Luftwaffe made no effort to intercept the 37th; four enemy aircraft were seen, but they did not approach. And despite the medium and heavy flak guns that defended the target, no aircraft were lost. By 0830 the formation was making their landing back at El Bathan.

This large armored column moving south from the area of Vizzini—probably the Hermann Göring panzer division—was to be targeted repeatedly by the Allied fighter-bombers in many subsequent missions on July 10.

The 48th Fighter Squadron had the second mission of the day—dive-bombing targets of opportunity in the region extending from Licata northeast toward Mazzarino. Taking off at 0645, the formation flew from their base at El Bathan to a point just east of Licata, then made a turn to the northeast to the road junction 5 miles south of Mazzarino. Targeting this was critical to the Allies because it ran roughly parallel to the coastline, where the major invasion beaches were located, and would be expected to be used heavily by the Axis defenders. At that road junction, the formation was jumped by two Me 109s. After driving off these interceptors, the formation wheeled back around toward Licata, and at 0800 found and engaged a concentration of guns. Heavy flak was encountered, though there was little movement on the roads. The flight made their return to base at 0905.

The 48th had flown in the vicinity of the Italian Livorno division, which was at that time moving in a southeasterly direction in order to position itself for a counterattack on the Allied forces at the Gela beachhead.

The third mission of the day was off at 0845 to dive-bomb targets of opportunity in the vicinity of Canicatti and Porto Embedocle—farther to the east from the mission that preceded it. Lieutenants Knepper and Deru were assigned to this mission as "spares," and when Lieutenant Bitter was forced to return home with a mechanical issue, Lieutenant Deru took his position as wingman to Captain Hageny. Lieutenant Bitter returned to base at 0905. Lieutenant Knepper, flying as an additional spare, but not needed for the mission, returned to base at 1115.

For this mission, Knepper again flew aircraft #45. This had been a well-maintained and reliable aircraft for the 49th. It was the favored mount of Bob Riley, who flew it on ten missions from May 8 through June 18, when Knepper took over as primary pilot. From restart to July 10, it had been flown by six other pilots, including Bland, completing twenty-three missions without an early return. The aircraft had been flawless.

The mission had difficulty locating a good target. Crossing Sicily near Licata, the formation flew north 40 miles before turning east to a point just south of Mount Etna. Still not finding a target, the squadron retraced their way back to Canicatti, where they began a dive-bombing attack at 1015 on railroad yards there, destroying three locomotives and several freight cars. So few good targets were found that one P-38 did not drop its bomb. The squadron's flight plan had taken it circumferentially around the enemy concentrations at Caltanissetta and Enna, but at a distance and altitude that apparently prevented it from seeing ground targets.

Turning toward the coast and still searching for strafing targets, the formation was jumped by six German Me 109s from what was left of

JG 53—the "Ace of Spades" wing just south of Campobello. The German fighters concentrated on the four-plane flight led by Lieutenant Leikness. Leikness and his wingman, Lieutenant Ellis, turned into the attacking aircraft, as did Lieutenant Manlove, leading the second element with his wingman, Lieutenant Booth. In the ensuing dogfight, Manlove and Leikness each shot down two Me 109s. Lieutenant Booth was last seen as he turned with Manlove to engage the German aircraft. He is presumed to have been shot down in the melee that followed, his sixteenth combat mission.

Still full of fight, the remaining eleven planes strafed an antiaircraft position at Porto Embedocle as they returned to base.

Although both the second and third missions flown by the 14th Fighter Group achieved good results, neither mission found and engaged the main column of Italian forces moving south toward the beachhead at Gela during the morning of D-Day. This, despite the fact that the first mission of the day for the 1st Fighter Group had observed and reported a column of seventy-five trucks moving in the direction of the battle line at 0725. This formation, most likely the Italian Livorno Division, was one of the Axis's primary defensive forces on Sicily. Engaging them effectively early on D-Day could have had a big effect on operations that day, and in the ensuing month of the Battle of Sicily. Clearly, had this intelligence been made available to the 14th, and providing that the commander of the 14th had had the authority to make targeting changes, the two morning missions of the 14th need not have been "targets of opportunity" sweeps, but targeted attacks.

The fourth mission was given to the 37th FS, who took off at 1045 on a dive-bombing mission to the region north and west of Comiso, to just south of Gerbini. Thirteen P-38s were armed with 500-pound bombs—the standard issue for the day—and they flew right into the lion's den. The squadron found good targets in the Comiso region. Five trucks were destroyed, and the road junction just north of Comiso was blocked. The radar station near Grammichele was bombed and strafed by a four-plane flight of the squadron. A bivouac area and truck park west of Comiso was strafed, destroying one JU 87 aircraft on the ground. Other buildings and motor cars, and one command car, were also strafed in a very full mission. The mission reported moderate flak from trucks and tanks, accurate at times, and flak was reported around the aerodrome at Comiso.

Turning back to base, the squadron reported seeing fifty or more vehicles, including several German medium tanks, parked in trees along the roadway just west of Comiso aerodrome. An additional twenty vehicles, including several tanks, were parked at the road junction just north of Comiso. What the 37th's pilots spotted appears to have been one of the attacking formations of the Hermann Göring panzer division—quite likely the same tanks and trucks spotted by the 37th squadron at 0700 that morning on the first mission of the day. By noon of D-Day, the Intelligence officers of the 14th Fighter Group would have developed a fairly clear idea of the direction in which German ground forces were moving.

In fact, the earlier intelligence estimates related to the likely movement of German assets was proven to be precisely correct. By noon the German Hermann Göring Division had launched a two-pronged counterattack from its position near Caltagirone, had been repulsed, had moved rearward, and was making preparations for a second counterattack that afternoon.

Just prior to their return of the 37th FS, the 48th FS took off on the fifth mission of the day for the 14th FG. Off at 1250, the squadron was again targeting any Axis asset in the southeastern portion of Sicily. Just over an hour into their mission, the formation spotted a convoy of twenty to thirty trucks heading in a southerly direction between Caltagirone and Grammichele, obviously bound for the battlefront. The P-38s commenced their dive from 2,500 feet, with results that must have been disappointing to the squadron. Nine near misses. One truck was seen to explode, and one bomb caused part of the roadbed to cave away. The mission reported light machine-gun fire from the truck convoy, but no enemy aircraft were seen. A train, station house, and other buildings just east of Canicatti were also strafed and left ablaze.

Again, mission intelligence would have further refined the position of the German forces, making additional interdiction missions much more likely to achieve success. The German forces had been engaged

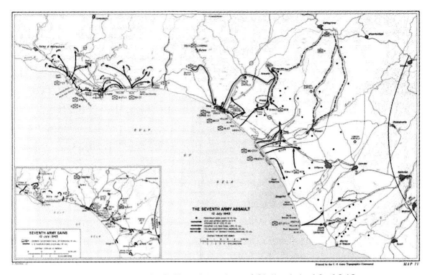

American amphibious assault, D-Day, Invasion of Sicily, July 10, 1943.
U.S. ARMY IN WORLD WAR II, MEDITERRANEAN THEATER OF OPERATIONS, SICILY AND THE SUR-RENDER OF ITALY, PART II, OPERATIONS AND NEGOTIATIONS, CHAPTER VI, THE ASSAULT.

several times already, and the fighter-bombers of the 14th and 1st FGs seemed poised for a knockout punch.

The sixth mission left El Bathan about thirty minutes before the return of the 48th FS's mission. Assigned to the 49th FS, the objective of the mission was to search for targets of opportunity in the area from Licata to Gerbini. Off at 1450, this was the second mission of the day for Lieutenants Bitter and Knepper. In the earlier mission, Bitter had a mechanical issue with his aircraft and returned to base. On this flight, he had mounted a different aircraft. Knepper flew the same aircraft as he had in the earlier mission. Lieutenants Ogle and Foster were assigned to the mission as "spares." Lieutenant Richard's aircraft developed a mechanical issue just ten minutes after takeoff. Lieutenant Foster took his position as wingman to Captain Decker. Lieutenant Ogle, the remaining spare, was not needed for the mission and returned to base before the formation made their attack.

With Foster in position, the formation included ten of the squadron's most experienced pilots, each having already logged more than half of their 50-mission combat tour. The two replacement pilots—Kocour and Knepper—had each completed a handful of combat missions, and their competence in combat was growing with each mission.

Unaccountably, during the preflight briefing for this mission the squadron was apparently not apprised of the intelligence received earlier in the day from their sister squadron at El Bathan, the 37th. Returning from two prior missions that day, the 37th had reported large concentrations of German armor, vehicles, and troops in the Vizzini-Caltagirone corridor. In the last mission of the day, the 37th—taking off shortly after Decker's flight departed—was sent on a final dive-bombing mission, targeting those same concentrations at Vizzini for the third time that day. Had Captain Decker known of the location of this concentration of forces, his flight course and mission would have taken a much different direction and probably had a much different outcome.

What was said during the mission briefing is not recorded. It is certainly possible that Decker was sent as far as Catania in order to intercept reinforcing troops potentially moving south from Catania or Messina; a second Italian reserve division was known to be in the area south of Catania, and it was not known whether this force would be sent against the American landing forces at Gela, or against the British forces near Syracuse. It is also known that roughly one-third of the Hermann Göring Division was located in the vicinity of Catania, and it is plausible that Decker's mission was to seek out and attack that concentration.

The formation flew "on the deck" as it crossed the Mediterranean toward the coastline of Sicily. As it neared the Sicilian coastline at Gela, it increased altitude and continued on a generally northeastern course over Ponte Olivo, to and beyond the landing complex at Gerbini, and continuing to the port city of Catania. Not finding targets at any point on their outbound leg, Decker wheeled the formation back around and continued their visual search for targets on a southwestern track, intending to fly over Vizzini and Comiso before returning to base.

The inbound route for the squadron took them slightly to the west of the region in which the Hermann Göring Division was staging its decisive counterattack against the American forces landing at Gela on

D-Day—the same German forces that had been reported twice that day in post-flight briefings by the 37th squadron.

As recounted by Lt. William Gregory, flight leader for the Blue flight, "We flew over the coastline of Sicily at altitude. And there were all these ships lined up for what seemed like 50 miles. When we flew over these ships on the way in, we were about 10,000 feet, maybe 7,500. We had been briefed that they [the U.S. Navy] might shoot at us, but they shouldn't, since we were P-38s, and they probably would have identified us. But they sure did. Fortunately no one got hit, and we didn't lose anyone from that. That is why we were so high when we went in. We went all the way to Mount Etna inland, then we turned around 180 degrees and were coming back. It seemed like there was no war on for most of that mission. Of course, our own ships shot at us, be we did not receive any ground fire going over from the Germans."[17]

The formation had flown across most of the southeastern part of Sicily without having encountered any enemy aircraft, without receiving any enemy ground fire, and without spotting any suitable targets for their 500-pound bombs.

About the time that Captain Decker had turned his formation back around, headed southwest in the direction of the beachhead at Gela, the seventh and final mission for the 14th Fighter Group was taking off from its base at El Bathan. That mission, assigned to the 37th FS, was the third mission they would fly on this date. The 37th flew off in search of targets in the region between Gerbini and Comiso aerodromes. The aircraft were on a roughly parallel and opposite path to the 49th FS formation, led by Decker, and were also flying directly over one of the main battle-fronts of the invasion. The 37th found good targets just west of Scordia, and made their drop later in the afternoon, destroying munition dumps, warehouses, a railroad station house, railroad tracks, and nearby buildings. The mission reported seeing heavy German tanks and quite a lot of truck traffic along the roads in the vicinity of Vizzini.

As Decker's squadron continued in the direction of the beachhead at Gela, he "jumped down" low as they continued to search for a target of opportunity. Their course took them in the direction of Vizzini—the exact location where the Hermann Göring Division had just retreated following their mauling by the U.S. Army and Navy at the Gela beachhead. The formation was jumped by two Me 109s as it neared the vicinity of Vizzini. One fired at "Charley"—the last P-38 in the formation—but the German fighters were driven off when the formation turned into them. At this point in the mission, the aircraft were still in formation, flying at 3,000 feet altitude, and spanning a distance of roughly a quarter-mile from the far left to the far right of the formation.

Lt. William "Greg" Gregory recalls: "And that is where, near the coastline, the Germans had this heavy concentration—in this kind of valley, as I recall. There were a lot of trees in that area—could have been an olive grove. We didn't see all of this going in." The squadron had overflown a hidden column of twenty German tanks and twenty-five trucks northwest of Vizzini along the Vizzini-Buccheri road. The German concentration took the squadron completely by surprise. It was not an ambush—the Germans had no way of knowing the 49th's squadron was approaching. But they were certainly on high alert, having just been beaten back at the Gela beachhead, and were ready to throw up a wall of antiaircraft fire. Flying in close formation, at a low altitude, the P-38s were huge targets for the experienced German gunners.

Lt. Harold Harper, flying on Lieutenant Gregory's right side, remembers: "We flew over a grove of trees when all of a sudden the situation 'lit up.' We had encountered a GAF AA battery."[18] The P-38s immediately dove, strafing as they neared the vehicles, the pilots hurrying to release their bombs.

Greg: "There was no signal from the flight leader. It was not a typical dive-bombing run. It was more of a strafing run, but we dropped our bombs as we were approaching. A few trucks, tanks, and other vehicles were spotted, and they were attacked successfully." Greg glanced to his right, and saw that his good friend Wallace Bland and his formation were also in a dive, strafing as they went.

Harper: "Decker was leading at around 2,500 to 3,000 feet, looking for something to shoot at. I don't think we ever did see anything. We dropped our bombs on the trees when the fire came up. They saw us before we saw them. I never did see them. They were in thick trees. We dropped and kept going. Decker did not swing around to make another pass at the ground targets. As soon as the ground fire started coming up, the squadron dropped [its bombs]. I got hit right away. The AA fire was not [just] ground fire; it was 30/40mm cannon fire—the four-barrel AA guns. Everybody got hit, and when you get hit, you better drop your bomb and get the hell out of there. We were not in attack mode; we were still looking, and still in our formation. The GAF AA knew what was going on, on the rest of the island, and were on alert."

The German gunners found the entire squadron. According to official reports, six aircraft were damaged by flak, and two pilots—Lt. Harold Harper and Lt. Herman Kocour—had one engine shot out and had to nurse their aircraft back to base on the remaining engine.

Harper: "Yes, they just opened up. So you can see how many guns they [must have] had, to hit that many aircraft. So at this point, [everyone was shot up]. There was no thought of completing the mission. It was a matter of getting back to base if possible. My wingman [Lieutenant Boatman] was still with me when I got hit, and was still in element formation. I called Decker and told him that I was hit and was going down. I dove down and my engine started to get hot, so I feathered it up." Diving down got him out of the way of the AA fire—he was right on the deck. "If you are right on the deck, and someone is shooting at you, anything that is between you as you are going past him, he has got to swing that gun around [like a tree], and it would give a bit of cover."

Adding to the swirling action, B-26s from the 320th Bomb Group were on their final approach in a bombing mission to nearby Vizzini, targeting troop and armor concentrations that had been reported there. Harper's plane was hit in front of the cockpit, and one engine was shot out. "It's a wonder that on this mission that was all shot up, a bullet didn't hit me," says Harper. "It hit right in front of the cockpit, and missed the nosewheel; how it did that, I don't know. It flew back on the right engine and knocked it out, and shrapnel stopped on the aluminum skin on the left engine. That's pretty close."

Harper had to limp back to the base at El Bathan, and while passing back over the invasion fleet, the U.S. Navy shot at him again. "I was thinking about bailing out," Harper recalls. "When we got over the water,

I got up to about 2,500 feet. I thought if I had to bail out, I would have time to get things together. Mostly guys who parachuted would go out over the wing, and go under the tail booms."

Flying on Harper's left, Greg remembers: "I saw Bland get hit. He was pretty low, when I saw him."

According to Lieutenant Lovera, flying just behind Bland: "I saw Lieutenant Bland's plane going down and the left engine was smoking. He called over the radio that the airplane was out of control, and about that time the left engine caught fire and the plane peeled off and did a wing-over to the left and blew up. As the plane started over, I saw an object go past the tail assembly, but I did not see a parachute open."

Lieutenant Evans, also flying just behind Bland, reported: "I saw Lieutenant Bland's left engine smoking and tried to call him on the radio and tell him about it, but he didn't reply. Then he called and said he was going to bail out. His plane turned over and started down. I saw him bail out, but his parachute didn't open, and I saw him hit the ground."[19]

Harper's understanding—unconfirmed, but based on what he heard at the debriefing—was that Lieutenant Bland's parachute had gotten wrapped around the tail boom of his aircraft. Bland was killed on his twenty-sixth combat mission; he'd just turned twenty-four years of age.

Knepper's good friend Herman Kocour, flying as Bland's wingman, was also hit by ground fire. Knepper, Lieutenant Evan's wingman, was also pouring cannon fire into the German armored column when he was hit by flak. His plane peeled up, made a half-roll, and crashed straight into the ground.[20]

CHAPTER 14

Aftermath

"Good hunting, Lieutenant." With these words, and an unspoken prayer, many of the crew chiefs in the 14th FG had wished success to their pilots. Flying the P-38 required a team, and the ground crew assigned to each plane thought of it as "their" plane, and of the pilot as "their pilot." On each mission, as the estimated return times for the aircraft came closer, the crews began to assemble at the flight line to welcome back their plane and pilot. This came to be called "sweating out" the return—not knowing who would return, or what their condition would be. Throughout this day, with aircraft returning riddled with holes, and some on one engine, it became clear that some of the day's missions had run into trouble on their "target of opportunity" sweeps to the island.

On this day, three crews waited and watched as other pilots on the mission returned. Waiting, and seeing other returned pilots talking to their crew chiefs, catching the glances back to the empty hardstands. Finally, their buddies walked slowly over. "Your pilot didn't make it . . . Heavy flak . . . Two more lost . . ." A horrible day. Since restarting combat operations in early May, the squadron had never lost three men in a single day.

Knepper's good friend Lt. Herman Kocour had returned to base after the 49th's last mission on D-Day, not knowing what had become of his friend or the rest of the squadron. When the antiaircraft fire bloomed in front of them near Vizzini, the entire formation was blown apart, each man struggling to maintain control of his own damaged aircraft. Of the twelve-ship formation, two had been shot down, and six more received damage. Two pilots—Harper and Kocour—struggled home on one engine. The remnants of the formation straggled back to base a couple of hours before sunset, some having reconnected in the air to give mutual cover.

Captain Decker and Lieutenant Foster returned to base at 1745. Lieutenants Kocour, Evans, Harper, and Boatman were down at 1815—slowed somewhat, with Kocour and Harper having had an engine shot out by ground fire. Lieutenants Gregory, Bitter, Lovera, and Harris were down at 1820. Meeting with the squadron Intelligence officer, the pilots shared what they knew and learned the fate of Lieutenants Bland and Knepper.

The loss of Bland was tough on his tentmates, Lieutenants Gregory, Manlove, and DeMoss, all the more because of Neely's tragic death just a few days before. For Neely, a funeral at the military cemetery at Constantine was possible. For Bland, there would be no funeral and no time to come to terms with the loss of this good man.

And the loss of Lieutenant Knepper, on his fifth combat mission, was especially tough for Lieutenant Kocour. The two had been together for well over a year, had attended the same flight schools, had learned to fly the P-38 together during Transition training, had traveled together across the United States and the Atlantic Ocean to North Africa, and had reported together to the 14th Fighter Group for assignment. As any veteran pilot will attest, friendships already strong were forged more deeply by combat, and by shared losses.

Lieutenant Kocour would later write: "I never saw his plane go in and thought he was okay, till we got home. I found then from one of the other fellows who tagged on behind that Knep went in the same way the leader did. We had been together so much, and he was, and is, the best fellow I ever knew. That was the hardest thing I had to take."[1]

The War Diary of the 49th and the squadron's Mission History recorded the losses factually and without comment. Stapled to the diary was a personal message from General Doolittle, commander of NASAF: "Wish to express appreciation of enthusiasm, spirit, and skill shown by pilots of First and Fourteen [sic] Fighter Groups during operations 10 July—their work has been magnificent."

The 1st Fighter Group lost two of its pilots on D-Day, and the 82nd and 325th each lost one. Doubtless reflecting on the loss of seven fighter pilots, NAAF headquarters would have also realized how much more extensive the losses would have been had air superiority still been contested.

As the afternoon eased into evening, the pilots knew that there would be no pause to reflect on their losses: Now entering D-Day +1, everyone expected Axis counterattacks against the invading British and American troops, and no one was expecting any respite. Once more, the pilots of the 49th had to steel themselves against their own personal feelings, choke back the rising grief that they may have allowed themselves to feel under other circumstances, and put their minds back in the cockpits.

The loss of three pilots in a single day was a blow for the 49th Fighter Squadron, but in the context of overall losses on that day, or of losses incurred during the Battle of Sicily, the loss of three men was scarcely noted in military reports. The surviving pilots in the 49th might well have been struck by the knowledge that an event that was so significant to them would scarcely register beyond the squadron.

There is strong evidence that the 49th's second mission on D-Day had flown over the rear elements of the Hermann Göring Division on the afternoon of July 10—one of the best equipped and most capable elements of the German army. The pilots on that mission would never learn of the apparent intelligence lapse during the preflight briefing that had failed to include important information about troop and armor locations, and which contributed to their losses over Vizzini. Only seventy years after the fact were pilots Gregory and Harper apprised of the location of the Hermann Göring Division, to their great surprise.

On D-Day +1 the expected Axis counteroffensive was launched, with the Hermann Göring Division attacking from its overnight position at Ponte Olivo airfield and the region around Niscemi. Though the German and Italian counterattack was beaten back, the area around Vizzini and Grammichele was to be strongly defended by the Axis forces in the following three days, and the Vizzini-Grammichele road was to become an important withdrawal route for German forces as they continued their defense of the island in a series of holding actions.

The 14th Fighter Group put up seven more missions on July 11. Most of the pilots who had flown on July 10 were flying again on the following day. With a dozen aircraft in each mission, and at least two missions for each squadron, there was no downtime for any plane or pilot. Everyone had a mission to fly, and some had two.

New aircraft were ordered up to replace those lost with Booth, Bland, and Knepper, and the lost pilots' crew chiefs were assigned to those new planes, introduced to the new replacement pilots as they arrived. For the ground crews, there seemed to be no end to replacement planes and pilots, and no stopping the losses.

And so, less than twelve hours after being nearly blown out of the sky over Vizzini, Captain Decker and Lieutenants Harper, Evans, Kocour, Gregory, Harris, Lovera, and five other pilots were again flying together in a twelve-plane formation at 0645, on a dive-bombing mission back to Vizzini—another low-level operation, against the same seasoned, well-equipped, and alert German defenders.

The second mission of that day for the 49th was off at 1315, and included Lieutenants Leikness, Foster, Bitter, Boatman, and Richard. Lieutenants Harper, Lovera, and Kocour also flew this mission—their second combat mission of the day. The loss of three pilots the day before meant that some of the 49th's pilots would have to step up to fill the gap. On this mission, Lieutenant Manlove engaged enemy fighters and shot down two, and Lieutenant Leikness downed one.

At El Bathan, orders were passed to collect the personal belongings of the pilots who had been lost the day before. Government-owned material was separated from personal effects and distributed to whoever had a need for them. Blankets, helmets, mess kits. Personal effects were boxed for shipment back home, a job no one wanted. It was a harsh intrusion, a violation of their friends' privacy, but it was also the last kindness that they could extend to their fallen comrades. And when the task was done, the last vestige of their fellow officers and squadron mates would be gone.

None of the pilots had much gear with them—a small carton at most. In addition to a bit of clothing, each pilot's family would receive their insignia, flight logs, photos and letters, packet of orders, and a saved souvenir or two. Knepper's wallet included a single photograph, and four money order receipts, evidence of his having sent money home to his family. Ever the student, Lieutenant Knepper's effects included four dictionaries, a phrase book, and an officer's guide. And the personal effects of all three of the lost pilots included a copy of the New Testament.

The ground war in Sicily surged ahead, and with it the air forces continued their pounding of Axis ground and aviation forces. As the American and British armies moved forward, former German and Italian air bases came under Allied control. NATAF and NASAF units began to move forward almost immediately, making it possible for fighters and bombers to range farther into the field, and to remain longer over the combat theater.

For the three squadrons of the 14th Fighter Group, the relentless pace of combat missions continued. Pilots flew high-level bomber-escort missions or low level fighter bombing sweeps nearly every day. Pilot fatigue grew. Stress continued to mount. Friends and fellow pilots were killed or went missing. Completing a fifty-mission tour seemed very unlikely.

One of the 49th's most experienced pilots, a captain with over thirty missions already completed, may have reached his emotional limit by mid-July. Having flown eleven combat missions in the prior ten days, the pilot seemed dazed and unengaged.

According to one of the group's crew chiefs:

> *"A group of airmen had just completed work on a P-38 plane when this . . . officer arrived to test-fly the aircraft. He looked somewhat sad and was very quiet . . . different than the other pilots who were always in a pleasant mood. We offered to take off the auxiliary gas tanks, but he declined and said he was just going to fly around."*[2]

The pilot circuited El Bathan airfield for 20 minutes. Then, from an altitude of 2,000 feet, he started a steep dive.

Lt. William Gregory witnessed what followed:

> *"I saw the whole thing. He did a slow roll over the base and crashed. He just lost control. If you are going to do (a slow roll), you should do*

it at high speed and higher altitude. He was a good pilot and he knew better than that. I just thought what a waste that was. I had a strange feeling—that it was not a total accident. It was almost like he knew it was going to happen. I just wonder if he meant for it to happen."

The Squadron's War Diary records the pilot's death without attributing a cause. Within the squadron it was rumored that the pilot had just received a "Dear John" letter. Whether it was an accidental death or a suicide will never be known, and in the inexorable grind of the air war, the squadron mounted another mission the next morning. Later in the day, the group's chaplain conducted a funeral service at Constantine.

By July 13 the first Allied fighters began to arrive at captured Sicilian airfields and landing grounds. Within a few days there were eighteen and a half squadrons of NAAF planes—both British and American—operating from the fields at Pachino, Comiso, Ponte Olivo, and Licata.[3] The 14th was not part of the move to Sicily. Their longer-range P-38s allowed them to continue operations from North Africa, though they did move forward to a new base at Sainte-Marie du Zit, 50 kilometers south of Tunis and 300 or so miles closer to the battle lines.

In mid-July, Capt. Frank Clark, operations officer of the 14th Fighter Group, was asked to provide a summary of operations for the group since it had first re-commenced combat operations in early May. Paraphrasing his report: "Since commencing combat operations on 5 May 1943, and until 17 July 1943, the Group has received 96 pilots and 75 airplanes. In this 74-day period, the Group has flown 210 missions, including 4,349 sorties. We have destroyed 122 enemy aircraft. We have lost 35 pilots."[4] Thirty-five pilots out of ninety-six; an attrition rate of 36 percent.

From D-Day forward, the losses for the 14th Fighter Group, and for the 49th Fighter Squadron, continued to mount. As if to punctuate the dangers of flight operations, Capt. Mark Hageny, one of the original "restart" pilots and a squadron leader on many combat missions, was killed on July 15 in a plane crash at the 49th's base at Sainte-Marie du Zit. Hageny had completed forty-nine combat missions and was due to be reassigned stateside after just one more mission. Four weeks later, another experienced pilot was lost when Lt. Walter Hoke, a veteran of an estimated forty combat missions, was killed in a plane crash at the squadron's base.

By mid-July, the surviving pilots who had originally come to North Africa to restart the 14th Fighter Group numbered just fifteen. At that point, they had completed an average of thirty-two missions, and would reach their fifty-mission limit by the end of August.[5] As their combat tour continued, some of the pilots became flight leaders and were promoted to captain, including Lieutenants DeMoss, Gregory, Knott, and Leikness.

As the Sicily invasion continued, so too did heavy combat duty for the 49th. Following a few more days of dive-bombing interdiction missions, the 49th reverted to its primary role as bomber escorts, now focusing on targets beyond Sicily in preparation for the next ground action that would follow—the invasion of Italy. Their losses continued to mount, and new replacement pilots continued to arrive. Missions were flown, new pilots checked out, replacement aircraft tested and prepared.

Captain Trollope continued to lead the squadron, and during the 108 days of his command, thirteen pilots were lost (KIA, MIA, POW, and accidental losses), ten of them unrecovered.[6]

Trollope, Decker, and Blount continued to be vigilant regarding battle fatigue in their pilots, and by mid-August, they had become concerned about Lieutenant Lovera.

The frequency of missions assigned to combat pilots had varied over the course of that summer. In the first sixty-one days of his combat tour, Lieutenant Lovera flew twenty-four combat sorties. He had flown a combat mission about every 2.5 days, and within that period were some 5–7 day stretches with no combat. By early July his tour was about halfway complete, and at the rate he was flying he could look forward to orders home by early September.

Starting with the ramp-up to the invasion of Sicily, the squadron's combat assignments became particularly intense. There was essentially no let-up between July 9 and August 20; over that forty-two day period Lieutenant Lovera flew twenty-five missions, about one every day-and-a-half.

The type of mission changed as well. The majority of missions Lieutenant Lovera flew in the first half of his tour were bomber-escort missions. While these missions carried a high level of risk, they were generally less dangerous than the low level bombing and strafing missions that characterized the missions conducted by the squadron after July 9, during the Sicilian Campaign. On those missions, the 49th's aircraft were well within range of the greatly feared 40mm German antiaircraft guns, and close-to-the-ground missions carried a greater risk of pilotage errors leading to crashes.

Losses continued to mount during the summer, and most of the losses were pilots Lieutenant Lovera had come to know well. During the summer of 1943, twenty of his fellow pilots were killed or went missing in combat, or were killed in accidents. Many of these young pilots were men Lieutenant Lovera had trained with, men who relied on each other during combat. Many of them he would have come to know as friends.

As he neared the end of his combat tour, Lieutenant Lovera continued to fly a mix of missions: bomber escort, search and rescue, and dive-bombing/strafing. On August 18 he took part in a fighter bombing raid on Siderno. On August 19, having just been promoted to first lieutenant, Lovera was assigned to a combat mission escorting B-17s to the railroad yards at Foggia. On this mission, Lieutenant Moak developed engine trouble, dropped from the returning flight, and was not seen again. The next day Lieutenant Lovera was assigned to a search mission, escorting a PBY, presumably to look for Lieutenant Moak. On takeoff, Lieutenant Hoke's aircraft lost both engines. His plane flew into the ground, and he was killed.

The following day, August 21st, Lieutenant Lovera was assigned to an all-squadron mission escorting B-17s targeting the railroad yards at Aversa, near Naples. The squadron's Mission History cites: "Lt. Lovera did not take off." As far as the available records indicate, he never again was to fly a combat mission.

Lieutenant Lovera was hospitalized in North Africa sometime after the Aversa mission. Medical records are not available, and the reason for his hospitalization cannot be confirmed. It is known that he returned to the squadron on August 31.

He remained with the squadron, but was assigned to no further combat missions. In fact, no other flight time of any kind is shown on his sortie log. Lieutenant Lovera departed from the squadron on September 18 and returned to the States, credited with having completed 48 combat missions during his 104 days as a combat pilot.

It can only be speculated why Lieutenant Lovera was removed from combat status, or the reason for his hospitalization. His fellow pilot, Lt. William Gregory, would later recall:

> *I always had the feeling that Lovera was a little more tense than the rest of us. I just felt like he was really uncomfortable in combat, but to his credit he never turned down a flight. Every time he was scheduled, he went.*
>
> *I kind of felt for him, like he had more anxiety than the rest of us. We all had some. He was in my flight, and I was always concerned about him, and tried to look out for him and give him special attention. He made it though.*[7]

Lieutenant Harper succinctly recalled: "He had some kind of mental thing, he got so he did not like to fly too well."[8]

Neither Gregory nor Harper knew that Art Lovera did not complete his combat tour; both believed that he finished his fifty missions like the rest of them, and had been assigned home.

It is possible that the accumulation of combat stress overcame Lieutenant Lovera, preventing him from continuing his combat tour. It is also possible that Lieutenants Moak and Hoke were close friends, and that their loss brought Lieutenant Lovera to the tipping point.

The commanders and pilots who had been with the group and squadron since its "restart" in the early spring began to transition out and return home. Squadron Commander Trollope, who along with Captain Decker had recently been promoted to Major, passed his command to Major McKenzie on Sept. 21, and Lieutenant Colonel Keith relinquished command of the 14th Fighter Group on September 26 to Col. Oliver Taylor.

Majors Trollope and Decker, recently promoted Captains Gregory, DeMoss and Leikness, and Lieutenants Boatman, Evans, Knott, Homer, Bitter, Harper, Deru, Vogelsong and Flight Officer Richard all received their orders home on Sept. 26th. By the time they began the journey back to the 'States, they were leaving a squadron that they barely recognized.

With the departure of the original pilots, Lt. Herman Kocour became the "old man" of the squadron. He completed his fifty combat missions, compiling 218 combat flying hours. "Koc" flew his last mission on October 22, escorting B-25s on a mission to Grosseto, Italy. Prior to returning to the States, Lieutenant Kocour was given a final physical examination by the squadron physician, Capt. Lester Blount. In his remarks, Captain Blount noted that Kocour was "Healthy, but showing signs of combat fatigue . . ."

In a rare personal notation, the squadron mission report contains this:

Twelve P-38s flew escort for B-25's to Grosseto, Italy. Today was the last mission of Lt. Kocour with this squadron. He has completed his 50th mission and shall be missed by the squadron for his leadership and ability.[9]

Although unknown, it's not likely that Herman ever forgot his friend Allan. After his return to the United States, he wrote to Allan's sister, Christina, in careful script: "I think I could go back to the spot he went in, as it was beside a little church that I don't think I'll ever forget. I can still see it very plainly, as we were very low at the time. Later on we were based in Sicily, and I wanted to go over to the spot where he went in to see if I could learn anything. I thought I might be able to find out something from the natives if I couldn't learn anything any other way. I'm sorry to say I never got that chance, as we had no means of transport outstation and we were so busy that we got very little time off."

In a later letter, he wrote of Allan's occasionally curt demeanor, but his kind heart. "He was gruff but grand. A year ago Xmas we were at Williams Field. We both went to town the afternoon before Xmas. I had such a bad cold that I just [settled] for a hotel room and went to bed till time for Midnight Mass. [I] went to Midnight Mass and back to bed, and then got up and went back to the field about noon. It was my first Xmas away from home, and with the cold and all, I wasn't feeling very imbued with the spirit of Xmas. When I got in my room there was a sock hanging above my bed. I took it down and found a bar of soap with a rope so it could be hung around my neck. That little thing made Xmas a much better one for me, thanks to Allan."[10]

The 49th Fighter Squadron continued its service during the war, moving to the large aerodrome complex at Foggia, Italy, on December 12. From that base, the squadron supported ground forces and conducted many dive-bombing and strafing missions against railroads, road convoys, bridges, and enemy airfields. The squadron operated briefly from Corsica in the waning days of the war, supporting the Allied invasion of southern France, and was demobilized during the summer and fall of 1945.

The 14th Fighter Group lost 141 pilots in 1944, and another 32 during the final months of the war in 1945. In the war's duration, the Group lost 277 pilots—75 of whom flew with Lieutenant Knepper's 49th Fighter Squadron.

Lieutenant Knepper's status as missing in action was common for pilots in that era. Six months after his loss, the Intelligence officer for the squadron, Capt. Howard Wilson, was asked to prepare a "Special Report on Operations" for the 14th Group HQ. His report confirmed that, since the squadron first arrived in North Africa in November of 1942, fourteen of the squadron's pilots had been declared missing in action. At that time in the war, with aerial combat occurring over open water and over territory controlled by the enemy, crash sites were often undiscoverable, and remains of downed pilots unreported.

Following normal air forces procedure, Captain Trollope issued Missing Air Crew Reports for Lieutenants Booth, Bland, and Knepper on July 13, 1943. Within ten days, the War Department notified each pilot's next of kin as to their status, typically by telegram.

The Bland Family's Long Wait
Captain Trollope's MACR for Lieutenant Bland appended eyewitness statements from two of that fateful mission's pilots: Lts. Anthony Evans and Arthur Lovera. In their statements, it was reported that Lieutenant Bland successfully exited his stricken aircraft, but that his parachute did

not deploy. Lieutenant Evans reported that he saw Lieutenant Bland hit the ground. Captain Trollope's MACR concluded that the "pilot is believed not to have survived." Since the crash site was on enemy-held territory, no search was instigated at that time.

A week later, Lieutenant Bland's father, Grady Bland, would have received a telegram from the adjutant general informing him that his son, Lt. Wallace Grady Bland, was reported to be missing in action since July 10. The telegram informed Grady that "if further details or other information of this status are received you will be promptly notified."

On December 24, 1943 the adjutant general sent a second telegram to Grady, apparently based on the eyewitness reports and evidencing the lack of any confirmation that Lieutenant Bland had been taken prisoner. That telegram advised that "the Secretary of War desires that I tender his deep sympathy to you in the loss of your son First Lieutenant Wallace G Bland who was previously reported missing in action. Report received states that he was killed in action on 10 July. Letter follows."

Grady Bland with Lt. Wallace Bland's daughter, Jessica.
ART TAPHORN

Grady was terribly hurt by the loss of his only child, his strong young son with a loving wife and child and an unbridled future. Grady had great difficulty dealing with this unresolved loss, living with a grief that was palpable, and seemingly perpetual.

A year later, frustrated by what he apparently perceived as insufficient action on the part of the army in providing details about his son's crash or about the whereabouts of his remains, Grady Bland contacted his congressional representative, Congressman Carter Manasco, requesting assistance in obtaining any information about his son. This request generated an official Congressional Inquiry into the matter.

When another year passed with no further substantive information, Grady continued to press his inquiry with Manasco. In late September 1945 Grady Bland wrote: "I have spent more than two years in imagination about whether my son was ever found. It would be a great relief to me to know if he was found and buried."[11] Within days, the congressman repeated his request for further information from the adjutant general, which in turn generated an urgent request from the AG to the director of the Memorial Division of the Quartermaster Corps.

By early May 1946 an extensive ground search had been made of the region around Palagonia, Mineo, Rammacco and Militello, including interviews with carabinieri at Palagonia and Mineo, and a review of cemetery records in Mineo and Palagonia. All towns and villages surrounding Palagonia were searched for isolated burials and air crashes. No crash- or gravesite was located, but the commandant of the carabinieri at Mineo reported that on July 10, 1043 he had seen an airplane crash in which the parachute had opened just enough to break the pilot's fall, and that the pilot was immediately taken prisoner by the Germans. The QMC report concluded that an exhausting search of (German) prison records was called for.

Pursuing that line of inquiry, by early June, the QMG had reported that Lieutenant Bland's name did not appear on an official prison of war lists received through the International Red Cross or on captured German records.

June 20, 1946 QMC reported to Manasco that "an extensive search has been made of the area where Lt. Bland's plane was supposed to have gone done," with no results. While offering no encouragement it did reference an ongoing investigation.

In an August 1946 report, the QMC reported that a further intensive field search had been conducted over a broad swath between Enna and Palagonia. It further confirmed that an administrative search had been made of any unknown American deceased reportedly disinterred from that region. The report concludes: "Every effort has been expended, both fieldly and administratively, to locate the grave or remains of the officer,"[12] however it left open the possibility that Lieutenant Bland, following capture by the Germans, was evacuated onto the Italian mainland into a German POW stockade or hospital whereat the subject officer later could have died and been interred in a German military cemetery somewhere in Italy.

Grady persisted, and in October 1946 pressed his request for information with the headquarters of the American Graves Registration Service Command. His request led to no discernable action by the army. In June 1947 he was again informed by the Memorial Division of the QMG that no further information had been received regarding the fate of Lieutenant Bland.

In April 1948, the American Graves Registration Service convened a special Board of Officers in Rome to review the record regarding the likely fate of Lieutenant Bland. It was their finding that Lieutenant Bland had not survived the crash of his aircraft and been taken prisoner, but rather had been killed in the action of July 10, 1943. It recommended that no further action be taken, that Lieutenant Bland's remains be declare unrecoverable, and the case closed.

But in April 1949 the Memorial Division, finding discrepancies involving the areas searched in prior field work, requested that the American Graves Registration Service undertake yet another investigation. This investigation's report, completed on June 13, 1949, clarified the discrepancy and confirming that no remains had been located.

In July 1949 the Memorial Division confirmed its findings to Grady Bland that his son's remains were "not recoverable." It continued, "Realizing the extent of your grief and anxiety, it is not easy to express condolences to you who gave your loved one under circumstances so difficult that there is no grave at which to pay homage. May the knowledge of your son's honorable service to his country be a source of sustaining comfort to you."[13]

As late as October 1950, the Memorial Division continued to attempt to correlate the dental records of Lieutenant Bland with those of unidentified deceased servicemen, again with negative results.

For Grady Bland, and for Lieutenant Bland's wife Carolyn, the long investigation was concluded. With all options now exhausted, Lieutenant Bland's family was forced to accept the hard truth that his story would never be fully told, that there would be no closure for a life that began so hopefully. Lieutenant Bland was simply gone.[14]

Enduring Lieutenant Knepper's Loss

Allan Knepper's parents were relaxing on a Sunday morning when the phone rang in their grocery store, adjacent to their home. Jess Knepper left to take the call, and returned to his wife in tears, completely overcome by the news of his son's loss.

Arriving later, the War Department telegram, now lost to time, would have read:

> *I regret to inform you that the Commanding General, Mediterranean area, reports your son, Second Lieutenant Allan Knepper, missing since July 10. If further details or other information of his status are received, you will be promptly notified.*

While this status did not necessarily mean that Allan had been killed, it was widely known that few airmen designated as MIA were ever recovered. Still, clinging to some small hope, Jess Knepper continued to believe that his son might be located. In a letter to the War Department, Jess wrote: "I am enclosing papers that should prove that Allan W. Knepper would desire that I store his property. Allan is not married. I believe he would desire that I store his things. I would be willing . . . at any time to return them to him."[15] The army complied with his request, and in the fall of 1943 sent his son's belongings to Jess in Lewiston, Idaho. His family has said that to the end of his days, Jess could never bring himself to open the carton of Allan's things. His grief lasted the rest of his life.

Lieutenant Kocour's mother, who knew Allan well from the stories related by her son, later wrote to Allan's aunt: "Mrs. Rosevear, though the loss of Knep hurts terribly, you must be proud of him, and you can be sure these boys don't go down in fear; they are just a grand bunch of boys, and we must not spend too much time grieving, and pray and pray some more [that] this horrible slaughter will end soon."[16]

The family would eventually receive a letter from President Roosevelt. Formulaic though it might have been, the sentiment contained in the president's message might have given some comfort to Allan's family: "In grateful memory of Second Lieutenant Allan W. Knepper, A.S.No. 0-737801, who died in the service of his country in the North African Area, July 11, 1944. He stands in the unbroken line of patriots who have cared to die that freedom might live, and grow, and increase its blessings. Freedom lives, and through it, he lives—in a way that humbles the undertakings of most men."

The experience of the Knepper family was repeated in many homes in his hometown of Lewiston, Idaho, and its sister city of Clarkston, Washington, just across the Snake River, and in each one's surrounding county. Eighty-eight servicemen from the region were killed during the war, apparently including three men who received CPT flight training at Lewiston Normal in 1941: Hazen D. (Dale) Eastman, Donald W. Ham, and John D. Pratt.

Following standard army practice, after an interval of one year, servicemen originally classified as MIA but not recovered were reclassified as KIA (killed in action). For Lieutenant Knepper, this action came on July 11, 1944.

For pilots of the 49th squadron who flew combat missions during the summer of 1943 the losses continued after returning home.

Most of the 49th's veteran pilots were assigned as flight instructors, an occupation that was itself inherently risky. Over the next few months,

Lieutenants DeMoss, Harris, and Manlove were killed in training accidents. Each of these exceptional pilots had completed his assigned fifty-mission combat tour, had compiled over 200 combat hours, overcome unaccountable hazards, and had been credited with a combined nine aerial victories. For Captain Gregory, these losses were especially hard-felt: within a year after entering combat, all four of his closest friends and tentmates had been killed: Lieutenant Bland in combat and Lieutenants DeMoss, Neely, and Manlove in training accidents.

Following the war, the American government consecrated fourteen permanent sites on foreign soils to receive the remains of those killed in the conflict. The Sicily-Rome American Cemetery and Memorial was completed in 1956, and is located in Nettuno, adjacent to the landing beaches at Anzio. It is the final resting place for the remains of 7,861 servicemen, most of whom were killed in the bitter fighting on Sicily, in the landings and subsequent fighting at Salerno and Anzio, or in the air and naval operations in the area. These gravesites include both identified and unidentified remains. It is also the place of commemoration for 3,095 servicemen whose remains were never recovered. The names of these missing servicemen are recorded in the Tablets of the Missing, located in the Chapel of the Memorial. Lieutenant Knepper's name is included in those Tablets, along with his fellow pilots Wallace Bland, Sidney Booth, and other pilots downed but never recovered during this period of the war.

It is possible, though not likely, that the remains of these three men were recovered but not identified, and interred at Nettuno. In that case, their remains would be among the gravesites, but their names recorded on the Tablets of the Missing.

VICTORY IN SICILY

The amphibious assaults on Sicily by American and British troops succeeded on all beachheads, and by midday of July 10, the Allied forces had beaten back a determined if somewhat uncoordinated Axis counterattack. The Axis counteroffensive the next day at Gela was also repulsed by the American invasion force, and by evening of the second day, the Allied forces were in strong positions. American forces, led by Lt. Gen. George Patton, moved toward the northwestern shore of Sicily, then turned east toward Messina. British forces led by Gen. Bernard Montgomery pushed up the eastern coast of Sicily.

The Battle of Sicily raged for thirty-eight days. During the fighting, the Axis's strategy involved a series of delaying actions, effectively trading space for time. Withdrawing to the northwest in a controlled retreat, by the end of July the Axis forces were seemingly trapped in the vicinity of Messina. As Patton and Montgomery began what they thought would be a final and decisive offensive, Axis forces began an extraordinary evacuation through Messina to the Italian mainland. By the time Patton arrived in Messina on August 17, the Axis armies had disappeared.

The battle for Sicily was complete, but the German losses had not been severe, and their escape to Italy strengthened the German assets there, making further Allied advances in the Italian mainland more time-consuming and costlier in terms of men and materiel.

HISTORICAL REFLECTION

Historians have had the time, and access to key military documents from both Allied and Axis sources, to conduct many exhaustive evaluations of the Allied efforts in Operation Torch, the Tunisian Campaign, and Operation Husky. Though expert opinions differ on some points, there appears to be a broad consensus that the Allied efforts were marked by both high levels of success and clear failures.

The campaigns met many of the objectives laid out by Allied planners in the spring and summer of 1942, when military planners had finally settled the debate about where to take on the Axis forces first. Mediterranean sea lanes were open to Allied shipping, Italy surrendered, and German forces in Italy would soon face Allied landings there. German forces were diverted from the Russian front, its Luftwaffe had been decimated, and Allied strategic bombing had been perfected. In addition, Allied losses had been less than anticipated.

Historians also generally agree on the failures of Operation Husky. Clearly, AAF commanders did not yet understand how to provide effective close air support for ground troops, and the planning, communications, command, and control employed by Allied commanders were found wanting. Interdiction missions flown by NASAF and NATAF were inconsistent, leaving important Axis ground forces and reserve units inadequately targeted during crucial points in the invasion.

The most glaring failure of Husky was a lack of an end-game strategy at Messina. Both the American commander, Eisenhower, and the British commander, Alexander, expected a major battle there, with the same result that had been achieved in Tunisia in May—the surrender of Axis forces in huge numbers. But the commanders had failed to anticipate an ordered withdrawal. Defended by over two hundred large- and medium-caliber antiaircraft weapons, the region around Messina was effectively impregnable to either air or naval assault. Under the brilliant leadership of Fregattenkapitän Gustav von Liebenstein and Colonel Baade, Germany was able to evacuate over 102,000 troops, 10,000 vehicles, and over 17,000 tons of stores.[17]

REVIEW OF AIR FORCES OPERATIONS

In retrospective studies, the air forces were strongly commended for achieving many of their objectives preliminary to, and during, the Battle of Sicily. Most notably, the number-one priority set for the North African Air Force—air superiority—was achieved, and most Axis air assets were pummeled prior to the invasion, with many withdrawing to temporary safe havens in Italy. Naval and ground commanders, however, leveled strong criticisms about other aspects of air forces operations during Husky, and the air forces pushed back with their own assessment of operations during this phase of the war, providing data refuting the purported deficiencies in its support of naval and ground forces, and contending that it met its mission adequately in all respects.

In fact, there is truth on both sides of the argument. The harsh criticisms leveled at the air forces for their handling of certain aspects of air operations during the Battle of Sicily are all the more difficult to contemplate given the similarly negative reviews given to the conduct of air operations following Operation Torch and during the initial days of the

Tunisian Campaign. On first review, it would appear that the war policy planners had learned little from the experiences of the invasion of North Africa and the Tunisian Campaign.

The Allied air plan for Husky was designed around four primary missions: neutralizing enemy air forces, disrupting lines of communication, isolating the battlefield, and providing close air support. Important secondary tasks included protecting the Allied naval armada, coordinating naval and air operations, reinforcing convoys, performing airborne assaults, protecting rear areas from enemy air attacks, and conducting air-sea rescues.[18] Historians have demonstrated that roughly half of these objectives were met.

Certainly the secondary tasks identified above were accomplished well, with the exception of the performance of airborne assaults. The commander of the Western Naval Task Force, Admiral Hewitt, commended the air forces coverage of the 3,000-plus-vessel invasion fleet as it moved with the assault forces toward Sicily. That coverage was provided by the Coastal Air Force's 31st, 33rd, and 79th Fighter Groups, "the most carefully planned and most successfully executed phase of Husky."[19] Admiral Cunningham, commander in chief, Mediterranean, declared that the navies and armies "owed a great debt to the air for the effectiveness of the protection offered them throughout the operation."[20]

And high marks can be given to the air forces for neutralizing the enemy air forces. On D-Day the Axis forces were able to muster between 150 to 200 air missions against the invading Allied naval and ground forces from their nearly destroyed aerodromes and primitive satellite landing grounds, "a very respectable number considering their handicaps."[21] However, in the days that followed, the German and Italian air assets were largely inconsequential, and Allied forces enjoyed air superiority that approached supremacy.

INTERDICTION

Generations to come would debate how well the air forces performed with regard to disrupting lines of communication and isolating the battlefield.

Regarding lines of communication, the NAAF efforts—essentially interdiction missions—were primarily assigned to the NASAF, supplemented by additional missions by A-36 tactical bombers from NATAF and the 9th Air Force. It can be shown that effective bombing campaigns were waged against port and rail systems within Sicily, and to a lesser extent, the Italian mainland. However, the ability of the Wehrmacht to transfer the entire Hermann Göring Division in June from Italy to Sicily in the days leading up to the Allied invasion of Sicily, without interdiction by the air forces, was to have profound implications later in the Sicilian Campaign. Despite repeated missions against the primary trans-shipping port of Messina, the heavy air defenses there prevented Allied bombers from inflicting the level of damage that would have shut down the movement of troops into—and later, out of—Sicily.

Efforts to prevent German reinforcements from reaching the landing beaches began well before the actual landings.

Air Force planes during the closing daylight hours of D-Day minus 1 undertook in repeated bombing attacks to soften resistance at and adjacent to the beaches, to prevent the movement of enemy reserves to the threatened areas, and to pin down German and Italian aircraft. RAF through the night hours struck at a variety of targets in southeastern Sicily, most of them in the Syracuse area. With daylight, B-17 and B-25 bombers took over again to hit the Gerbini, Trapani/Milo, and Sciacca airfields and also the town of Palazzolo ahead of the Eighth Army.[22]

On D-Day, NASAF's interdiction missions had yielded good results. The P-38 missions in eastern Sicily, and the A-36 missions to the western and central regions, launched every half-hour from dawn to near dusk, had been especially effective along the eastern coastal road and on roads radiating from the Axis concentrations area around Enna in central Sicily.

Heavy and medium bombers also took on tactical missions during and after D-Day. However, the target selection for these missions appears to have been less than optimal, and may have been due to an uncertainty as to the location of key German and Italian defensive units on the island.

The continued bombing campaign against Axis airfields was probably unnecessary. The airfields were largely unoccupied, unusable, and undefended on D-Day. German air assets were continuing their evacuation from the island and little was to be gained with continued bombing. NASAF bombing efforts would have been better directed against troop concentrations nearer to the battle line, most particularly the German and Italian forces that counterattacked the Allied landings on D-Day and D-Day +1.[23]

> *Air support did little to impede the advance of the Hermann Goering and Livorno Divisions on 10 July and even less on the crucial day of 11 July. Conversely, on 11 July, 198 Italian and 283 German aircraft flew missions against the Allied beachhead (at Gela).*

> *The panzers on the Gela plain were sitting ducks had air support appeared to assist the hard-pressed ground forces. Their absence at the critical moment revealed the ineffectiveness of close air support and justified Admiral Hewitt's comment that "close support of aircraft in amphibious operations, as understood by the Navy, did not exist in this theater."*

> *Allied aircraft roamed far to the Axis rear, bombing Sicilian roads, Gerbini, Trapani/Milo, and Sciacca but not the positions just in front of the invading infantry. Nor were the rapidly advancing Mobile Group E, Brigade Schmaltz (German forces held in reserve near Catania), or the Hermann Goering Panzer Division seriously attacked.[24]*

Through the course of the Sicilian Campaign, the Allies flew hundreds of sorties under conditions of absolute air superiority. However quick-response close air support was never fully mastered by either tactical or strategic air forces, a failing that effectively squandered the Allies' hard fought victories against the Luftwaffe. Even small-scale strike missions often required up to 12 hours to plan and prepare, and the air commanders' inability to independently direct missions to meet the immediate requirements of ground commanders made timely support of ground units impossible.[25]

It was later argued that the air arm commanders were unwilling to consider any change that might lead to a loss of control to another unit. This rigidity, and the ineffective close air support that was its consequence, would later be the focus of sharp criticism of the air forces by other service units.

CLOSE AIR SUPPORT

As has been noted, the evolution of close support doctrine had been an intractable issue since the first days of combat aircraft. "Air and ground leaders struggled with interservice rivalry, parochialism, employment paradigms, and technological roadblocks while seeking the optimum balance of missions given the unique speed, range, and flexibility of aircraft." Close air support at this time in the war operated in what has been called a "doctrinal void."[26]

The strongest criticism leveled at NAAF was surely related to the perception that the close air support (CAS) provided by the North African Tactical Air Force had been a failure. In part, this failure may be attributed to the failure of NATAF to promulgate a clear plan as to what air support was likely to be provided. Air commanders now planned operations independent of ground commander interference, yet that same separation also produced plans that were not "integrated in detail with ground and naval plans,"[27] as demonstrated by the glaring absence of invasion-day CAS.

The air campaign overemphasized air dominance and interdiction, while CAS was scarcely mentioned. As noted by author Carlo D'Este, "what became increasingly worrisome to the ground and naval commanders was the absence of specific details about how the air force intended to support the invasion forces. During May and June these and other questions were repeatedly raised but satisfactory answers were not forthcoming from the air chiefs." Ground forces were "deeply concerned that the air forces had presented them with only the vaguest description of their plans for the air support of the invasion. The plan outlined by

[Arthur] Tedder [air commander in chief of MAC] was less a plan than a concept,"[28] writes D'Este. "It was almost as if the air forces were fighting their own war. Allied tactical air forces were under the command of . . . a man [Coningham] who had little use for either Montgomery or Patton. Coningham's North African Tactical Air Force was indifferent and even hostile to requests for air support from ground units, and routinely turned down even the most justifiable requests for aerial reconnaissance."[29]

American ground commander Patton complained to his naval counterpart, Admiral Hewitt, just before the landings: "You can get your navy planes to do anything you want, but we can't get the air force to do a goddamn thing!"[30] Historians Mitcham and von Stauffenberg opined: "With their 4,300 aircraft, the Allied air superiority over the beaches should never have been in question; yet, after having done a magnificent job of defeating the Luftwaffe and the Italian Royal Air Force, the Allied air forces did an absolutely miserable job of protecting the American convoys and beachheads and supporting the ground troops during the critical first three days of the invasion. While the army was enjoying success of the beaches . . . they did so without support from the Allied air forces."[31]

The poor close air support probably had as much to do with equipment and logistics as intent. The responsibility for close air support was NATAF's, and with the longer-range P-38s assigned to an interdiction role, the CAS missions had to be accomplished by the shorter-range Spitfires and P-40s. Their limited range meant that the aircraft could provide cover over their assigned sectors for very short windows of time, as little as thirty minutes. Further refueling and servicing of these aircraft was done at Pantelleria and Malta, which had definite limits as to the numbers of aircraft they could accommodate. And finally, NATAF fighters were also charged with providing fighter cover for bombing missions to Sicily.

CONCLUSIONS ABOUT OPERATION HUSKY

For all its achievements, the Sicilian Campaign also demonstrated some weaknesses in Allied capabilities, particularly in the realm of joint operations. None of the Allied commanders had much experience in joint air-land-sea operations, and consequently, the three services did not always work together as well as they might have. Ground commanders complained about the lack of close air support and the inaccuracy of airborne drops; air commanders complained of their aircraft being fired upon by Allied ground and naval forces; and naval officers chided the land commanders for not fully exploiting the fleet's amphibious capabilities to outflank the enemy once the campaign had begun. Similarly, General Alexander's unfortunate decision to broaden the Eighth Army's front at the expense of the Seventh Army can be attributed to the newness of combined operations, for the decision reflected the British Army's proclivity toward underestimating American military capabilities—an attitude that American GIs proved unjustified during the Sicilian Campaign.

Sicily was thus an important victory for the Allies, but not a decisive one. Coalition politics and the innate conservativeness of men who were still learning how to work the intricate machinery of joint, multinational operations tied Allied armies to a strategy which achieved the physical objective while letting the quarry escape. Nevertheless, Axis forces did not escape unscathed, and the experience Allied commanders gained in orchestrating airborne, amphibious, and ground combat operations during the campaign would serve them well in the months ahead, first in Italy, and then at Normandy.[32]

Post-Husky

The endgame could not yet be seen, but the outcome of the war was becoming evident. The dire situation for the Reich was especially clear to the Luftwaffe, for whom it was quite evident that they lacked the ability to withstand the inexorable advances of the combined Allied air forces. Göring's assertion to Hitler that German skies would never see Allied bombers was soon shown to be hollow bravado.

As Galland realized, in the face of overwhelming numbers of Allied aircraft, all tactical experiments tried by the GAF "led back to the old realization, seemingly almost banal now, that nothing could be done either in the air or on land without air superiority."[33]

The air war was costly to both sides. America lost 23,000 aircraft in combat during the war. On average, 6,600 American servicemen died each month during the war—about 220 a day. Over 40,000 airmen were killed in combat, 12,000 were missing in action, and 41,000 were captured.[34]

While the Battle of Sicily was raging, Allied bombers conducted a protracted campaign against Hamburg. "Operation Gomorrah" ran from July 24 to August 3, practically destroying the entire city. Over 42,000 civilians were killed, and 37,000 wounded. As Luftwaffe chief Galland notes in his memoirs: "After Hamburg in the wide circle of the political and the military command could be heard the words: 'The war is lost.'"[35]

CHAPTER 15

The Search for Allan Knepper

REACHING AN END TO GRIEF IS VERY HARD FOR FAMILIES WHOSE LOVED ones are listed as missing in action. As has been noted, the army declared the lost serviceman or -woman killed in action if their remains were not recovered for twelve months following their initial report of loss. For Allan Knepper, that determination came on July 11, 1944. But an official military declaration, while somehow meaningful in itself, still left an open wound. A funeral, a graveside ceremony, and a coming together of the families was needed, and for these families, none of that could be truly meaningful without the recovery of their loved one.

And so the Knepper family continued to live through the bright sunshine of Lewiston with an emotional cloud of grief that would not dissipate. Allan's father took his loss very hard. Allan was his firstborn, and they were evidently very close. Allan's mother had passed away in 1938, making the loss all the more heartfelt for his father.

The recovery of remains for servicemen who had gone missing in action has been a relatively rare event. In the case of the Mediterranean Theater, a high percentage of the losses occurred over open water, with no possible recovery. Losses over land made recovery more feasible, but the possibility of finding the missing airmen was strongly influenced by the local topography and the events of the day.

Allan was lost on what was surely the busiest day of the war up to that time for the Allies, and equally busy for the Axis forces on Sicily. The rural Sicilians who may have witnessed a plane coming down or a pilot parachuting to earth were not well equipped to deal with a capture, a rescue, or a burial, and perhaps even less equipped to document the event or report it to local authorities. In Sicily on July 10, with General Patton's army storming from the south and the British Army from the east, with the German army conducting a controlled retreat, and Italy surrendering to the Allies, the local citizenry could be excused if their only thought was to hunker down and hope for a quick resolution.

No record of Allan Knepper's loss has been discovered beyond the Missing Air Crew Report that Captain Trollope filed on July 13; any chance of recovering his remains was slim. But, having recorded the events of Allan's life—his joining the Army Air Corps, his completion of flight school and assignment to combat duty in North Africa—reaching a point of closure for what has come to be called the Allan Knepper Project has led to a fair effort to locate his crash site, hoping beyond reason to recover and repatriate his remains. Much more important than reaching a point of closure for his family was the clear realization that Allan himself, having given his life in service to his country in this most brutal war, deserved a faithful effort to recover him.

Having reached a point in the research where a recovery effort could be considered, the standard investigative steps were considered first, specifically, contacting local churches, cemeteries, and municipal governments to determine if any records existed from 1943. The first small step was made on June 29, 2014, when a letter was mailed to three churches in Mineo, selected for two reasons: Mineo is the closest town to the point where Lieutenant Knepper's plane was thought to have crashed; and in Lieutenant Kocour's letter to Allan's sister, he mentioned that Allan's plane went down next to a small church.

The initial inquiry resulted in one response acknowledging receipt, but no further word was received. At this point, it was decided to revert to the most powerful information-gathering technology ever developed— social networking. The reasoning was that even though the readers of social networking sites may not include eyewitnesses to the events of 1943, they may well include children and grandchildren of people who were eyewitnesses and who may have shared stories around the dinner table over the years.

In mid-April 2015 a quick Internet search of informational blogs within Sicily turned up several possible candidates for a social media campaign. Among them: BlogSicilia, a robust Internet platform with offices in six Sicilian cities and a network of correspondents and editors. BlogSicilia was contacted by e-mail on April 21, provided a brief background of the Allan Knepper Project, and asked if they believed a posting to their site would be appropriate and productive. The response from BlogSicilia was immediate. Mr. Francesco Lamiani, chief reporter for the blog in Catania, replied that a post would be made. Incredibly, the same day that the blog went live, a response was received from Salvo and Annalisa Fagone from Palagonia, Sicily: "This afternoon I talked with two people that remember this event. One of these is eighty-one years old, and he explained to me that he saw the plane falling into his garden. The second one is the son of a witness that is dead, unfortunately. He remembers that his father often told him about an airplane falling in that area. At the moment we have no information about the pilot, but we hope to find more information as soon as possible."

Salvo with his wife and son visited the farmstead owned by Mr. Giuseppe Gulizia four days later, and reported: "Mr. Giuseppe Gulizia, the witness of the crash, told us that Allan Knepper was first buried close to the place of the crash by them [Mr. Gulizia's family], and that one year later, more or less, the U.S. Army recovered the rest of the body. So, he confirms that the body is no longer in that place. As far as the aircraft was concerned, he told us that it was dismantled and all of the parts recycled by the residents. We hope to find some residual piece of the plane by using a metal detector, but for this we have to wait [until] the harvest." Mr. Fagone also attached photos from his visit with Mr. Gulizia.

As mentioned in Salvo's e-mail, the harvest was soon to commence in the region of the crash site. With crops high, and the farmers not willing to have them threatened, a sweep of the area using metal detectors had to be delayed.

On April 30, 2015, Salvo was supplied with Lieutenant Knepper's Missing Air Crew Report (MACR) and other military maps of the region dating to that time period. It was apparent that there was a strong correlation between what Mr. Gulizia had reported to Salvo and what was contained in the U.S. military records. In Missing Air Crew Reports, witnesses to the loss are identified, and supplemental information about the location of the event is included. In Lieutenant Knepper's MACR, a witness statement was provided by Capt. Richard Decker that included a simple map showing the approximate location of the crash sites for Lieutenants Bland and Knepper. The straight-line difference between the site pointed out by Mr. Gulizia and the estimate based on the MACR map is less than 1 mile.

On May 2, Salvo delivered an additional discovery: "A [piece of] good news is that Mr. Giuseppe Gulizia has a brother, one year younger. Mr. Giuseppe didn't [tell] me this because in the past he had words with him. I've just talked with his brother, Mr. Raimondo Gulizia. He remembered very well the crash, and he indicated to me the [location] of it. It corresponds exactly with the place that his brother pointed out. I want to underline that they don't talk to each other, and this is very important because they indicated the same place."

It was becoming clear that the event of July 10 was well remembered by at least two eyewitnesses, and that the location as indicated by both corresponds very closely to the location mentioned in the MACR. Intriguingly, there is an important discrepancy with regard to the young lieutenant's remains. While Giuseppe Gulizia believed that the body had been removed by the U.S. Army, his brother Raimondo believed that the remains were still located in the original gravesite.

Salvo also confirmed that the harvest was beginning, and that on the following day he was planning to visit the cemetery located in the nearby town of Mineo, searching for whatever additional information could be discovered there.

At this point, there appeared to be enough corroborated information to confirm—at least tentatively—that an airplane crash had occurred on or about July 10, 1943, and with a provisional location. There was still no confirmation that it was a P-38 crash site, and certainly no evidence to suggest that it was Lieutenant Knepper's plane that the Gulizia brothers were referring to.

Between May 8 and 10, 2015, the University of Catania and several private Sicilian companies were contacted to inquire into the feasibility of conducting ground penetrating radar (GPR) sweeps of the suggested crash site. After several e-mail exchanges, it was apparent that it would not be feasible to use GPR to locate Lieutenant Knepper's remains. The cost was steep. One company offered to rent our team the necessary equipment at a cost of 1,000 euros per day, along with a whopping deposit of 15,000 euros. Other firms submitted proposals whereby the sweep would be conducted by their personnel, at a cost that was also prohibitive.

It had also been suggested that GPR might be a suitable technology for locating the airplane remnants, but not the remains of the pilot. Dr. Alessandro Monacchi at CIS Geofisica advised: "If your need is to find the remains of the aircraft . . . this is simple . . . but it is difficult to find human remains buried in an agricultural land after seventy years. Very difficult, especially if the person was not buried in a real tomb or closed before in a case of metal or wood and then buried within in the casing."[1]

A leading U.S. expert was contacted to clarify the point made by Dr. Monacchi. Dr. Jim Doolittle, a research soil scientist with the National Soil Survey Center, confirmed Dr. Monacchi's opinion, and noted: "[In using GPR] the radar operator will look for 'anomalies' on radar records. Anomalies are reflections or patterns that are different and stand out from the rest of profiled materials. Detection of the burial will depend on its contrast with the surrounding soil matrix. As the officer's body was not placed in a coffin, detection will be more difficult. With the passage of time, features weather and become more similar to the surrounding soil matrix; this results in lower contrast and radar reflections with lower amplitudes. I concur with your feelings that the use of GPR will be unproductive and ineffective."[2]

With this information, by mid-May it had become apparent that the only affordable technology that held out any possibility of progress was metal detection. Concurrently, Salvo made a follow-up visit to the Gulizia farm, accompanied by the younger Gulizia brother, Raimondo. Salvo later reported: "He told me about the crash. He remembers that it happened in the afternoon, that his father [ran] toward the crash site immediately after the crash, hoping to find someone still alive, but the fire was too strong, and he couldn't. When the fire [was] extinguished, the airplane was shattered. He doesn't remember [anything] about the body."[3]

Importantly, during this visit to the site, Salvo discovered that the location of the crash appeared to be on two properties, not just one. A property adjacent to the Gulizia farm was owned by Mr. Salvatore Sipala and contained a citrus orchard. Mr. Sipala extended permission to Salvo to enter the property for this project. Having concurred that GPR was not feasible, on May 17 Salvo brought his own metal detector, a system capable of reaching 50 to 60 centimeters into the soil to identify medium-size objects. Salvo also mentioned a metal detectors club in Sicily that could possibly provide advice and on-site assistance in the coming days and weeks.

Realizing that the search for Allan's aircraft, and possibly his gravesite, was now entering a phase that would be more intrusive on the landowner's private property, letters of introduction and thanks were sent to the three key individuals contacted by Salvo: Giuseppe Gulizia, his brother Raimondo, and Salvatore Sipala.

On May 27, initial contact was made with the Air Force Mortuary Affairs Division to ask if there was a central point where unidentified remains were taken on Sicily. This question related to Mr. Gulizia's statement that, in his recollection, the U.S. Army had come one year after the plane crash to remove the victim's remains. A referral was made to Mr. Greg Gardner, who confirmed that any remains of unknowns from Sicily were consolidated into the Sicily-Rome American Cemetery in Nettuno, Italy, run by the American Battle Monuments Commission (ABMC). The Allan Knepper Project was referred to that cemetery, and to the Defense POW/MIA Accounting Agency (DPAA). Mr. Jason Blount, the assistant superintendent of the ABMC cemetery at Nettuno, was consulted.

In a very cordial and informative conversation, it was learned:

Lt. Knepper's name is included in the Tablet of the Missing at Nettuno, indicating that either his remains had not yet been recovered, or that they had been recovered but were unidentified.

*The cemetery itself has 7,861 gravesites, each holding remains—
both identified and unidentified.*

*It is possible that Lt. Knepper's name is included in the Tablet of
the Missing, but with his unidentified remains interred in a gravesite.*

*Remains, when recovered, were assigned an "X Card," on which
was recorded information related to the recovery of the remains. Apparently the information was quite variable, and somewhat limited.*

Concurrently, with the increased energy that his early findings generated, Salvo confirmed that he was intending to involve the local metal
detecting club in his search of the crash site.

The next day a "blind" call was made to Mrs. Martha Sell at the
ABMC office in Arlington. An extremely helpful and well-informed
resource, Mrs. Sell referred the Knepper Project to Mr. Joshua Fennell of
DPAA, and to Mr. Kyle R. Charrington, director of the U.S. Mortuary
Affairs office for Europe. An e-mail was sent to Mr. Fennell on May 28,
which brought an immediate reply and a phone conversation on May
29. Mr. Fennell confirmed that the DPAA was the correct office to work
with, and further confirmed his strong interest in the project. As a result
of this conversation, the photographs taken by Salvo on May 23 were
forwarded to Mr. Fennell, together with other background information
on the project and army materials related to Lieutenant Knepper's service
and loss. On June 1 Josh Fennell indicated that he would also be doing
a search for any after-action reports for the 14th Fighter Group and the
49th Fighter Squadron.

Subsequent contact was made with Mr. Joshua Frank, a DPAA
research analyst assigned to cases in Italy. Mr. Frank had been referred to
the Knepper Project by Mr. Fennell, and confirmed that the search for
Lieutenant Knepper looked "promising." On June 9, he mentioned that a
crash site had been reported in 2007–2008 by DPAA's predecessor organization, at coordinates 37.285623, 14.620299, roughly 4 miles from the
crash site indicated by the Gulizia brothers. It was his opinion that this
crash site could have been Lieutenant Bland's aircraft. He also reported:
"I have done a quick comparison of unknowns that were recovered in the
area, in an effort to see if Lt. Knepper's remains could be buried as an

unknown in either Nettuno or Florence. I do not see any indication that this is the case. There are no unknowns that could be associated with a pilot that were recovered within 25 miles of the crash area."

About this time, Salvo reported that Mr. Sipala had begun to show some concern about further searches on his property. The orchard is equipped with an underground irrigation system, and Mr. Sipala was unwilling to jeopardize either his trees or his watering system. The search was halted for what was initially hoped would be a few days, but which stretched into many months.

After doing a bit of cleanup on one of the components found in his first sweep, Salvo found that one of the items appeared to contain numbers and letters. Serial numbers are critical in crash-site investigations. Aircraft contain dozens of components that are marked with serial numbers, and they can be used to trace back to the manufacturer of the component, and to the type of aircraft in which the component was installed.

On June 21, Salvo returned from another sweep of Mr. Gulizia's farm lot and forwarded images of items he had found, including a trailer ball, what appears to be a brake component, several fragmented pieces, an intriguing bearing plate, and a spent cartridge casing. The shell casing caused some interest within the Knepper Project, with speculation that it may have come from the aircraft.

These photos were also uploaded to Josh Fennell and Josh Frank at DPAA. As it happened, Josh Fennell confessed to having been "noodling around" with cartridge headstamps for a few years. On the basis of photos that clearly showed the headstamp "K1940 VII," and reflecting the breadth of competence within the DPAA, Josh was able to confirm that this round was made by the British firm, Kynoch, in 1940. It is a casing from a .303 caliber round, possible dropped by a soldier in the British Eighth Army as he passed through this region in the first half of June 1943.

Important news came on July 14, 2015, when Josh Fennell reported the results of a review conducted by DPAA's aircraft analysis laboratory at Wright-Patterson Air Force Base: "They made a connection between two of the parts that Salvo found. In picture DSC01552, the circular part on the far left and the metal block slightly to the right of center frame were matched, respectively, to a cooling system flange mount and a connecting rod bearing cap. Both parts would be found on an Allison V-1710 engine, such as the ones used in P-38 aircraft. Without knowing more specifically which engine it is, we can bear in mind that the same power source was used for the P-39, P-40, and P-51 aircraft. But the site Salvo has found is almost certainly a U.S. airplane, and, given that there is a known P-38 crash in the vicinity, the circumstances would seem to suggest he is uncovering a Lightning."

Over many months, Salvo continued to meet with Mr. Sipala, attempting to determine if there were any conditions under which permission to continue the surface search on the Sipala property could continue. After careful negotiations, in May 2016 Salvo received approval from Mr. Sipala for a limited search on his property. A limit was imposed on the depth to which Salvo and his team could search, and with great care the metal detection search continued.

Salvo and his team returned with their metal detectors and were quickly rewarded with an astonishing number of metallic components. Photos of the components were sent to the Defense POW/MIA

Salvatore Fagone and associates conducting metal detection sweeps at the location believed to be the site of Lieutenant Knepper's crash in 1943.

FAGONE

Metallic artifacts discovered by Salvatore Fagone and associates at the location believed to be the site of Lieutenant Knepper's crash in 1943.

FAGONE

Accounting Agency, and in June Joshua Frank confirmed that the images had been forwarded to appropriate army and air force experts, and were being reviewed.

By December, the results of the analysis confirmed that the new metallic components uncovered by Salvo and his team on the Sipala property were that of a British Spitfire. It was definitely not Lt. Knepper's crash site.

Back in Lewiston, Allan's half-sister Shirley Dawn (Knepper) Finn is coordinating family efforts that could one day provide conclusive evidence of Allan's remains. DNA samples have been obtained and forwarded to the Army's Casualty and Mortuary Affairs Operations Center at Ft. Knox where they will be stored in the event that remains are discovered at the crash site in Sicily.

On December 19, 2016, DPAA's Josh Frank advised that the agency had recently added new research personnel, and that new information was emerging from the National Archives, including documents related to captured German Flak reports concerning the events of July 10. This new data suggests what might be very productive additional field investigations in the vicinity of Caltagirone, southwest of Palagonia.

Mr. Frank has announced that he and his DPAA team will visit Sicily in February–March, 2017 to conduct new field investigations. All parties are hopeful that these new efforts, led by experienced DPAA professionals, and aided by Salvo Fagone and his team, will uncover critical information about both Lieutenant Knepper's and Lieutenant Bland's crash site, as well as other potential crash sites in the vicinity.

This recovery and investigative work being done in Sicily goes beyond professional interest. And neither can it be explained as a hobbyist's curiosity. The personal and professional commitment to recovering the remains of servicemen lost in World War II is a continuing passion for the men and women involved. This passion, when married to DPAA's exceptional resources, could very well lead to a final and successful resolution to the question of what happened to Lt. Allan Knepper.

Chapter 16

After Combat

As mentioned previously, the combat pilots of the 49th Fighter Squadron continued their hard duty through the months of July and August, 1943, returning home at the conclusion of their fifty-mission combat tours.

Of the ten surviving members of the mission in which Lieutenants Bland and Knepper were killed, all survived their combat tour in North Africa. The next chapters in their own personal stories are filled with honor, achievement, and, in too many instances, tragedy. Brief biographies of those ten pilots, and of the squadron commander, are included below.

Red Flight

Lt. William "Greg" Gregory

Greg's fifty-mission combat tour ended as it had begun—escorting bombers. But in the 105 intervening days, he had grown from a novice to an experienced combat pilot and a leader within the squadron. In that time, he had flown every sort of mission possible with the P-38, had made many friends in the squadron, and had quietly endured the losses as they came. In recognition of his service, he had been awarded the Air Medal, a decoration awarded to pilots upon completion of five combat missions in recognition of meritorious achievement in flight. Following each subsequent five combat missions, pilots' Air Medals were appended with an "oak leaf cluster" in further recognition of combat service. At the time Captain Gregory completed his combat tour in North Africa, he had accumulated a total of eight oak leaf clusters. In addition, he had been recommended for the Distinguished Flying Cross.

His combat missions completed, Greg returned to the States and was reassigned as an instructor pilot. Together with his close friend Lloyd DeMoss he also ferried P-38s around the country, and on one of these flights the two passed through Barksdale AFB in Shreveport, Louisiana. It was there that Greg first met Helen, and they were married about a year later. In time, they were blessed with two daughters, Gretchen Dwire Gregory (husband, Gene) and "Cookie" Gregory Ruiz (husband, Phil), and grandchildren J. R., Boo, and Greg.

Greg would eventually fulfill his early teaching ambitions by earning his undergraduate degree in education from Centenary College, and later a master's degree in international affairs from George Washington University.

Greg remained in the air force briefly following the end of the war, and in 1947 left the active service and remained in the Air Force Reserve. He and his wife moved back to Shreveport, and at nearby Barksdale AFB, Greg continued to fly—without pay—on weekends. Barksdale was a bomber base, and Greg switched from fighters first to the B-29 bomber, and then to the B-47. His reserve duty continued to involve occasional overseas postings, and it was after returning from a three-month assignment to Morocco that he was interviewed for a highly classified assignment with the high-altitude "Black Knight" Program. The interview was held at Turner AFB in Albany, and Greg was introduced to the aircraft that was at the center of the program—the Martin RB-57D Canberra, a specialized high-altitude strategic reconnaissance aircraft.

Black Knight was the U.S. military's early efforts at developing a capability for overflight and surveillance of the Soviet Union. In brief, the program would use the RB-57 as the basis for a new, more performant aircraft. The new plane would use the fuselage of the RB-57 with longer wings, a honeycombed construction, and a larger engine. The B57-D2 version was used for an interim intelligence program from 1956 to 1960. In a later evolution of the program, the aircraft used would be designated the U-2.

Just twenty of the B57-D2 aircraft were built. As is cited in the literature, "Little is known about their use."[1] Thirteen of the aircraft were equipped with cameras and six with the automatic ELINT system for collecting radar data, and one was equipped with the very first (experimental) infrared system.

After four years as commander of this squadron, in April of 1960 Greg was selected for the CIA's U-2 Program, and was named as operations officer for the U-2 squadron located in Atsugi, Japan. Almost concurrently, Gary Powers's U-2 was shot down over Russia. With chaos in Washington, Greg's orders were on hold for three months before he was assigned to Edwards AFB, where he took charge of a squadron of ten U-2 aircraft.

Greg's unit began to overfly Cuba on intelligence-gathering missions in October of 1960. In early 1961 his group began overflights of Vietnam—four years before the large buildup there.

Lt. Col. William J. Gregory, commander, 4025th Strategic Reconnaissance Squadron, 4080th SR Wing (SAC), Laughlin AFB, Del Rio, Texas, 1959.
COL. WILLIAM J. GREGORY (RET.)

Black Knight squadron commander
Lt. Col. William J. Gregory.
COL. WILLIAM J. GREGORY (RET.)

In late August of 1961, one of Greg's pilots, Bob Erickson, found the first surface-to-air missiles in Cuba. Identifying the SA-2s was important because they were normally deployed by the Soviet Union in a defensive circle around intercontinental ballistic missiles. Locating twenty of these SAM missiles on the western end of Cuba, it was evident what was coming next from the USSR. At this point, the intelligence missions were turned over to the U.S. Air Force, and on the basis of their confirmatory findings, the United States implemented a blockade leading to what is now known as the Cuban Missile Crisis.

In 1964 Greg was offered the position of operations officer for the new SR-71 spy plane. The position represented a phenomenal career opportunity for Gregory, but would take him away from his family almost entirely for two years, followed by three more years after that with scant contact. With his daughters in high school, and his wife dreading another long period of separations, Greg declined the position, and instead accepted a placement in the National War College.

After one year at the college—one of the most prestigious assignments in the air force—Greg accepted a position at the Pentagon, working on research and development for reconnaissance systems, including ground-breaking work on the early air force drone systems, and on systems that would later become "smart bombs." After five years at the Pentagon, Greg accepted a position as vice commandant of the Air Force Institute of Technology. At that time AFIT operated a graduate program at Wright Patterson in aeronautical engineering, and in management, and placed several thousand officers in colleges and universities around the country.

Over the course of his career, Greg piloted fifty-five different airplanes, including naval aircraft. He is one of a select few air force pilots to have attained the Aircraft Carrier Qualification, earned from the decks of the USS *Lexington*.

In addition to the combat decorations earned in World War II, Greg was awarded the CIA's Medal of Merit, together with a personal letter of commendation from President John F. Kennedy. For security reasons, the awards were retained at CIA Headquarters until his involvement in the Cuban Missile Crisis was de-classified in 1975.

Greg retired from what can only be described as an awe-inspiring career in the Air Force in 1975, but continued working as assistant director of Workers' Compensation for the Office of the Attorney General of the state of Texas for an additional 15 years. He and his wife Helen enjoyed fifteen years together after his retirement, before her death in 1990. "She was such a loyal person—she was a great wife," says Greg. "And she did a really great job with the girls. I am really proud of both my girls."

With time on his hands, Greg turned to cycling at the age of seventy-five. His passion for cycling grew, and he made extensive cycling tours in France, Germany, Belgium, the Netherlands, Austria, Denmark, and England. He cycles to this day, and is, by any standard that may be applied, a remarkable man.

Lt. Frederick James Bitter

Lt. Frederick James Bitter, known to his squadron mates as "Jim," was awarded the Distinguished Flying Cross in recognition of his valiant actions in what would be his final combat mission—a B-17 bomber escort over Orte, Italy in late August 1943. His commendation includes: "On many combat sorties his leadership, gallantry and selfless devotion to duty have reflected great credit upon himself and the Armed Forces of the United Stated (by command of Maj. Gen. James Doolittle)."

Lieutenant Bitter came very close to not surviving this final mission. Operating at 26,000 feet while escorting the B-17s, Bitter's wingman peeled out of formation when one of his motors failed. With three enemy fighters closing in on the crippled aircraft, Bitter went on the attack and shot down two of the German aircraft. At that point, he came into the sights of two other German fighters. His aircraft was hit with cannon shell, and he was only able to escape by throwing his P-38 into a steep, two-mile spinning descent.

On being interviewed later by his local newspaper, Bitter commented that he did not take much stock in prayers while taking his training in the United States, but after he went into his first battle he had all the faith in the world in a prayer when the going got rough. "At least my prayers were answered on my last mission; it was the only way that I could have gotten out of the mess."

In addition to the DFC, Lieutenant Bitter earned the Air Medal with nine oak leaf clusters during his tour in North Africa.

Lieutenant Bitter returned to his wife May Jane following his combat tour, and was reassigned as an instructor in the 443rd Training unit. Together they raised four children: Rick, Greg, Rebecca, and Amy. His

Mary Jane and Fred Bitter. Photo dated Sept. 19, 1942, just prior to Lieutenant Bitter's posting abroad.
RICK BITTER

Fred and Mary Jane Bitter with children Rick, Greg, and Rebecca. Daughter Amy still to come.
RICK BITTER

son was named after William "Greg" Gregory, Lieutenant Bitter's close friend and frequent wingman in the Mediterranean Theater.

Bitter continued his military career in the U.S. Air Force Reserves, retiring with the rank of lieutenant colonel.

Fred Bitter returned to the family business after the war, managing Bitter's Grocery Store with his brother Herman until 1965. He then worked as supervisor in the railroad and steel yard at Pullman Standard for fifteen years until his retirement in 1979. Not content to be idle, he then worked in the maintenance department at Friedman's market for five more years.

Fred Bitter died on February 10, 1994 at the age of 77.

Lt. Art Lovera

1st Lt. Art Lovera returned to the United States in mid-September, 1943. He was assigned to the 440th Base Unit as a flight instructor, along with Harold Harper and other returning combat veterans.

Lieutenant Lovera's life back home was troubled and unsettled. His son, Dusty, recalls:

> *As a kid coming up, my Dad never really spoke about the war any-time. Never told us anything about it. I never knew if that was right or wrong at the time. We never pushed him on it because he wasn't one that you could readily sit down and talk about it. He pretty well clammed up.*

By 1945 Art's family consisted of a wife, a stepson, a son. Two months later a third son was born, and at that point Art's wife deserted the family. He remarried twice more. Of his father's second wife, Dusty has nothing good to say. But Dusty fondly recalls Art's third wife, Norma, a kind and generous woman who was good for Art.

Dusty also has this to say: "If you relate it to guys in my time that went to Vietnam, they've been fighting it since they got back. A lot of the guys I golf with are Vietnam vets, and our getting together has done more for our vets here than going to any doctor has, to be honest with you. We went through that, and we heckle each other as we play. And after we play we'll sit down and shoot the breeze for an hour or an hour and a half. But it helps, and I don't think my Dad had anything like that when he got home. When you look at when our Dad grew up, and what he came through, they had it so much tougher than what we had."

First Lieutenant Lovera was discharged from the army on January 16, 1946 at the AAF Regional & Convalescent Hospital at Fort George Wright, Spokane, Washington. His service medals included the Air Medal, with eight oak leaf clusters—a testament to the many combat missions he flew from North Africa.

Art Lovera died on January 17, 1982. His Certificate of Service includes the notation: "Wounds Received in Action. . . None"—A cate-gorization that is tragically inaccurate.[2]

Lt. John Harris

Beryl Boatman with John Harris.
MICHELE BRANCH

Lt. John Harris completed his fifty combat missions with a fighter bombing sweep over Avellino, Italy.

On his return he commented that he "has failed to note any indication that German soldiers are weakening or that they have lost faith in their fuehrer and his blatant promises."[3]

He returned to the States in November 1943, and was assigned as flight instructor in Washington and California with the 443rd Base Unit. On May 20, 1944, having just received orders for a second combat assignment overseas, Lieutenant Harris's aircraft's engine failed during a routine training flight. He was able to control his plane just long enough to heroically guide it to a local park away from the businesses and residential areas of heavily populated Ontario, California, and was killed in the crash.

Lieutenant Harris had been awarded the Air Medal with ten oak leaf clusters and the Distinguished Flying Cross in recognition of his overseas combat duty.

Lt. Martin Foster

Lieutenant Foster arrived in North Africa in March 1943, having journeyed first to England with the other pilots who would "restart" the 14th Fighter Group. His combat service nearly ended on his fourth mission, on May 21, escorting B-17s on a raid to Castelvetrano aerodrome on Sicily. Joined by twelve aircraft each from the 37th and 48th Fighter Squadrons, the twelve P-38s from the 49th took off from Telergma at 0730. Lieutenant Little was leading the Blue Flight, with Lieutenant Foster as his wingman. The bombers made their drop amidst heavy but inaccurate flak over the target, and the combined bomber-fighter formation encountered and engaged enemy aircraft almost continuously on the return leg. At 1015, Lieutenant Foster and his leader, Lt. Albert Little, were last seen diving on an enemy Me109.

In Lieutenant Foster's words:

Another pilot (Lt. Little) and I made the beginner's error of going after what seemed to be a couple of easy ones. It turned out to be a Jerry trap and a couple of ME-109s proceeded to show us their fire power.

Lt. William Gregory, in Blue flight, recalls:

We got into a really big scrap. There were 12 of us, and . . . there must have been 20-30 enemy aircraft and we were back and forth and all of a sudden I was all by myself. I looked down and saw a P-38 with four 109s in a circle. I dove down through them, and made one pass, and got two of them on me. I did not know at the time, but it was Little. I got two of them on me, and one of them followed me all the way to the coast, to North Africa.

In the frantic aerial combat, Lieutenant Foster's left engine was shot out, and he lost use of his left aileron and left inboard flap. He limped his way back to the African coastline, and crash landed on a beach near Bizerte.

The plan was wrecked, but I wasn't hurt—not until two hours later. I had landed near a British camp. I went swimming with some English soldiers and then they took me for a ride in a captured Nazi reconnaissance car. We hit a bump and I sprained by wrists.

Lieutenant Little was never recovered.

Lieutenant Foster continued to fly combat missions, and in early September 1943 succeeded Captain Decker as Operations Officer of the 49th Fighter Squadron. His service tour ended with fifty-one combat missions, his last coming on October 11, 1943, also escorting B-17s, on a raid to Sardinia.

On his return to the States in January 1944, and his reunion with his wife Faye, Lieutenant Foster was reassigned as a flight instructor with the

Col. Martin A. Foster.

NATIONAL PERSONEL RECORD CENTER

4th Air Force at Santa Maria Army Air Base in California, teaching new flight cadets how to fly the P-38 and P-51 fighters. His squadron mate Harold Harper and his wife occupied the other half of the duplex Martin and Faye lived in while assigned to Santa Maria.

He remained in the service following the end of the war, and in August 1946 was named executive officer of the 39th Fighter Squadron (35th Fighter Group), and later would become the Group Operations Officer.

He was twice assigned to the Air University at Maxwell Air Force Base, served at air bases in Japan, England, and the United States, and completed one tour at Ton Son Nhut Air Base in Vietnam, serving as assistant deputy chief of staff.

In early 1970 he was named commander of the Niagara Falls Air Base. He retired with the rank of colonel on January 21, 1972, having been awarded the Bronze Star and numerous other campaign and service medals.

Martin and his wife Faye had five children: Marion Lee, Carolyn, Elizabeth, Dennis, and Michael.

Martin Foster died on April 9, 2003 at the age of 84.[4]

WHITE FLIGHT
Capt. Richard Decker

After completing his combat tour, Richard Decker returned to the United States in late 1943 and was assigned as director of operations and training at Abilene Air Base in Texas.

When the war ended he was assigned to Headquarters XII Tactical Air Command in Bad Kissingen, Germany. He returned to the States in 1947 to serve as squadron commander of the 307th Pursuit Squadron (31st Pursuit Group), based at Turner AFB in Albany, Georgia. In 1949, Colonel Decker was sent overseas for the third time, assigned to the 51st Fighter Wing as deputy for materiel. At the outbreak of the Korean conflict he was sent to Japan as tactical inspector for Far East Air Forces. He returned to the United States in 1951, assigned to the 4706th Interceptor Wing in Chicago, Illinois. In 1953 he was appointed air defense liaison officer to the U.S. Navy's Eastern Sea Frontier headquarters in New York City.

Colonel Decker was assigned next to Roslyn Air Force Station, Long Island, New York, as inspector general for the 26th Air Division. He left Roslyn in 1957 to attend the Jet All Weather Fighter School at Perrin Air Force Base in Texas, flying F-86 aircraft. Upon completion of the course, he was assigned to postings in Pittsburgh, Pennsylvania, and St. John's, Newfoundland. He retired from the air force at Lowry Air Force Base in Denver, Colorado, in 1961, a command pilot having been awarded decorations in both World War II and Korea, including the Distinguished Flying Cross, the Bronze Star, and the Air Medal with nine oak leaf clusters.

Richard and Louise split their time between their Colorado ranch near Anton and a home in Naples, Florida. For many years he owned and flew his own plane between Florida and Colorado.

Louise Decker passed away on February 23, 1998. Richard followed fifteen years later, on October 10, 2013.

Flight Officer Charles Richard

F/O Charles Richard returned to the United States after earning the Distinguished Flying Cross and the Air Medal with nine oak leaf clusters. He began instructing P-38 pilots at Salinas and Santa Maria. After one year, he was again posted overseas, transiting India over the Himalayas, en route to China.

He flew twenty-six missions out of Mengzi, China, into French Indochina. On one mission his plane was hit, knocking out one engine and shattering the gun sight in front of his face, sending shrapnel into his right hand, arm, and leg. For this action he was awarded the Purple Heart.

After the war, he returned to complete his education at McNeese College, and then earned a law degree from Louisiana State University. After graduation, he worked briefly as a corporate credit manager, and began his own law practice. He later joined the district attorney's office, and worked there for twenty-four years, retiring in 1984.

True to his roots, Charles was an avid hunter of deer, rabbits, ducks, and squirrel. And his culinary skills with wild game were widely praised: deer jerky, smoked ducks, smothered rabbit or squirrel, and his specialty— shrimp and okra gumbo.

Charles married Mary Margaret "Mimi" Stine and they raised three children: Charlane, Charles W. Jr., and Velarie. After Mimi passed, he married Jeanette Burge and became stepfather to her three children.

In a testimony to his service, in 2013 he received the Louisiana Medal of Honor.

Jeanette would later write of him: "I would describe my husband as a man's man, an honest man, highly intelligent, elegant, and as one who knew and practiced all social graces. He was truly a southern gentleman, but one who could and would stand his ground when necessary!"

Lt. Harold Harper

Lt. Harold Harper flew his last combat mission on August 28, 1943, leading the 14th FG's three squadrons on a B-17 escort mission to Terni, Italy. This mission was the farthest north that the group had ever flown, and when he returned, he had logged a total of 215 hours of combat flying in his fifty missions.

He was awarded the Distinguished Flying Cross for action just a few days before his final mission. On August 19, 1943, while escorting B-17s on a mission over Foggia, the formation was hit by enemy fighters. When fifteen of the enemy fighters attacked his formation, Lieutenant Harper saw an Me 109 directly pressing in to attack a crippled P-38. Realizing his fellow pilot was in danger, Harper "unhesitatingly turned his plane directly into the path of the hostile fighter, and by drawing the enemy fire to his own aircraft, enabled his comrade to parachute to safety. He then outfought the Me 109 and shot it down in flames."[5]

With several other pilots from the 49th squadron who had also completed their combat tour, Harper transited Rabat, Morocco, en route to England. There they boarded a C-54 transport for the long flight to Iceland, then Presque Island, Maine, and finally to Wright-Patterson AFB in Ohio. Lieutenants Harper, Knott, and Homer boarded

Capt. Harold Harper.
LT. COL. HAROLD HARPER (RET.)

the "Super Chief" to the West Coast and were treated to a heroes' welcome on their arrival at Bakersfield, where the local press dubbed them the "Three Musketeers." The three friends were assigned to the 371st Fighter Squadron (366th FG), first posted to Salinas, California, then to Santa Maria, where they remained for the duration of the war as instructors in P-38 fighter tactics.

Harper was especially pleased to complete his combat tour and return to the United States with his fellow flight school students, good friends, tentmates, and squadron pilots, Carroll Knott and Monroe Homer. He was also pleased that

Lts. Knott, Harper, and Homer.
BAKERSFIELD CALIFORNIAN, 21 OCT 1943

their other tentmates, Lieutenants Manlove and Evans, were able to complete their combat tour safely and return to the United States.

Harper was separated from the service in September of 1945, at Salinas, California. He returned to college and graduated from Oregon State University in 1947, with a BS degree in biology, and began a career as a research biologist with the California Department of Fish and Game.

He was called back to active duty when the Korean War erupted, flying P-51s at Tyndall AFB in Florida. He trained as an aviation physiologist at Gunter AFB in Alabama and was then assigned for the duration of the Korean conflict to Mather AFB in California, as commanding officer of the Physiological Training Section.

Harold was discharged from active duty in September 1953, returning to work with the State of California. He remained in the Air Force Reserves until retiring in 1968 with the rank of lieutenant colonel. In 1984 he retired from the California Department of Fish and Game.

Harold Harper,
August 15, 2014.
RICHARDSON

Lt. Beryl Boatman

Following his combat tour in North Africa, 1st Lt. Beryl Boatman returned home in the fall of 1943 to be reunited with his wife and to see his five-month old son for the first time. At the age of 21, Boatman was a hardened combat pilot, credited with having shot down two—and possibly as many as five—enemy aircraft, and logging more than 200 hours of aerial combat flying.

After a brief posting stateside, Beryl Boatman served a second combat tour with his old unit—the 49th Fighter Squadron—where he was promoted to squadron commander. Before ending this second tour, he completed 32 more combat missions, with a total of 361 combat hours, a remarkable achievement considering the great dangers associated with flying the P-38 in combat.

Boatman completed his baccalaureate degree in physics at the University of Oklahoma in 1950, and was soon teaching at the Air Force Institute of Technology at Wright-Patterson AFB in Dayton, Ohio.

In July 1952 he was assigned to Air Command and Staff School at Maxwell AFB, administering the Project RAND contract, a program designed by air force general "Hap" Arnold as a way of connecting military planning with research and development decisions.

In August 1953 the world learned that the Soviet Union had detonated a hydrogen bomb, resulting in an emergency program to develop America's first intercontinental ballistic missile with the primary planning and policy work for the program assigned to the Air Force Ballistic Missile Division, Headquarters Air Research and Development Command.

From 1954 to 1959, Beryl Boatman served with the Air Force Ballistic Missile Division. The resultant missile system, the Atlas ICBM, became operational in 1959. In addition to ICBM development, the research conducted through the ARDC led to scientific and engineering breakthroughs that allowed satellites to be launched into space, a capability spurred on by the launching of the Soviet Union's Sputnik 1 in October 1957.

Recognizing the immense potential of ballistic rocketry, Boatman's vision extended well beyond military applications. In 1955 he posed a curious question to his brother Karl, a cardiac surgeon, about the half-life of red blood cells. When asked what prompted the question, Boatman replied: "Because when I get this ballistic missile thing going I want to put a man on Mars and bring him back and I don't know how long it's going to take."

Following his successful contributions to this program, Boatman returned to the University of Oklahoma to complete his master's degree in nuclear physics in 1959.

From 1959 to 1961 Beryl Boatman was executive officer of the Air Force Systems Command. In 1961, at the age of 39, he was named military assistant to the assistant secretary of defense.

According to his daughter Michelle Branch, "He loved flying—that was his bliss." By the fall of 1961, realizing that his flying days with the air force were coming to an end, Beryl retired. At the time of his retirement, Beryl Boatman held the rank of colonel in the Regular Air Force and was a command pilot with over 2,000 hours in all types of aircraft.

His decorations included the Distinguished Flying Cross with one oak leaf cluster, the Air Medal with fourteen oak leaf clusters, the Legion of Merit, and many awards and commendations.

Beryl Boatman receiving the Legion of Merit from General Schreiber, 1961.

MICHELE BRANCH

After a distinguished career which saw fundamental changes in air force capabilities and doctrines, Beryl Boatman died of natural causes in 1983 at the age of 62.

BLUE FLIGHT

Lt. Herman Kocour

Lt. Herman "Koc" Kocour completed his fifty combat missions with a B-25 escort mission to Grosseto, Italy, on October 22, 1943. His combat hours totaled 218, and he received the Air Medal with nine oak leaf clusters. During his time with the squadron, he saw thirteen of his fellow pilots lost in action.

Herman received orders home on October 26, 1943, and almost immediately upon his return married his sweetheart, Agnes Josephine Finn, on Thanksgiving Day, 1943. He was assigned as an aircraft maintenance officer, and separated from the service on March 17, 1946. According to his family, he never flew a plane again.

Herman earned his degree from Wichita State University, putting himself through college working as a butcher. He became an accountant, first with the firm Coffman, Kocour and Taylor, which merged in 1961 with Fox & Co. to become one of the nation's largest accounting companies at the time. He became a leader in natural resource accounting.

He kept a few head of livestock on his 80-acre farm, and according to his family, he was most at ease wearing jeans and boots on the farm. Herman Kocour died in Kansas at the age of sixty-five.

Lt. Anthony Evans

Almost nothing is known of Lt. Anthony Evans. He completed his fiftieth combat mission on August 28, 1943, a B-17 bomber-escort mission to Terni, Italy. He completed his tour with a bang, destroying an Me 109 on his final flight. Tony Evans was a very effective fighter pilot. He has been credited with four confirmed kills during his service in North Africa.

Lieutenant Evans's orders sending him home to the States were received on September 26, 1943, and he joined many of his fellow pilots on the long homeward trek. From that point forward, no record is found.

The Bland Family

In the course of time, Bea and Grady Bland would later add two sons to their family, John and Bob. And in due course, Carolyn coped with the loss of her young husband, and like many young war widows, remarried. She settled with Jessica in Houston, and with her husband Joe added two more daughters to the family, Winifred and Janice. She and Joe were married until his death in 1995, and she died in May 2005.

Wallace Bland's parents, Bea and Grady Bland, with Carolyn (Bland) Clark and Joe Clark.

ART TAPHORN

Lt. Louis Ogle

Lieutenants Louis Ogle and Martin Foster were assigned as spares to the mission of July 10, 1943, when Allan Knepper and Wallace Bland were killed. When Lieutenant Richard's aircraft developed a mechanical problem, he peeled off the formation and Lieutenant Foster took his position as Lieutenant Decker's wingman. Richard and Ogle escorted each other back to base.

Lieutenant Ogle got a lot of flying in during the month of July, assigned to eight more missions between July 10 and 30. He was absent from the squadron for the month of August, for reasons that are not known. He returned to action on September 6, just in time for the next major American offensive of the war—Operation Avalanche.

The invasion of Italy began on September 3 with Operation Baytown, in which the British Eighth Army jumped across the Messina Strait to occupy the toe of Italy. A second invasion force, code-named Operation Slapstick, landed at Taranto on September 9. The main invasion force, consisting of the American 5th Army, landed at Salerno on that day.

As with the landings on Sicily during Operation Husky, the Allied air forces were assigned the task of attaining air superiority and supporting the ground offensive. Accordingly, the pilots of the 49th squadron flew at a pace that was little noted during the months of June, July, and August.

Lieutenant Ogle was assigned to twelve missions in the nine days from September 6 to 15. On four of those days he flew two missions each, a heavy load of combat assignments shared by other members of the squadron.

On September 15 Ogle was assigned to a dive-bombing mission on the road between Baiano and Monteforte, Italy, having already flown a dive-bombing mission earlier in the day to Montecorvino. According to his fellow pilots: "As we were approaching Salerno after leaving the target area we encountered flak. While weaving to avoid this flak I saw a puff of black smoke come out of Lieutenant Ogle's left engine. I looked away, watching the ground for a very short time, and when I next looked up I saw Ogle, apparently out of control, pull straight up and then over and hit the ground . . . in the town of Fisciana."[6]

Incredibly, Lieutenant Ogle was the only casualty sustained by all three squadrons of the 14th Fighter Group during the Allied invasion of Italy. An experienced combat pilot at the time of his death, Ogle was killed on his eighteenth mission, and was buried at the U.S. Military Cemetery at Mount Soprano, Italy. In 1948 his remains were repatriated, at his father's request, to his hometown of Pierce City, Missouri.

Maj. Lester Blount, probably
photographed at Foggia, Italy.
BLOUNT FAMILY COLLECTION

Capt. Lester L. Blount

Captain Blount remained with the squadron for nearly the entire war, and upon his return to the United States was assigned as psychiatrist at the El Toro Air Force Base. He narrowly avoided being reassigned to a combat unit in the Pacific Theater, and credited a compassionate clerk with "misfiling" his documents.

After the war, Lester Blount restarted his medical practice at Santa Ana, California. That area was to experience unprecedented growth, and his practice grew along with it. He later returned to school to study surgery, and his wife, Barbara, returned to teaching.

After the war, Dr. Blount continued his predilection for invention and pioneered the use of disposable plastic components for hospital use. Working out of his garage, and occasionally using his children as models for his pediatric prototypes, he developed the Blount Oxygen Mask, a pliant polyethene design that provided a closer and more comfortable patient fit.

Later, Dr. Blount became committed to not just limiting smoking in America, but to stamping it out. He developed the "Smoker's Kit," a smoking cessation system for which he received a patent and later commercialized.

For several years, Dr. Blount and his son Gary would board a military surplus C-47 operated by Southwest Airlines and fly up the

The three children of Lester and Barbara Blount: Gary, John, and Barbara Lynn.
BLOUT FAMILY COLLECTION

California coast, hopscotching airfields until they arrived at the grand-parents' home in Salina.

Lester was the sort of person who did not know how to slow down. On the day he was scheduled for his own cardiac surgery, he first completed hospital rounds to check on his patients. Dr. Blount did not recover from his own surgery, and died on March 3, 1988, at Santa Ana, California.

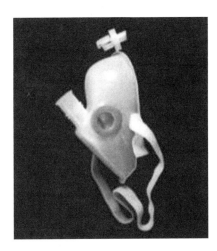

Blount Oxygen Mask.
BLOUNT FAMILY COLLECTION

Lester and Barbara Blount, and family.
BLOUNT FAMILY COLLECTION

Maj. Henry "Hugh" Trollope

Maj. Henry Trollope, the commander of the 49th Fighter Squadron during the summer of 1943, a time of intense combat and high losses, flew his last mission with the squadron on September 19, 1943. Along with many of his fellow pilots, he received orders to return home on September 26. His service in North Africa resulted in his being awarded the Distinguished Flying Cross and the Air Medal with eight oak leaf clusters. His travels home took him from North Africa through Rio de Janeiro to Miami, and by rail back to his wife Margaret in Casper. He arrived home on October 20.

On September 9, 1946 Hugh Trollope's P-80 went down shortly after takeoff from his base, and he was killed in the crash. According to his family, a mechanical failure caused his "bucket wheel" to come off, destroying the aircraft's stabilizer.

Major Trollope's accident was one of many that occurred during the introduction of the P-80. America's leading ace in World War II, Maj. Richard Bong, was killed during an acceptance flight of the P-80 in August 1945. In 1946 alone, eighty accidents were reported at home and abroad, with eight pilot fatalities.

Hugh's twin brother Harry married, and christened his son "Hugh" in honor of his lost brother.

Epilogue

The three young men from the Lewiston-Clarkston valley who joined the Army Air Corps in the spring of 1942 all began their service in the same way, but traveled vastly different paths, with ends that could not be predicted but were yet all too familiar.

Ralph Nichols became a C-47 pilot, flew with distinction, and was awarded service medals in recognition of his contribution to the war effort.

Leonard Richardson washed out of pilot school, became a navigator, and served with a C-47 group in the South Pacific in the early days of America's island-hopping northward. His brief period of overseas service ended with a plane crash in mid-September 1943, and the story of his ordeal is told in an unpublished 2012 manuscript, "A Mustering of Heroes."

Allan Knepper became a P-38 fighter pilot in North Africa. As reported in Richardson's brief memoir: "Al and I both went missing, and they never found Al." It was from this short phrase that the search for Allan Knepper was begun in 2011.

Allan's story is told imperfectly in the present book. Relating his service, and the circumstances of his loss, has been complicated by the almost total lack of surviving personal communication. One letter, written on his arrival in North Africa as he traveled to join his P-38 squadron, is all that has been recovered. So telling Lieutenant Knepper's story has required an exhaustive review of army documents, a thorough search for contemporaries, and a careful reading of historical literature.

The book was written for an audience of one: Allan's half-sister, Shirley Finn. Though she was born after Allan's death, through the stories and memoirs that spoke of the enduring loss felt by his family, his life became a part of her own. Although many years have passed since his death, Shirley and her family continue to wonder about his loss and to wish that more could be known about how he came to be in North Africa, who he fought, and who he fought alongside, and how and where he died. This book was written to answer those questions, and the chief regret of the author is that it comes too late for many of Shirley's kin.

Astonishingly, two pilots who participated in Allan's last mission were located and have made extensive contributions to this writing: William Gregory and Harold Harper. Both have vivid memories of their time of service in North Africa, and of this specific mission. Their recollections and confirming documents have been of inestimable help in completing the narrative of Lieutenant Knepper's service.

Allan, Ralph, and Leonard are clear examples of what has come to be called "the Greatest Generation"—three men responding to their country's call to arms, willing to leave their homes and loved ones to take paths that all three knew would be life-changing. They knew that their lives would be forever altered by the horrible conflict they were entering, that they were entering a branch of service known to be inherently dangerous, and also that others of their generation had already responded to their nation's call, young men and women whose sacrifice "humbles the undertakings of most men."

This quote is taken from the certificate the Knepper family received from President Roosevelt. The full text reads as follows:

In grateful memory of Second Lieutenant Allan W. Knepper, A.S.No. 0-737801, who died in the service of his country in the North African Area, July 11, 1944. He stands in the unbroken line of patriots who have dared to die that freedom might live, and grow, and increase its blessings. Freedom lives, and through it he lives—in a way that humbles the undertakings of most men.

The date given for his death is one year and a day after his actual loss. This was standard practice for the army at that time, in the belief that if he did not appear after one year, he had most probably been killed in action.

I presume that this same certificate was sent by the president to the next-of-kin to all servicemen who were killed in action, and is in addition to the Purple Heart award that Allan's family received.

Allan was killed on his fifth combat mission, but this should not suggest that he was unprepared for battle. At the time of his loss, he and his squadron mates were the most feared warriors history had ever produced, wielding the most devastating and technologically advanced weapons systems ever devised, ably prepared for precisely the sort of mission that would sadly take his life.

Had his formation been just slightly higher or lower, or moving just a bit faster or farther to the east or west, he might have survived the mission. One can just as easily imagine him completing his fifty combat missions and returning home to his loving family, with a chest full of medals and the Distinguished Flying Cross. Home to a life perhaps like his own brother's, when he returned from the war—a wife, children, and a career.

It is also easy to imagine that, coming home, Allan would have had the same reticence as his fellow pilots, men who had themselves lost many friends, had seen the terrible devastation of the war, and had come to understand the tragic losses on all sides among both combatants and civilians. For Allan, as with the young men with whom he flew, there was honor but no glamour. Those who survived combat and returned home, their duty fulfilled, could reflect that they had taken their piece of the action and that no one had shouldered their part of the load. They had earned the sense of pride that comes after a job well done.

The story of Lieutenant Knepper's brief career as an Army Air Forces pilot may be of no great significance in the context of the vast slaughter of that war, except to his family. But the arc of his life, from schoolteacher in rural Idaho to front-line aerial combat against the Luftwaffe, mirrors the lives of so many other young men of his generation. And the loss to his family is surely representative of the losses felt in countless homes around the country, and around the world, during the war.

There is satisfaction in telling Allan Knepper's story, but more gratifying is the possibility that his crash site may have finally been located on Sicily, with the hope that his remains will ultimately be found and repatriated to Lewiston. Allan Knepper, an admirable young man, deserves this effort, and more. His was a short life well-lived, remembered with love by his family and those who came to call him friend.

Notes

Chapter One

1. Much of the information related to pilot assignments and aircraft is taken from the squadron mission reports. For this chapter, see Mission Report, 49th Fighter Squadron, Mission #31, 18 June 1943. Also see "The Building of a Fighter Squadron," Marshall Cloke, Major, Air Corps, Merriam Press, Military Reprint 2, 2012, and Personal Correspondence, Robert Vrilakas, Dec. 5, 2015.

2. Pilot Training Manual for the P-38 Lightning, Headquarters, AAF Manual 51-127-1.

3. German Air Force (GAF) data sources: www.cgsc.edu/CARL/nafziger/943GG AB.pdf and www.ww2.dk/air/jadg/jg77.htm.

4. Authors Steve Blake and John Stanaway take a different view in their book, *Adorimini (Up and at 'Em): A History of the 82nd Fighter Group in World War II* (Marceline, MO: Walsworth Publishing, 1992). They posit that "Many American pilots and air crewmen were convinced that an elite German fighter unit was based at Gabes and that it could be identified by its Me 109s' distinctive white or yellow noses. This unit was often referred to as 'Göring's elite yellow-nosed squadron,' or by some similar appellation. In reality, none of the German fighter Gruppen in the MTO at that time were any more 'elite' than the others. Most of them had been in action almost continuously since the beginning of the war in Europe, and had been credited with the destruction of hundreds of Allied aircraft on various fronts. In truth, all the Luftwaffe fighter units then stationed in the Mediterranean could be considered elite."

5. The Messerschmitt Bf 109 fighters were designed by Willy Messerschmitt in the early 1930s. After the original manufacturer Bayerische Flugzeugwerke was renamed to Messerschmitt AG, later production of these fighters carried the designation Me 109, though this designation was used in only a few official Luftwaffe documents. The British also referred to them as Bf 109s; "By 1945, we were drowning in Bf 109 nameplates," said British aviation expert Bill Gunston, referring to the nameplates of numerous Bf 109 fighters shot down over Britain, "[T]here's no excuse for not referring to the aircraft by its right name." To the Americans, however, aircraft of this model were known as Me 109 since the start; "It will always be the Me 109 to me," said retired U.S. Air Force colonel James L. McWhorter, who fought against them as a pilot of the U.S. Army Air Forces 365th Fighter Group during World War II from the Normandy Campaign until the end of the European War. See: ww2db.com/aircraft_spec.php?aircraft_model_id=F18.

6. Interviews, William Gregory, October 12, 2014, and May 5, 2015.

7. Mission information is from the Air Force Historical Research Agency (hereafter, AFHRA): 1st FG Unit History 1st Fighter Group, GP-1-SU-RE-D (FI), 00077183; Unit History 27th Fighter Squadron, SQ-FI-27-SU, 00056064; Unit History 71st Fighter Squadron, SQ-FI-71-SU, 00057182; and Unit History 94th Fighter Squadron, SQ-FI-94-SU, 00057826; 82nd FG Unit History 82nd Fighter Group, GP-82-HI, 00080877-80880 and 00080936; Unit History 95th Fighter Squadron, SQ-FI-95-HI, 00057840 and -57870; Unit History 96th Fighter Squadron, SQ-FI-96-HI, 00075872; and Unit History 97th Fighter Squadron, SQ-FI-97-HI, 00057905; 325th FG Unit History 325th Fighter Group, GP-325-SU-OP(FI), 00058318; and Unit History 319th Fighter Squadron, SQ-FI-319- HI, 00058313.

8. 14th Fighter Group Monthly Statistical Summary, One Year of Continuous Operations, May 6, 1943–May 6, 1944, prepared by the Statistical Section.

9. "The Crew Chief's Lament," Clarence N. Hammes, 342nd Bomb Squadron, cited in "Magnificent Men of the B17s," *Washington Post*, July 29, 1985.

10. Mission Report, Form D-11, 37th Fighter Squadron, June 18, 1943, AFHRA.

11. The cross-over turn was a tactical innovation credited to German pilot Werner Mölders. This maneuver allowed an entire flight to quickly change direction without loss of formation and with reduced risk of collision.

12. Missing Air Crew Report #308 (Campbell) and #309 (Church). Missing Air Crew Reports of World War II, National Archives Identifier 305256.

CHAPTER TWO

1. Table of Organization and Equipment for a Twin-Engine Fighter Squadron, No. 1-37, War Department, July 1, 1942.

2. "Crew Chief Daze," *Lightning Strikes*, Newsletter of the P-38 National Association, Vol. 1, No. 4, September 1988. Memoirs of former crew chief Fred Montgomery.

3. "World War II: Japanese Military Aviation Training," Children in History, histclo.com/essay/war/ww2/cou/jap/force/air/w2jfai-train.html.

4. "Aerial Warfare and the Spanish Civil War," by Pamela Feltus, *U.S. Centennial of Flight Commission* (www.centennialofflight.net/essay/Air_Power/Spansh_CW/AP18.htm).

5. "Imperial Japanese Army Air Service" Wikipedia, en.wikipedia.org/wiki/Imperial_Japanese_Army_Air_Service.

6. Biennial Reports of the Chief of Staff of the U.S. Army to the Secretary of War, The President's Emergency Proclamation, September 8, 1939.

7. Stephen L. McFarland, *A Concise History of the U.S. Air Force, World War II— Global Conflict*, Air Force History and Museums Program, 1997.

8. RAF Tribute, raf-112-squadron.org/index3.html, 14th Fighter Group, 5th Wing, 15th Air Force Combat Squadrons of the U.S. Air Force, edited by Maurer Maurer, Albert F. Simpson Historical Research Center and Office of Air Force History, Headquarters USAF, 1982.

9. Frank N. Schubert, *Mobilization in World War II: The U.S. Army in World War II*, 50th Anniversary, U.S. Army Center of Military History, p. 290.

10. Stephen L. McFarland, *A Concise History of the U.S. Air Force*, Air Force History and Museums Program, 1997.

11. Army Air Forces Historical Studies, No. 2, "Initial Selection of Candidates for Pilot, Bombardier, and Navigator Training," Assistant Chief of Air Staff Intelligence Historical Division, November 1943.

12. Flight Training on the Eve of WWII, Article 196919, National Museum of the U.S. Air Force, Wright-Pattrson Air Force Base, Dayton, OH. http://www .nationalmuseum.af.mil/Visit/MuseumExhibits/FactSheets/Display/tabid/509/Article/196919/flight-training-on-the-eve-of-wwii.aspx

13. "Putt Putt Air Force: The Story of the Civilian Pilot Training Program and the War Training Service, 1939–1944," Department of Transportation, Federal Aviation Administration, Aviation Education Staff, GA-20-84. The interested reader is also referred to the following: Rebecca Hancock Cameron, *Training to Fly: Military Flight Training, 1907–1945* (CreateSpace, 2012); and the Virginia Aeronautical Historical Society (vahsonline.publishpath.com/).

14. The CPT program eventually included 1,132 educational institutions and 1,460 flight schools. By the time the CPT program was ended in 1944, it had provided flight training to 435,165 students, including several hundred female pilots. By mid-1942, CPT had trained over 125,000 pilots. For a complete list of schools, see *They Flew Proud*, by Jane Gardner Birch (2007).

15. Dominick A. Pisano, *To Fill the Skies with Pilots: The Civilian Pilot Training Program, 1939–1946* (Washington, DC: Smithsonian Institution Scholarly Press, 2001).

16. Southern Illinois Normal University Bulletin, April 1941 (archive.org/stream/ southernillinoi194142sout/southernillinoi194142sout_djvu.txt); Lawrence J. Hodgins Jr., "The Civil Aeronautics Administration Civilian Pilot Training Program (The CAA Course)," November 29, 1940 (archive.org/details/TheCivilAeronauticsAdmin istrationCivilianPilotTrainingProgramthe).

17. Ibid. Hodgins.

18. "Old Air Service Was Airline's Daddy," *Lewiston Tribune*, September 19, 2011 (lmtribune.com/mobile/article_fb5331c3-8191-57b9-91f6-3d1b3a4d77af.html).

19. Hodgins Jr., "The Civil Aeronautics Administration Civilian Pilot Training Program."

20. "U.S. Civil Aeronautics Authority," *Air Commerce Bulletin*, Vol. 11, #3, September 15, 1939.

21. Ibid.; "The Piper Cub," *History of Flight*, U.S. Centennial of Flight Commission (www.centennialofflight.net/essay_cat/10.htm).

22. *Popular Aviation*, March 1941.

23. Hodgins Jr., "The Civil Aeronautics Administration Civilian Pilot Training Program."

24. Lewiston Normal Annual, *Elesenes* yearbook, 1942.

CHAPTER THREE

1. William P. Mitchell, *From the Pilot Factory*, 1942 (College Station: Texas A&M University Press, 2005).

2. Information provided by Casey Jones at Andale High School (Andale, Kansas), January 9, 2015.

3. 1969 Comprehensive Plan for the City of Andale, Kansas. City Clerk, Andale, Kansas.

4. Riley Moffatt, *Population History of Western U.S. Cities and Towns, 1850–1990* (Lanham, MD: Scarecrow, 1996), 95.

5. Editorial, *Lewiston Tribune*, December 12, 1941.

6. Brig. Gen. H. H. Arnold and Maj. Ira Eaker, *This Flying Game* (New York and London: Funk and Wagnalls, 1936).

7. Aviation Cadet Training Manual for the AAF, undated. Aviation Cadet Manual, 1942, War Department, Adjutant General's Office, Washington, Recruiting Publicity Bureau, U.S. Army, Governors Island, NY, 1942.

8. AAFHS, No. 2, "Initial Selection of Candidates for Pilot, Bombardier, and Navigator Training."

9. Aviation Cadet Training Manual.

10. AAFHS, No. 2, "Initial Selection of Candidates for Pilot, Bombardier, and Navigator Training."

11. Ibid.

12. Ibid.

13. Aviation Cadet Training Manual for the AAF.

14. See paragraph below, for a description of the examination, including sample questions.

Sample questions from the AC exam: Army Air Forces Historical Studies No. 2, "Initial Selection of Candidates for Pilot, Bombardier and Navigator Training," Assistant Chief of air Staff Intelligence Historical Division, November 1943.

Vocabulary

Two circles which overlap but do not have the same center are

A   elliptical
B   eccentric
C   congruent
D   unequal
E   concentric

Mathematics

Logarithms are the least useful in which of the following processes?

A   Subtraction
B   Cube Root
C   Division
D   Square Root
E   Multiplication

Alertness to Recent Developments

After the German attack on Russia in June 1941, the United States

A   avoided sending any direct aid to Russia.

B   announced that Lend-Lease aid would be sent to Russia.

C   stated that aid to Russia would depend on the Russian attitude toward the Church.

D   encouraged Finland to recover the territory she lost to Russia in 1940.

E   announced that aid to Britain prevented Lend-Lease aid to Russia.

15. Cameron, *Training to Fly: Military Flight Training, 1907–1945*.

16. AAFHS, No. 2, "Initial Selection of Candidates for Pilot, Bombardier, and Navigator Training."

17. Ibid.

18. Dates are based on the similar records contained in the archives of Knepper's fellow enlistee, Leonard G. Richardson.

19. Dr. Bruce Ashcroft, staff historian, *We Wanted Wings: A History of the Aviation Cadet Program*, HQ AETC Office of History and Research, 2005 (www.afhso.af.mil/shared/media/document/AFD-150911-028.pdf).

20. Letter, Joseph C. Rollins, 1st. LT, Air Corps, Recorder, Air Base HQ, Aviation Cadet Examining Board, Geiger Field, Washington, March 12, 1942.

21. Enlistment Records, Herman Kocour, provided by Robert Kocour, July 3, 2014.

22. Correspondence with Dr. Theresa L. Kraus, agency historian, Federal Aviation Administration, Washington, DC, March 14, 2014.

23. AFHRA Historical Study No. 48, "Preflight Training in the AAF (1939–1944)."

24. Robert L. Richardson, *A Mustering of Heroes*.

25. "Historic California Posts, Camps, Stations, and Airfields," California State Military Museum (www.militarymuseum.org/SantaAnaAAB.html).

26. "The War Experiences of Arthur R. Driedger Jr., C-47 Radio Operator Mechanic," 13th Troop Carrier Squadron, 403rd Troop Carrier Group, 13th Air Force.

27. Aviation Cadet Training Manual for the AAF.

28. AFHRA Historical Study No. 48.

29. Loving, *Woodbine Red Leader: a P-51 Mustang Ace in the Mediterranean Theater*, 2003.

30. Mitchell, *From the Pilot Factory, 1942*.

31. *Students' Manual: Primary Flying*, AAFTC Army Air Forces Training Command, Visual Training Unit.

32. Robert Vrilakas, *Look, Mom—I Can Fly! Memoirs of a World War II P-38 Fighter Pilot* (Tucson, AZ: Amethyst Moon, 2012).

33. *Students' Manual: Primary Flying*.

34. Mitchell, *From the Pilot Factory, 1942*.

35. Ibid.; Samuel Hynes, *Flights of Passage: Recollections of a World War II Aviator* (New York: Penguin, 2003).

36. "Crossroads: Basic Flying School," Fact Sheet 1491, National Museum of the U.S. Air Force.

37. Capt. Bob Norris, *The Dust Bowl to World War II: One Young Man's Journey of Survival*: Xlibris, 2014).

38. Ibid.

39. See extended below, for comments related to the suitability of the BT-13 for aerobatic flight training.

Some sharp differences of opinions exist regarding the use and function of the BT-13. An advocate, Wayne G. Johnson, reports as follows in his book *Whitey, from Farm Kid to Flying Tiger to Attorney:*

> *That powerful engine made it a great aerobatic plane. We did slow rolls, a roll around a point, barrel rolls a roll around a circle in a coordinated roll, chandelles, a steep dive and then a pull-up while turning one-hundred eighty degrees, and lazy eights, similar to a chandelle, except you would continue on around in another type of chandelle until you flew a vertical figure eight. We did loops, a steep dive to pick up speed then pulling up until the plane was upside down then around and down into a complete vertical circle. Immelmens [sic] were another fun maneuver involving half a loop where the pilot would roll out to a level position at the top.*

George Loving felt quite differently, as he expressed in his book *Woodbine Red Leader:*

> *Given its sluggish performance, the BT-13 wasn't well suited to acrobatic flying, but that wasn't a problem because the curriculum concentrated on instrument, formation, and day and night cross-country flying.*

There appears to be general agreement that the BT-13 was difficult to fly, and for that reason was considered the perfect training aircraft for pilots who would later transition to the P-38 fighter.

40. Norris, *The Dust Bowl to World War II.*

41. Vrilakas, *Look, Mom—I Can Fly!*

42. Interview, William J. Gregory, October 12, 2014.

43. 63rd Army Air Forces Flying Training Detachment at Douglas, Georgia (wwii-flighttraining.org/AdvancedTraining.php).

44. AAF Training During World War II, Article 196138, National Museum of the U.S. Air Force, Wright-Patterson Air Force Base, Dayton, OH.

45. "Winning their Wings: Advanced Flying School," May 4, 2015, National Museum of the U.S. Air Force (www.nationalmuseum.af.mil/Visit/MuseumExhibits/FactSheets/Display/tabid/509/Article/196855/winning-their-wings-advanced-flying-school.aspx).

46. Harold Harper, commentary included in manuscript draft review, March 29, 2015.

47. *Silver Wings*, class yearbook for 43-B, Williams Field.

48. Mitchell, *From the Pilot Factory*.

49. W. F. Craven and J. L. Cate, *The Army Air Forces in World War II, Vol. VI, Men and Planes* (Chicago: The University of Chicago Press, 1983).

50. 63rd AAF Flying Training Detachment at Douglas, Georgia.

51. Harper, commentary, March 29, 2015.

52. Norris, *The Dust Bowl to World War II*.

53. George Loving, *Woodbine Red Leader: A P-51 Mustang Ace* (Novato, CA: Presidio Press, 2003).

54. Honorable Discharge, Allan W. Knepper, 19033105, February 5, 1943.

55. "Army Air Corps Flight Training in WWII," National Museum of the U.S. Air Force (www.scharch.org/Dick_Baer/_RFB%20AAF%20Training/AAF.htm); Cameron, *Training to Fly: Military Flight Training, 1907–1945*.

56. "Forging Combat Pilots: Transition Training," Fact Sheet, National Museum of the Air Force (www.nationalmuseum.af.mil/Visit/MuseumExhibits/FactSheets/Display/tabid/509/Article/196854/forging-combat-pilots-transition-training.aspx).

57. *LIFE* magazine, August 16, 1943, P-38, by William P. Gray, p. 51.

58. "AAIR Search Result for Squadron 83," AAIR Aviation Archaeological Investigation and Research, (www.aviationarchaeology.com/src/dbasqdn.asp?squad=83&Submit5=Go&offset=625).

59. Ibid.; Craven and Cate, *The Army Air Forces in World War II, Vol. VI, Men and Planes*.

60. Vrilakas, *Look, Mom—I Can Fly!*

61. Blake and Stanaway, *Adorimini*.

62. *The Army Air Forces in World War II*, Volume Six, Men and Planes, Chapter 18, Combat Crew and Unit Training, Wesley Craven and James Cate, editors, Office of Air Force History, Washington D.C., 1983

63. "The *Muroc Maru*: Practice Target," Histomil Historica (histomil.com/viewtopic.php?t=14601#ixzz3PwugWwDb).

64. "USAAF/USAF Accident Report Monthly List," AAIR Aviation Archaeological Investigation and Research (www.aviationarchaeology.com/src/AFrptsMO.htm).

65. Form 5, Individual Flight Record, Herman J. Kocour, 337th FS, 329th FG.

66. John Underwood, *Grand Central Air Terminal* (Images of Aviation) (Charleston, SC: Arcadia Publishing, 2006).

67. Orders, Lt. Herman Kocour, April 11, 1943.

68. Ibid.

69. "The Summer of '42," Writings of Art Ayotte (www.fugawee.com/summer_of.htm).

70. Vmail dated May 18, 1943, from Lt. Allan Knepper to his father, J. W. Knepper, Lewiston.

71. Ibid.

72. History of the 82nd Fighter Group, AFHRA Document 80879.

73. Wayne G. Johnson, *Whitey: From Farm Kid to Flying Tiger to Attorney: A Memoir* (Minneapolis, MN: Langdon Street Press, 2011).

74. Ibid.

Chapter Four

1. W. F. Craven and J. L. Cate, eds. *The Army Air Forces in World War II, Vol. 2, Europe: Torch to Pointblank, August 1942 to December 1943* (Washington, DC: Office of Air Force History, 1983).

2. Maurer, ed., *Air Force Combat Units of World War II* (Washington, DC: Office of Air Force History, 1983).

3. *History of the 14th Fighter Group* (TE), AAF, January 15, 1941–May 1943, AFHRA Documents 00077884 and 00077885.

4. Leo J. Meyer, *The Decision to Invade North Africa (TORCH)* (Washington, DC: Center of Military History, U.S. Army, 1990).

5. "Operation TORCH: Allied Invasion of North Africa," originally published by *World War II* magazine. Published online June 12, 2006 (www.historynet.com/operation-torch-allied-invasion-of-north-africa.htm).

6. Meyer, *The Decision to Invade North Africa (TORCH)*.

7. Ibid.

8. Ibid.

9. The following notations are drawn primarily from Meyer. Even in retrospect, it is debatable whether the decision to invade North Africa was the soundest strategic decision that could have been made at the time, and under the existing circumstances. The real question therefore remains: Was it wise to embark on an operation in the northwest African area in 1942 at the expense of a possible direct attack against the Continent in 1943? The British as a group, and some Americans, notably the president, believed it was; most of the American military leaders and strategic planners thought otherwise. The preference of the British for Operation Torch undoubtedly stemmed fundamentally from their opposition to an early frontal assault on *Festung Europa*. Their inclination for a peripheral strategy was based in part on tradition, in part on previous experience in the war, in part on the desirability of opening up the Mediterranean, and in part on the need of bolstering their bastions in the Middle East. The American military leaders believed the war could be brought to an end more quickly if a main thrust was directed toward the heart of the enemy. Marshall and his supporters contended with equal vigor that had not Torch and the preparations for subsequent operations in the Mediterranean drained off men and resources, depleted the reserves laboriously built up in the United Kingdom under the Bolero program, wrecked the logistical organization in process of being established there, had given the enemy an added year to prepare his defenses, a cross-Channel operation could have been carried out successfully in 1943 and the costly war brought to an end earlier. Whose strategy was the sounder will never be known. Adolf Galland, commandant of the Luftwaffe, also noted that the effect of opening a third front resulted in the Luftwaffe being stretched to the breaking point. Four fighter groups protected the Reich, five were fighting on the Eastern Front, and three in Sicily. The Luftwaffe was being degraded on all fronts—an effect that was to have profound consequences in the later battles in Italy and northern Europe.

10. Tentative Manual for the Employment of the Air Service, Lt. Col. William C. Sherman, 1919.

11. Field manuals issued in the immediate prewar years—*FM 1-10* and *FM 1-15*—failed to clarify either the use of aviation forces or the organization in which they operated; *FM 31-35*, issued just prior to the United States' entry into the war, also failed to clarify the role of air forces in combat operations.

12. The successes in the eastern desert campaign were largely attributed to the effective relationship between the RAF and the British Eighth Army, for which the RAF commander, Air Marshal Arthur Coningham, is credited.

13. Army Field Manual *FM 31-35*, Aviation in Support of Ground Forces.

14. Winston Churchill, in a speech at the Lord Mayor's Day Luncheon at the Mansion House, London, November 10, 1942.

15. W. F. Craven and J. L. Cate, *The Army Air Forces in World War II, Vol. VI*, Men and Planes (Chicago: The University of Chicago Press, 1983).

16. USAF Historical Study No. 114, "The Twelfth Air Force in the North African Winter Campaign, November 11, 1942, to the Reorganization of February 18, 1943," Air Force Historical Studies Agency.

17. AFHRA Study No. 88: "Employment of Strategic Bombers in a Tactical Role, 1941–1951," USAF Historical Division, Research Studies Institute, Air University, 1953.

18. John L. Frisbee, "The Lessons of North Africa," *Air Force Magazine*, The Online Journal of the Air Force Association, September 1990.

19. *The First and the Last, The rise and fall of the Luftwaffe*: 1939-45, Adolf Galland.

20. *The German Air Force in the Mediterranean Theater of War*, Lt. Gen. (General d. Flieger) (Retired) Hellmuth Felmy, unpublished manuscript, 1955, U.S. Air Force Historical Study 161, AFHRA file K113.107-161.

21. The *Courier-Journal*, Louisville, KY, Wednesday, February 3, 1943, "Roving Report from Africa," by Ernie Pyle.

22. Maurer, *Air Force Combat Units of World War II*.

23. John W. Lambert, *The 14th Fighter Group in World War II* (Atglen, PA: Schiffer Publishing, 2008).

24. Robert W. Shottelkorb, *From Model T to P-38 Lightning: Celebrating the Life of William Frank Shottelkorb* (Missoula, MT: Pictorial Histories Publishing, 2003).

25. Frisbee, "The Lessons of North Africa."

26. Aircraft operating under NATAF included: Bombers: B-25 medium bombers A-20, A-36, Baltimore and Mosquito light attack bombers; Fighters: Spitfires, P-40s, P-51s, Beaufighters, and Hurricanes. Also included various reconnaissance and transport aircraft.

27. Aircraft operating under NASAF included: Bombers: B-25, B-26, and Wellington medium bombers; B-17 heavy bombers; Fighters: P-38 and P-40 fighters.

28. Aircraft operated under NACAF included: Bombers: Halifax heavy bombers, B-24, B-26, and Wellington medium bombers, Beaufort, Swordfish, and Albacore torpedo bombers, Blenheim, Ventura and Hudson light bombers; Fighters: Spitfires, Beaufighters, Hurricanes, P-39s. Also included were Walrus air-sea rescue aircraft.

29. Frisbee, "The Lessons of North Africa."

CHAPTER FIVE

1. These dates are surmised based on orders issued to Knepper on June 4, 1943, and on their confirmed arrival date at the 49th squadron on June 9, 1943.

2. Combat Crew Rotation, World War II and Korean War, Historical Studies Branch, USAF Historical Division, Aerospace Studies Institute, Air University, Maxwell AFG, Alabama, January 1968.

3. Fredric Arnold, *Doorknob Five Two* (S. E. Maxwell Publishing, 1984).

4. Interview, William J. Gregory, October 12, 2014.

5. Transcript of conversation with William Gregory, October 12, 2014.

6. Op. Cit. *Adorimini*; 37th Fighter Squadron Summary Report for 1943, AFHRA Document IRIS 56284.

7. 37th Fighter Squadron Summary Report for 1943, AFHRA Document IRIS 56284.

8. 14th FG Monthly Statistical Summary, One Year of Continuous Operations, 6 May 43 – 6 May 1944, prepared by the Statistical Section.

9. Mission History, 49th Fighter Squadron, Sgt. Ralph Holt, AFHRA Document IRIS 56631.

10. Roy Grinkler and John Spiegel, Men Under Stress, J. & A. Churchill, 1945. This information on combat stress is not intended to be an accurate representation of battle stress as understood in the current era, but rather a reflection of what constituted stress and battle fatigue as reckoned during World War II.

11. *Once There Was a War*, John Steinbeck, 1943

12. "The Building of a Fighter Squadron," Marshall Cloke, Major, Air Corps, Merriam Press, Military Reprint 2, 2012, and personal correspondence, Robert Vrilakas, Dec. 5, 2015, and to "Memoires, Royal Clarence Gilkey," Veterans History Project, American Folklife Center, Library of Congress Collection AFC/2001/001/20875.

13. Maurer, *Air Force Combat Units of World War II*. Note that this document has an incorrect date for the arrival of the 14th FG to Telergma. Other sources verify the correct date.

14. Biography of George Underwood, S/Sgt, 381st Bomb Squadron, 310th Bomb Group, 57th Bomb Wing, 12th AF, USAAF, James F. Justin Museum; Blake and Stanaway, *Adorimini*.

15. Mission History, 49th Fighter Squadron, entry for June 7, 1943.

16. Personal correspondence, Mike Howell, June 2014.

17. Weekly Squadron and Operations Report, 37th Fighter Squadron, 14th Fighter Group, June 20–26, 1943. AFHRA Document 56321.

18. Blake and Stanaway, *Adorimini*.

19. NAVAER, Interview of Maj. John W. Mitchell, USAAF, and Capt. Thomas G. Lanphier, USAAF, P-38 Pilots—Guadalcanal in the Bureau of Aeronautics, June 18, 1943.

20. Col. Harold J. Rau, Commander 20th Fighter Group to Commanding General, VIII Fighter Command, 3 June 1944.

21. William B. Colgan, *Allied Strafing in World War II: A Cockpit View of Air to Ground Battle* (Jefferson, NC: McFarland, 2010).

22. Vrilakas, *Look, Mom—I Can Fly!*

23. Target Priority Lists, A-2 Section, XII Air Force, AFHRA Document 232881.

24. Strategic Analysis—Air, prepared by Lt. Col. Robert C. Lowe, Assistant Chief of Staff, A-2, NAAF, May 13, 1943.

25. Part IV of Detailed Interrogation Report on P/W Adalbert Steininger, CSDIC File 281, May 29, 1943, AFHRC Document 232885.

26. Mission Reports , 49th Fighter Squadron, AFHRC Document IRIS 56630.

27. Matthew G. St. Clair, "Air Support of the Allied Landings in Sicily, Salerno, and Anzio," Joint Force Quarterly, October 1, 2005, ISSN 1070-0692.

28. Lt. Col. Albert Garland and Howard Smyth, *U.S. Army in World War II, Mediterranean Theater of Operations, Sicily and the Surrender of Italy*, Chapter IV, The Axis Situation, Pantelleria (Washington, DC: U.S. Army Center of Military History, 1993) (www.history.army.mil/html/books/006/6-2-1/CMH_Pub_6-2-1.pdf).

29. Garland and Smyth, *Sicily and the Surrender of Italy.*

30. Mission Reports Document IRIS 56630.

31. The *Daily Telegram*, Adrian, Michigan, Wednesday, June 9, 1943.

32. Interviews, William Gregory, October 12, 2014, and May 5, 2015. Also see phone notes based on Gregory's review of an early manuscript copy.

33. AAF Historical Study No. 37: Harry L. Coles, "Participation of the Ninth and Twelfth Air Forces in the Sicilian Campaign" (1945), AAF Historical Office, AFHRC Document 467628.

34. Mission History, 49th Fighter Squadron.

35. Craven and Cate, *The Army Air Forces in World War II, Vol. 2, Europe: Torch to Pointblank*, p. 170.

36. Foreign Airport Description, El Bathan, 3.6 miles SE of Tebourba, A-3 Section, III ASAC (SP). NARA Document 00244738.

37. El Bathan, Tunisia, NARA Document Folder 638.9351, Reference 00244738, June–September 1943.

38. Maurer, *Air Force Combat Units of World War II.*

39. Basic Airdrome Report, El Bathan, June 13, 1943, Capt. John C. Gillespie, NARA Document Folder 638.9351, Reference 00244738, June–September 1943.

40. AFHRA Document 638.9351.

41. "The Building of a Fighter Squadron."

42. Lloyd A. Guenther, *Under the Wings of a P-38 in North Africa*, May 2005 (guenther.sterbenz.org/lloyd-guenther-memoirs.pdf).

43. Notes from M/Sgt. Norman G. Schuller, 12045371 48th Fighter Squadron, RAF No. 112 Squadron Tribute website (www.raf-112-squadron.org).

44. Blake and Stanaway, *Adorimini.*

45. Guenther, *Under the Wings of a P-38 in North Africa.*

46. Loving, Woodbine Red Leader.

47. Samuel W. Mitcham Jr. and Friedrich von Stauffenberg, *The Battle of Sicily: How the Allies Lost Their Chance for Total Victory* (Stackpole Military History Series) (Guilford, CT: Stackpole Books, 2007).

48. Adolf Galland, *The First and the Last: The Rise and Fall of the Luftwaffe, 1939–45* (New York: Ballantine Books, 1968).

49. Form 5s for Lt. Herman Kocour, provided by Robert Kocour.

50. Op. Cit. Mitcham.

51. Johannes Steinhoff, *Messerschmitts Over Sicily: The Diary of a Luftwaffe Fighter Commander* (Guilford, CT: Stackpole Books, 2004).

52. Ibid.

53. German Air Forces in Italy, Sicily, and Sardinia, July 10, 1943, U.S. Army Combined Arms Center, Combined Arms Research Laboratory, NFZIGER Collection of Orders of Battle, Document 943GGAB. Also see "The Luftwaffe, 1933–1945," at www .ww2.dk/air/jagd/jg53.htm and www.ww2.dk/air/jagd/jg77.htm.

54. John Dell, Dinger's Aviation Pages, German Fighter Organization, Joint Chiefs of Staff, Outline Plan for the Seizure of Sardinia, FDR Presidential Library and Museum.

55. Steinhoff, *Messerschmitts Over Sicily.*

56. Ibid.

57. Op. Cit. Steinhoff.

58. Op. Cit. Steinhoff.

59. "German Antiaircraft Defense, FLAK," Lone Sentry (www.lonesentry.com).

60. "Flak 30" (en.wikipedia.org/wiki/2_cm_Flak_30/38/Flakvierling).

61. Nona Hengen, *Palouse Pilot* (Paragon, IN: Celerus Books, 2009).

62. "German Antiaircraft Defense, FLAK."

Chapter Six

1. "Human Meteor," Lt. Troy Keith, *New Castle News* article, Monday, Feb. 13, 1939, and "Army flier Alive After 4-Mile Dive," Washington C.H. *Record-Herald*, Tuesday, Feb. 7, 1939.

According to his family, the Army did not have oxygen masks in 1936, and pilots breathed from a distasteful rubber oxygen tube. Pilots would remove the foul-tasting tube until they started to feel light-headed, and then reinsert it. Keith, apparently waiting too long, passed out and his plane went into a high-speed dive. He recovered his senses as a lower altitude was reach, bailed out at a low altitude, and reportedly (but unofficially) set a new high-speed record in the process. Also see: AAIR Database, Aviation Archaeology, August 25, 1936

2. Information about the life and service of Henry "Hugh" Trollope comes from numerous sources, including family interviews, high school and college yearbooks, the Western History Center at Casper College, military service records, and several newspaper articles.

3. Information and photographs about the life and service of Richard Decker come primarily from the exceptionally complete obituary prepared by his family. Additional information was found through census information and military sources.

4. Autobiography of Richard Decker, undated.

5. Information about the life and service of Frederick James Bitter is based primarily on materials received from his family and from standard military sources.

6. The primary source for information on Wallace Bland is the report received from the National Personnel Records Center, St. Louis, MO, Reference numbers 92.70.0001, 1014, 9-16-00-11. Additional sources include numerous citations in the Cullman *Banner* and Cullman *Democrat* newspapers, including Cullman *Banner*, August 5, 1943.

7. Information, including photographs, related to the life and service of Beryl Boatman include report received from NPRC, Request No. 2-119085022921, and family information.

8. Information related to the life and service of Anthony Evans includes NPRC Request No. 2-119085022893, family information, standard military records, and newspaper citations from the Mansfield, Ohio *News Journal* and the *Marion Star*.

9. Op. Cit. Harper interview, August 14, 2014.

10. Information related to the life and service of Martin Foster is derived from standard military sources and news clippings.

11. Information related to the life and service of William Gregory is primarily derived from interview transcripts, documents provided by William Gregory, and standard military sources.

12. Information is based on commentary Greg based on reading of March 2015 draft manuscript.

13. Information related to the life and service of Harold Harper is primarily derived from interview transcripts, documents provided by Harold Harper, and standard military sources.

14. Information related to the life and service of John Harris is primarily derived from genealogical data, university yearbook, and NPRC, Request No. 2-19055337217.

15. Information for Arthur Lovera was provided by family members, high school and university yearbook, and census information.

16. Information related to the life and service of Charles Richard is primarily derived from family sources and from high school and college yearbooks.

CHAPTER SEVEN

1. Specific model confirmation for B-25C at: MACR 14580, National Archives, NARA Catalogue No. 305256 and Mission Report, 310th Bomb Group, July 4, 1943

2. For consistency, aircraft specifications are taken from the works of Mr. Joe Baugher, www.joebaugher.com, except as indicated in separate notes.

3. FM 30-30, Military Intelligence, Aircraft Recognition Pictorial Manual, June 1943, Training Division, Bureau of Aeronautics, Navy Department, Washington D.C.

4. Specific model confirmation for B-17F at: "The Second Was First," History of the 2nd Bomb Group, mission report May 5, 1943 and MACR 2817, National Archives, NARA Catalogue No. 305256

5. For consistency, aircraft specifications are taken from the works of Mr. Joe Baugher, www.joebaugher.com, except as noted in separate notes.

6. FM 30-30, Military Intelligence, Aircraft Recognition Pictorial Manual, June 1943, Training Division, Bureau of Aeronautics, Navy Department, Washington D.C.

7. Specific model confirmation for B-26B at: B-26 Marauder Historical Society, B-26 Marauder Variants, www.b-26mhs.org.

8. For consistency, aircraft specifications are taken from the works of Mr. Joe Baugher, www.joebaugher.com, except as noted in separate notes.

9. FM 30-30, Military Intelligence, Aircraft Recognition Pictorial Manual, June 1943, Training Division, Bureau of Aeronautics, Navy Department, Washington D.C.

10. National Museum of the Air Force, Fact Sheet, Article 196310.

11. Hill Air Force Base Fact Sheet, Number 5649, Hill Air Force Base Library, Ogden, Ut.

12. Cost of the B-26 Marauder, Robert Harwell, Marauder Historical Society, Tucson, AZ.

13. "Tactics and Technique of Air Fighting," Army Air Forces Field Manual *FM 1-15*, April 10, 1942, War Department.

14. Ibid.

15. 1st Fighter Group in North Africa and Italy, Dick Catledge, undated.

16. Robert Vrilakas, *Look Mom—I Can Fly*

17. Personal correspondence, Robert Vrilakas, March 2015

18. 5th Wing Combat Manual, Brig. Gen. J.H. Atkinson, Commander, undated.

19. Correspondence with Harold Harper, member of the 49th Fighter Squadron during the summer of 1943. August 14, 2014.

20. Interview first posted on Geocities. With the demise of Geocities, hard copy maintained by the author. Interview with Maurice Nickle, a lieutenant and combat pilot who served with the 14th Fighter Group, 48th Fighter Squadron in Italy in 1945. The name of the interviewer is unknown.

21. "Bombs on the Target," War Diary of the 319th. Air Force Historical Research Agency, IRIS No. 00082327, 1945

22. "B-17 Flying Fortress: The Queen of the Skies" (www.b17flyingfortress.de).

23. A primary source for this chapter is "Combat Tactics in the Southwest Pacific Area" by Maj. Thomas B. McGuire Jr. (www.rhinobytes.com/haze/mcguire.htm).

24. Harold Harper, interview, August 14, 2014.

25. Interview with William Gregory, October 12, 2014.

26. 12th Air Force, 57th Bombardment Wing, 321st Bombardment Group, History: May 1943.

27. Comments by Herb Ross, combat pilot, 48th Fighter Squadron, Prop Talk, Golden Gate Wing, www.goldengatewing.org/proptalk/speaker.cfm?ID=55.

28. *P-51 Pilot: A Day in the Life*, William Lyons.

29. Sources here are the telephone mission reports—Form D-11, for each of the units involved, including the 37th, 48th, and 49th Fighter Squadrons, the 14th Fighter Group, and the 17th, 319th, and 320th Bomb Groups.

30. Reference to "Injuns" is contained in Raymond F. Toliver, *The Interrogator: The Story of Hanns Joachim Scharff, Master Interrogator of the Luftwaffe* (Atglen, PA: Schiffer Publishing, 1997).

31. 320th Bomb Group Missions (320thbg.org/mission_pdfs/mission_037.pdf).

32. Harold Harper, interview, August 14, 2014.

33. Interview, William J. Gregory, Oct. 12, 2014

34. The unpublished mission diary of William J. Gregory.

35. Capt. William J. Gregory, by Col. Troy Keith, Commander, 14th Fighter Group, 2 Sept. 1943.

CHAPTER EIGHT

1. Biennial Reports of the Chief of Staff of the U.S. Army, July 1, 1941–June 30, 1943, to the Secretary of War.

2. Interview, Harold Harper, August 14, 2014.

3. "Honor Roll for the 14th Fighter Group," RAF No. 112 Squadron Tribute website (www.raf-112-squadron.org).

Also note that in his autobiography Capt. Decker indicated that Lt. Neely's high speed dive resulted in his aircraft experiencing a "compressibility" condition from which he could not recover. Compressibility was known to occur in P-38s at very high speeds, and arose when airflow was deflected above and below the leading edge of the wing, preventing proper flow of air over the wing's control surfaces. Apparently, the cause of Lt. Neely's crash was never confirmed

4. Interview with Col. William J. Gregory (Ret.), November 2, 2014.

5. Mission Reports for the 37th, 48th, and 49th Fighter Squadrons, June 28, 1943. Also see Headquarters 2686 Medium Bombardment Wing (Prov), A-2 Section, Daily Summary No. 11, June 28, 1943.

6. Reference mission reports for all NASAF Bombardment Groups.

7. Abandoned, Forgotten, and Little Known Airfields in Europe (www.forgotten airfields.com/italy/sicily/palermo/boccadifalco-s596.html).

8. Regia Aeronautica in WWII, Units, Bases, and Assigned Aircraft, 1940–1943, Carl Nafziger (www.cgsc.edu/CARL/nafziger/940IXAL.pdf).

9. Summary of Target Analysis, Sicily, 12th AF, 20141016_140039.jpg.

10. Diary of W. Harold Plunkett, included in Witness to War: Preserving the Oral Histories of Combat Veterans (www.witnesstowar.org).

11. Data compiled from mission reports and other sources. Pilots lost included 2nd Lts. Wayne M. Chaves (10 May), John F. Burton (13 May), Burton J. Snyder (22 May). The loss of experienced pilots was especially hard felt by the squadron. 1st Lt. John L. Wolford, killed in action over Trapani on 19 May, was one of the pilots from the 1st Fighter Group who had already completed a combat tour, and who had been given the task of restarting the 14th FG earlier that spring. 1st Lts. Frank C. Howk (killed 19 May) and Albert Little (killed 21 May) were part of the "restart" cohort for the 14th FG, and each had probably flown six or more combat missions when they were downed.

12. *Defenders of Liberty: History of the 2nd Bomb Group* (www.2ndbombgroup.org/ Defenders%20of%20Liberty.htm), p. 145.

13. "German Training Regs for AA Flak," Assistant Chief of Air Staff, Intelligence, Informational Intelligence Summary, July 30, 1944.

14. *Defenders of Liberty*, pp. 101–50.

Chapter Nine

1. "P-38 Design," USAAF Resource Center (www.warbirdsresourcegroup.org/comments.html).

2. Der Gabelschwanz Teufel, Assessing the Lockheed P-38 Lightning, Technical Report APA-TR-2010-1201, Dr. Carlo Kopp, December 2010.

3. Warbirds Resource Group (www.lockheedmartin.com/us/100years/stories/p-38.html).

4. Specifications for the P-38G model are taken from the works of Joe Baugher. http://www.joebaugher.com/usaf_fighters/p38_11.html.

5. These are the 1942 production costs. By the war's end, the cost for the P-38 had decreased to $97,147, and to $50,985 for the P-51. *Army Air Forces Statistical Digest*, World War II, Table 82. Office of Statistical Control, U.S. Army Air Forces, 1945, AFHRC, Iris No. 00111991

6. The Aviation History (New Aircraft I) Color, Petrescu and Petrescu, Norderstedt: Books on Demand, 2012.

7. Steinhoff, *Messerschmitts Over Sicily.*

8. Interview with World War II Luftwaffe Eagle Johannes Steinhoff, HistoryNet, June 12, 2006.

9. Lockheed, "Of Men and Stars," 1958, p. 11

10. "Lockheed P-38G/F-5A Lightning," Joe Baugher.com (www.joebaugher.com/usaf_fighters/p38_11.html).

Chapter Ten

1. "Commitment of German Air Forces on Sardinia and Corsica," Headquarters, European Command, Office of the Chief Historian, General Hubertus Hirshold, Document D-038.

2. History of the 325th Fighter Group, AFHRA Document 83716.

3. The squadron records for this date are uniquely imperfect, and the assignments for the three squadrons of the 14th FG on this day are in some instances estimates. However, the assignments for the 49th squadron, in particular, are exact and confirmed.

4. AFHRA Study No. 88.

5. Despite their awareness of the importance of strategic bombing in future conflicts, Germany did not develop an effective strategic bomber. The primary German proponent of a strategic bomber force, Gen. Walther Wever, died in mid-1936, and the concept of strategic bombing never again developed any prominence. The Heinkel He 177A was developed in the late 1930s as a strategic bomber intended to support long-range bombing against Russia, but technical problems limited its use during the early years of the war. A usable design eventually evolved, but too late to be of significance during the war.

6. Craven and Cate, *The Army Air Forces in World War II, Vol. 2, Europe: Torch to Pointblank.*

7. Ibid.

8. Mission Reports and Unit Histories for the 14th Fighter Group and its squadrons: the 37th, 48th, and 49th Fighter Squadrons.

9. U.S. Air Force Historical Study No. 88, The Employment of Strategic bombers in a Tactical role, 1941–1951, USAF Historical Division, Research Studies Institute, Air University, April 1954.

10. AFHRA Study No. 88:

11. Bernard L. Montgomery, "Some Notes on the Use of Air Power in Support of Land Operations and Desert Air Support" (Holland: 1944); also, unpublished manuscript, "The Employment of Air Forces in Support of Land Operations," in document entitled, "Operations in North West Africa" (CARL, Fort Leavenworth, KS, MS # N3497).

12. Coningham is frequently lauded as the "architect of modern airpower doctrine regarding tactical air operations." His three operating principles—necessity of air superiority as first priority, centralized command of air operations co-equal with ground leadership, and innovative tactics in support of ground operations—were immensely successful in the western desert during the British Eighth Army's battle against Rommel and the Afrika Korps. His assumption of command over NATAF in early February 1943 resulted in a vastly clearer mission, and led to rapid and positive improvements in tactical airpower effectiveness. The contributions of the Allied air forces to the defeat of Axis forces in the North African Campaign are a case in point. Prior to and during Operation Husky, the effectiveness of NATAF in satisfying Coningham's call for air superiority and air interdiction is widely accepted. The Allies operated not merely with air superiority; their command of the skies approached air supremacy. And NATAF's interdiction efforts also received high marks for its effectiveness.

13. Even after the air forces reorganization that resulted from Casablanca, air forces planners bridled at the lack of supporting doctrine. In a March 1943 letter to AAF headquarters, Col. Charles Williamson noted that the "lack of an authoritative and concise statement of AAF doctrine and employment policies" was responsible for many failures and for conditions that were "almost chaotic" in the air operations he had observed in combat zones. By May 1943 theater and overseas commanders had begun to receive a series of informally written pamphlets which were eventually codified in July as *Field Manual 100-20*, "Command and Employment of Air Power." Finally, the "learned doctrine" that emerged from the bitter experience during and immediately after Operation Torch was officially enunciated. And it was this document that guided tactical operations for the rest of World War II. With regard to operations, the run-up to the invasion of Sicily was conducted in a less-than-lucid environment. Doctrine governing tactical operations would continue to evolve out of Coningham's HQ, and would eventually provide strong guidance for the conduct of the air operations for the remainder of the war. But that doctrine arrived too late to be of much guidance to military planners in the run-up to the invasion of Sicily. And still unclear was the precise role of strategic forces, particularly considering, as will be shown later, that the operations of strategic forces over Sicily were essentially tactical in nature. In brief, the American army began the invasion of Sicily with little practical guidance on the use of airpower in support of ground troops, on the use of strategic air assets, and on the issues of command and control.

14. AAF Historical Study No. 37.

15. Target Priority Lists, February–September 1943, XII Air Force, A-2 Section, AFHRC Document 00232881.

16. AAF Historical Study No. 37.

17. Benjamin Franklin Cooling, ed., *Case Studies in the Development of Close Air Support* (Washington, DC: Office of Air Force History, 1990) (www.afhso.af.mil/shared/media/document/AFD-100924-035.pdf).

18. B. Michael Bechthold, "A Question of Success: Tactical Air Doctrine and Practice in North Africa, 1942–43," *The Journal of Military History*, Vol. 68, No. 3, July 2004.

19. AFHRA Study No. 88:

Chapter Eleven

1. USAAF Chronology: Mediterranean Theater of Operations (MTO), Monday, July 5, 1943.

2. Samuel W. Mitcham and Friedrich von Stauffenberg, *The Battle of Sicily*, Orion Books.

3. "Chapter 7: Sicily," *New Zealanders with the Royal Air Force*, Vol. III, nzetc.victoria.ac.nz/tm/scholarly/tei-WH2-3RAF.html.

4. AAF Historical Study No. 37.

5. Steinhoff, *Messerschmitts Over Sicily.*

6. AFHRA, Mission reports for the 14th FG, and 37th, 48th, and 49th Fighter Squadrons.

7. Mission Report, 37th Fighter Squadron, July 5, 1943, Capt. John McCarthy, Intelligence Officer

8. AFHRA, History of the 2nd Bomb Group, IRIS No 00077215.

9. AFHRA, History of the 1st Fighter Group, IRIS No. 77183.

10. Unit Citation, 99th Bombardment Group, General Order 896, June 7, 1944, Col. R.K. Taylor, Chief of Staff, Headquarters, Fifteenth Air Force.

11. 99th Bomb Group Historical Society: Thunder from the South, 99th Bomb Group Citations and Records (www.99bombgroup.org/).

12. Steinhoff, *Messerschmitts Over Sicily.*

13. *Pantechnicon* was a term applied by the GAF to the B-17 Flying Fortress. Originally a term dating to the early 1800s to describe furniture-removal vans drawn by horses, by 1943 the term was used to describe high-capacity but cumbersome trucks.

14. By the end of the war, Steinhoff had been shot down twelve times. In all cases but one he flew his damaged aircraft to an emergency landing. "I only bailed out once. I never trusted the parachutes. I always landed my damaged planes, hoping not to get bounced on the way down when I lost power." Colin D. Heaton, "Interview: Luftwaffe Eagle Johannes Steinhoff," *Military History Magazine* (February 2000).

15. Steinhoff, *Messerschmitts Over Sicily.*

16. Cited in Denis Richards and Hilary St. G. Saunders, *The Royal Air Force 1939–1945, Vol. II, The Fight Avails* (London: HMSO, 1954).

17. Galland, *The First and the Last.*

Chapter Twelve

1. Brendan Phibbs, *The Other Side of Time: A Combat Surgeon in World War II* (Boston: Little, Brown & Co., 1987), p. 149.

2. Kenneth Poolman, *The Winning Edge: Naval Technology in Action, 1939–1945* (Stroud, England: Sutton Publishing, 1997).

3. Target Priority Lists, February–September 1943, XII Air Force, A-2 Section, AFHRC Document 00232881.

4. Steve Chalker, "World War II, Aerial Counterflak Tactics," Scribd (www.scribd .com/document/33690091/WWII-Aerial-Counterflak-Tactics).

5. Correspondence, Harold Harper, February 19, 2015.

6. "How to Dive-Bomb in World War II Aircraft–1943," U.S. Navy Training Film, Military Arts Pictures, ZenosWarBirds (www.youtube.com/watch?v=lOz_i_2USkY).

7. Pilot Training Manual for the P-38 Lightning, AAF Manual 51-127-1, Headquarters Army Air Forces, AAF Training Command.

8. Interview, James Graham, June 14, 2014.

9. Col. Nathaniel G. Raley (Ret.), memoirs, Experiencing War: Stories from the Veterans History Project, Library of Congress Veterans History Project (memory.loc.gov/diglib/vhp-stories/loc.natlib.afc2001001.00449/).

10. Interview, Harold Harper, August 14, 2014.

11. Charles Everard Dills, "It Just Wasn't My Time" (memoirs), 27th Fighter-Bomber Group, Veterans History Project, American Folklife Center, Library of Congress, Collection No. AFC/2001/001/56290.

12. *Flying Magazine*, 1946. Vol. 38 No. 2, February 1946, p. 108, Ziff-Davis Publishing Company.

13. Arnold, *Doorknob Five Two.*

14. William B. Colgan, *Allied Strafing in World War II: A Cockpit View of Air to Ground Battle,* Jefferson, NC: McFarland, 2010. An excellent source for strafing operations and tactics employed during World War II, used as source material for much of the information that follows in this chapter.

15. Ibid.

16. Ibid.

17. The Combat Strategy and Tactics of Major Gregory Boyington, USMC, Commanding Officer of VMF214, Report to HQ Marine Aircraft, South Pacific, Fleet Marine Force, Intelligence Section, January 19, 1944.

18. 5th Wing Combat Manual, Brig. Gen. J. H. Atkinson, commander, date unknown.

19. Phone interview, July 31, 2014, Mr. B. W. Curry.

20. Squadron History, 49th Fighter Squadron, May 24, 1943, and Group History, 14th Fighter Group, May 24, 1943.

21. Interview, William Gregory, Nov. 4, 2014

CHAPTER THIRTEEN

1. 57th Bomb Wing Association, 321st Bomb Group, http://57thbombwing.com/index2.php.

2. AAF Historical Study No. 37.

3. Ibid.

4. War Diary, 27th Fighter Squadron, 1st Fighter Group, Jan 1943–Mar 1945, Air Force Historical Research Agency IRIS Number 00056064, Call SQ-FL-28-HI, entry for July 2, 1943.

5. Lida Mayo, *The Ordnance Department: On Beachhead and Battlefront* (Washington, DC: U.S. Army Center of Military History, 1991) (www.history.army.mil/html/books/010/10-11/CMH_Pub_10-11.pdf).

6. AAF Historical Study No. 37.

7. Craven and Cate, *The Army Air Forces in World War II, Vol. 2, Europe: Torch to Pointblank*, pp. 434–45.

8. Op. Cit. AFHRA Study 37, p. 24.

9. AAF Historical Study No. 37.

10. David W. Dengler, *Seeing the Enemy: Army Air Force Aerial Reconnaissance Support of U.S. Army Operations in the Mediterranean in World War II* (www.dtic.mil/cgi-bin/GetTRDoc?AD=ADA501753).

11. C. Peter Chen, ed., World War II Database (ww2db.com/image.php?image_id=12157).

12. Ernie Pyle, *Brave Men* (Lincoln: University of Nebraska Press, 1944).

13. *Lewiston Morning Tribune*, Monday, July 12, 1943.

14. Ibid.

15. War Diary of the 49th Fighter Squadron, AFHRC Document 56630, pp. 1264–65.

16. The details of missions flown on July 10, 1943, are taken from the mission reports of the units involved. This includes the 14th Fighter Group, the individual squadron reports for all three squadrons of the 14th, the 1st Fighter Group, the individual squadron reports for all three squadrons of the 1st, and the mission reports for all bomb groups involved: 2nd, 97th, 99th, and 301st BGs flying B-17s; 310th and 321st BGs flying B-25s; 17th, 319th, and 320th BGs flying B-26s. All reports were secured from either the Air Force Historical Research Office at Maxwell AFB, or from the National Archives. The 1st FG flew eight missions on D-Day, with each P-38 carrying a 500-pound bomb attacking targets of opportunity in the central part of southeastern Sicily. Sources: 57826, 57828, 57327 Unit History 94th FS, 57182 Unit History 71st FS, 77183 History 1st FG and 56054 WSOR 27th FS.

17. Interview, Lt. Col. William J. Gregory (Ret.), October 12, 2014.

18. Op. Cit. Harper interview, August 14, 2014.

19. Missing Air Crew Report No. 100, 1st Lt. Wallace Bland, 13 July 1943, Henry H. Trollope, Captain, A.C, commander, 49th Ftr. Sq.

20. Missing Air Crew Report No. 74, 2nd Lt. Allan Knepper, 13 July 1943, Henry H. Trollope, Captain, A.C, commander, 49th Ftr. Sq.

CHAPTER FOURTEEN

1. Letter from Herman Kocour to Mrs. Rosevear, Allan Knepper's aunt, Jan. 28, 1944.

2. Hangman's News, Vol. 13, Issue 1, January 2015, and Interview, Antonio Villegas, January 3, 2016.

3. Craven and Cate, *The Army Air Forces in World War II, Vol. 2, Europe: Torch to Pointblank.*

4. Weekly Operational Report, July 19, 1943, Capt. Frank Clark.

5. Operational Report for the 49th FS, Richard Decker, July 19, 1943.

6. Pilots lost during this interval were: 1st Lt. Bruce Campbell, 2nd Lt. George B. Church, 1st Lt. William D. Neely III, 2nd Lt. Sidney R. Booth, 1st Lt. Wallace G. Bland, 2nd Lt. Allan W. Knepper, 1st Lt. Mark C. Hageny, 2nd Lt. Jack L. Moak, 2nd Lt. Walter L. Hoke, 1st Lt. William K. Hester, F/O John D. McCoy, 1st Lt. Louis D. Ogle, 1st Lt. Martin Faust.

7. Interview, William Gregory, Feb. 24, 2016.

8. Interview, Harold Harper, October 1, 2014.

9. War Diary, 49th Fighter Squadron, Air Force Historical Research Agency, IRIS document 56630.

10. Letter from Herman Kocour to Mrs. R.W. (Chris) Giegler, Allan Knepper's sister, March 8, 1944.

11. Letter from Grady Bland to Congressman Carter Manasco, Sept. 20, 1945," included in Individual Deceased Personnel File for Lt. Wallace Bland, Ref. 114215.

12. Report from Maj. Steven F. Capasso, Commander QMC, 2621 Graves Registration Unit, to Commanding Officer, American Graves Registration Service, Mediterranean Theater Separate Zone Command, Aug. 9, 1946. Included in Individual Deceased Personnel File for Lt. Wallace Bland, Ref. 114215.

13. Letter from Lt. Col. W.E. Campbell, Memorial Division, QMC, to J. Grady Bland, July 21, 1949, Included in Individual Deceased Personnel File for Lt. Wallace Bland, Ref. 114215.

14. Missing Air Crew Report No. 100, 13 July 1943, Henry H. Trollope, Captain, A.C. commander, 49th Ftr. Sq. Details regarding the search for Lt. Bland are taken from the Individual Deceased Personnel Form, 92-70-0001, 1014, 9-16-00-1-1, U.S. Army Human Resources Command, Casualty & Memorial Affairs Operations Division, Fort Knox, KY.

15. Letter from Jess Knepper to Kansas City Quartermaster Depot, date uncertain. Written sometime between Oct. 13 and Dec. 13, 1943. Included in the Individual Deceased Personnel File for Lt. Allan Knepper, Request Ref. 14-0607.

16. Letter from Mrs. Kocour to Mrs. Rosevear, Jan. 26, 1944.

17. Geoffrey M. McKenzie, Operation Husky: Seeking an Operational Approach to Decisive Victory (www.dtic.mil/get-tr-doc/pdf?AD=ADA611984).

18. St. Clair, "Air Support of the Allied Landings in Sicily, Salerno, and Anzio."

19. Ibid.

20. Craven and Cate, *The Army Air Forces in World War II, Vol. 2, Europe: Torch to Pointblank.*

21. Galland, *The First and the Last*, p. 25.

22. Craven and Cate, *The Army Air Forces in World War II, Vol. 2, Europe: Torch to Pointblank, Chapter 14.*

23. Mitcham and von Stauffenberg, *The Battle of Sicily*, p. 103.

24. The Battle of Sicily," Samuel W. Mitcham, Jr. and Friedrich von Stauffenberg.

25. Mitcham and von Stauffenberg, *The Battle of Sicily*, p. 103.

26. Philip W. Wielhouwer, *Trial by Fire: Forging American Close Air Support Doctrine, World War I through September 1944*, U.S. Army Command and General Staff College, U.S. Air Force Academy, Colorado: BiblioScholar, 2012).

27. Carlo D'Este, *Bitter Victory: The Battle for Sicily, 1943* (New York: Harper Perennial, 2008).

28. Ibid.

29. Ibid.

30. Ibid.

31. Mitcham and von Stauffenberg, *The Battle of Sicily*.

32. "Sicily, 1943," U.S. Army Center of Military History (www.history.army.mil/brochures/72-16/72-16.htm).

33. Galland, *The First and the Last*.

34. World War II Foundation. WWII Aircraft Facts, http://www.wwiifoundation.org/students/wwii-aircraft-facts/.

35. Galland, *The First and the Last*.

CHAPTER FIFTEEN

1. E-mail correspondence, Dr. Alessandro Monacchi, CIS Geofisica Srl, Casalpusterlengo, Italy, May 15, 2015.

2. E-mail correspondence, Dr. Jim Doolittle, Research Soil Scientist, National Soil Survey Center, June 1, 2015.

3. E-mail correspondence, Mr. Salvatore Fagione, May 12, 2015.

CHAPTER SIXTEEN

1. Martin B-57 Canberra, https://en.wikipedia.org/wiki/Martin_B-57_Canberra.

2. Correspondence and Telephone Interviews, Dusty Lovera, 2014–2016.

3. Yakima Daily Republic, Nov. 12, 1943.

4. Interview, William Gregory, October 12, 2014. News article, "Camp Hill Fighter Pilot Flies Into Jerry Trap, Shot Badly, Forced Down," *Harrisburg Telegraph*, 4 April 1944, Report, National Personnel Records Center, Request No. 2-11908502925, Martin A. Foster, O 733862, 26 August 2014.

5. Distinguished Flying Cross Citation, General Orders No. LGC 4, 29 December 1943, By command of Major General Doolittle, Headquarters Army Air Forces.

6. Missing Air Crew Report No. 707, 16 Sept. 1943, National Archives, NARA Catalog No. 305256.

INDEX

Page numbers in italics indicates illustrations.